North Carolina

Communities Around Our World

www.harcourtschool.com

Communities Around Our World

Printed in the United States of America

ISBN-13: 978-0-15-356642-4

ISBN-10: 0-15-356642-6

2 3 4 5 6 7 8 9 10 059 13 12 11 10 09 08

Contents

COMMUNITIES AROUND OUR WORLD

TABBED SECTION

Program Contributors

SERIES AUTHORS

Dr. Michael J. Berson
Professor
Social Science Education
University of South Florida
Tampa, Florida

Dr. Tyrone C. Howard
Associate Professor
UCLA Graduate School of Education & Information Studies
University of California Los Angeles
Los Angeles, California

Dr. Cinthia Salinas
Assistant Professor
Department of Curriculum and Instruction
College of Education
The University of Texas at Austin
Austin, Texas

NORTH CAROLINA CONSULTANTS AND REVIEWERS

Jenny Bajorek
Teacher
Northwoods Elementary School
Cary, North Carolina

Dan Barber
Teacher
Idlewild Elementary School
Charlotte, North Carolina

Brianne Beck
Teacher
Allen Jay Elementary School
High Point, North Carolina

Melissa Blush
Teacher
Allen Jay Elementary School
High Point, North Carolina

Ardelia Brown
Teacher
Pearsontown Elementary School
Durham, North Carolina

Alice M. Cook
Teacher
Paw Creek Elementary School
Charlotte, North Carolina

Lori D. Davis
Teacher
C. Wayne Collier Elementary School
Hope Mills, North Carolina

John D. Ellington
Former Director
Division of Social Studies
North Carolina Department of Public Instruction
Raleigh, North Carolina

Laura Griffin
Teacher
Sherwood Park Elementary School
Fayetteville, North Carolina

Sharon Hale
Teacher
Hillandale Elementary School
Durham, North Carolina

Dr. Ted Scott Henson
Educational Consultant
Burlington, North Carolina

Charlotte Heyliger
Teacher
C. Wayne Collier Elementary School
Hope Mills, North Carolina

Tony Iannone
Teacher
Nathaniel Alexander Elementary School
Charlotte, North Carolina

Judith McCray Jones
Educational Consultant
Former Elementary School Administrator
Greensboro, North Carolina

Gwendolyn C. Manning
Teacher
Gibsonville Elementary School
Gibsonville, North Carolina

Courtney McFaull
Teacher
Sherwood Park Elementary School
Fayetteville, North Carolina

Lydia Ogletree O'Rear
Teacher
Elmhurst Elementary School
Greenville, North Carolina

Marsha Rumley
Teacher
Brooks Global Studies
Greensboro, North Carolina

Dean P. Sauls
Teacher
Wayne County Public Schools
Goldsboro, North Carolina

Melissa Turnage
Teacher
Meadow Lane Elementary School
Goldsboro, North Carolina

Joseph E. Webb
Educational Consultant
Adjunct Professor
East Carolina University
Greenville, North Carolina

Harcourt Social Studies North Carolina . . .

▶ *Aligns with the North Carolina Standard Course of Study*

In *Harcourt Social Studies North Carolina,* **each unit and each lesson at each grade level is built upon the North Carolina Standard Course of Study.** Each unit addresses one competency goal, and each lesson addresses one or more objectives under that competency goal. Competency goals and objectives are introduced and taught through rich content, illustrations, and graphics that connect to students' experiences.

NORTH CAROLINA STANDARD COURSE OF STUDY

COMPETENCY GOAL 1
The learner will apply the five themes of geography to North Carolina and its people.

OBJECTIVES
1.01 Locate, in absolute and relative terms, major landforms, bodies of water and natural resources in North Carolina.
1.02 Describe and compare physical and cultural characteristics of the regions.
1.03 Suggest some influences that location has on life in North Carolina such as major cities, recreation areas, industry, and farms.
1.04 Evaluate ways the people of North Carolina used, modified, and adapted to the physical environment, past and present.
1.05 Assess human movement as it relates to the physical environment.

Through an integrated study of the students' families, homes, schools, neighborhoods, communities, state, and nation, *Harcourt Social Studies North Carolina* **teaches concepts and generalizations from history, geography, economics, and the other key social studies disciplines.** Students not only learn facts but also understand the themes that flow through these disciplines.

Understanding key social studies themes allows students to grasp how their own lives connect to the peoples and cultures of the past as well as to the peoples and cultures of other places. Students learn to examine the perspectives of people in other times and places, and they begin to build a knowledge base of history, economics, and government that will help them to better understand the present and to plan for the future as active, responsible citizens. By focusing students' learning, creating dynamic and interactive learning experiences, and providing options for planned formal assessments, *Harcourt Social Studies North Carolina* broadens students' social understanding while laying the groundwork for their civic efficacy.

BACKGROUND

Requirements for Public Office The Constitution of North Carolina outlines the requirements for most state public offices. To be eligible to serve as governor or lieutenant governor of North Carolina, a person must ... of the United States for ... Carolina for two years.

BUILD SKILLS

Problem Solving Have students discuss the problems involved in moving the state capitol. Explain to students that they can use the following steps to solve problems.

1. Identify the problem and its causes.
2. G... ...ble solutions.
3. T... ...ges of ...
4. C...

Global Connections Economic relationships formed with international trade also help nations form stronger cultural connections. For example, many Americans play video games that are produced in other countries, and those games affect culture in the United States. At the same time, American movies and television shows affect cultures in other nations.

▶ *Builds 21st Century Skills*

Harcourt Social Studies North Carolina **helps students acquire the knowledge and skills needed for success in the global economy,** an economy that is marked by rapid technological change, a rapid accumulation of knowledge, increased competition, and rising workplace requirements. Through program components, classroom practice and instruction, and instructional activities, **students develop the competencies needed for the 21st century:**

- global awareness
- financial, economic, business, and entrepreneurial literacy
- civic literacy
- critical-thinking and problem-solving skills
- creativity and innovation skills
- communication and collaboration skills
- information and media literacy skills

Technology/Digital Resources

Spotlight on Goals and Objectives

North Carolina Interactive Presentations

Like the units in the Student Edition, each North Carolina Interactive Presentation focuses on a North Carolina competency goal. The presentation provides an entertaining visual overview of the competency goal and its objectives. Teachers can use the interactive presentation to preview a competency goal for the whole class before beginning a unit, or they may wish to use it throughout the unit to reinforce individual objectives. A North Carolina Interactive Presentation is available for each unit in your North Carolina Student Edition.

The first slide in each interactive presentation is clearly labeled with the grade and unit.

All objectives in the unit are listed and reviewed in the presentation.

Discussion questions, background, project activities, and more can be found in the presentation notes.

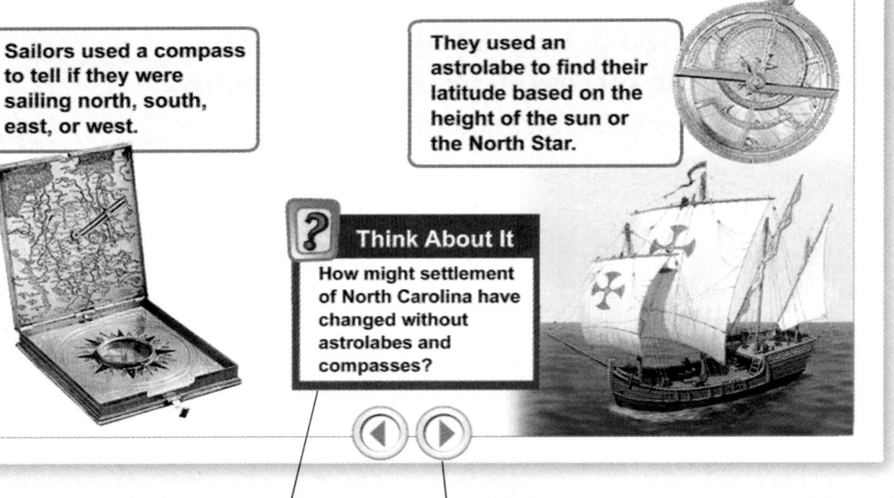

Each objectives slide includes the correlating lesson and objective number for ease of use.

A linked table of contents makes navigation between lessons easy.

Think About It boxes prompt students for discussion and critical thinking.

On each slide, new text and images appear at the click of a mouse to allow for a point-by-point discussion of each objective.

North Carolina Adventures

The North Carolina Adventures games, offered both on CD and online, provide an entertaining first-person-player method of content review. When students have completed the unit, they can review its competency goal and all objectives through the game.

Students can use their knowledge of what they have learned in the unit to solve cases in a detective agency, get the scoop on stories as a reporter, and more! Along the way, "Help" buttons in the game refer students to pages in their textbooks if they need help answering the questions.

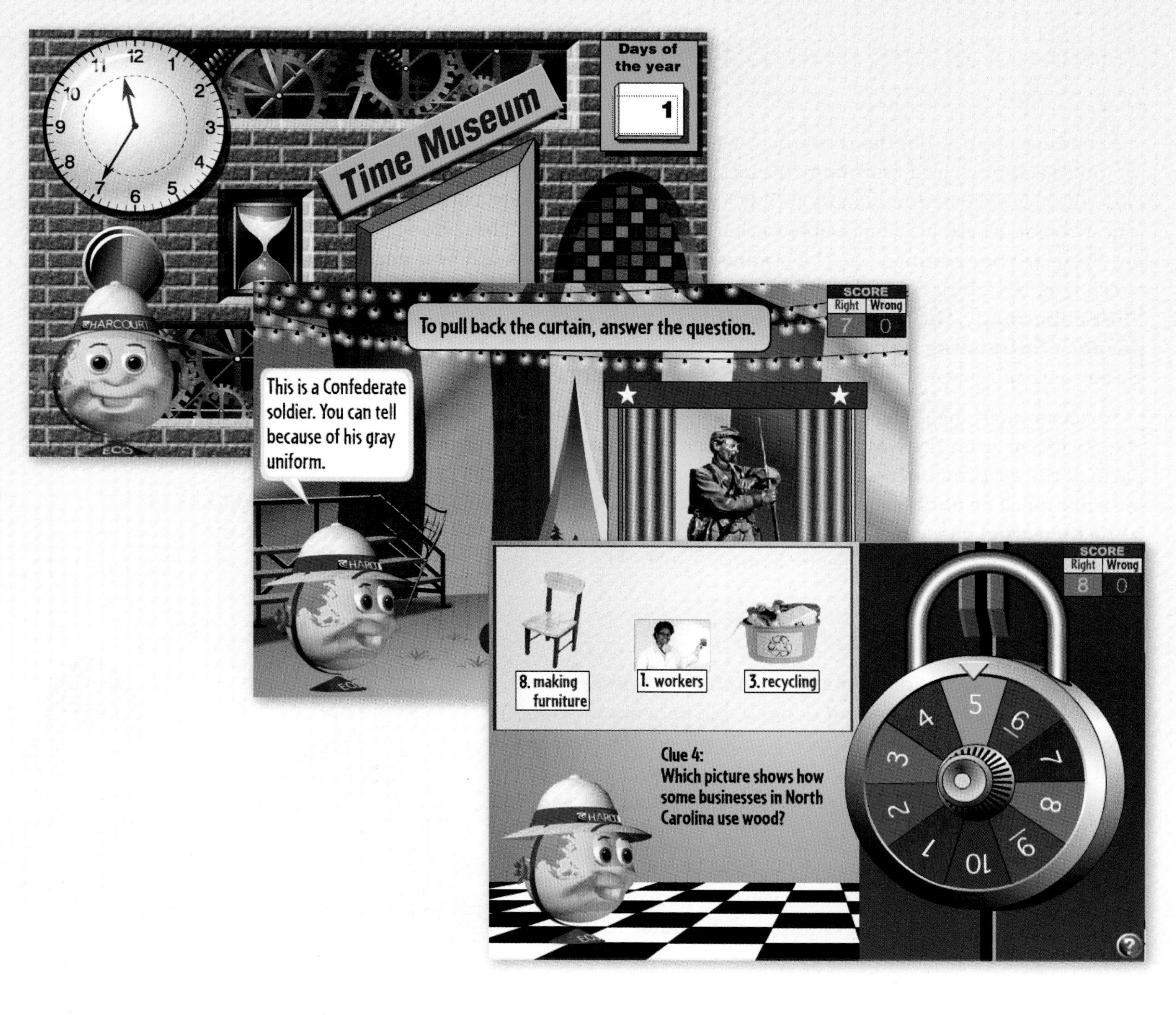

Help Students Become Smarter About Content-Area Reading

Meaningful Interaction with Text

Harcourt Social Studies North Carolina **helps students learn, practice, and apply research-proven strategies for interacting with text.** The series is based on a systematic, developmental sequence of interaction that is informed and guided by a valid and reliable assessment tool—the SSSMART™ test. While the series is entirely based on the North Carolina Standard Course of Study for social studies, **it is also designed to make students better readers in ALL content areas.**

Reading Content Area Textbooks Is Not the Same as Reading Stories

Reading required in the content areas is very different from the reading that has been taught to establish and maintain "literacy." The narrative forms that make up the bulk of early literacy instruction usually follow a story line. Conversely, content-area textbooks do not follow a plot. There may be people in them, but there are no "characters." There are places, but there are no "settings." Social studies concepts and issues can be complex and require a specialized vocabulary that may not be part of students' listening and speaking vocabularies. Most importantly, **the purpose for reading expository text differs greatly from the purpose for reading narratives.** Readers of expository text learn about a specific topic, gather and apply information, or gain understanding of events and their causes.

To accomplish the goals of textbook reading, a reader engages with the material in a way different from the way used with narrative. Skimming and scanning are important parts of the reading process, requiring students to know how and where to locate needed information. The abilities to extract and interpret information from graphic sources and to navigate textual cues are critical. The reader uses unique textbook structures and relies on graphics and typographic clues to acquire information.

What Is the SSSMART™ Test?

SSSMART™ is a valid, reliable, research-based assessment tool that provides accurate and dependable data about students' comprehension of expository texts, academic vocabulary, and ability to locate information within and across resources. The data predicts success on high-stakes content-area and reading tests, helping teachers make instructional decisions based on students' individual needs.

- The **Comprehension** test determines how effectively students read and understand social studies text selections.

- The **Vocabulary** test identifies a student's knowledge of content-specific terms and background knowledge of concepts.
- The **CUES** test determines how well students read and understand such things as maps, tables, graphs, illustrations, and typographical features.
- The **Skimming and Scanning** test indicates how well students can locate information quickly and accurately.

How Does the SSSMART™ Test Help Inform Instruction?

SSSMART™ test scores are not merely numbers; instead, **they provide guidance for planning instruction.** Scores determine whether students can read the textbook

- with *ease*
- with *some teacher guidance*, or
- with *extensive assistance.*

Score results are provided for each skill area: Comprehension, Vocabulary, CUES, and Skimming and Scanning. In *Harcourt Social Studies North Carolina*, each lesson page features TextWork activities or questions for students to complete. Teacher support provides scaffolding to be used with individual students, small groups, or the whole class to help students succeed with the question or activity. **The teacher can thus adjust instruction at the group or individual level.**

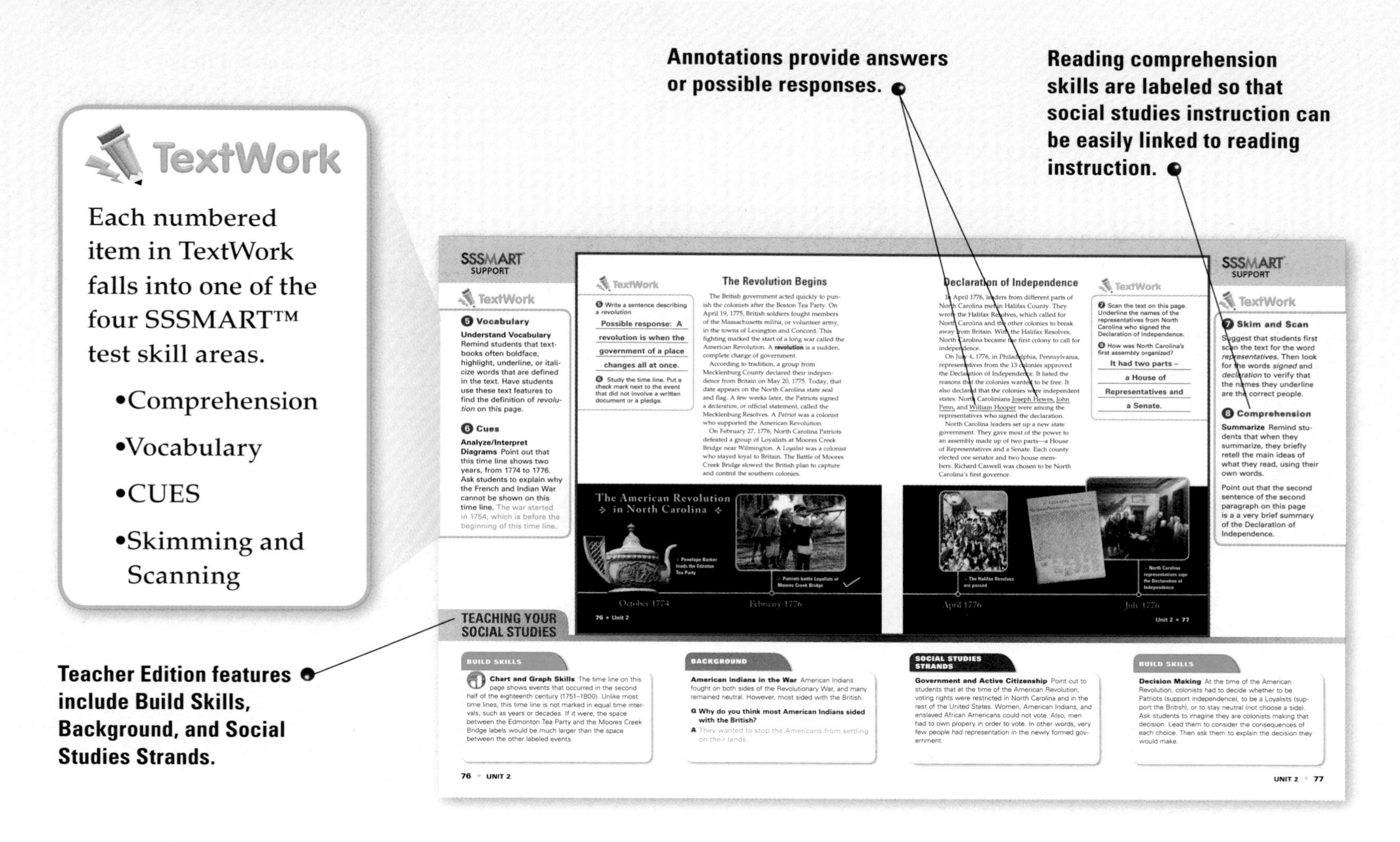

Planning and Assessment

Harcourt Social Studies North Carolina recognizes that **the time you have for teaching social studies is limited,** so the Teacher Edition provides **the support you need for effective planning and instruction.**

Unit Planning

Unit planning guides list vocabulary; the unit competency goal and objectives; support for Teaching Your Social Studies and for SSSMART™; and key program resources. Suggestions for lesson pacing and management for long-term planning are also given.

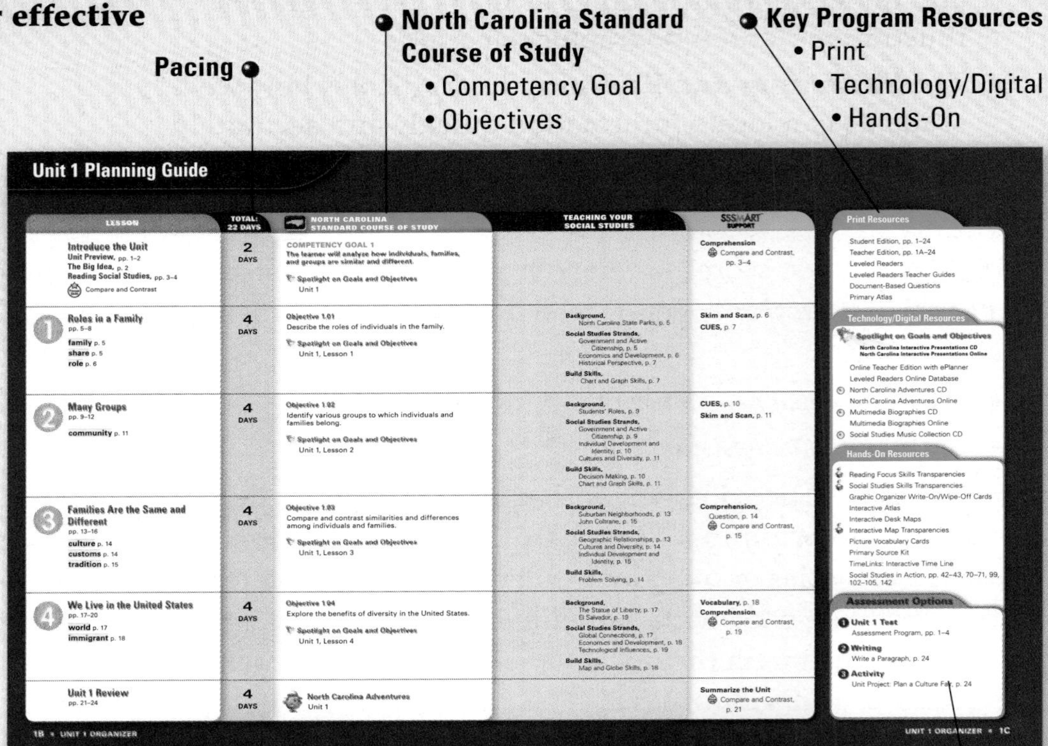

Lesson Planning

Teacher Edition pages at the beginning of each lesson provide ideas for starting a lesson, preteaching vocabulary, reaching diverse learners, and integrating social studies across the school curriculum.

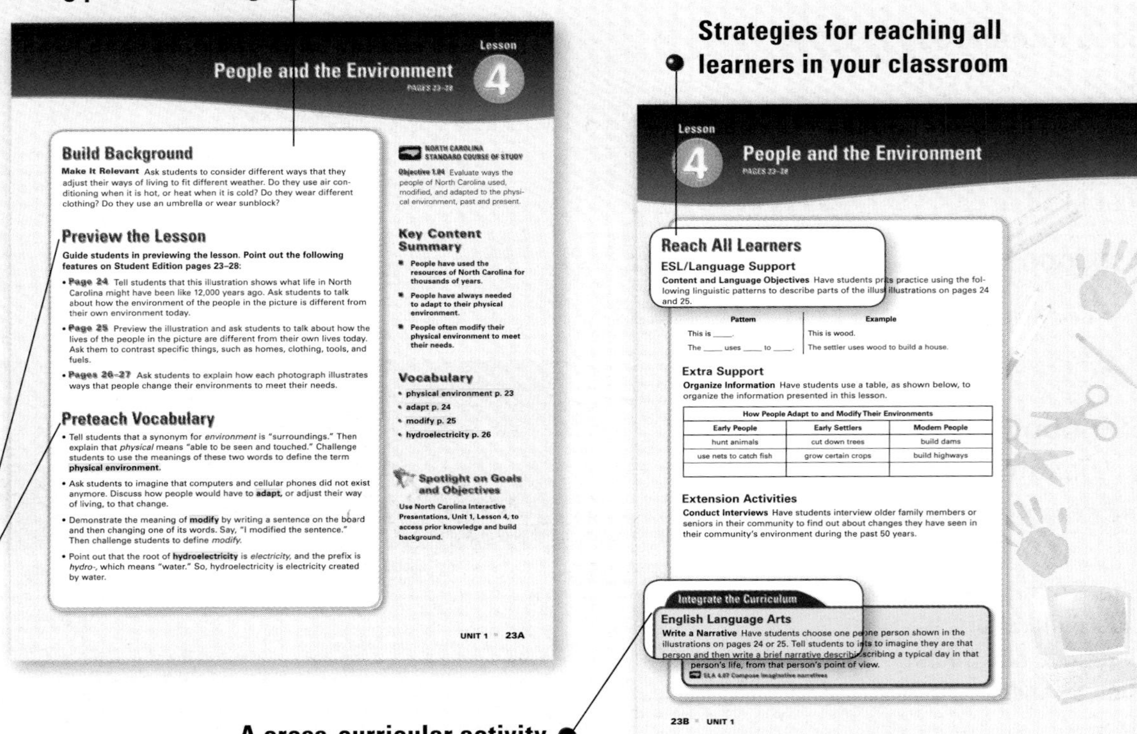

Teaching Your Social Studies

Harcourt Social Studies North Carolina provides you with the **background information and instructional strategies needed to teach every lesson.** It provides direct instruction of social studies strands as well as key skills.

TEACHING YOUR SOCIAL STUDIES

BACKGROUND

The Fall Line Extending from New Jersey to Alabama, the Fall Line separates the flat, low land of the Coastal Plain from the higher, rocky land of the Piedmont. It is called a fall line because rivers drop from higher to lower land, forming many waterfalls. Early settlers used the power of those waterfalls to run mills and factories. As a result, many cities grew along the Fall Line, including Raleigh.

- **Additional teacher information about important people, places, and events**

SOCIAL STUDIES STRANDS

Geographic Relationships Silt, or the fine sand and soil that rivers carry from the mountains, contains minerals that enrich soil.

Q Why do you think many farms are located on floodplains?

A Floodplains have fertile soil and a nearby source of fresh water.

- **Historical Perspectives**
- **Individual Development and Identity**
- **Technological Influences**
- **Cultures and Diversity**
- **Economics and Development**
- **Geographic Relationships**
- **Global Connections**
- **Government and Active Citizenship**

BUILD SKILLS

MAP SKILL **Map and Globe Skills** The map on this page is a latitude and longitude map of North Carolina. It has a grid formed by lines of latitude and lines of longitude. Lines of longitude are measured in degrees east or west of the prime meridian (0°). Lines of latitude are measured in degrees north or south of the equator (0°).

- **Chart and Graph**
- **Decision Making**
- **Map and Globe**
- **Problem Solving**

An Active Approach

Hands-On Projects and Activities

Apart from or along with print and technology, **social studies content and skills can be delivered through projects and activities.** *Harcourt Social Studies North Carolina* offers **short- and long-term projects** to meet your curriculum goals.

Writing

Harcourt Social Studies North Carolina also provides many **opportunities for students to demonstrate their command of social studies through writing.**

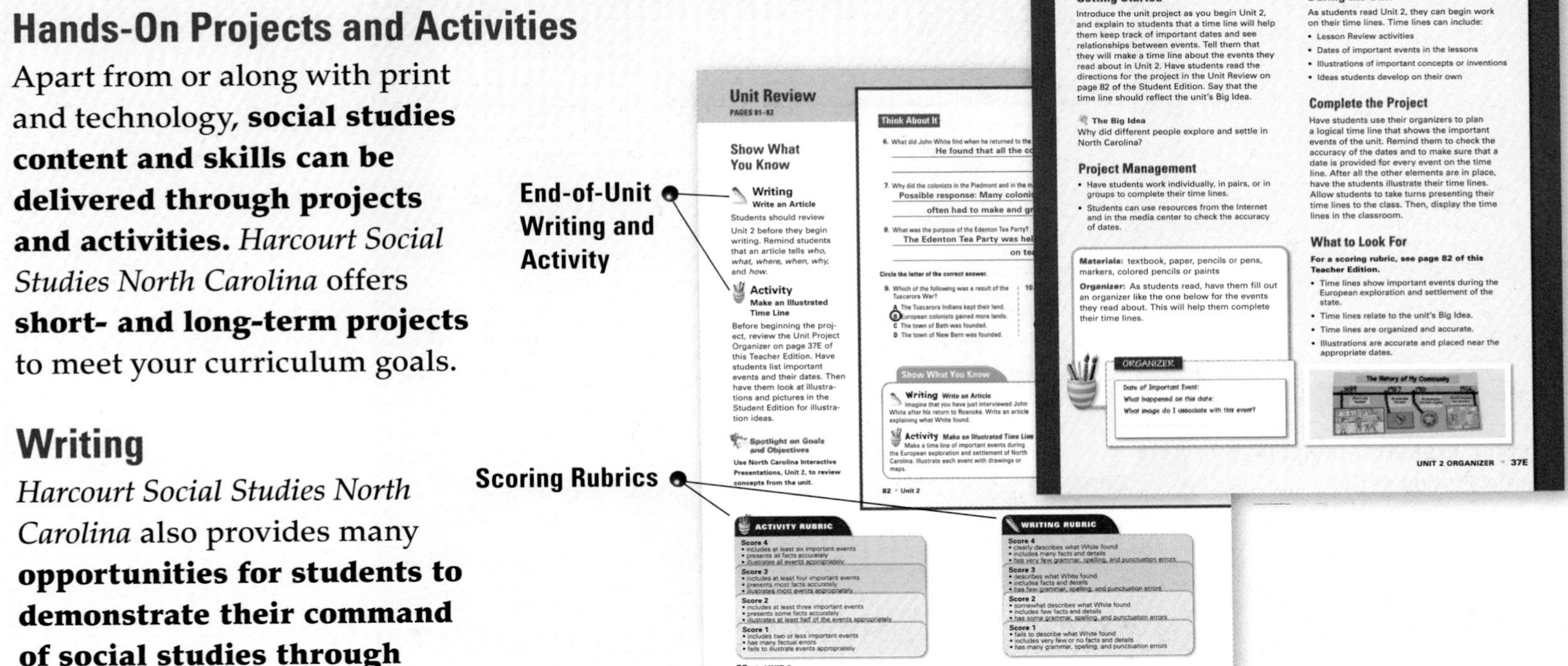

Unit Project: Hands-On Activity

Make an Illustrated Time Line

Getting Started

Introduce the unit project as you begin Unit 2, and explain to students that a time line will help them keep track of important dates and see relationships between events. Tell them that they will make a time line about the events they read about in Unit 2. Have students read the directions for the project in the Unit Review on page 82 of the Student Edition. Say that the time line should reflect the unit's Big Idea.

The Big Idea
Why did different people explore and settle in North Carolina?

Project Management

- Have students work individually, in pairs, or in groups to complete their time lines.
- Students can use resources from the Internet and in the media center to check the accuracy of dates.

Materials: textbook, paper, pencils or pens, markers, colored pencils or paints

Organizer: As students read, have them fill out an organizer like the one below for the events they read about. This will help them complete their time lines.

ORGANIZER
Date of Important Event:
What happened on this date:
What image do I associate with this event?

During the Unit

As students read Unit 2, they can begin work on their time lines. Time lines can include:

- Lesson Review activities
- Dates of important events in the lessons
- Illustrations of important concepts or inventions
- Ideas students develop on their own

Complete the Project

Have students use their organizers to plan a logical time line that shows the important events of the unit. Remind them to check the accuracy of the dates and to make sure that a date is provided for every event on the time line. After all the other elements are in place, have the students illustrate their time lines. Allow students to take turns presenting their time lines to the class. Then, display the time lines in the classroom.

What to Look For

For a scoring rubric, see page 82 of this Teacher Edition.

- Time lines show important events during the European exploration and settlement of the state.
- Time lines relate to the unit's Big Idea.
- Time lines are organized and accurate.
- Illustrations are accurate and placed near the appropriate dates.

UNIT 2 ORGANIZER ▪ 37E

Leveled Readers

Accompanying *Harcourt Social Studies North Carolina* is a series of nonfiction Leveled Readers. At each grade level, three topical Readers correlate to each North Carolina Standard Course of Study competency goal. The Readers reinforce social studies vocabulary and reading focus skills. Lesson plans for each Reader are included in the Teacher Edition as well as in the Leveled Readers Teacher Guides.

- Activities to reinforce social studies vocabulary
- Critical-thinking questions
- Writing prompts
- Graphic organizer to apply reading focus skills

Leveled Readers

BELOW-LEVEL

North Carolinians

Summary *North Carolinians.* This Reader examines how people with different backgrounds have helped form North Carolina's culture.

Vocabulary Power Have students define the following words. Help them write one sentence for each word as it relates to North Carolina's history and culture.

culture
slaves
ethnic group
festival
pottery

Critical Thinking Lead students in a discussion about some ways people in North Carolina celebrate their cultures.

Write a Song Have students write a song about life in North Carolina.

Main Idea and Details

ON-LEVEL

A Musical Heritage

Summary *A Musical Heritage.* This Reader explores the roots of American music in the Southeast.

Vocabulary Power Have students define the following words. Help them write one sentence for each word as it relates to the roots of American music in the Southeast.

tourism
high-tech
ballad
spiritual
improvise

Critical Thinking Lead students in a discussion about the musical roots of some of their favorite songs.

Write a Description Have students write a description about a style of music they like and how it might have been influenced by earlier music.

Compare and Contrast

ABOVE-LEVEL

North Carolina Crafts

Summary *North Carolina Crafts.* This Reader examines the history of North Carolina crafts and identifies the groups who have influenced North Carolina's craft heritage.

Vocabulary Power Have students define the following words. Help them write one sentence for each word as it relates to the history of North Carolina's crafts.

potteries
generation
quilting
basketry

Critical Thinking Lead students in a discussion about how crafts help describe the history and culture of North Carolina.

Write Instructions Have students write instructions on how to quilt, using facts from the Reader and/or the Student Edition.

Main Idea and Details

Complete a Graphic Organizer

Have students complete the graphic organizer to show that they understand the main idea and details about culture and religion in North Carolina.

Main Idea: North Carolina's culture is very diverse.

Details: Scottish clans hold festivals. | People of many religions live in North Carolina. | People of different backgrounds make crafts.

Leveled Readers Teacher Guides include complete lesson plans, copying masters, and project cards.

Harcourt Leveled Readers Available Online! www.harcourtschool.com

187D ■ UNIT 6 ORGANIZER

Meeting People

Ben's Room

iii

Unit 2

Good Citizenship

Competency Goal 2

iv

Unit 3

Changing People and Places

Unit 4

Special Days

v

Unit 5

Where People Live

Welcome To NORTH CAROLINA

vi

Unit 6

The Marketplace

vii

Unit 7

Technology We Use Today

Geography Review

The Five Themes of Geography

The story of people is also the story of where they live. When scientists talk about Earth, they think about five themes, or main ideas.

Location

Everything on Earth has its own location.

Place

Every place has features that make it different from other places.

GEOGRAPHY

I2

Geography Review

The Five Themes of Geography

The story of people is also the story of where they live. When scientists talk about Earth, they think about five themes, or main ideas.

Location

Everything on Earth has its own location.

Place

Every place has features that make it different from other places.

GEOGRAPHY

THEMES

Human-Environment Interactions

People can change the environment or change their ways to live in it.

Movement

People, goods, and ideas move every day.

Regions

Areas of Earth have features that make them different from other areas.

I3

Looking at Earth

The shape of Earth is shown best by a globe. A **globe** is a model of Earth.

On a map of the world, you can see all the land and water at once. A **map** is a flat drawing that shows where places are.

Much of the world is covered by large bodies of water called oceans.

A continent is one of seven main land areas on Earth.

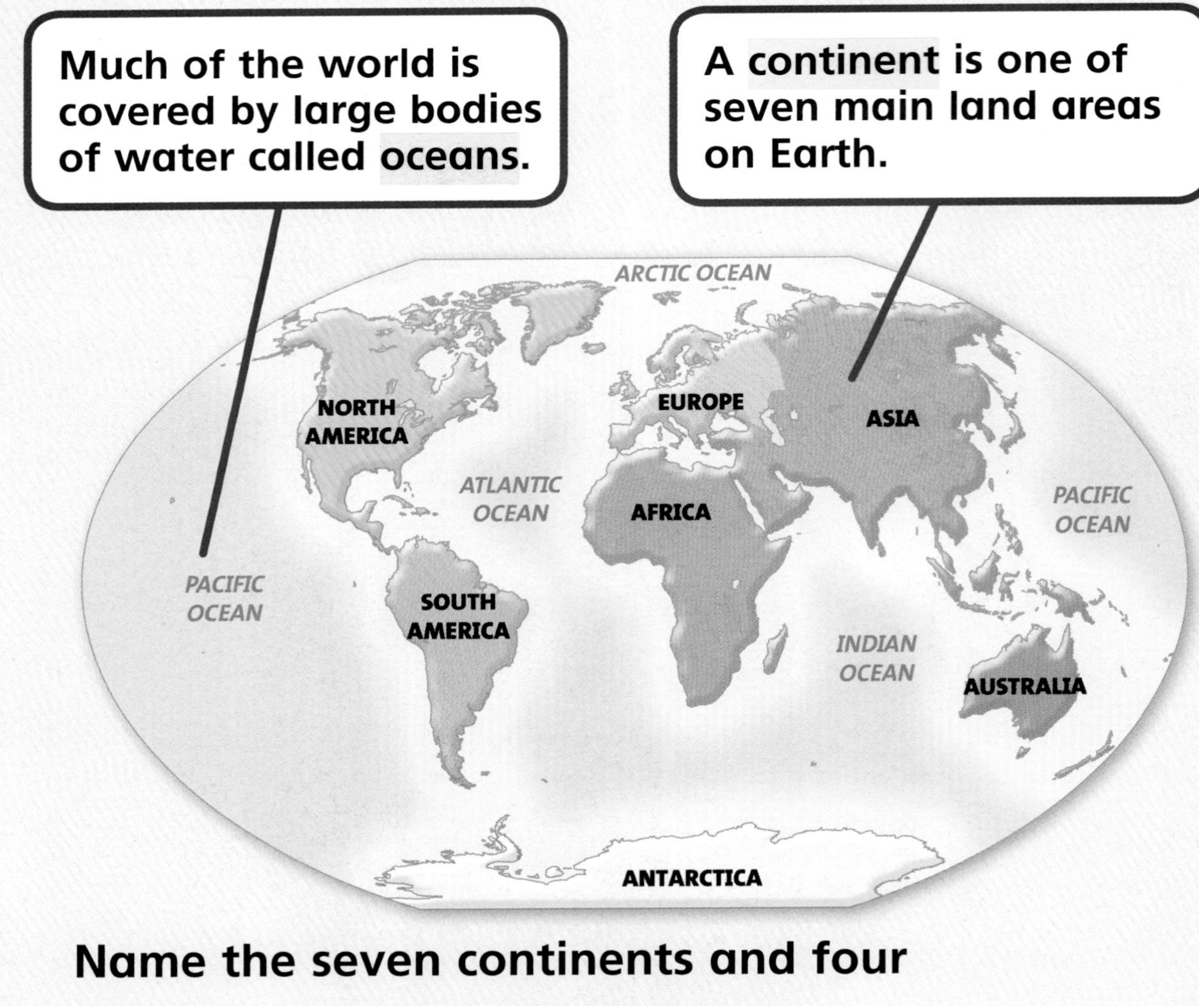

Name the seven continents and four oceans you see on the map.

Your Address

You live on the continent of North America in a **country** called the United States. Your address names the **city** and **state** in which you live.

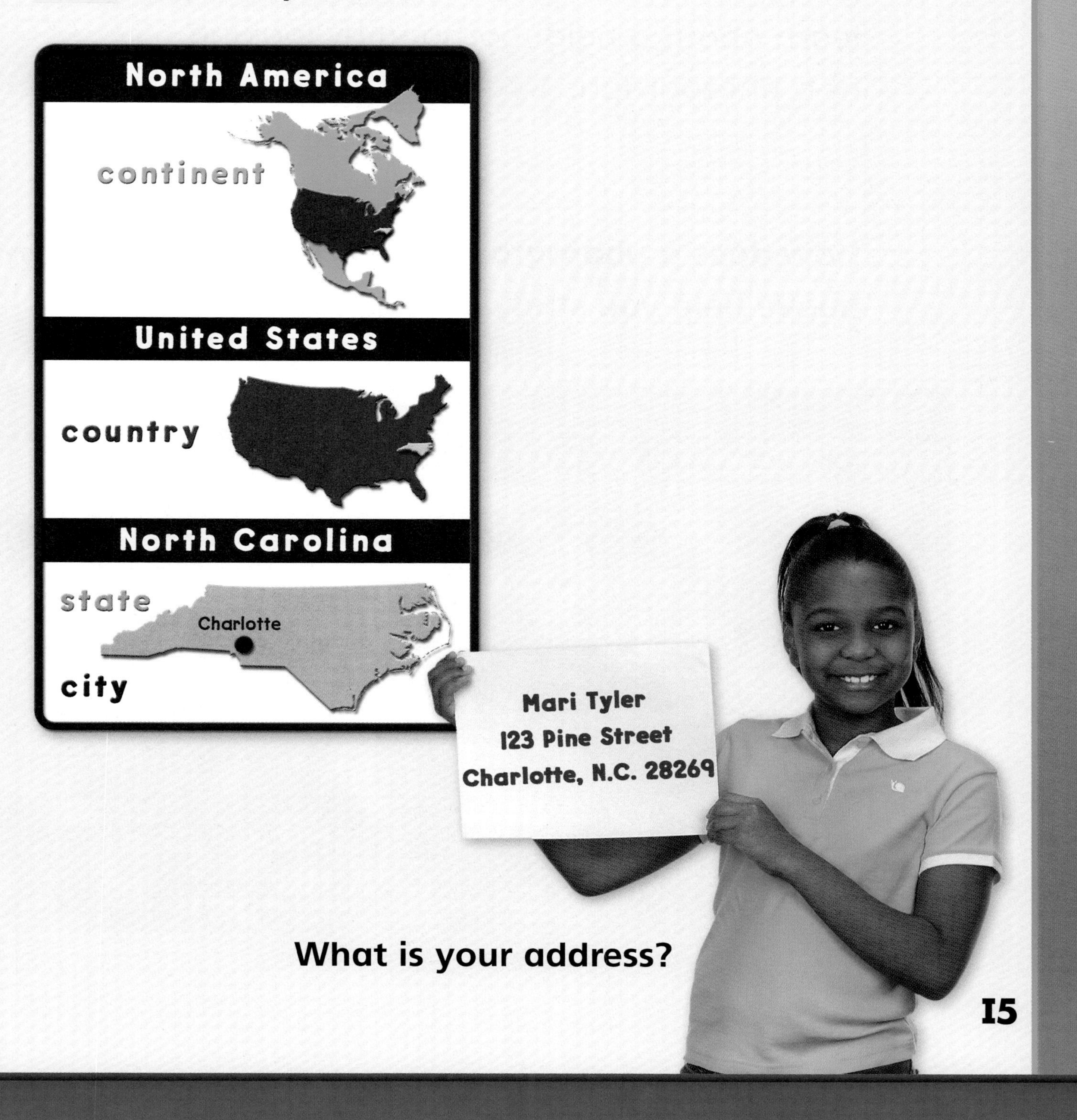

What is your address?

15

View from Above

Does your neighborhood have a school, a grocery store, a library, a fire station, a park, and a bank? These are places that people share in a neighborhood. You can learn about a neighborhood by looking at a photograph.

How does a photograph taken from above help you study a neighborhood?

16

Your Address

You live on the continent of North America in a **country** called the United States. Your address names the **city** and **state** in which you live.

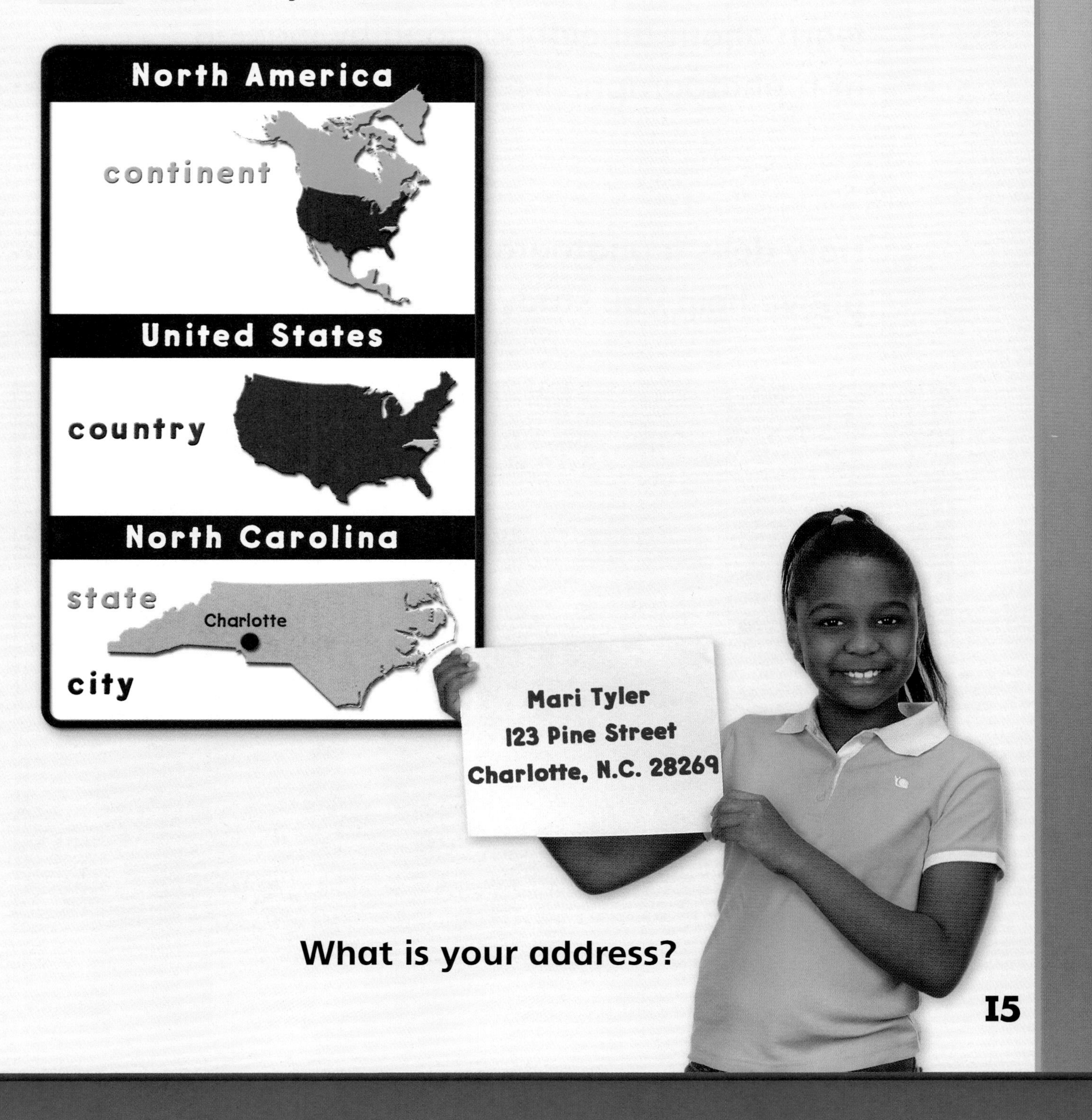

What is your address?

View from Above

Does your neighborhood have a school, a grocery store, a library, a fire station, a park, and a bank? These are places that people share in a neighborhood. You can learn about a neighborhood by looking at a photograph.

How does a photograph taken from above help you study a neighborhood?

I6

You can also learn about a neighborhood by looking at a map. Mapmakers draw symbols to help you find places on the map. A **map symbol** is a small picture or shape that stands for a real thing. The **map title** tells you what the map shows.

How is this map like the photograph? How is it different?

17

Reading Maps

Maps are used to show many different kinds of information. This is a map of the United States. On this map, you can use the map key to find our national capital, or our country's capital. You can also use the key to find each state's capital and borders. A **border** is a line that shows where a state or country ends.

Locate the state of North Carolina on the map. What is the state capital? Name the states that border North Carolina.

18

You can also learn about a neighborhood by looking at a map. Mapmakers draw symbols to help you find places on the map. A **map symbol** is a small picture or shape that stands for a real thing. The **map title** tells you what the map shows.

How is this map like the photograph? How is it different?

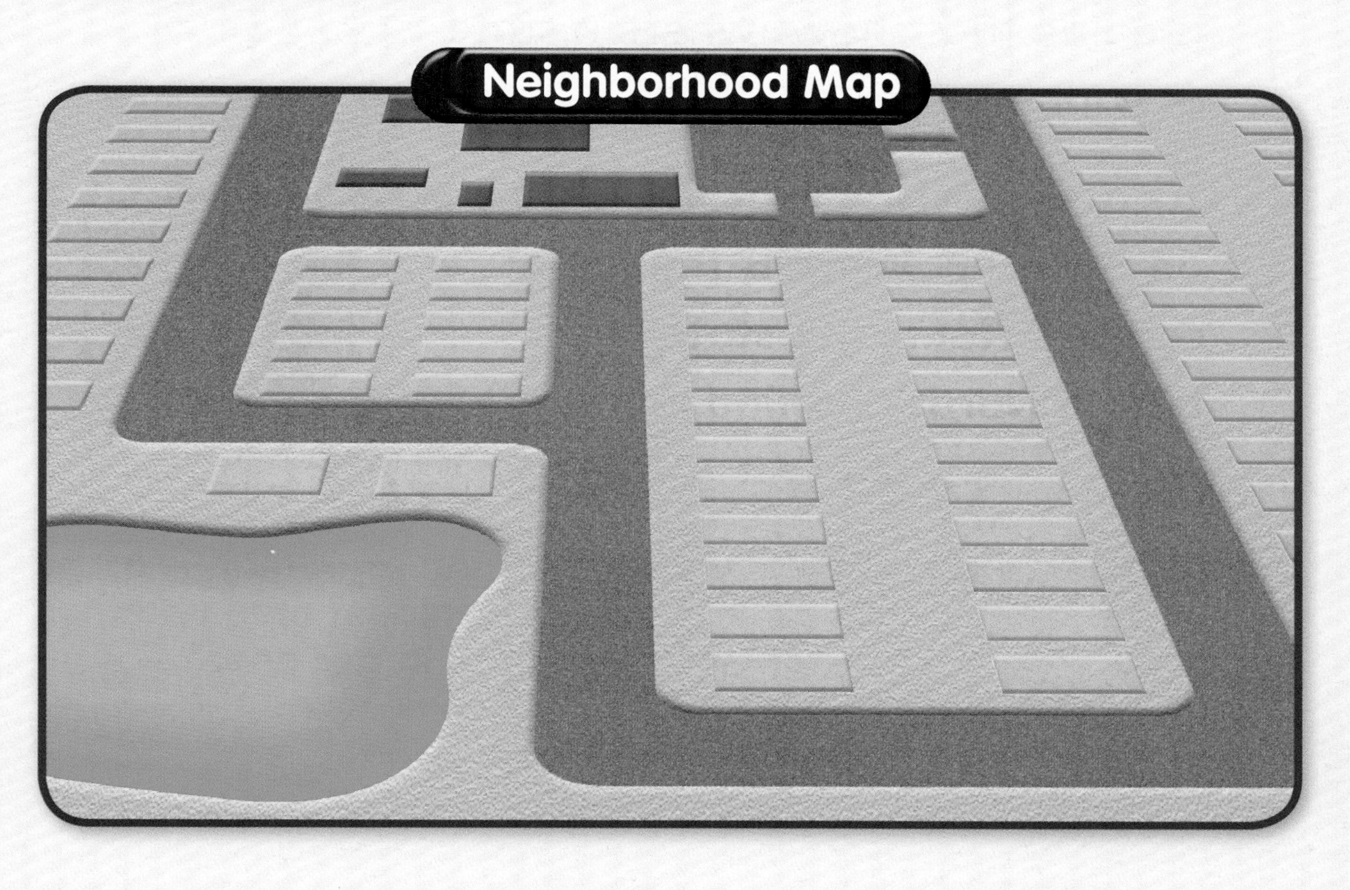

17

Geography Review

Reading Maps

Maps are used to show many different kinds of information. This is a map of the United States. On this map, you can use the map key to find our national capital, or our country's capital. You can also use the key to find each state's capital and borders. A **border** is a line that shows where a state or country ends.

Locate the state of North Carolina on the map. What is the state capital? Name the states that border North Carolina.

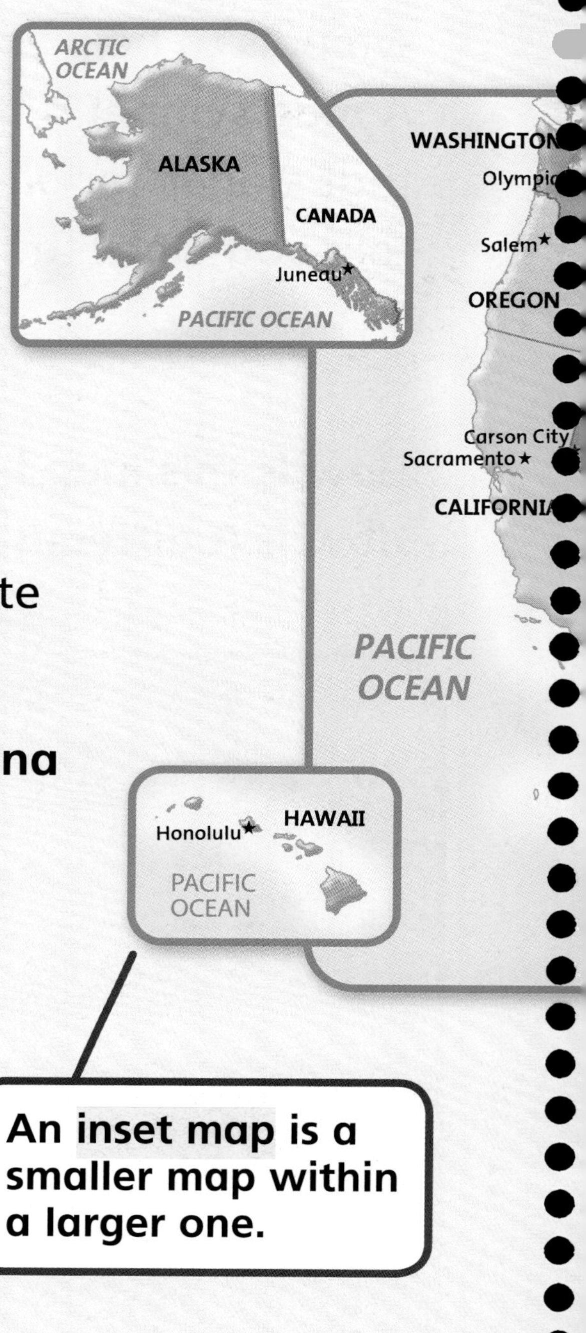

An inset map is a smaller map within a larger one.

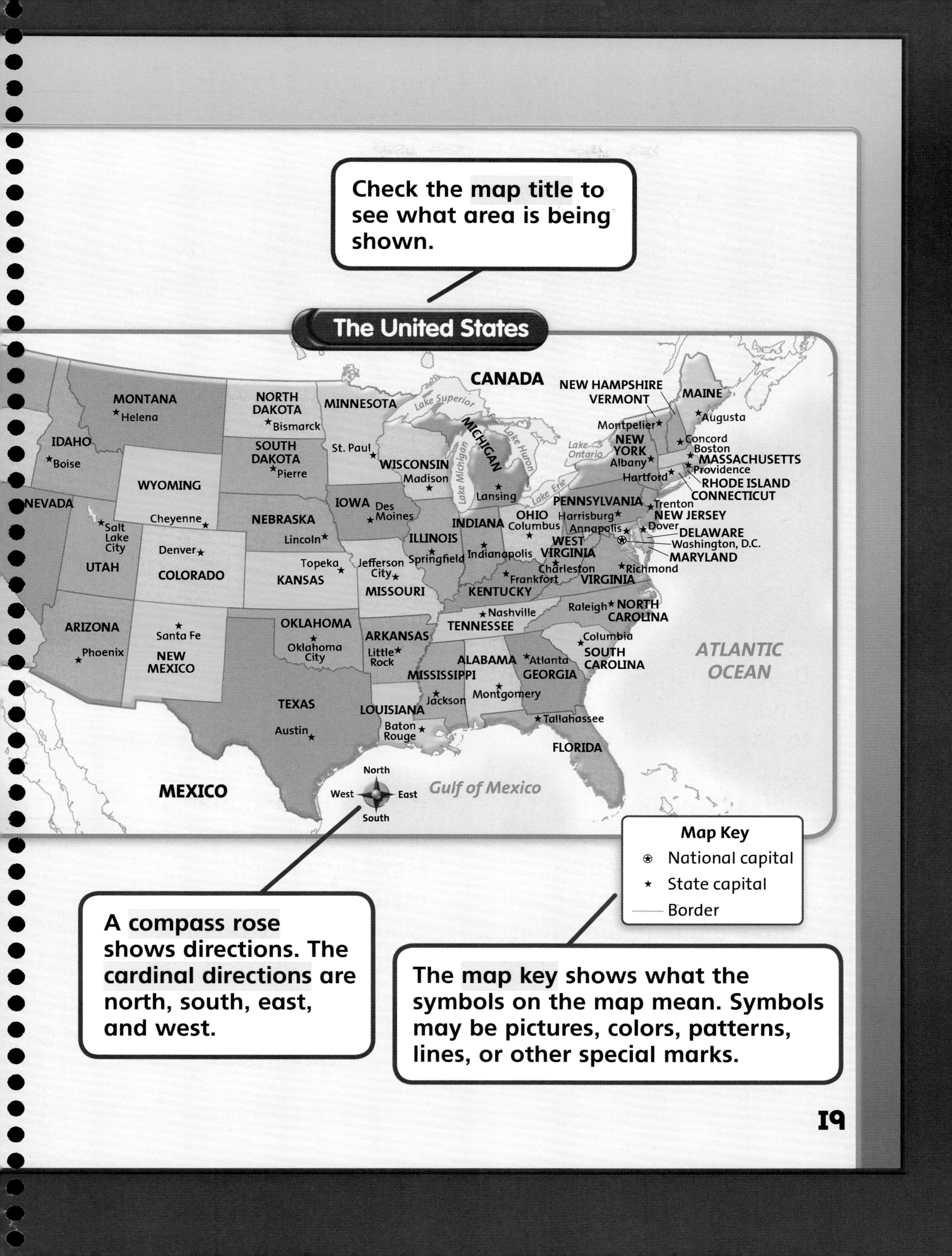
Check the map title to see what area is being shown.
The United States
CANADA
MONTANA
Helena
NORTH DAKOTA
Bismarck
MINNESOTA
Lake Superior
NEW HAMPSHIRE
VERMONT
MAINE
Augusta
IDAHO
Boise
SOUTH DAKOTA
Pierre
St. Paul
WISCONSIN
Madison
MICHIGAN
Lake Michigan
Lake Huron
Lansing
Montpelier
Concord
Boston
MASSACHUSETTS
Providence
RHODE ISLAND
CONNECTICUT
Lake Ontario
NEW YORK
Albany
Hartford
WYOMING
Cheyenne
NEVADA
Salt Lake City
UTAH
NEBRASKA
Lincoln
IOWA
Des Moines
Lake Erie
PENNSYLVANIA
Harrisburg
Trenton
NEW JERSEY
Dover
DELAWARE
Washington, D.C.
MARYLAND
Annapolis
OHIO
Columbus
INDIANA
Indianapolis
ILLINOIS
Springfield
WEST VIRGINIA
Charleston
Richmond
VIRGINIA
Denver
COLORADO
Topeka
KANSAS
Jefferson City
MISSOURI
KENTUCKY
Frankfort
Raleigh
NORTH CAROLINA
Nashville
TENNESSEE
ARIZONA
Phoenix
Santa Fe
NEW MEXICO
OKLAHOMA
Oklahoma City
ARKANSAS
Little Rock
Columbia
SOUTH CAROLINA
ALABAMA
Atlanta
GEORGIA
MISSISSIPPI
Jackson
Montgomery
ATLANTIC OCEAN
TEXAS
Austin
LOUISIANA
Baton Rouge
Tallahassee
FLORIDA
MEXICO
North
West
East
South
Gulf of Mexico
Map Key
National capital
State capital
Border
A compass rose shows directions. The cardinal directions are north, south, east, and west.
The map key shows what the symbols on the map mean. Symbols may be pictures, colors, patterns, lines, or other special marks.
19

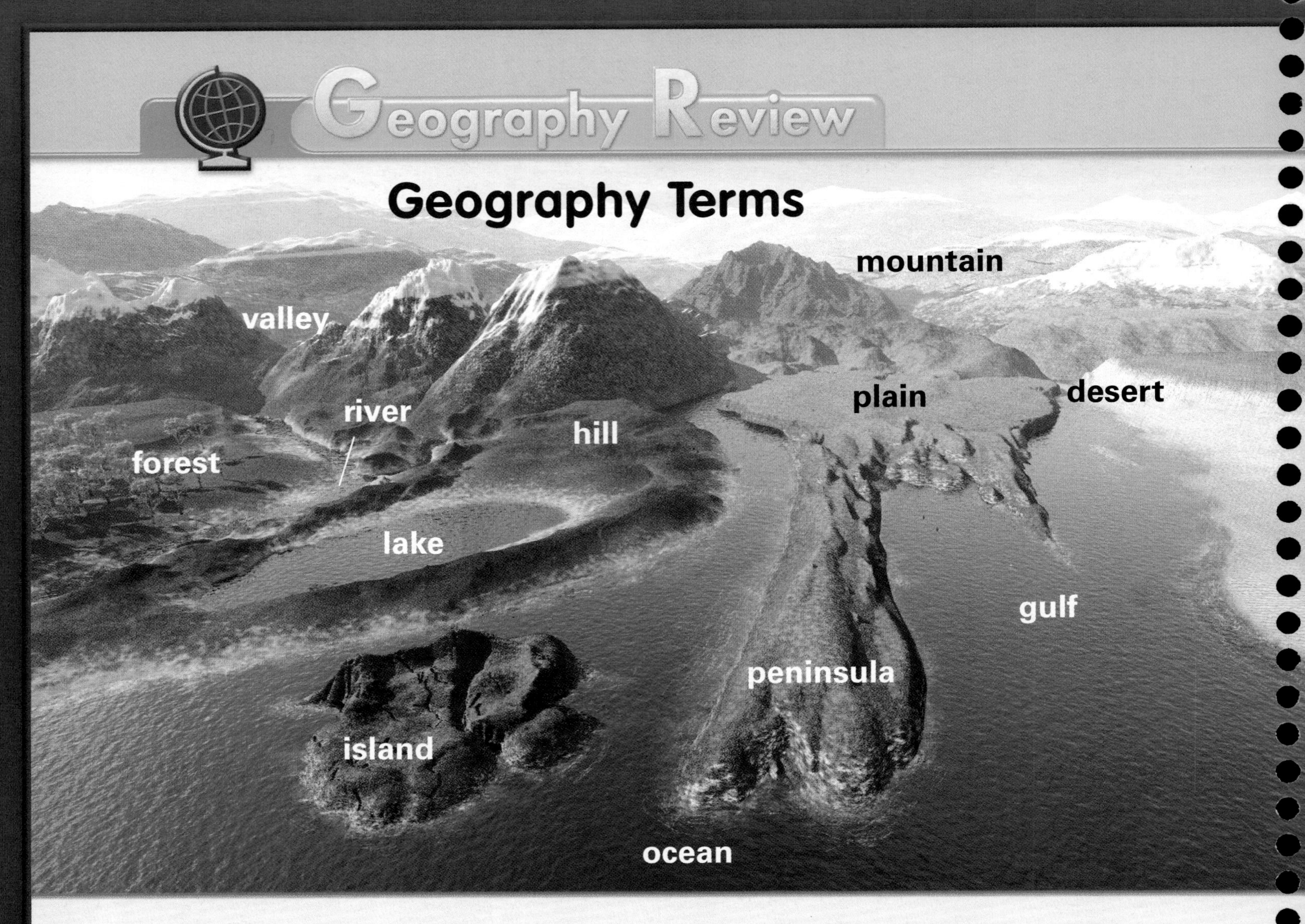

desert a large, dry area of land

forest a large area of land covered with trees

gulf a large body of ocean water that is partly surrounded by land

hill a landform that rises above the land around it

island land with water all around it

lake a body of water with land all around it

mountain the highest kind of landform

ocean a body of salt water that covers a large area

peninsula land that is surrounded on only three sides by water

plain flat land

river a large stream of water that flows across the land

valley low land between hills or mountains

110

Unit 1

Unit 1
Meeting People

NORTH CAROLINA STANDARD COURSE OF STUDY

COMPETENCY GOAL 1

The learner will analyze how individuals, families, and groups are similar and different.

OBJECTIVES

1.01 Describe the roles of individuals in the family.

1.02 Identify various groups to which individuals and families belong.

1.03 Compare and contrast similarities and differences among individuals and families.

1.04 Explore the benefits of diversity in the United States.

LESSON	TOTAL: 22 DAYS	NORTH CAROLINA STANDARD COURSE OF STUDY
Introduce the Unit **Unit Preview,** pp. 1–2 **The Big Idea,** p. 2 **Reading Social Studies,** pp. 3–4 Focus Skill: Compare and Contrast	2 DAYS	COMPETENCY GOAL 1 **The learner will analyze how individuals, families, and groups are similar and different.** **Spotlight on Goals and Objectives** Unit 1
1 **Roles in a Family** pp. 5–8 **family** p. 5 **share** p. 5 **role** p. 6	4 DAYS	**Objective 1.01** Describe the roles of individuals in the family. **Spotlight on Goals and Objectives** Unit 1, Lesson 1
2 **Many Groups** pp. 9–12 **community** p. 11	4 DAYS	**Objective 1.02** Identify various groups to which individuals and families belong. **Spotlight on Goals and Objectives** Unit 1, Lesson 2
3 **Families Are the Same and Different** pp. 13–16 **culture** p. 14 **custom** p. 14 **tradition** p. 15	4 DAYS	**Objective 1.03** Compare and contrast similarities and differences among individuals and families. **Spotlight on Goals and Objectives** Unit 1, Lesson 3
4 **We Live in the United States** pp. 17–20 **world** p. 17 **immigrant** p. 18	4 DAYS	**Objective 1.04** Explore the benefits of diversity in the United States. **Spotlight on Goals and Objectives** Unit 1, Lesson 4
Unit 1 Review and Test Prep pp. 21–24	4 DAYS	**North Carolina Adventures** Unit 1

TEACHING YOUR SOCIAL STUDIES	
	Comprehension Compare and Contrast, pp. 3–4
Background, North Carolina State Parks, p. 5 **Social Studies Strands,** Government and Active Citizenship, p. 5 Economics and Development, p. 6 Historical Perspective, p. 7 **Build Skills,** Chart and Graph Skills, p. 7	**Skim and Scan,** p. 6 **CUES,** p. 7
Background, Students' Roles, p. 9 **Social Studies Strands,** Government and Active Citizenship, p. 9 Individual Development and Identity, p. 10 Cultures and Diversity, p. 11 **Build Skills,** Decision Making, p. 10 Chart and Graph Skills, p. 11	**CUES,** p. 10 **Skim and Scan,** p. 11
Background, Suburban Neighborhoods, p. 13 John Coltrane, p. 15 **Social Studies Strands,** Geographic Relationships, p. 13 Cultures and Diversity, p. 14 Individual Development and Identity, p. 15 **Build Skills,** Problem Solving, p. 14	**Comprehension,** Question, p. 14 Compare and Contrast, p. 15
Background, The Statue of Liberty, p. 17 El Salvador, p. 19 **Social Studies Strands,** Global Connections, p. 17 Economics and Development, p. 18 Technological Influences, p. 19 **Build Skills,** Map and Globe Skills, p. 18	**Vocabulary,** p. 18 **Comprehension** Compare and Contrast, p. 19
	Summarize the Unit Compare and Contrast, p. 21

Print Resources

Student Edition, pp. 1–24
Teacher Edition, pp. 1A–24
Leveled Readers
Leveled Readers Teacher Guides
Document-Based Questions
Primary Atlas

Technology/Digital Resources

Spotlight on Goals and Objectives

North Carolina Interactive Presentations CD
North Carolina Interactive Presentations Online

Online Teacher Edition with ePlanner
Leveled Readers Online Database
North Carolina Adventures CD
North Carolina Adventures Online
Multimedia Biographies CD
Multimedia Biographies Online
Social Studies Music Collection CD

Hands-On Resources

Reading Focus Skills Transparencies
Social Studies Skills Transparencies
Graphic Organizer Write-On/Wipe-Off Cards
Interactive Atlas
Interactive Desk Maps
Interactive Map Transparencies
Picture Vocabulary Cards
Primary Source Kit
TimeLinks: Interactive Time Line
Social Studies in Action, pp. 42–43, 70–71, 99, 102–105, 142

Assessment Options

1 Unit 1 Test
Assessment Program, pp. 1–4

2 Writing
Write a Paragraph, p. 24

3 Activity
Unit Project: Plan a Culture Fair, p. 24

Leveled Readers

BELOW-LEVEL

Many Cultures

Summary *Many Cultures.* This Reader focuses on the cultures of the United States and how these cultures are similar and different.

Vocabulary Power Have students define the following words. Help them write one sentence for each word as it relates to learning about people's ways of life.

culture
history
immigrant
folktale
custom

Critical Thinking Lead students in a discussion about the beliefs shared by people who live in the United States.

Write a Poem Have students write a poem about the special beliefs and customs of their families or a family they know.

Focus Skill **Compare and Contrast**

ON-LEVEL

Tell Me a Story

Summary *Tell Me a Story.* This Reader examines the art of storytelling and how, through stories, people can learn about right and wrong, history, and culture.

Vocabulary Power Have students define the following words. Help them write one sentence for each word as it relates to learning about people's ways of life.

culture
history
world

Critical Thinking Lead students in a discussion about some of their favorite stories.

Write a Story Have students write stories about important events in their lives. Remind them that their stories should have a beginning, a middle, and an end.

Focus Skill **Compare and Contrast**

ABOVE-LEVEL

Games People Play

Summary *Games People Play.* This Reader illustrates how people around the world enjoy playing games and identifies some specific games that people play.

Vocabulary Power Have students define the following words. Help them write one sentence for each word as it relates to learning about people's ways of life.

culture
history
world

Critical Thinking Lead students in a discussion about why students play different games in different countries.

Write a Report Have students write a report about one of their favorite games. Have them write a paragraph about how the game is played, the rules of the game, and why they like the game.

Focus Skill **Compare and Contrast**

Complete a Graphic Organizer

Have students complete the graphic organizer to show that they understand how to compare and contrast people's ways of life.

Topic 1	Similar	Topic 2
Native Americans First people to live in North America	**Both** Shared their cultures	**Early Settlers** Came to North America later

Leveled Readers Teacher Guides include complete lesson plans, copying masters, and project cards.

Harcourt Leveled Readers Available Online! www.harcourtschool.com

Plan a Culture Fair

Getting Started

Introduce the Hands-On Activity on page 24 in the Unit Review as you begin Unit 1. Begin planning elements of the culture fair as students learn about our diverse country. Point out that fairs often have food, art, music, games, and other elements unique to a culture. Explain that this fair will celebrate the cultures represented in their school and community. The fair should reflect students' understanding of the unit's Big Idea.

The Big Idea
How are people, families, and groups the same? How are they different?

Project Management

- Organize students into small groups. Work with each group to help them research an assigned culture to celebrate at the fair.
- Provide instructional support and materials for art and props as needed.

Materials: Social Studies textbook; posterboard; construction paper; markers, crayons, or colored pencils; paper; recordings of cultural music; game boards and pieces; musical instruments (if available); ethnic foods from volunteers

Organizer: Have each group use an organizer like the one below to list the types of food, art, music, and games that group members will bring to the fair.

ORGANIZER

Food	Art	Music	Games

During the Unit

As students read Unit 1, they can begin work on their culture fair ideas. Fairs may include the following:

- Lesson Review activities
- Your own favorite activities
- Ideas students develop on their own

Complete the Project

Have students practice dances, games, and other activities of the assigned cultures. Then have students invite other classes, faculty, and family members to the fair. Encourage guests to ask questions and participate in activities. When the fair is over, encourage students to describe what they learned about each of the cultures presented.

What to Look For

For a scoring rubric, see page 24 of this Teacher Edition.

- Students recognize the diversity of people in their school and community.
- Each group prepares and maintains a booth that presents the assigned culture.
- Activities and other fair elements relate to the cultures and are clearly presented.

Technology/Digital Resources

START

North Carolina Interactive Presentations

Purpose

The North Carolina Interactive Presentation Unit 1 can be used to preview Unit 1. This presentation provides a concise, visual overview of Competency Goal 1 and its objectives. You can use it to preview the unit for the class, or throughout the unit to introduce and reinforce individual objectives.

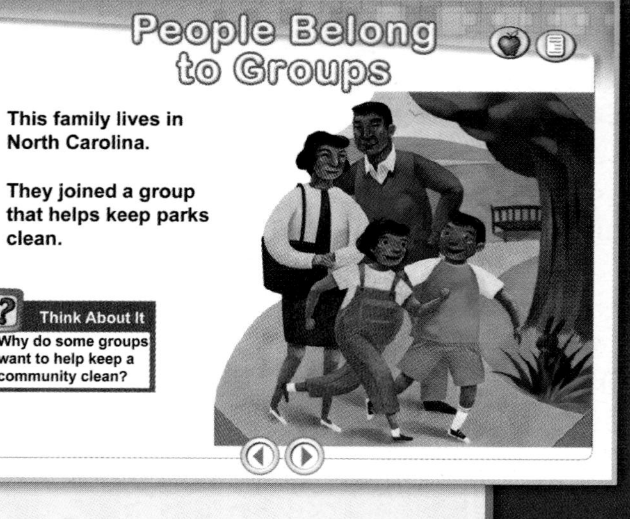

Contents

The Unit 1 presentation includes an introduction to Competency Goal 1, including a vocabulary preview and a visual introduction to individuals and family. In addition, the presentation covers all the unit's objectives lesson by lesson, giving students a broad overview of North Carolina's communities and neighborhoods.

REVIEW

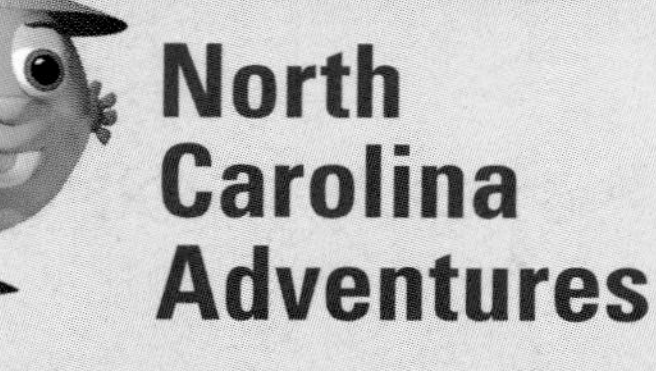

North Carolina Adventures

Purpose

The North Carolina Adventures games, offered both on CD and online, provide an entertaining first-person-player method of content review. When students have completed the unit, they can review its competency goal and all objectives through the Unit 1 game.

Contents

Tell students they will use their knowledge of families to help Eco and Eco's friend, Macy, make it to the cultural fair. Throughout, students will review what they have learned about people, the groups they belong to, and immigration. Explain that the "Help" buttons in the game will refer them to pages in their textbooks if they need additional information.

Additional Resources

For Teachers

Free and Inexpensive Materials are listed on the Social Studies website at **www.harcourtschool.com/ss1**

- Addresses to write to for free and inexpensive products
- Links to unit-related materials
- Internet maps
- Internet references

The eTE with ePlanner provides the following components

- A calendar tool for scheduling Social Studies lessons and displaying all scheduled lessons and activities
- TE pages and additional resources for easy online reference

For Students

When students visit **www.harcourtschool.com/ss1** they will find internal resources such as

- Our Multimedia Biographies database
- Skills activities
- Additional research tools
- Information about all 50 states

Children play a game together.

Unit 1 Preview

PAGES 1–2

Start with the Competency Goal

Competency Goal 1 The learner will analyze how individuals, families, and groups are similar and different.

Make It Relevant

Ask the following question to help students understand the differences among people who live in the United States.

Q In what ways do people differ from one another?

A Students may mention ethnic groups, languages, cultures, and abilities.

Discuss the Photograph

Have students look at the photograph and explain how the children are the same and different.

Q What does the photograph show about people in the United States?

A It shows that people from different cultures live in the United States.

Instructional Design

START WITH THE GOAL AND OBJECTIVES

NORTH CAROLINA STANDARD COURSE OF STUDY

- competency goal
- objectives

PLAN ASSESSMENT

Assessment Options

- Option 1–Unit 1 Test
- Option 2–Writing: Write a Paragraph, p. 24
- Option 3–Activity: Plan a Culture Fair, p. 24

PLAN INSTRUCTION

Spotlight on Goals and Objectives
North Carolina Interactive Presentations, Unit 1

Unit 1 Teacher Edition
- resources
- activities
- strategies

Unit 1 Leveled Readers Teacher Guides

Unit 1 Preview

PAGES 1–2

The Big Idea

Have students read The Big Idea question and then preview the ways in which people, families, and groups are the same and different.

Access Prior Knowledge

Draw a two-column compare-and-contrast chart on the board. Label one column *Same* and one column *Different*. Have students name ways in which the people in their school are the same. Record these responses in the *Same* column of the chart. Then have students name ways in which people in their school are different from one another. Record those responses in the *Different* column. Discuss the similarities and differences. Then, have students read the paragraph and complete the activity.

The Big Idea

How are people, families, and groups the same? How are they different?

There are many kinds of groups of people. A group is a number of people who do things together. A group can be as big as all the people in a community. A group can be as small as a family. Even though people belong to different groups, the groups are the same in many ways.

Draw a picture of a group you belong to.

Drawing should show that student understands the concept of groups.

2

READ MORE

Encourage independent reading with these books or books of your choice.

Basic

The Quilt Story by Tony Johnston. Putnam Juvenile, 1996. A quilt's comforting presence is shown through changes in two different generations of families.

Proficient

All Kinds of People: What Makes Us Different by Jennifer Waters. Spyglass Books, 2002. This book explores the diversity of all people.

Advanced

Coming to America: The Story of Immigration by Betsy Maestro. Scholastic Press, 1996. Offers a brief history of American immigration.

Reading Social Studies

Compare and Contrast

Focus Skill

Learn

- You compare two things by thinking about how they are the same.
- You contrast two things by thinking about how they are different.

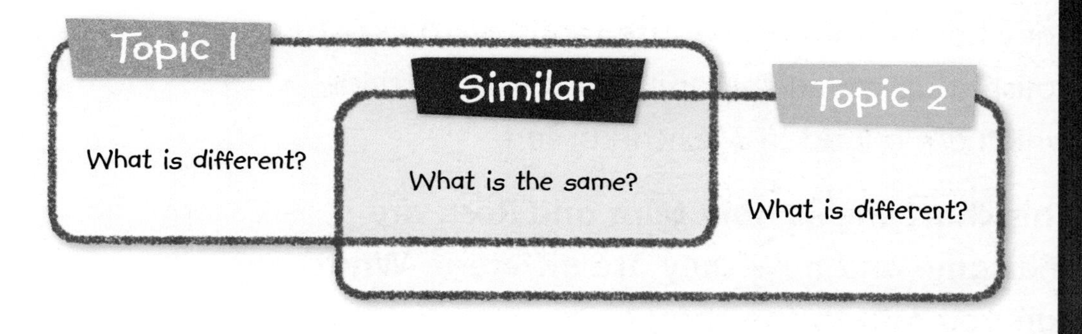

Practice

Read the paragraph below. Underline the sentence that tells how Ian and Jack are the same.

Ian and Jack both belong to the book club. Ian also belongs to the cooking club. Jack belongs to the art club.

Topic 1

Topic 2

3

Reading Social Studies PAGES 3–4

Learn

Have students read the Learn section and examine the graphic organizer. Point out that by listing ways in which two things are the same and different, students can better understand the relationship between those things. Explain that words such as *both* and *but* show compare-and-contrast relationships.

Practice

Read the paragraph with students. Ask to which club both Ian and Jack belong. Then ask students to identify the clubs to which only one boy belongs. Help students write the information in the graphic organizer.

READING FOCUS SKILLS

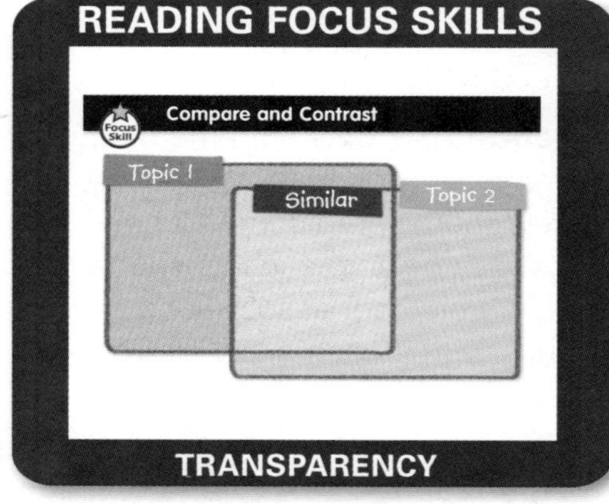

TRANSPARENCY

Graphic Organizer Write-On/ Wipe-Off Cards available

INTEGRATE THE CURRICULUM

ENGLISH LANGUAGE ARTS Classify Words Create pairs of index cards naming or showing comparable items, such as apple and orange, motorcycle and bicycle, clock and watch, and radio and television. Organize students into groups. Give each group one pair of cards. Have each group list how the two items are the same and how they are different.

ELA 3.02 Recognize and relate similar vocabulary use and concepts across experiences with texts.

Reading Social Studies PAGES 3–4

Apply

This selection provides students with opportunities to compare and contrast characteristics of Mira and Rosa. Have students identify the girls' favorite foods. Ask students whether those foods are the same or different. Tell students to write the information in the graphic organizer.

Unit 1 provides many opportunities for students to practice comparing and contrasting different items and ideas. As students read the unit, challenge them to think about similarities and differences in the information.

Apply

Read the paragraphs.

Mira and Rosa are best friends. They live in Greenville, North Carolina. Mira's family is from Poland. She speaks Polish and English. Rosa's family is from Mexico. She speaks Spanish and English.

Mira and Rosa both like to play basketball. They have different favorite foods. Mira likes a Polish soup called chlodnik. Rosa likes tortillas, which are a kind of Mexican bread.

This chart shows how Mira and Rosa are the same and how they are different. What can you add to the chart?

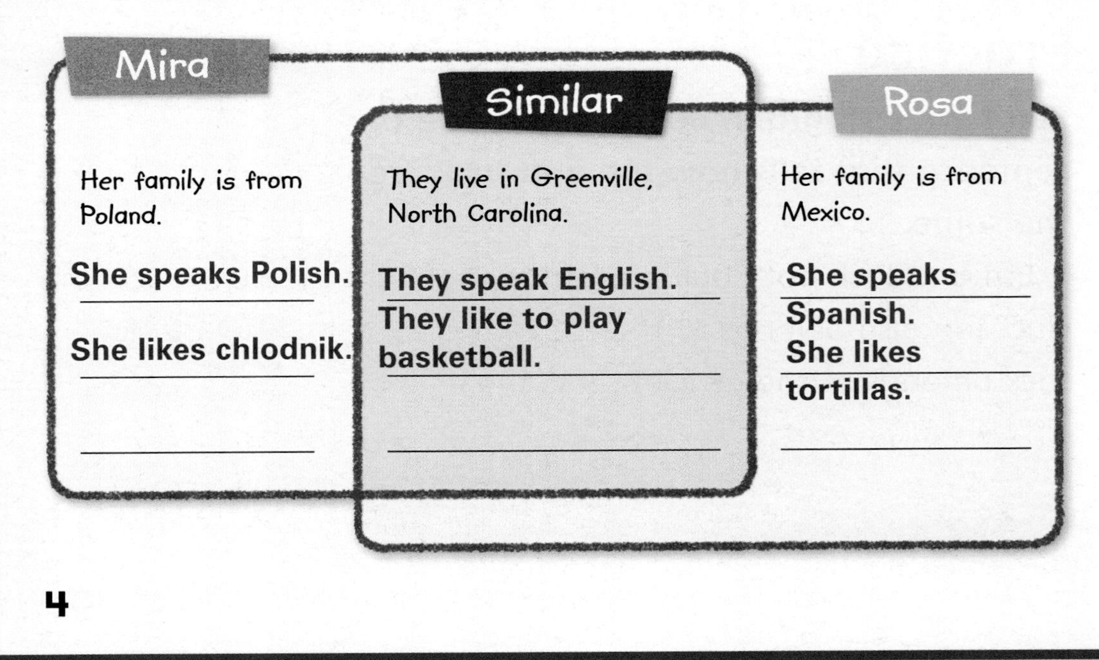

4

ESL/LANGUAGE SUPPORT

Vocabulary Development As they read the unit, help students create a word wall. Have each student write a word to describe his or her family. Display the words on a large area, grouping together words that are the same.

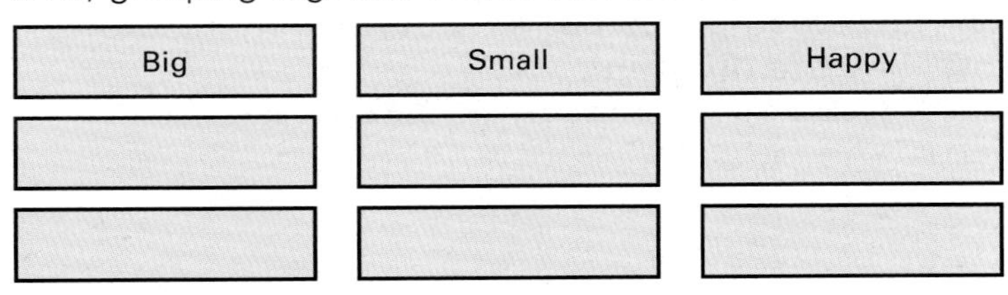

Prior Learning and Experiences As they read the unit, ask students to think about community groups to which they or people they know belong. Help them name some clubs or organizations to which people may belong, such as sports teams, summer reading groups, or volunteer associations. Write these on the board. Discuss with students any similarities among the groups or organizations.

Build Background

Make It Relevant Ask students to think of the different roles that family members may have. Have them list these roles. These roles may include a mother, a father, brothers and sisters, a grandparent, an aunt, and an uncle.

Preview the Lesson

Guide students in previewing the lesson. Point out the following features on Student Edition pages 5–8:

- **Page 5** Discuss the photograph of the family enjoying a trip to the park. Ask students what activity they see the family doing. What other activities can families do at a park?
- **Page 6** Explain that parents play a different role in the family than children do. Ask students to name some of the roles a parent has.
- **Page 7** Preview the photographs and ask students to discuss the role that each child is taking. Have students compare and contrast what the children are doing in each of the photographs with the roles that the students have in their own homes.

Preteach Vocabulary

- Point out that a **family** can have many different characteristics. Explain that a family can be big or small and that family members may be good at different things. Invite students to draw a picture of their family or of a family that they know.
- Explain that family members **share**, or use, many of the same objects. Show students a circle cutout and say that it represents a pizza. Tell students that four students want to share the pizza. Cut the pizza to show how four students can share the pizza.
- Tell students that the words *part* and **role** are synonyms, and that each member of a family has a different part or role to play. Read aloud a story about a family, and discuss the roles that family members play in the story.

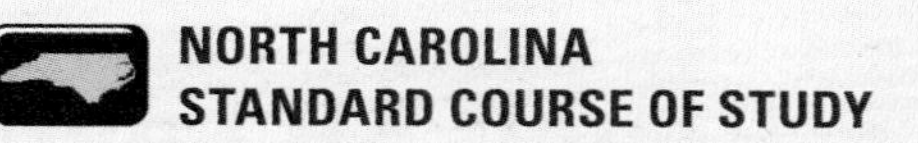

NORTH CAROLINA STANDARD COURSE OF STUDY

Objective 1.01 Describe the roles of individuals in the family.

Key Content Summary

- **A family is a group of people who live, work, and play together.**
- **Each person in a family has a role.**
- **Parents work and take care of their children. Children help around the house.**

Vocabulary

- **family,** p. 5
- **share,** p. 5
- **role,** p. 6

Spotlight on Goals and Objectives

Use North Carolina Interactive Presentations, Unit 1, Lesson 1, to access prior knowledge and build background.

Reach All Learners

ESL/Language Support

Content and Language Objectives Have students think about the roles they play in the classroom. Have them list on a sheet of paper the different types of roles they may have. Encourage students to think of different roles, such as line leader, person watering class plants, and helper picking up art supplies. Then have each student share his or her list with the class.

Extra Support

Use the Photographs The photographs on page 7 show children in different roles. Have students review those roles. Make activity cards with pictures cut from magazines that show family members engaged in various roles or activities. Ask students to choose a card randomly and act out the role on the card.

Extension Activity

Perform a Skit Have students review the section called The Roles of Parents on page 6. Then have pairs of students write a brief skit that shows some roles that parents might play. Invite volunteers to act out their skits for the class.

Integrate the Curriculum

Second Languages

Learn Different Languages Tell students that people from other cultures often speak different languages. Teach students to say the words *mother, father, brother,* and *sister* in several different languages. Invite students to add other languages they know.

Spanish: madre, padre, hermano, hermana

French: mère, père, frère, sœur

Italian: madre, padre, fratello, sorella

German: mutter, vater, bruder, schwester

Roles in a Family

Lesson 1

A **family** is a group of people who live together. People in a family share things. We **share** when we use something with others. Families also work and play together. **What will you learn about families?**

Possible response: Families are groups of people who work and play together.

A family enjoys a park in North Carolina.

NORTH CAROLINA STANDARD COURSE OF STUDY

1.01 Describe the roles of individuals in the family.

5

Start with the Objectives

Objective 1.01 Describe the roles of individuals in the family.

Set a Purpose for Reading

Read aloud the introduction. Call attention to the highlighted words (family, share). Ask students to provide definitions and examples of each. To help students set a purpose for reading, ask volunteers to answer the question. Finally, use the Think Aloud to model thinking about families for students.

Think Aloud

I know that in my family, each person has different jobs, but sometimes we help one another with our jobs. I will read the lesson to learn more about the jobs in families.

BACKGROUND

North Carolina State Parks There are twenty-nine state parks in North Carolina. Each park has a variety of recreational and educational activities. Visitors are able to hike, camp, fish, and visit historical sites. People visiting Crowders Mountain State Park near Charlotte, NC, might see some animals that are often found in the park, such as an American beaver, a red fox, or a white-tailed deer.

SOCIAL STUDIES STRANDS

Government and Active Citizenship Have students name people at school and their roles (teacher, principal, nurse, and so on). Then have students consider their own role in school. Guide students to recognize that they have many roles, including those of learner, helper, and friend. Point out that we have similar roles in our families. Students can draw two pictures to show a role they have at school and at home.

SSSMART™
SUPPORT

1 Skim and Scan

Tell students that when they skim a text, they will read it quickly to find facts. They will not read each word. Ask students how they can use headings and words in bold type to skim a text. Ask students to scan the first paragraph to find the highlighted word *role*.

1 Underline one sentence that tells about a parent's role in the family.

The Roles of Parents

There are many kinds of families. A family may be big or small. Each person in a family has a role. A **role** is the part a person plays in a group.

Parents work at jobs to earn money. They use this money to buy things for their families. Parents also take care of their children.

6

TEACHING YOUR SOCIAL STUDIES

SOCIAL STUDIES STRANDS

Economics and Development Discuss the fact that some parents work in a home office. When both parents work outside of the home, babies and young children may attend day care or have a babysitter. Parents pay for these services. Some parents who stay home to care for their children may not work for pay.

The Roles of Children

Children have many roles in their families. Most children help around the house. They may wash the dishes, make their beds, or set the table. Older children may help care for their younger brothers and sisters.

TextWork

❷ Look at the pictures. Circle the jobs children can do.

7

SSSMART™ SUPPORT

TextWork

❷ **CUES**

Analyze/Interpret Photographs Engage students in a discussion about the job depicted in each photograph. Take an informal class survey, in the form of raised hands, to find out how many students in the class do each job. Write the numbers on the board.

SOCIAL STUDIES STRANDS

Historical Perspective With students, compare and contrast the roles of children in families today with those of children long ago. If possible, show students historical images of children doing household chores, such as spinning wool or churning butter.

BUILD SKILLS

Chart and Graph Skills Remind students of the survey they took to see how many of them have the roles shown on the page. With students' help, turn the survey into a chart showing the number of students who perform each job depicted.

Lesson Review

Summary Have students work in pairs to summarize the lesson's key content before they complete the Lesson Review. Students should practice skimming and scanning as they summarize.

- A family is a group of people who live, work, and play together.
- Each person in a family has a role.
- Parents work and take care of their children. Children help around the house.

Lesson 1 Review

1. **SUMMARIZE** What roles do people play in a family?

   Possible response: People can be parents or children in a family. Parents work at jobs and take care of their children. Children may help around the house.

2. What is a **family**?

   A family is a group of people who live together.

3. How is a child's role in a family different from a parent's role?

   Possible response: Children help around the house and go to school. Parents go to work and take care of children.

Writing

Write two sentences about your roles in your family.

8

WRITING RUBRIC

Score 4
- identifies two or more family roles
- clearly understands the purpose of their role in the family
- shows a developed understanding of sentence structure

Score 3
- identifies at least one family role
- understands the purpose of their role in the family
- shows a basic understanding of sentence structure

Score 2
- identifies a role but does not connect it to family
- does not clearly understand the purpose of their role in the family
- shows a beginning understanding of sentence structure

Score 1
- does not clearly describe a family role
- does not understand the purpose of their role in the family
- fails to show an understanding of sentence structure

Build Background

Make It Relevant Explain that different people belong to different groups. Students can belong to a family, a school, and a classroom, as well as to other groups. Ask students to think about some of the other groups they belong to, both inside and outside of school. Have students list the groups in which they are members. Write their responses on the board. These responses may include groups such as a choir, a sports team, or a club.

Preview the Lesson

Guide students in previewing the lesson. Point out the following features on Student Edition pages 9–12:

- **Page 9** Discuss the photograph of Macy. Ask students to identify the group that Macy is with on this page.
- **Page 10** Explain that Macy has a different role in each of the groups to which she belongs. Ask students what roles they have in the different groups to which they belong.
- **Page 11** Preview the photograph, and ask students to discuss what activity this group is enjoying. What are some of the group members' specific roles? What is Macy doing in this group?

Preteach Vocabulary

- Explain that a **community** is a large group to which individuals or entire families belong. Ask students to compare and contrast the things Macy does in her community with the things they do in their own communities.

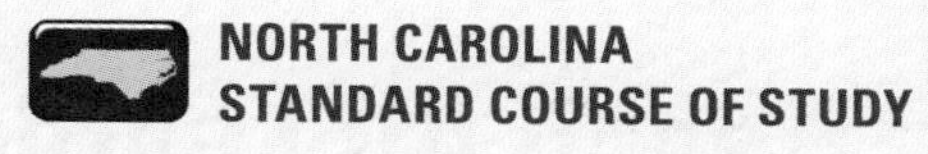

Objective 1.02 Identify various groups to which individuals and families belong.

Key Content Summary

- **People can belong to many groups.**
- **Macy has different roles in each group to which she belongs.**
- **Macy's family is part of a community.**

Vocabulary

- **community,** p. 11

Spotlight on Goals and Objectives

Use North Carolina Interactive Presentations, Unit 1, Lesson 2, to access prior knowledge and build background.

Reach All Learners

ESL/Language Support

Active Learning Draw a two-column chart on the board. Label one column *Person* and the other column *Family*. Make cards to illustrate groups for individuals and groups for families. For example, for individuals, you might suggest an art club, a baseball team, or a theater group. For families, you might suggest a community, a volunteer group, or a neighborhood. Draw or use magazine pictures to illustrate each group. Ask students to name the group that they see on each card and tell you in which column that group belongs. Categorize the groups in the chart on the board.

Person	Family

Extra Support

List Different Groups Help students create lists of groups to which they or their families belong. Then have students choose one of the groups from the list and write a sentence explaining what that particular group does.

Extension Activity

Make a Poster Have students think about the different groups of which they are members. Then have them choose a group and make a poster about it. Invite students to display their posters in the classroom.

Integrate the Curriculum

Healthful Living

Learn a Dance Ask a music or physical education teacher to show students the steps of a traditional folk dance, such as the Mexican Hat Dance, an Irish jig, a polka, or the hula. When students have learned the dance, invite other classes to watch the performance. Have student dancers begin by telling about the origins of the dance.

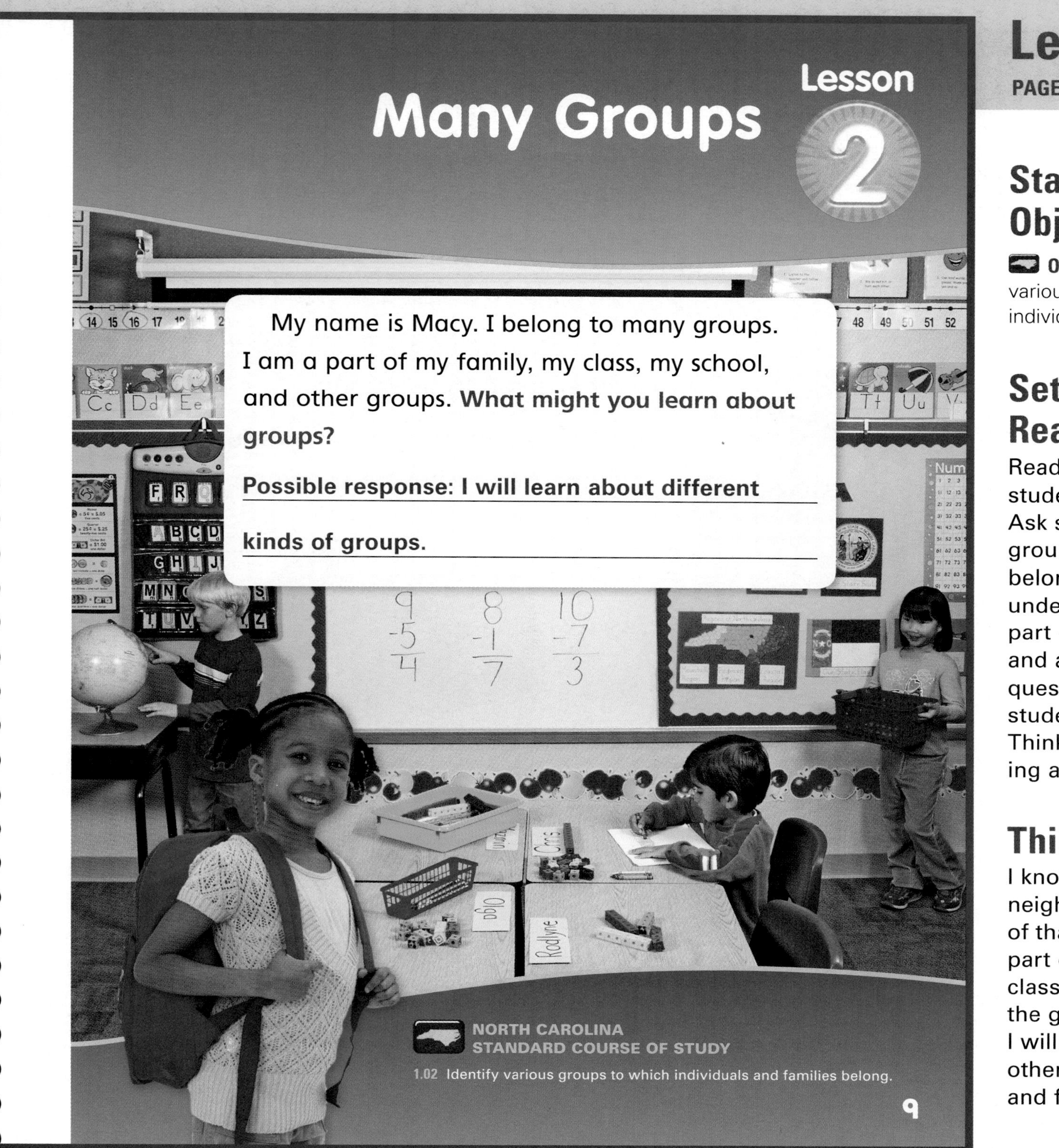

Lesson 2

PAGES 9–12

Start with the Objective

Objective 1.02 Identify various groups to which individuals and families belong.

Set a Purpose for Reading

Read the text aloud as students follow along. Ask students to name the groups to which Macy belongs. Help students understand that Macy is part of a family, a class, and a school. Reread the question aloud, and have students answer it. Use the Think Aloud to model thinking about groups.

Think Aloud

I know that I live in a neighborhood. I am a part of that group. I am also a part of a family and this class. These are some of the groups I belong to. I will read to learn about other groups that people and families belong to.

BACKGROUND

Students' Roles Students in North Carolina are part of a class. Students in the classroom may have different roles. One student may be a line leader. Another student may be responsible for watering the plants. Another student may be responsible for looking after art supplies.

SOCIAL STUDIES STRANDS

Government and Active Citizenship Show students various photographs of service groups and community helpers, such as firefighters and police officers. Ask students to identify the group to which the people in each photograph belong and to explain how each group works to help the community.

SSSMART™ SUPPORT

TextWork

1 CUES

Analyze/Interpret Photographs Remind students of the different groups that Macy belongs to. One group is the art club. Ask students to describe materials that people in an art club would use. Invite a volunteer to skim the text to identify Macy's role in the art club. Then ask students to identify the photograph that shows Macy in the art club. Point out that thinking about what they already know about art can help students choose the correct photograph.

1 Circle the picture that shows Macy in the art club.

Groups I Belong To

I am a daughter in my family. I set the table for dinner.

I am in first grade. I water our class plants.

I am a soccer goalie. I keep the other team from scoring.

I am in an art club. I make sure there are brushes for everyone.

10

TEACHING YOUR SOCIAL STUDIES

BUILD SKILLS

Decision Making Tell students that Macy has a decision to make. The art club is having an art show next Saturday. The art show is at the same time as her next soccer game. Macy must decide which event she will attend. Ask students which event they think Macy should attend. Encourage them to explain their decision-making process and the reasons for their response.

SOCIAL STUDIES STRANDS

Individual Development and Identity Ask students to think about different groups to which they belong. Invite them to discuss how belonging to a group makes them feel. Have students draw a picture showing them engaged in an activity with a group they belong to. Have each student write or dictate a completion to the following sentence starter: When I am with the group, I feel ________ .

Groups My Family Belongs To

My family is part of many groups. We belong to the **community** where we live and work.

We go to the community center. We are in the swim club.

We are also part of a larger family group. We have aunts, uncles, cousins, and grandparents.

TextWork

2 Underline the sentences that name groups Macy's family belongs to.

SSSMART™ SUPPORT

TextWork

2 Skim and Scan

Tell students that skimming text can help them find information they need to answer a question or complete an activity. Invite volunteers to identify each sentence in the text that names a group to which Macy's family belongs. Make sure students underline the entire sentence. This is a good opportunity to review sentence structure, including beginning with a capital letter and ending with a period.

SOCIAL STUDIES STRANDS

Cultures and Diversity Draw a word web on the board. Write *Groups I Belong To* in the center. Complete the web with groups that you belong to at school, at home, and in the community. Think aloud as you do so. (At school, I belong to the group of first-grade teachers. I also belong to this class.) Then have each student complete a similar word web. Compare and contrast the various groups. Help students recognize and appreciate the differences.

BUILD SKILLS

Chart and Graph Skills Lead students in skimming the text, noting all the groups to which Macy and her family belong. With students' help, transfer the information into a chart. Be sure to include a chart title. You may wish to present the groups in a single column or divide them into two columns for individual and family groups.

Lesson Review

Summary Have students work in pairs to use the lesson headings and images to summarize the lesson's main ideas. Then have them complete the Lesson Review independently.

- People can belong to many groups.
- Macy has different roles in each group to which she belongs.
- Macy's family is part of a community.

1. **SUMMARIZE** What kinds of groups do people and families belong to?

   Possible response: People and families belong to their community, school, larger family groups, and other groups.

2. What are some groups in your **community**?

   Answers will vary depending on different groups found in the student's community. Possible response: My community has families, schools, teams, and clubs.

3. What groups does Macy belong to?

   Macy belongs to her family, her class, her school, and the art club.

Activity

Think about the groups you belong to. Draw pictures to show these groups.

12

ACTIVITY RUBRIC

Score 4
- drawing includes groups at school, at home, and in the community
- material contains no errors or very few errors

Score 3
- drawing includes groups in two of the following places: at school, at home, or in the community
- material contains few errors

Score 2
- drawing includes only one group
- material contains some errors

Score 1
- no groups are shown
- drawings are incomplete

Build Background

Make It Relevant Explain that people can be part of different cultural groups. They may eat different foods or listen to different music. Groups of people, like families, may also practice different traditions. Ask students to think about their own families or a family they know. What traditions do their families or the family they know have? Do students know how these traditions got started?

Preview the Lesson

Guide students in previewing the lesson. Point out the following features on Student Edition pages 13–16:

- **Page 13** Discuss Ben and the fact that he and his family have just moved to a new city. Ask whether any students have ever moved to a new home or a new city. What did those who moved want to learn about their new city right away?
- **Page 14** Ask students to preview the photograph. What are Ben and the other students doing? How can music represent a group's culture?
- **Page 15** Explain that traditions are things that are shared by families. Traditions can exist in many different forms. Some families have holiday activities, and other families share special foods. What tradition does Ben's family have?

Preteach Vocabulary

- Explain that a **culture** is a group's way of life. Tell students that cultures can include many things, such as beliefs and history. Ask students to suggest other things that help make a group's culture special.
- Point out that every family has **customs**, and that customs may be different from one family to the next. Ask students to share some of their family customs or the customs of a family they know.
- Ask students to explain the word **tradition**. Point out that families share and pass along special family traditions. Have students compare and contrast some of their family traditions or the traditions of a family they know.

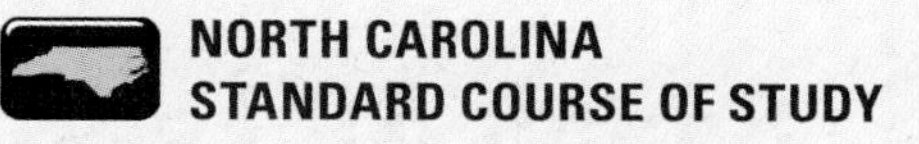

NORTH CAROLINA STANDARD COURSE OF STUDY

Objective 1.03 Compare and contrast similarities and differences among individuals and families.

Key Content Summary

- **Some people and families are the same, and others are different.**
- **People come from different cultures and also practice different customs.**
- **Families share special traditions.**

Vocabulary

- **culture,** p. 14
- **custom,** p. 14
- **tradition,** p. 15

Spotlight on Goals and Objectives

Use North Carolina Interactive Presentations, Unit 1, Lesson 3, to access prior knowledge and build background.

Reach All Learners

ESL/Language Support

Scaffolding Content Construct a word web. In the center circle write the word *Family*. Make two branches off the center and write the word *Culture* in one branch and the word *Tradition* in the other. Provide an example of each, such as a branch coming from *Culture* that says *History*, and a branch coming from *Tradition* that says *Special Foods*. Have students create other branches using other words that they associate with culture and tradition.

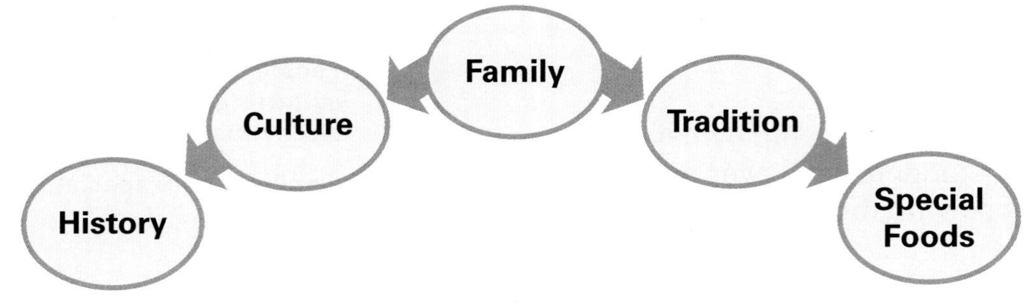

Extra Support

Draw Traditional Clothing Have small groups of students work together. Have the groups use school-approved resources to research the traditional clothing worn by people from different cultures. Have each group draw a picture of a person wearing traditional clothing and provide a caption for the picture.

Extension Activity

Share a Recipe Have students work in pairs. Have each pair use school-approved resources to research a traditional recipe made by people of another culture. Ask pairs to write out the recipe's steps and describe what they think the food might taste like.

Integrate the Curriculum

Arts

Learn About Music Find songs that represent different cultures in your class or community. Point out that music is an important part of many cultures. Play the music selections. Then have students discuss their reactions. Ask questions like these: What does the music make you think of? How are the songs alike and different?

Families Are the Same and Different

In many ways, people and families are the same. They can be different, too. Ben has just moved to a new city. He is learning about the people there. **What will you learn about people and families?**

Possible response: I will learn that people and families are alike and different.

Ben's Room

NORTH CAROLINA STANDARD COURSE OF STUDY

1.03 Compare and contrast similarities and differences among individuals and families.

13

Lesson 3

PAGES 13–16

Start with the Objective

Objective 1.03 Compare and contrast similarities and differences among individuals and families.

Set a Purpose for Reading

Read aloud the introduction as students follow along. Have students suggest ways people are alike and different. Read aloud the question. Use the Think Aloud to model thinking about similarities and differences among families.

Think Aloud

I know that my family likes to do certain things. We like to cook together on weekends. My friends' and neighbors' families are different. Some speak different languages. Some have more people. I will read to learn more about how families are alike and different.

BACKGROUND

Suburban Neighborhoods Many people move to the suburbs. Often, suburban homes are larger than city homes and have larger yards. Generally, suburbs have less traffic and are quieter than cities. Many families with children live in suburban neighborhoods.

SOCIAL STUDIES STRANDS

Geographic Relationships Show students a map of the United States. Explain that the map shows the country in which we live. Point out North Carolina. Explain that this is the state we live in.

Q Look at the map. Find the states that border, or touch, North Carolina.

A Virginia, Tennessee, Georgia, South Carolina

SSSMART™ SUPPORT

TextWork

1 Comprehension

Question To help students understand what they have read, model for them the practice of asking questions while reading. For example, you might say this: *I ask myself, "What is a culture?" I should be able to answer if I understand correctly what I have just read. A culture is a group's way of life. Another question I might ask is "What is one thing that is part of a group's culture?" If I cannot remember the answer, I can scan to find it. I will look for the highlighted word* culture. Students' responses may include either food or clothing.

1 Name one thing that is part of a group's culture.

Possible responses: food, clothing

Different Cultures

Ben likes learning about the cultures in his new city. A **culture** is a group's way of life. Things such as food and clothing are parts of a group's culture.

Ben has also learned about different customs. **Customs** are ways of doing things. The children in his new school come from different cultures. Their families have different customs.

14

TEACHING YOUR SOCIAL STUDIES

SOCIAL STUDIES STRANDS

Cultures and Diversity Have students discuss the question "What is culture?" Remind students that a culture is a group's way of life. Culture includes the way people dress, the language they speak, the foods they cook and eat, their beliefs, the holidays they celebrate, and their history. Explain that different cultures are found around the world. Different cultures exist within North Carolina, too.

BUILD SKILLS

Problem Solving Tell students to imagine that Ben has a problem. He does not have a musical instrument, and he doesn't know where to get one. Walk students through the problem-solving steps (name the problem, list different choices, think about and choose the best choice, and then solve the problem) and decide on the best way to solve Ben's problem.

Sharing Traditions

A **tradition** is something that is passed on from older family members to children. Ben's family makes a sweet bread on special days. Hailey's family has a special quilt. Learning about different cultures, customs, and traditions helps people get along.

TextWork

❷ How are Ben's family traditions different from Hailey's?

Ben's family makes bread and Hailey's has a blanket.

❷ **Comprehension**

Compare and Contrast Explain that to complete this activity, students must know what a tradition is. Ask a volunteer to locate the highlighted word on the page. Read aloud the definition. Encourage students to provide examples of traditions or define the term in their own words. Then help students locate the two specific traditions mentioned in the text and tell how they are different.

Biography
Caring

John Coltrane

John Coltrane was a jazz musician from North Carolina. He played the saxophone and recorded many songs. He used music from different cultures. He spent his life sharing their different musical traditions.

SOCIAL STUDIES STRANDS

Individual Development and Identity Remind students of the terms *culture* and *customs*. Point out that a tradition can be unique to a family. Some traditions may be eating a special meal at a holiday or reading a special book with a parent. With students, brainstorm a list of other traditions, such as going to the library once a week or going to the lake every summer. Then have students think of one tradition in their family and draw a picture of it.

BACKGROUND

John Coltrane John Coltrane grew up in High Point, North Carolina. He learned to play different instruments, including the saxophone. He once played in a military band, and he later played with famous jazz musicians Dizzy Gillespie and Miles Davis. Coltrane achieved fame with his own jazz group. He became known as a talented composer and musician.

Lesson Review

Summary Have students use the highlighted words to help them summarize the main ideas in the lesson. Then have them complete the Lesson Review.

- Some people and families are the same, and others are different.
- People come from different cultures and also practice different customs.
- Families share special traditions.

1. **SUMMARIZE** How are families the same? How are they different?

   Possible response: Families may be members of the same community. Families may have different customs or traditions.

2. Why do the children in Ben's school have different **customs**?

   Possible response: They come from different cultures.

3. Why is it important to learn about different cultures, customs, and traditions?

   Possible response: Learning about different cultures, customs, and traditions helps people get along.

Writing

Write about a tradition you share with your family members.

16

WRITING RUBRIC

Score 4
- clearly understands the term *tradition*
- accurately describes a family tradition
- shows a developed understanding of sentence structure

Score 3
- shows an understanding of the term *tradition*
- generally describes a family tradition
- shows a basic understanding of sentence structure

Score 2
- demonstrates incomplete understanding of the term *tradition*
- describes an aspect of family, but not necessarily a tradition
- shows little understanding of sentence structure

Score 1
- does not understand the term *tradition*
- fails to describe a family tradition
- shows no understanding of sentence structure

Build Background

Make It Relevant Point out that many people come from other countries to live in the United States. These people are called immigrants. Tell students that many Americans have relatives who were immigrants at some point. These people brought their customs to America. Ask students whether any of their relatives came to the United States from another country.

Preview the Lesson

Guide students in previewing the lesson. Point out the following features on Student Edition pages 17–20:

- **Page 17** Point out that many countries make up the world. Display a globe, and ask students to locate the United States.
- **Page 18** Have students preview the small globes above the photographs of Kweli and Anahat and the larger globe below the photographs. Ask students why the globes are shown.
- **Page 19** Explain that immigrants who come to the United States bring their cultures with them. Ask students to name some well-known holidays in the United States. Encourage students to think of holidays that many people celebrate, regardless of their culture, such as Saint Patrick's Day, the Chinese New Year, and Cinco de Mayo. Ask students to name the culture from which each celebration comes.

Preteach Vocabulary

- Explain that the **world** is made up of every person and every place on Earth. Display a globe. Ask students to make a drawing of it on a separate sheet of paper.
- Point out that almost every family has or has had a member who was an **immigrant** to the United States. Ask volunteers to tell what they think it would be like to move to a new country. Some students in the class may have immigrated to the United States. Encourage them to share their stories.

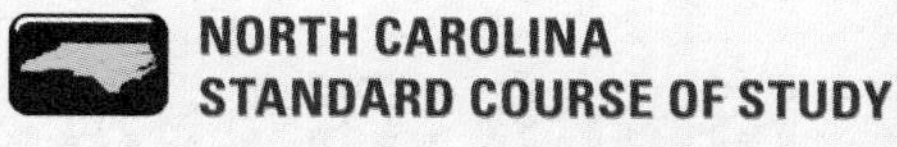

Objective 1.04 Explore the benefits of diversity in the United States.

Key Content Summary

- **People come from around the world to live in the United States.**
- **Immigrants are people who come from another part of the world to live in a country.**
- **Immigrants share their customs and cultures.**

Vocabulary

- **world,** p. 17
- **immigrant,** p. 18

Use North Carolina Interactive Presentations, Unit 1, Lesson 4, to access prior knowledge and build background.

Reach All Learners

ESL/Language Support

Active Learning Have students review the photographs on pages 18 and 19. Read aloud the captions for those photographs. Invite students to choose one of the pictured children for a role-play. Students should imitate some activities that the child is likely to do. For example, a student using Anahat for his or her role-play might act as though he or she is helping in Anahat's family's restaurant.

Extra Support

Write a Journal Entry Have students suppose that they have immigrated to the United States and are new students at their school. Ask them to write words or draw pictures that describe their school day. Remind students to describe things that are a part of American culture, such as games and books.

Extension Activity

Draw a Cartoon Give each student a sheet of paper with three boxes drawn on it. Have students draw a comic strip with cartoon characters. The characters should be a family moving to the United States from another place in the world. Tell students to write what their characters might think or say during their move. Students may want to use their cartoons to show the culture or customs of the family moving to the United States.

Integrate the Curriculum

English Language Arts

Make a List Ask students to create a list of foods and food-related terms that come from other cultures. Examples include spaghetti, tortillas, bagels, hummus, lo mein, and others. Create a multicultural word wall for use on a continuing basis. **ELA 3.01 Elaborate on how information and events connect to life experiences.**

We Live in the United States

People have come from around the world to live in the United States. The **world** is all the people and places on Earth. People from other places make the United States interesting. **What will you learn about people from different places?**

Possible response: People have come from different places to live in the United States.

The Statue of Liberty in New York Harbor

NORTH CAROLINA STANDARD COURSE OF STUDY

1.04 Explore the benefits of diversity in the United States.

Lesson 4

PAGES 17–20

Start with the Objectives

Objective 1.04 Explore the benefits of diversity in the United States.

Set a Purpose for Reading

Have students follow along as you read aloud the introduction. Draw students' attention to the highlighted word *world*. Ask students to provide definitions of the word. Then read aloud the question, and ask volunteers to share their answers. To further set a purpose for reading, share the Think Aloud, modeling a way of thinking about different cultures in the United States.

Think Aloud

Every year I go to Charlotte for the Saint Philip Neri Italian Festival. I eat Italian food and dance to Italian music. I learn about Italian American culture. I will read this lesson to learn more about other cultures in the United States.

BACKGROUND

The Statue of Liberty France gave the Statue of Liberty to the United States more than 100 years ago. The statue was a symbol of friendship between the two countries. Today, it is also a symbol of freedom and democracy. Standing over 150 feet tall, the Statue of Liberty has welcomed millions of immigrants to the United States.

SOCIAL STUDIES STRANDS

Global Connections Display a world map. Point out North Carolina in the United States. Then locate other countries, including the countries discussed in this lesson. Tell students that people in different countries have different cultures. Discuss with students that when people move to the United States, they bring much of their culture, such as their recipes and clothing styles, with them. Over time, their native culture blends with the traditions they learn in their new country.

SSSMART™ SUPPORT

TextWork

1 Vocabulary

Understand Vocabulary Tell students that new words in a text often appear in dark letters. Definitions for such words may appear in the surrounding sentences. Definitions may also appear in the glossary. Have students scan the text to find the highlighted word *immigrant* and read the sentence containing it.

1 Underline the sentence that tells you what an immigrant is.

Immigrants in the United States

Kweli, Anahat, Yana, and Juan are making a scrapbook. They are immigrants to the United States. An **immigrant** is a person who comes from another place to live in a country.

Anahat is from India. Anahat's family owns an Indian restaurant.

Kweli is from Kenya. Kweli's family sells African art.

18

TEACHING YOUR SOCIAL STUDIES

BUILD SKILLS

Map and Globe Skills Have students locate all of the globes on the page. Ask students to explain why the small globes appear with each child's photograph. Help students recognize that the globes highlight the country from which the child's family emigrated. As you read aloud each caption, have students point to the corresponding country on the globe and say that country's name.

SOCIAL STUDIES STRANDS

Economics and Development Guide students to recognize that each family uses a part of their home country's culture to earn money in the United States.

Q What part of Anahat's culture does her family share with others?

A Indian food

Families who come to the United States bring their cultures. They share their cultures with others. Immigrants have brought many new customs to our country.

People of different cultures live and work together. This makes the United States an interesting place.

TextWork

❷ How are Yana's family and Juan's family alike?

Both are immigrants.

Yana's mother teaches ballet, which she learned in Russia.

Juan's grandmother sells cloth that she learned to make in El Salvador.

❷ Comprehension

Compare and Contrast Remind students that when you contrast, you tell how things are different. When you compare, you tell how things are alike. Have volunteers find the pictures of Yana and Juan. Read aloud the accompanying captions. Have students tell how Yana and Juan are different. Then have them think about the lesson's main idea and tell ways in which Yana and Juan are alike.

SOCIAL STUDIES STRANDS

Technological Influences Immigrants often leave family members and friends in their home country. Today, there are many ways to communicate with people in other parts of the world. Yana's family may use a telephone to call family and friends. Juan's family may use the Internet to send photographs or e-mail to people in El Salvador. However, not all countries, or all places in a country, have widespread use of phones or computers.

BACKGROUND

El Salvador Students may recognize North America on the globe on this page. Explain that El Salvador is a small country in Central America. Spanish is El Salvador's official language. The largest city in El Salvador is San Salvador. It is also the capital city. More than 2 million people live in San Salvador. El Salvador sells clothing and foods to the United States.

Lesson Review

Summary Ask students to work in pairs to retell the important parts of the lesson. Then have students work independently to complete the Lesson Review.

- People come from around the world to live in the United States.
- Immigrants are people who come from another part of the world to live in a country.
- Immigrants share their customs and cultures.

Lesson 4 Review

1. **SUMMARIZE** How have people from different countries made the United States more interesting?

   Possible response: They bring their own cultures and customs.

2. Where do **immigrants** come from?

   Possible response: Immigrants come from around the world to live in the United States.

3. How are Anahat, Kweli, Juan, and Yana like you?

   Possible response: They are children, like me.

   How are they different from you?

   Possible response: They come from another part of the world.

Activity

What countries did people in your family live in before they came to the United States? Mark the places on a map.

20

ACTIVITY RUBRIC

Score 4
- correctly names country of origin
- accurately locates the country on a map or globe

Score 3
- correctly names country of origin
- locates the country of origin within a small area

Score 2
- knows some information about cultural origin, but cannot name country
- locates the general region of country

Score 1
- cannot name the country of origin
- cannot locate the area near the country on a map or globe

Unit Review

PAGES 21–24

Review and Test Prep

Unit 1

The Big Idea

People come from different places. They may also belong to different groups. They still share many things.

Summarize the Unit

Compare and Contrast Fill in the chart. Show what you have learned about the roles of children and the roles of parents.

Children	Similar	Parents
go to school pick up my room, wash the dishes, set the table	help around the house, be part of a family	go to work, take care of children

21

The Big Idea

Ask students to review the unit's Big Idea. Have students discuss that while people may come from different places and may belong to different groups, they still share many similarities.

Summarize the Unit

Compare and Contrast Ask students to review the Reading Social Studies at the beginning of the unit. Then ask students to think about what they have learned about family roles in this unit. Have students list examples of parents' roles and children's roles. Ask students how these roles are similar and different.

READING FOCUS SKILLS

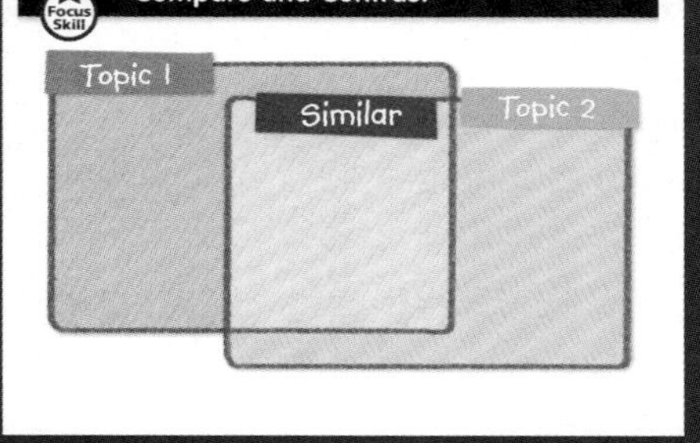

TRANSPARENCY

Graphic Organizer Write-On/ Wipe-Off Cards available

ASSESSMENT

Use the **UNIT 1 TEST** on pages 1–4 of the Assessment Program.

Use Vocabulary

Fill in the blanks with the correct words.

Word Bank
family p. 5
share p. 5
community p. 11
customs p. 14
world p. 17

1. A group of people who live together is called a **family**.
2. Most families are part of a larger **community** made up of other families.
3. People have come from all over the **world** to live in the United States.
4. People in a family **share** with one another.
5. Some people may have special **customs**, or ways of doing things.

22

VOCABULARY POWER

Syllables Help students say and remember each word by clapping the syllables. Sort the words into one-, two-, three- and four-syllable words. You may wish to write multi-syllable words with the syllable breaks to help children with pronunciation. Start with a one-syllable word, such as *share*. Have the students say the word aloud while clapping the syllable. Once students have identified the one-syllable words, move on to recognizing the two-, three- and four-syllable words.

Think About It

Circle the letter of the correct answer.

6. Which is a role that a child would have?
   - **(A)** going to school
   - **B** buying food
   - **C** going to work
   - **D** driving a car

7. Which is a part of a group's culture?
   - **A** the playground
   - **B** computers
   - **(C)** clothing
   - **D** television

8. Which is a kind of tradition?
   - **(A)** making a special food
   - **B** reading a book
   - **C** going to school
   - **D** playing outside

9. Which is a person who comes from another place to live in a country?
   - **A** a role
   - **B** a group
   - **C** a culture
   - **(D)** an immigrant

READ MORE

Encourage independent reading with these books or books of your choice.

Basic

The Quilt Story by Tony Johnston. Putnam Juvenile, 1996. A quilt's comforting presence is shown through changes in two different generations of families.

Proficient

All Kinds of People: What Makes Us Different by Jennifer Waters. Spyglass Books, 2002. This book explores the diversity of all people.

Advanced

Coming to America: The Story of Immigration by Betsy Maestro. Scholastic Press, 1996. Offers a brief history of American immigration.

Unit Review

PAGES 21–24

Show What You Know

Writing

Write a Paragraph

Review with students the parts of a paragraph, including the topic sentence and supporting details. Encourage students to brainstorm similarities and differences between their own culture and another.

Activity

Plan a Culture Fair

Before beginning the project, put students into groups to complete the tasks needed at each booth.

North Carolina Adventures

Remind students that this game will review the concepts in the unit.

Spotlight on Goals and Objectives

Use North Carolina Interactive Presentations, Unit 1, to review concepts from the unit.

Answer each question in a complete sentence.

10. Why do you think traditions are important to families?

Possible response: I think traditions are important to families because they are something special that families share.

11. Why do you think immigrants come to the United States?

Possible response: I think some immigrants come to the United States to find a better life.

Show What You Know

Writing **Write a Paragraph** Think about your culture and another culture. Write about how they are the same and different.

Activity **Plan a Culture Fair** Find out about a culture in your community. Make a booth with activities and displays. Hold the culture fair.

Go online To play a game that reviews the unit, join Eco in the North Carolina Adventures online or on CD.

24

WRITING RUBRIC

Score 4
- accurately compares and contrasts cultures with many details
- uses well-developed sentences
- writes neatly with no or few errors in grammar and punctuation

Score 3
- accurately compares and contrasts cultures with some details
- uses fairly well-developed sentences
- writes neatly with some errors in grammar and punctuation

Score 2
- compares and contrasts but uses few details
- uses minimally developed sentences
- writes somewhat illegibly with multiple errors in writing

Score 1
- does not compare and contrast
- uses incomplete sentences
- writes illegibly with errors in writing that prevent comprehension

ACTIVITY RUBRIC

Score 4
- recognizes diversity of people in the community
- shares many details about a culture's customs and traditions
- is a highly organized, well-prepared, and cooperative group

Score 3
- recognizes some diversity of people in the community
- shares some details about a culture's customs and traditions
- is an organized, prepared, and cooperative group

Score 2
- recognizes little diversity of people in the community
- shares few details about a culture's customs and traditions
- is a somewhat organized, prepared, and cooperative group

Score 1
- does not recognize diversity in the community
- shares no details about a culture's customs and traditions
- is not an organized, prepared, and cooperative group

Unit 2

Good Citizenship

Unit 2

NORTH CAROLINA STANDARD COURSE OF STUDY

COMPETENCY GOAL 2

The learner will identify and exhibit qualities of good citizenship in the classroom, school, and other social environments.

OBJECTIVES

2.01 Develop and exhibit citizenship traits in the classroom, school, and other social environments.

2.02 Identify the roles of leaders in the home, school, and community such as parents, mayor, police officers, principal, and teacher.

2.03 Participate in democratic decision-making.

2.04 Recognize the need for rules in different settings.

2.05 Identify the need for fairness in rules by individuals and by people in authority.

2.06 Predict consequences that may result from responsible and irresponsible actions.

LESSON	TOTAL: 26 DAYS	NORTH CAROLINA STANDARD COURSE OF STUDY
Introduce the Unit **Unit Preview,** pp. 25–26 **The Big Idea,** p. 26 **Reading Social Studies,** pp. 27–28 Focus Skill Main Idea and Details	2 DAYS	COMPETENCY GOAL 2 **The learner will identify and exhibit qualities of good citizenship in the classroom, school, and other social environments.** **Spotlight on Goals and Objectives** Unit 2
1 **Rules and Laws** pp. 29–32 **citizen** p. 29 **rule** p. 29 **law** p. 31	4 DAYS	**Objective 2.04** Recognize the need for rules in different settings. **Spotlight on Goals and Objectives** Unit 2, Lesson 1
2 **Leaders** pp. 33–36 **leader** p. 33 **principal** p. 34 **mayor** p. 35	4 DAYS	**Objective 2.02** Identify the roles of leaders in the home, school, and community such as parents, mayor, police officers, principal, and teacher. **Spotlight on Goals and Objectives** Unit 2, Lesson 2
3 **Following the Rules** pp. 37–40 **fair** p. 37 **consequence** p. 39	4 DAYS	**Objective 2.05** Identify the need for fairness in rules by individuals and by people in authority. **Objective 2.06** Predict consequences that may result from responsible and irresponsible actions. **Spotlight on Goals and Objectives** Unit 2, Lesson 3
4 **Being a Good Citizen** pp. 41–44 **right** p. 41 **responsibility** p. 41 **freedom** p. 42 **volunteer** p. 43 **respect** p. 43	4 DAYS	**Objective 2.01** Develop and exhibit citizenship traits in the classroom, school, and other social environments. **Spotlight on Goals and Objectives** Unit 2, Lesson 4

TEACHING YOUR SOCIAL STUDIES	SSSMART™ SUPPORT
	Comprehension, Main Idea and Details, pp. 27–28
Background, Rules, p. 29 Traffic Signs, p. 31 **Social Studies Strands,** Government and Active Citizenship, pp. 29, 31 Individual Development and Identity, p. 30 **Build Skills,** Chart and Graph Skills, p. 30	**Comprehension,** Main Idea and Details, p. 30 Review/Reflect, p. 30 **CUES,** p. 31
Background, Leadership, p. 33 William Bell, p. 35 **Social Studies Strands,** Individual Development and Identity, p. 33 Historical Perspectives, p. 34 Cultures and Diversity, p. 35 **Build Skills,** Problem Solving, p. 34	**Vocabulary,** p. 34 **Skim and Scan,** p. 35
Background, Following the Rules, p. 37 Fairness of Rules, p. 38 **Social Studies Strands,** Government and Active Citizenship, pp. 37, 39 Individual Development and Identity, p. 38 **Build Skills,** Decision Making, p. 39	**Comprehension,** Main Idea and Details, p. 38 **Skim and Scan,** p. 39
Background, Habitat for Humanity, p. 41 The Bill of Rights, p. 42 **Social Studies Strands,** Economics and Development, p. 41 Government and Active Citizenship, p. 43 **Build Skills,** Chart and Graph Skills, pp. 42, 43	**CUES,** p. 42 **Comprehension,** Review/Reflect, p. 43

Print Resources

Student Edition, pp. 25–52
Teacher Edition, pp. 25A–52
Leveled Readers
Leveled Readers Teacher Guides
Document-Based Questions
Primary Atlas

Technology/Digital Resources

Spotlight on Goals and Objectives
North Carolina Interactive Presentations CD
North Carolina Interactive Presentations Online

Online Teacher Edition with ePlanner
Leveled Readers Online Database
North Carolina Adventures CD
North Carolina Adventures Online
Multimedia Biographies CD
Multimedia Biographies Online
Social Studies Music Collection CD

Hands-On Resources

Reading Focus Skills Transparencies
Social Studies Skills Transparencies
Graphic Organizer Write-On/Wipe-Off Cards
Interactive Atlas
Interactive Desk Maps
Interactive Map Transparencies
Picture Vocabulary Cards
Primary Source Kit
TimeLinks: Interactive Time Line
Social Studies in Action, pp. 6–11, 14–17, 24–25, 46–47, 68–69, 86–87, 90–91, 112–113, 124, 134–135, 139

Assessment Options

1. **Unit 2 Test**
   Assessment Program, pp. 5–8
2. **Writing**
   Write a List, p. 52
3. **Activity**
   Unit Project: Plan a Campaign Rally, p. 52

LESSON		NORTH CAROLINA STANDARD COURSE OF STUDY
5 Make a Choice By Voting pp. 45–48 **vote** p. 45 **government** p. 45 **ballot** p. 46	4 DAYS	**Objective 2.03** Participate in democratic decision-making. **Spotlight on Goals and Objectives** Unit 2, Lesson 5
Unit 2 Review and Test Prep pp. 49–52	4 DAYS	**North Carolina Adventures** Unit 2

TEACHING YOUR SOCIAL STUDIES

Background,
Polling Places, p. 45
Voting Rights, p. 45
Elizabeth Dole, p. 46

Social Studies Strands,
Technological Influences, p. 46
Government and Active Citizenship, p. 47

Build Skills,
Decision Making, p. 47

SSSMART™ SUPPORT

Vocabulary, p. 46
CUES, p. 47

Summarize the Unit,
Focus Skill: Main Idea and Details, p. 49

Print Resources

Student Edition, pp. 25–52
Teacher Edition, pp. 25A–52
Leveled Readers
Leveled Readers Teacher Guides
Document-Based Questions
Primary Atlas

Technology/Digital Resources

Spotlight on Goals and Objectives

North Carolina Interactive Presentations CD
North Carolina Interactive Presentations Online

Online Teacher Edition with ePlanner
Leveled Readers Online Database
North Carolina Adventures CD
North Carolina Adventures Online
Multimedia Biographies CD
Multimedia Biographies Online
Social Studies Music Collection CD

Hands-On Resources

Reading Focus Skills Transparencies
Social Studies Skills Transparencies
Graphic Organizer Write-On/Wipe-Off Cards
Interactive Atlas
Interactive Desk Maps
Interactive Map Transparencies
Picture Vocabulary Cards
Primary Source Kit
TimeLinks: Interactive Time Line
Social Studies in Action, pp. 6–11, 14–17, 24–25, 46–47, 68–69, 86–87, 90–91, 112–113, 124, 134–135, 139

Assessment Options

1. **Unit 2 Test**
   Assessment Program, pp. 5–8
2. **Writing**
   Write a List, p. 52
3. **Activity**
   Unit Project: Plan a Campaign Rally, p. 52

Leveled Readers

BELOW-LEVEL

Rules and Laws Keep Me Safe

Summary *Rules and Laws Keep Me Safe.* This Reader discusses how rules and laws keep schools and communities safe and clean and how people can be responsible citizens.

Vocabulary Power Have students define the following words. Help them write one sentence for each word as it relates to the rules and laws people follow.

law
vote
rule
community
leader

Critical Thinking Lead students in a discussion about how rules in their school help students. Ask them to name one or two classroom rules that help them get along with their classmates.

Write a Rhyme Have students write a rhyme about following rules. Remind them that rhyming words have the same sound at the end.

Focus Skill **Cause and Effect**

ON-LEVEL

Let's Vote!

Summary *Let's Vote!* In this Reader a student learns that voting is a fair and good way for people to make a decision.

Vocabulary Power Have students define the following words. Help them write one sentence for each word as it relates to the rules and laws people follow.

law
vote
teacher
fair

Critical Thinking Lead students in a discussion about why voting is a fair way to make choices. Ask them how the United States would be different if we did not vote.

Write an Opinion Have students write down which pet they would vote for—a frog or a rabbit. Then ask them to write a sentence supporting their opinion. Their opinions should be based on facts from the Reader.

Focus Skill **Cause and Effect**

ABOVE-LEVEL

Strange Laws

Summary *Strange Laws.* This Reader discusses how countries, states, cities, and towns can make and change laws. It points out laws that seem strange because they were put in place many years ago.

Vocabulary Power Have students define the following words. Help them write one sentence for each word as it relates to the rules and laws that people follow.

law
vote
rule
country
government

Critical Thinking Lead students in a discussion about how laws keep people safe. As a class, talk about some of the laws from long ago that seem strange today. Ask students how they think these old laws may have kept people safe.

Write a Law Ask students to write a law that would help keep students in their school safe. Have them use the laws in their Reader as examples.

Focus Skill **Cause and Effect**

Complete a Graphic Organizer

Have students complete the graphic organizer to show that they understand the causes and effects of rules and laws.

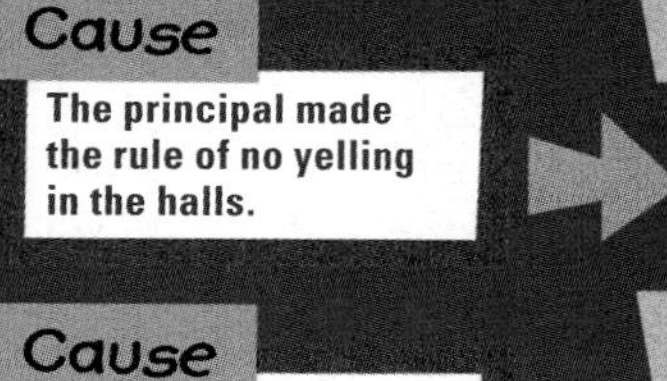

Cause	Effect
The principal made the rule of no yelling in the halls.	Students can hear their teachers because the halls are quiet.
The law says people must use crosswalks to cross the street.	People cross the street safely.

Leveled Readers Teacher Guides include complete lesson plans, copying masters, and project cards.

Harcourt Leveled Readers Available Online! www.harcourtschool.com

Plan a Campaign Rally

Getting Started

Introduce the Hands-On Activity on page 52 of the Unit Review as you begin Unit 2. Have students develop the project components as they learn about the rights and responsibilities of citizenship. Explain that rallies are filled with speeches, songs, and visual presentations that explain the ideas that candidates want to share. The final presentation should reflect students' understanding of the Unit's Big Idea.

The Big Idea
How do people show they are good citizens?

Project Management

- Divide students into small groups. Work with each group to assign tasks and direct research efforts.
- Provide instructional support and materials for art and props as needed.

Materials: Social Studies textbook; posterboard; markers, crayons, or colored pencils; blank adhesive labels; musical selections and CD/tape player; pencil; paper

Organizer: Assign to several students parts as performers in the rally, and work with them to develop oral and visual presentations. Ask them to use an organizer like the one below to help them plan the order of events for the campaign rally.

ORGANIZER

Schedule of Events

1. Greeting
2. Song: "Star-Spangled Banner"
3. First candidate's speech
4. Second candidate's speech
5. Closing

During the Unit

As students read Unit 2, they can begin work on their campaign rally. Rallies can include:

- Lesson Review activities
- Your own favorite activities
- Ideas students develop on their own

Complete the Project

Have the class perform the rally for other classes and for family members. When the rally is complete, invite audience members to ask students questions about what they saw and heard. Lead a discussion about what might happen next in a campaign. Have students share what they know about voting and elections.

What to Look For

For a scoring rubric, see page 52 of this Teacher Edition.

- Students understand the role of leaders.
- Campaigns are creative and well organized.
- Posters and other components relate to the rally and are clearly presented.

Technology/Digital Resources

START

North Carolina Interactive Presentations

Purpose

The North Carolina Interactive Presentation Unit 2 can be used to preview Unit 2. This presentation provides a concise, visual overview of Competency Goal 2 and its objectives. You can use it to preview the unit for the class, or throughout the unit to introduce and reinforce individual objectives.

Contents

The Unit 2 presentation includes an introduction to Competency Goal 2, including a vocabulary preview and a visual introduction to identifying and exhibiting qualities of good citizenship. In addition, the presentation covers all the unit's objectives lesson by lesson, giving students a broad overview of rules, laws, and leaders.

REVIEW

North Carolina Adventures

Purpose

The North Carolina Adventures games, offered both on CD and online, provide an entertaining first-person-player method of content review. When students have completed the unit, they can review its competency goal and all objectives through the Unit 2 game.

Contents

Tell students they will use their knowledge of good citizenship to help Eco in the classroom. Throughout, students will review what they have learned about leaders, rules, and problem solving. Explain that the "Help" buttons in the game will refer them to pages in their textbooks if they need additional information.

Additional Resources

For Teachers

Free and Inexpensive Materials are listed on the Social Studies website at **www.harcourtschool.com/ss1**

- Addresses to write to for free and inexpensive products
- Links to unit-related materials
- Internet maps
- Internet references

The eTE with ePlanner provides the following components

- A calendar tool for scheduling Social Studies lessons and displaying all scheduled lessons and activities
- TE pages and additional resources for easy online reference

For Students

When students visit **www.harcourtschool.com/ss1** they will find internal resources such as

- Our Multimedia Biographies database
- Skills activities
- Additional research tools
- Information about all 50 states

Students take turns voting in a class election.

Unit 2 Preview

PAGES 25–26

Start with the Competency Goal

Competency Goal 2 The learner will identify and exhibit qualities of good citizenship in the classroom, school, and other social environments.

Make It Relevant

Help students think about the importance of being a good citizen. Ask them the following question:

Q What are some ways that you can show good citizenship at home?

A Students might discuss respecting others' privacy and possessions.

Discuss the Photograph

Have students look at the photograph and explain what they see. Point out that being good citizens helps us get along.

Q How are the children in the photograph being good citizens?

A They are voting and waiting their turn.

Instructional Design

START WITH THE GOAL AND OBJECTIVES

NORTH CAROLINA STANDARD COURSE OF STUDY
- competency goal
- objectives

PLAN ASSESSMENT

Assessment Options
- Option 1–Unit 2 Test
- Option 2–Writing: Write a List, p. 52
- Option 3–Activity: Plan a Campaign Rally, p. 52

PLAN INSTRUCTION

Spotlight on Goals and Objectives
North Carolina Interactive Presentations, Unit 2

Unit 2 Teacher Edition
- resources
- activities
- strategies

Unit 2 Leveled Readers Teacher Guides

The Big Idea

Have students read The Big Idea question and then preview how people show they are good citizens.

Access Prior Knowledge

Begin a K-W-L chart about being a good citizen. Ask students what they know about good citizenship. Then ask them what they would like to learn. Record their responses in the chart, and post the chart for use after reading each lesson. Then have students read the paragraph and complete the activity.

The Big Idea

How do people show they are good citizens?

A citizen lives in and belongs to a community. We follow rules at home, at school, and in our community. When we do this, we are being good citizens. Good citizens also help others in their community.

Draw a picture that shows a child being a good citizen.

Drawing should show that student understands the concept of good citizenship.

26

READ MORE

Encourage independent reading with these books or books of your choice.

Basic

Vote! by Eileen Christelow. Clarion Books, 2004. This lively introduction to voting covers every step in the process, from the start of the campaign all the way to the voting booth.

Proficient

Following Rules by Robin Nelson. Lerner Publications, 2003. This book shows the importance of following rules at home, at school, and in the community.

Advanced

Serving Your Community by Christin Ditchfield. Children's Press, 2004. Students learn ways to reach out and help others.

Reading Social Studies

Main Idea and Details

Learn

■ The main idea tells you what you are reading about. It is the most important idea.

■ A detail gives more information. The details explain the main idea.

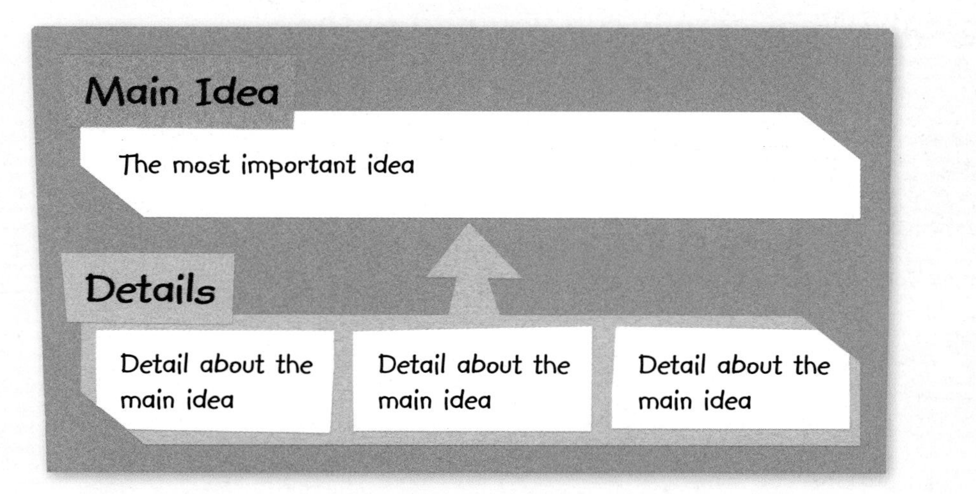

Practice

Read the paragraph below. Underline one of the sentences that tells a detail.

There are many kinds of rules. We follow rules at home. We follow rules at school. We follow rules in our community.

Main Idea

Detail

Reading Social Studies PAGES 27–28

Learn

Have students read the Learn section and look at the graphic organizer. Point out that the graphic organizer shows that many details support one main idea. Tell students that by thinking about what the details have in common, they can find the main idea of a text.

Q What is one detail that supports the main idea *Our school has different classes*?

A Possible response: Our school has a first-grade class and a second-grade class.

Practice

Ask students to read the paragraph. Then, help them identify three details about places where people follow rules.

READING FOCUS SKILLS

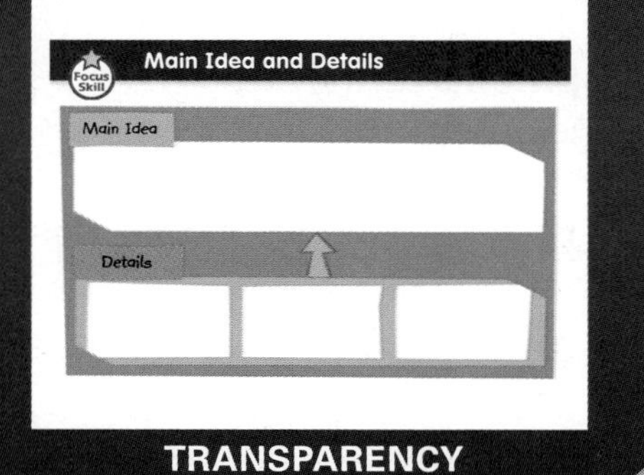

TRANSPARENCY

Graphic Organizer Write-On/ Wipe-Off Cards available

INTEGRATE THE CURRICULUM

ENGLISH LANGUAGE ARTS Write a Journal Entry Have students write short journal entries describing something they have done that they are proud of. Explain that the accomplishment will be the entry's main idea. Tell students to select details that explain how the event or activity happened and why it was important. Have volunteers share their entries with the class.

ELA 4.06 Compose a variety of products (e.g., stories, journal entries, letters, response logs, simple poems, oral retellings) using a writing process.

Reading Social Studies PAGES 27–28

Apply

This selection has many details that support the main idea *Anna follows rules at home for helping her family.* Ask students to identify this as the main idea. Tell them that the main idea often appears at the beginning or end of a passage. Help students find two details in the passage to complete the graphic organizer.

Unit 2 provides many opportunities for students to practice identifying main ideas and details. As students read the unit, challenge them to think about main ideas and details.

Apply

Read the paragraph.

Anna follows rules at home for helping her family. She puts her things away and keeps her room clean. She reads to her little brother. Anna also sets the table before dinner.

The chart below shows the main idea of the paragraph. What details can you add to the chart?

Main Idea

Anna follows rules at home for helping her family.

Details

Anna puts her things away and keeps her room clean.	**Anna reads to her little brother.**	**Anna sets the table before dinner.**

28

ESL/LANGUAGE SUPPORT

Vocabulary Development As students read the unit, have them create a word-sort organizer. Ask students to think about the kinds of rules they follow at home, at school, and in their community. Have them list words under the categories *Home*, *School*, and *Community*.

Home	School	Community

Prior Learning and Development As they read the unit, have students identify some school rules. Ask them why they think the school has those rules. Explain that the reason for the rules is the main idea and that the rules are the supporting details.

Build Background

Make It Relevant Explain to students that there are many different types of rules and laws. People follow rules at home, at work, at school, and even when playing. People in communities follow laws so everyone can live together safely. Ask students to list some rules they have to follow. Students might list rules they follow at home, in the classroom, or when playing sports.

Preview the Lesson

Guide students in previewing the lesson. Point out the following features on Student Edition pages 29–32:

- **Page 29** Discuss with students the park sign in the photograph. Ask students why the rules on the sign are important. Tell them that citizens in a community have to follow certain rules and laws. Ask students why they think communities make rules and laws for their citizens to follow.
- **Page 30** Have students preview the photographs of students following rules. Ask students why each school rule is important.
- **Page 31** Have students preview the photographs of signs. Ask students to predict what these signs mean. Why are these signs important? How might these signs help citizens in a community?

Preteach Vocabulary

- Explain that a **citizen** is a person who lives in and belongs to a community. Have students draw pictures of citizens in their classroom or community interacting with one another.
- Ask students to explain the word **rule** in their own words. Point out that all citizens follow rules. Ask students to name the rules that they follow in the classroom.
- Explain that a **law** is a rule that people in a community must follow. Ask students to think of some of the signs they see in their neighborhoods. Ask whether students know what laws these signs are asking citizens to follow.

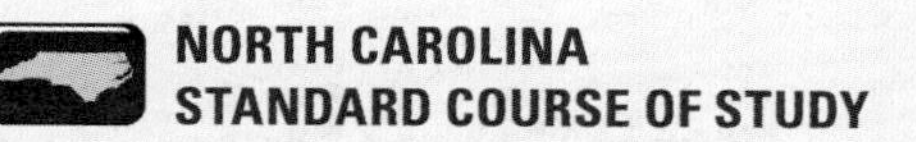

NORTH CAROLINA STANDARD COURSE OF STUDY

Objective 2.04 Recognize the need for rules in different settings.

Key Content Summary

- **Citizens must follow rules.**
- **Rules help people learn and stay safe.**
- **Communities have laws to help people live together safely.**

Vocabulary

- **citizen,** p. 29
- **rule,** p. 29
- **law,** p. 31

Spotlight on Goals and Objectives

Use North Carolina Interactive Presentations, Unit 2, Lesson 1, to access prior knowledge and build background.

Reach All Learners

ESL/Language Support

Active Learning Make illustrated cards showing various rules. Make a second set of cards that shows the different settings in which those rules would be appropriate. Invite students to choose a card and act out that rule. Then have them match the rule cards to the appropriate setting.

Extra Support

Draw Pictures Encourage students to draw pictures to help a new student remember rules in a new school. Invite volunteers to share their pictures with the class.

Extension Activity

Make a List Have students make a list of rules for different parts of the school. This list should include rules for the playground and cafeteria and any other relevant part of the school. Encourage students to think of rules that will make the school environment safe and orderly.

Integrate the Curriculum

Arts

Make a Poster Make a list of laws, such as wearing a seat belt, stopping at a stop sign, and using a crosswalk. Invite children to choose one law and create a poster showing why it is important to follow the law. Encourage children to use a variety of lines, shapes, colors, and textures when creating their posters. Display the posters on a safety-related bulletin board.

Rules and Laws

A person who lives in and belongs to a community is a **citizen**. Citizens must follow the rules of their community. A **rule** tells people how to act. We follow rules when we work and play. **What might you learn about rules?**

Possible response: I might learn about rules in my community.

All dogs must be on leash. Clean up after your dogs.

NORTH CAROLINA STANDARD COURSE OF STUDY

2.04 Recognize the need for rules in different settings.

29

Lesson 1

PAGES 29–32

Start with the Objective

Objective 2.04 Recognize the need for rules in different settings.

Set a Purpose for Reading

Read and discuss the lesson objective and the lesson introduction with students. Draw students' attention to the highlighted words. Ask them to identify examples of a *citizen* and a *rule*. Then have students answer the question to set a purpose for reading. Model student thinking about the question by using the Think Aloud below.

Think Aloud

I know that people who live in a community have rules to follow. These rules are made to keep people safe. I will read to find out how rules are made and why people follow rules in a community.

BACKGROUND

Rules Tell students that people follow rules every day. Draw students' attention to the photograph. Invite students to tell you the rules the mother and son are following as they walk their dog. Then ask students what other rules they follow in their community each day. What rules do they follow at the park? On the bus? When they visit friends? In the grocery store?

SOCIAL STUDIES STRANDS

Government and Active Citizenship Have children identify rules that they follow at home, at school, and when playing with friends. Ask them who makes these rules.

Q What are some rules that you follow at your home?

A Students should discuss rules followed in their homes.

SSSMART™ SUPPORT

TextWork

1 Comprehension

Main Idea and Details Help students find the details that support the main idea that we have rules in school. Ask them to read the first paragraph and circle the three details listed there.

2 Comprehension

Review/Reflect First, have students reread the rules already posted on the bulletin board. Then, give them an opportunity to think of another rule that they follow in class. As they reflect, invite them to think about different times of the school day. All rules students write should be accepted as long as they are reasonable class rules.

TextWork

1 Circle the reasons we have rules at school.

2 Draw and write a class rule. Add it to the bulletin board.

Rules at School

At school, rules help us learn and get along. Rules also help us stay safe.

We have different rules for different parts of the school. When we walk in the hall, we have to be quiet. When we play outside, we do not have to be quiet.

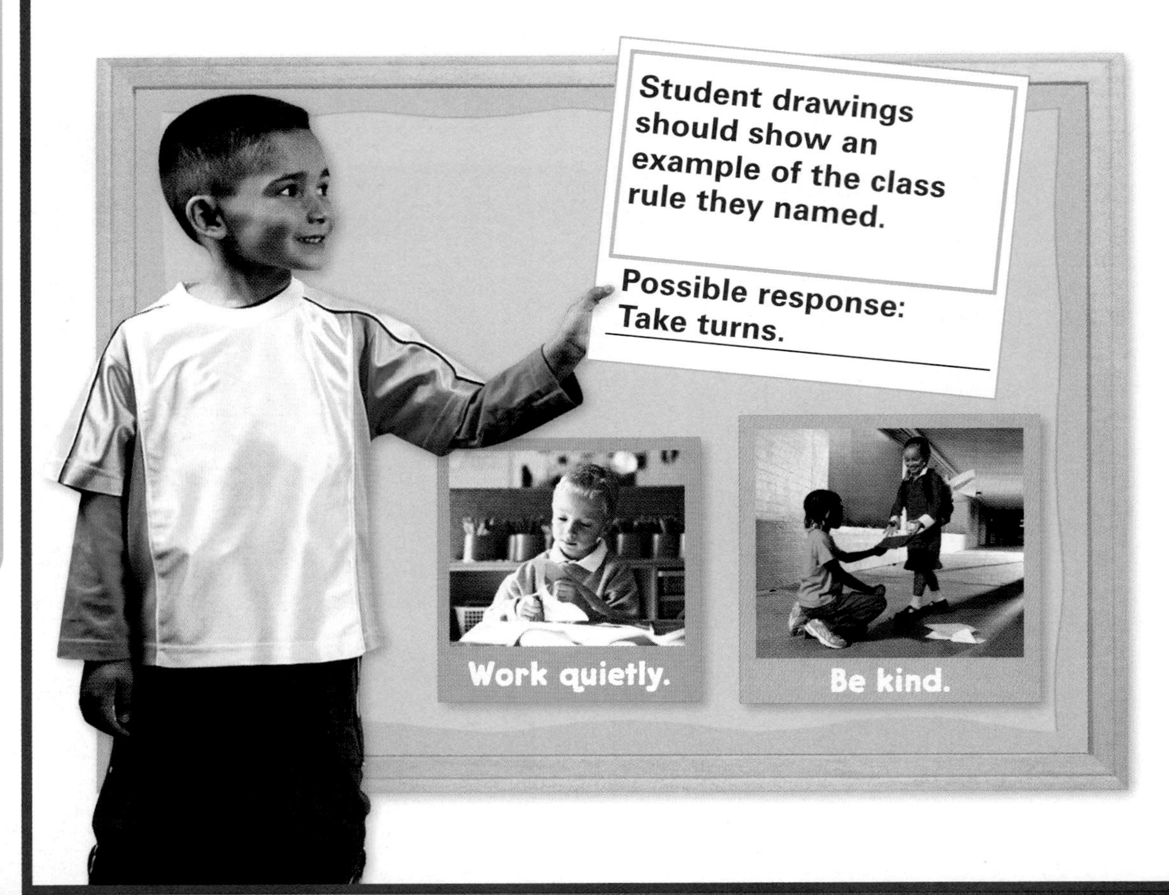

TEACHING YOUR SOCIAL STUDIES

BUILD SKILLS

Chart and Graph Skills After students have made rules to add to the bulletin board, use this chart activity. Have them organize their rules according to purpose, using a chart like the one below.

To help us learn	To help us get along	To keep us safe

SOCIAL STUDIES STRANDS

Individual Development and Identity Ask students to choose their favorite school rule. Have them reflect on what they like about that rule. One student might like using quiet voices because it helps her concentrate. Another might like the rule about taking turns because it helps people get along.

Rules in a Community

Communities have rules called laws. A **law** is a rule that people in a community must follow.

Communities have many kinds of laws. Laws are important for citizens in a community. They tell people how to live together safely. They also help keep communities clean.

❸ Circle the sign that tells where people might be crossing the street.

PARKING BY DISABLED PERMIT ONLY

STOP

31

SSSMART™ SUPPORT

TextWork

❸ **CUES**

Analyze/Interpret Photographs Remind students that most signs use pictures to give people a message. Have students look at each sign shown on this page. Tell them to find the one that uses a picture of a person crossing the street.

SOCIAL STUDIES STRANDS

Government and Active Citizenship Have students work in pairs to make a sign for the classroom that reminds students of a class rule. Have them use pictures and one or two words on their signs to depict the rule.

BACKGROUND

Traffic Signs Point out the traffic signs shown on this page. Tell students that most traffic signs use large pictures and few words to give drivers a message. The color and shape of each sign quickly lets drivers know the rule to follow. Red signs, including the stop sign in this picture, tell drivers that they have to do something, such as stop. Yellow signs give drivers warnings. Rectangular signs are for rules about parking and the speed limit.

Lesson Review

Summary Have students work individually to summarize the lesson's key content before they complete the Lesson Review.

- Citizens must follow rules.
- Rules help people learn and stay safe.
- Communities have laws to help people live together safely.

Lesson 1 Review

1. **SUMMARIZE** Why do we need rules and laws?

   Possible response: We need rules and laws to help us get along and stay safe.

2. What is a **citizen**? Use your own words to tell.

   Possible response: A citizen is someone who is part of a community.

3. What are some rules that your class follows?

   Answers will vary, but students should include some of the rules followed in your classroom. Possible response: Some of the rules in my classroom are working quietly, being kind, and taking turns.

Activity

Draw a picture that shows someone following a law.

32

ACTIVITY RUBRIC

Score 4
- clearly shows a person following a law
- has no errors

Score 3
- shows a person following a law
- has few errors

Score 2
- shows a person following a rule instead of a law
- has some errors

Score 1
- fails to show a person following a law or a rule
- has many errors

Build Background

Make It Relevant Explain to students that leaders are people who help a group follow rules and laws. Leaders also help organize events and activities. Ask students to list different types of leaders. Point out that a leader can work in his or her community or home or even in a classroom.

Preview the Lesson

Guide students in previewing the lesson. Point out the following features on Student Edition pages 33–36:

- **Page 33** Have students preview the photograph. Ask them to point out the leader. Explain that there are many different types of leaders.
- **Pages 34–35** Tell students that there are different types of leaders in their community. Ask students to name people whom they consider to be leaders either at home or at school. Ask students to list other people who act as leaders in their communities.

Preteach Vocabulary

- Point out to students that the base word of **leader** is *lead*. What does *lead* mean? (to go in front, head, direct) Ask students to draw a picture of ways in which they can act as leaders in the classroom.
- Explain to students that a **principal** is a person who leads a whole school. Invite your school's principal into your class. Encourage students to prepare in advance questions about how the principal acts as a leader.
- Point out that a **mayor** has to look out for his or her whole community. Ask students what they think are important things a mayor should do to make his or her community a good place to live.

NORTH CAROLINA STANDARD COURSE OF STUDY

Objective 2.02 Identify the roles of leaders in the home, school, and community such as parents, mayor, police officers, principal, and teacher.

Key Content Summary

- **Many kinds of leaders help make sure people follow rules and laws.**
- **Parents, teachers, and principals are all different types of leaders.**
- **Mayors, police officers, and firefighters are leaders within a community.**

Vocabulary

- **leader,** p. 33
- **principal,** p. 34
- **mayor,** p. 35

Spotlight on Goals and Objectives

Use North Carolina Interactive Presentations, Unit 2, Lesson 2, to access prior knowledge and build background.

Reach All Learners

ESL/Language Support

Scaffolding Content Have students fill out a three-column graphic organizer. The top three columns should have the headings *Leaders at Home*, *Leaders at School*, and *Leaders in the Community*. Have students draw pictures and write words giving examples of these types of leaders and what they do.

Leaders at Home	Leaders at School	Leaders in the Community

Extra Support

Write Sentences Ask students to write or dictate a sentence for each of the following words: *parent, teacher, principal, mayor,* and *police officer.* Encourage students to use their sentences to show how each of these people is a leader.

Extension Activity

List Responsibilities Encourage students to learn more about the jobs of a principal and a mayor. Have them list the responsibilities of each.

Integrate the Curriculum

Arts

Vote for a Song Leader Have students vote for a song leader who will choose a song for the class to sing. Explain that the class will choose their leader and their leader will then choose a song for them. Point out that this is how government leaders, such as mayors, make choices for people.

Leaders

A **leader** is a person who works to help a group. There are many kinds of leaders. Leaders make sure people follow rules and laws. **What might you learn about leaders?**

Possible response: I might learn about different kinds of leaders.

A coach is the leader of a team.

NORTH CAROLINA STANDARD COURSE OF STUDY

2.02 Identify the roles of leaders in the home, school, and community such as parents, mayor, police officers, principal, and teacher.

Lesson 2

PAGES 33–36

Start with the Objective

Objective 2.02 Identify the roles of leaders in the home, school, and community such as parents, mayor, police officers, principal, and teacher.

Set a Purpose for Reading

As a group, read the lesson introduction aloud. Point out the highlighted word *leader*. Ask students to give examples of a leader. Have students answer the question to set a purpose for reading. Model thinking for students by using the Think Aloud below.

Think Aloud

I know that leaders help the people whom they lead. I also know that there are different types of leaders, such as mayors and parents. I will learn about the ways different leaders help the people whom they lead.

BACKGROUND

Leadership Remind students that a leader is a person who works to help a group. Ask them to describe what is happening in this photograph. Use the following questions to guide students' interpretation of the photograph and to help them connect its contents to the lesson objective: "Who is the leader in this picture?" "What group is he leading?" "Why does this group need a leader?" "What might happen if the team did not have a coach to lead them?"

SOCIAL STUDIES STRANDS

Individual Development and Identity Have students think about what they might be like as leaders. List these examples on the board: nice, bossy, unfair, good listener. Discuss with students how each type of leader would make his or her group members feel.

Q What makes a person a good leader?

A Answers will vary, but students should add to the list of leadership qualities.

TextWork

1 Vocabulary

Use Context Clues Point out the clue words *leaders* and *school* in the TextWork directions. Tell students to look for these words as they reread the second paragraph and to circle the leaders at school. Have students repeat this strategy for the third paragraph, where they will find another type of leader at school.

1. Circle the names of the people who are leaders at school.
2. Name one kind of leader in a community. **Possible responses: mayor, police officer, firefighter**

Leaders in the Community

Parents are leaders at home. They make rules to keep children safe.

Teachers are leaders at school. Our teacher helps make the class rules.

A principal leads the whole school. Our principal works with parents and teachers to make our school safe.

34

TEACHING YOUR SOCIAL STUDIES

BUILD SKILLS

Problem Solving Ask students to think about how leaders can help this student solve his problem: Jerome has a field trip today. When he opens his backpack, he cannot find his permission slip.

Q What should Jerome do?

A Possible response: Jerome can call his parents and ask them to bring him the permission slip. Jerome can ask his teacher for help.

SOCIAL STUDIES STRANDS

Historical Perspectives In colonial North Carolina, there were few schools. Parents who could read and write taught their children and neighbors' children at home. Families that could afford to do so paid tutors to teach their children. However, most colonial children did not learn to read and write. They helped their families with the farmwork.

A **mayor** is the leader of a community. Our mayor works to make our community a good place to live.

Communities have other leaders, too. Police officers make sure that people follow the laws. Firefighters help when there is a fire.

Mayor William Bell of Durham, North Carolina, with citizens

SSSMART™ SUPPORT

TextWork

2 Skim and Scan

Remind students that a heading can give them clues about the text that comes after it. Have them read the heading to find out that all of the leaders discussed on these pages are community leaders. Tell them to fill in the blank with a community leader. Accept any reasonable answer that identifies a leader.

SOCIAL STUDIES STRANDS

Cultures and Diversity All cultures have leaders, but they have different types. In our culture, the President leads by sharing power with the people. Other cultures have a king or queen who makes all the decisions. Some cultures are led by generals; they make decisions for their people as well.

BACKGROUND

William Bell William "Bill" Bell was elected mayor of Durham in 2001. As mayor, he led the people of the city and the members of the city council. He voted on city issues. He put people on committees to help solve city problems. He also ran the Mayor's Summer Youth Work Program. This program gives summer jobs to high school students who want to learn how to be leaders.

Lesson Review

Summary Have students work individually to summarize the key content before they complete the Lesson Review.

- Many kinds of leaders help make sure people follow rules and laws.
- Parents, teachers, and principals are all different types of leaders.
- Mayors, police officers, and firefighters are leaders within a community.

1. **SUMMARIZE** How do leaders help people?

   Possible response: Leaders help people follow rules and laws.

2. What is the job of a **principal**?

   Possible response: A principal leads a school.

3. Who are some leaders in a community?

   Answers will vary, but students should name leaders in their community. Possible response: Some leaders in my community are teachers, a mayor, police officers, firefighters, and principals.

Write a sentence that tells about a leader in your community.

36

WRITING RUBRIC

Score 4
- correctly identifies a community leader
- clearly describes the leader
- shows a developed understanding of sentence structure

Score 3
- identifies a community leader
- describes the leader
- shows a basic understanding of sentence structure

Score 2
- identifies a community leader
- provides a partial description of the leader
- shows a beginning understanding of sentence structure

Score 1
- fails to identify a community leader
- does not describe a community leader
- fails to show an understanding of sentence structure

Build Background

Make It Relevant Point out to students that it is important to be fair and that rules and laws help people be fair. Ask students to think about some games they play on the playground. What are some rules for these games? Why is it important to play fair?

Preview the Lesson

Guide students in previewing the lesson. Point out the following features on Student Edition pages 37–40:

- **Page 37** Have students preview the photograph. Ask students what the children in the picture are doing. Explain that waiting in line allows everyone to have a turn. Why is it fair to wait in line?
- **Page 38** Explain to students that it is important to be fair when you do things with others. Have students make a list of activities that require them to be fair.
- **Page 39** Tell students that classroom rules have consequences. Explain that consequences can be bad or good. If students follow rules, they may be rewarded, but if they do not, they may miss something fun. Point out that rules at home work the same way. Ask students to name some rules and consequences.

Preteach Vocabulary

- Explain that being **fair** means acting in a way that is right for all. Point out that some people do not always act fairly. Ask students to think of examples of people not acting fairly. Answers might include cutting in line or not taking turns.
- Ask students what they think of when they hear the word **consequence**. Explain that consequences can be good or bad. Have students list some good and bad consequences.

NORTH CAROLINA STANDARD COURSE OF STUDY

Objective 2.05 Identify the need for fairness in rules by individuals and by people in authority.

Objective 2.06 Predict consequences that may result from responsible and irresponsible actions.

Key Content Summary

- **Rules and laws help people be fair.**
- **It is important for people to act fairly when doing things with others.**
- **Consequences happen when a person does or does not do something.**

Vocabulary

- **fair**, p. 37
- **consequence**, p. 39

Spotlight on Goals and Objectives

Use North Carolina Interactive Presentations, Unit 2, Lesson 3, to access prior knowledge and build background.

Reach All Learners

ESL/Language Support

Content and Language Objectives To ensure students understand the word *fair*, have students supply responses for this sentence frame describing the photograph on page 37: The children are standing in line at the drinking fountain because ____ .

Extra Support

Role-Play Following the Rules Post classroom or school rules for children to review. Organize students in groups of three, and assign a rule. Appoint one of the students in the group the "teacher." Have each group role-play to demonstrate the right and wrong way to follow the rule. The "teacher" should then assign consequences for each situation.

Extension Activity

Write Questions and Answers Post classroom or school rules for students to review. Then have students change each rule to a question and an answer. For example, a rule might be that students keep their hands and feet to themselves. Model writing a question, such as "What should I do with my hands?" and an answer, such as "I should keep them to myself." After they have written their own questions and answers, pair students and have them use their questions and answers to have a discussion about school rules.

Integrate the Curriculum

Healthful Living

Make Safety Rules Organize students in groups. Assign each group a familiar playground game, such as tag, kickball, or freeze tag. Have children choose three safety rules that everyone should know before playing their game. Then invite groups to present their rules to the class. If possible, allow students time to practice playing by the rules.

Lesson 3 Following the Rules

Rules and laws help us be fair. Being **fair** means acting in a way that is right for all. Sometimes people do not follow rules. This causes problems for everyone. **What do you think you will learn about following rules?**

Possible response: I will learn about why it is important to follow the rules.

NORTH CAROLINA STANDARD COURSE OF STUDY

2.05 Identify the need for fairness in rules by individuals and by people in authority.

2.06 Predict consequences that may result from responsible and irresponsible actions.

37

Start with the Objectives

Objective 2.05 Identify the need for fairness in rules by individuals and by people in authority.

Objective 2.06 Predict consequences that may result from responsible and irresponsible actions.

Set a Purpose for Reading

Draw students' attention to the highlighted word *fair*. Have students keep the highlighted word in mind as they answer the question to set a purpose for reading. Model thinking for students by using the Think Aloud below.

Think Aloud

I know that rules should be fair and that people are supposed to follow them. I think I will read about why we have rules and what happens when people do not follow them.

BACKGROUND

Following the Rules Help students make the connection between the photograph and the lesson introduction. Ask them to describe what is happening in this picture. How are the students in this picture being fair to one another? What might happen if someone were to cut in line? How do you feel when someone breaks the rules?

SOCIAL STUDIES STRANDS

Government and Active Citizenship Explain to students that some rules may not seem fair until we think about what can happen if people break them. Have students work in pairs. Ask each pair to write, draw, or dictate one rule that they do not think is fair. Then have them draw a picture of what could happen if people did not follow the rule. Finally, have them write a sentence explaining why the rule is fair after all.

SSSMART™ SUPPORT

TextWork

1 Comprehension

Main Idea and Details Help students find the reason that it is important to play fairly. Ask them to read the paragraph and circle the sentence that contains the word *fairly*.

TextWork

1 Circle the main reason it is important to play fairly.

Playing Fairly

It is important to be fair when you do things with others. When you play games fairly, everyone can have fun. If you do not play fairly, other children may not want to play with you.

38

TEACHING YOUR SOCIAL STUDIES

BACKGROUND

Fairness of Rules Have students examine the photograph on this page. Ask: "What is the rule for the people who are walking?" and "What is the rule for nearby cars?" Then remind students that rules should be fair. Ask whether students think it is fair to make people use a crosswalk to cross the street and whether they think it is fair to make drivers stop so that people can cross the street. Have students explain their responses.

SOCIAL STUDIES STRANDS

Individual Development and Identity Invite students to think of a time when they were playing a game with a group of friends. Have them recall the rules of the game.

Q How did the rules of the game make things fair?

A Possible responses: The rules ensured that everyone got a turn. They helped us get along. They helped solve problems.

SSSMART™ SUPPORT

Consequences

People who break laws face consequences. A **consequence** is something that happens because of what a person does or does not do.

Consequences can be bad or good. Children who break a rule might have to miss something that is fun. Children who follow rules might get more playtime.

TextWork

❷ What can happen if you break a rule?

Possible response: You might miss something fun.

People who cross a street at the wrong place may get hurt.

39

TextWork

❷ Skim and Scan

Remind students that a consequence is something that happens because of what a person does or does not do. To find out what happens when a person does not follow the rules, students can scan the second paragraph and look for the consequence. Student answers may vary, but answers should show that students understand they may face a consequence if they break a rule.

SOCIAL STUDIES STRANDS

Government and Active Citizenship Use a chart like the one below to further students' understanding of the consequences of following and breaking rules and laws. Have students consider why the consequences differ.

	Good Consequences	Bad Consequences
Rules	cooperation, safety	time out, arguments
Laws	cooperation, safety	tickets, fines, jail

BUILD SKILLS

Decision Making Organize students in small groups. Have each group make up a skit about the consequences of following and breaking rules. In their skits, students should show two people in the same situation. One person should be shown making the decision to follow the rule; the other should decide to break the rule. Tell groups that their skits should also show the consequences of each student's decision.

Lesson Review

Summary Have students work individually to summarize the key content before they complete the Lesson Review.

- Rules and laws help people be fair.
- It is important for people to act fairly when doing things with others.
- Consequences happen when a person does or does not do something.

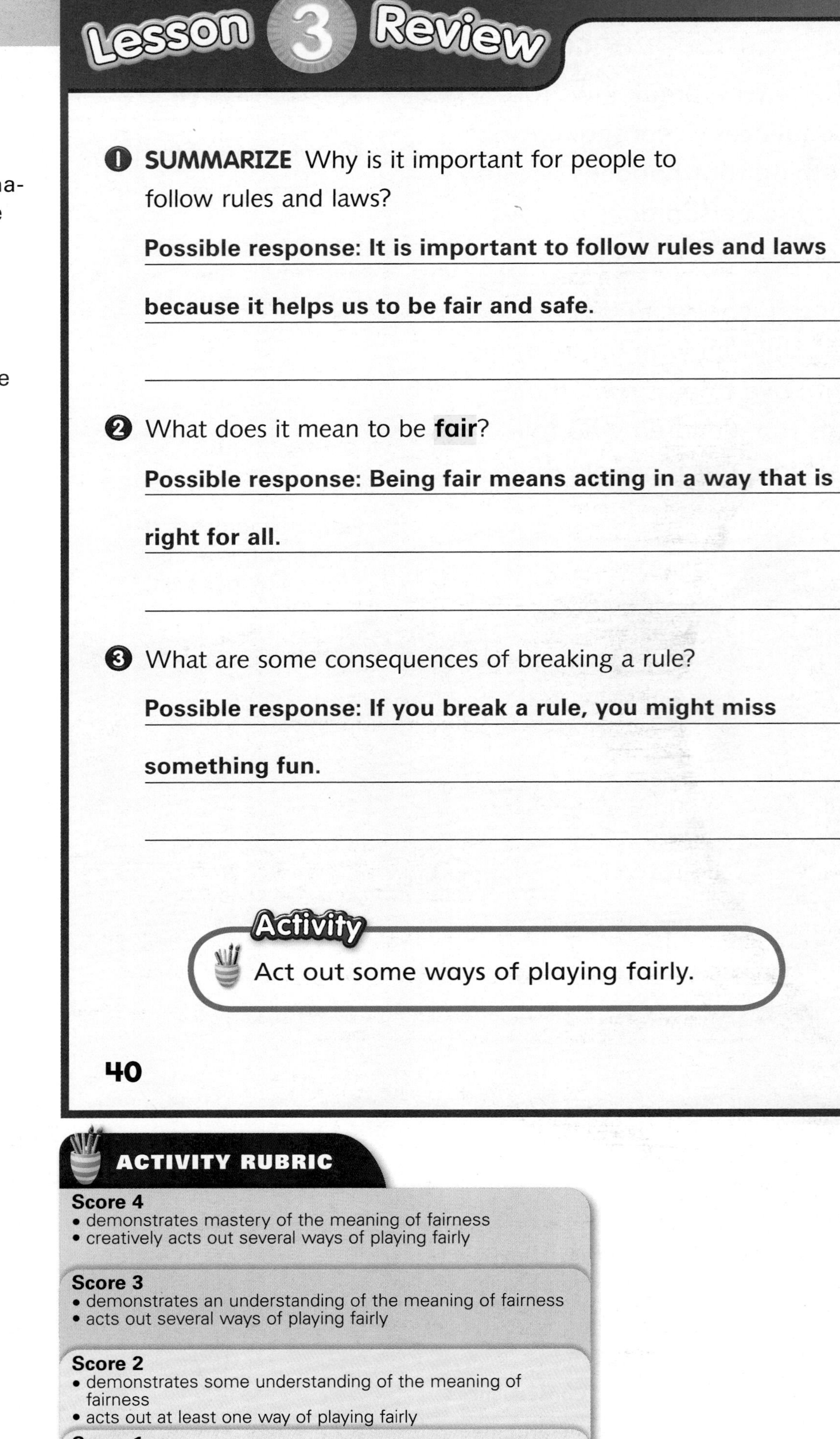

Lesson 3 Review

1. **SUMMARIZE** Why is it important for people to follow rules and laws?

   Possible response: It is important to follow rules and laws because it helps us to be fair and safe.

2. What does it mean to be **fair**?

   Possible response: Being fair means acting in a way that is right for all.

3. What are some consequences of breaking a rule?

   Possible response: If you break a rule, you might miss something fun.

Activity

Act out some ways of playing fairly.

40

ACTIVITY RUBRIC

Score 4
- demonstrates mastery of the meaning of fairness
- creatively acts out several ways of playing fairly

Score 3
- demonstrates an understanding of the meaning of fairness
- acts out several ways of playing fairly

Score 2
- demonstrates some understanding of the meaning of fairness
- acts out at least one way of playing fairly

Score 1
- fails to demonstrate any understanding of the meaning of fairness
- does not act out one way of playing fairly

Build Background

Make It Relevant Ask students whether they have ever heard the word *responsibility*. Explain that a responsibility is something a person should do. Ask students what responsibilities they have at home.

Preview the Lesson

Guide students in previewing the lesson. Point out the following features on Student Edition pages 41–44:

- **Page 41** Explain to students that citizens of the United States have certain rights. Citizens also have responsibilities. Tell students that they have both the right and the responsibility to go to school.
- **Page 42** Direct students to preview the photographs on the page. Tell them that each image illustrates a freedom. What are the people in the photographs doing?
- **Page 43** Tell students to read the heading on this page. What is the child doing in each photograph? Is he being a good citizen?

Preteach Vocabulary

- Explain that a **right** gives people the freedom to do something. Have students think of some rights they have at home and at school. Create a class list.
- Tell students that the base word of **responsibility** is *responsible*. Tell them that they have different responsibilities at home and at school. Ask student volunteers to share some of the different kinds of responsibilities they have.
- Have students look for the word *free* in **freedom**. Point out that a freedom is a kind of right.
- Explain to students that a **volunteer** is a person who works without pay to help other people. Have students think about the kinds of things they could do to help others.
- Tell students that treating something or someone well shows **respect**. Remind them that when we treat others with respect, they will often treat us respectfully in return.

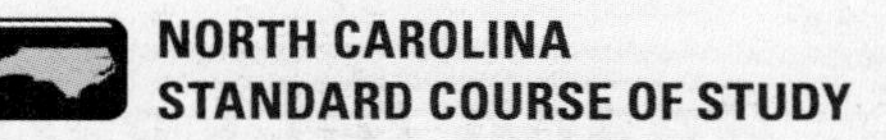

Objective 2.01 Develop and exhibit citizenship traits in the classroom, school, and other social environments.

Key Content Summary

- **Citizens of the United States have rights and responsibilities.**
- **People in the United States also have freedoms.**
- **Good citizens are responsible in many different ways.**

Vocabulary

- **right,** p. 41
- **responsibility,** p. 41
- **freedom,** p. 42
- **volunteer,** p. 43
- **respect,** p. 43

Spotlight on Goals and Objectives

Use North Carolina Interactive Presentations, Unit 2, Lesson 4, to access prior knowledge and build background.

Reach All Learners

ESL/Language Support

Active Learning Have pairs of students look through magazines and newspapers to find pictures of people showing good citizenship. Ask students to cut out the pictures they select and then paste them on a sheet of posterboard to create a collage. Invite partners to add such labels as *rights, responsibility, freedom, volunteer,* and *respect* to the images in their collage.

Extra Support

Guess the Vocabulary Write lesson vocabulary words on sentence strips, and display them on a wall. Make statements to students such as, "I'm thinking of a word that means...," completing the statements with definitions. Have students guess which vocabulary word corresponds to your definition statement by pointing to the correct word on the wall. When all words have been identified, challenge students to play the game in reverse by giving you the definition of each word you name.

Extension Activity

Create a Poster Talk with students about the fact that rights come with responsibilities. Remind them that they have the right to go to school, but they also have the responsibility to do all of their schoolwork. Invite students to think of other rights and responsibilities they have at home, at school, or in their community. Have each student choose an example and make a drawing to represent both elements. Tell students to include a brief caption to explain the drawing and to identify both the right and the responsibility.

Integrate the Curriculum

Arts

Paint a Picture Make a list of rights, such as freedom of the press, freedom of religion, and the right to attend school. Invite students to choose one right and create a painting showing people practicing that right. Then have students present their pictures and explain to the class why the right is important.

Being a Good Citizen

Lesson

Citizens of the United States have rights. A **right** is something people are free to do. People also have responsibilities. A **responsibility** is something you should do. **What do you think you will learn about being a good citizen?**

Possible response: I will learn what responsibilities I have as a good citizen.

Volunteers help Habitat for Humanity build houses for people.

NORTH CAROLINA STANDARD COURSE OF STUDY

2.01 Develop and exhibit citizenship traits in the classroom, school, and other social environments.

41

Lesson 4

PAGES 41–44

Start with the Objective

Objective 2.01 Develop and exhibit citizenship traits in the classroom, school, and other social environments.

Set a Purpose for Reading

Read the lesson introduction to the class. Point out the highlighted words *right* and *responsibility*. Tell students that they will learn about the difference between these words. Have students answer the question to set a purpose for reading. Model thinking for students by using the Think Aloud below.

Think Aloud

I know that there are things that a good citizen has to do. I also know that there are things a good citizen should do to help others. I will read to learn more about what people can do to be good citizens.

BACKGROUND

Habitat for Humanity This photograph shows volunteers working for Habitat for Humanity, a group that builds houses for people who need them. Citizens in the community donate money and building supplies to help Habitat provide these houses. Others offer their time and abilities to help build the houses. The family who will live in the house also takes part in building it. Habitat for Humanity has built houses in this way for more than one million people all over the world since 1976.

SOCIAL STUDIES STRANDS

Economics and Development Help students apply the concept of economics to the activities done by Habitat for Humanity volunteers. Ask: Is it a right or a responsibility to help others? Why would people work without pay to help others?

SSSMART™ SUPPORT

TextWork

1 CUES

Analyze/Interpret Photographs Have students look at each photograph and think about what the people are doing. Direct students to read each caption carefully. Provide reading help to students who may need it.

TextWork

1 Circle the person who is using the right of freedom of speech.

Rights

People in the United States have many rights. They also have many freedoms. A **freedom** is a kind of right.

Freedom of the press is the right to write about ideas in newspapers.

Freedom of assembly is the right to meet in groups.

Freedom of speech is the right to speak about our ideas.

42

TEACHING YOUR SOCIAL STUDIES

BACKGROUND

The Bill of Rights The rights of Americans were very important to the people who created our government. Many of them insisted that a section called the Bill of Rights be added to the United States Constitution. This section outlined each of the rights held by every American citizen. The three freedoms discussed on this page are part of the Bill of Rights. Explain that freedom of the press applies to television, radio, and other media. This includes but is not limited to newspapers.

BUILD SKILLS

Chart and Graph Skills Have students use a word web like the one below to identify the ways they exercise their rights in the classroom and at home.

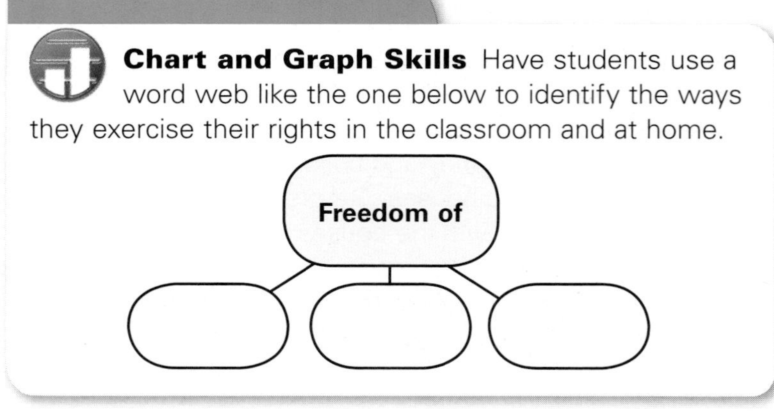

Good Citizens

Good citizens are responsible. You are being responsible when you do the things you should do.

One way to be responsible is to help others. A **volunteer** works without pay to help people. Another way is to show respect for people and things. To show **respect** is to treat someone or something well.

TextWork

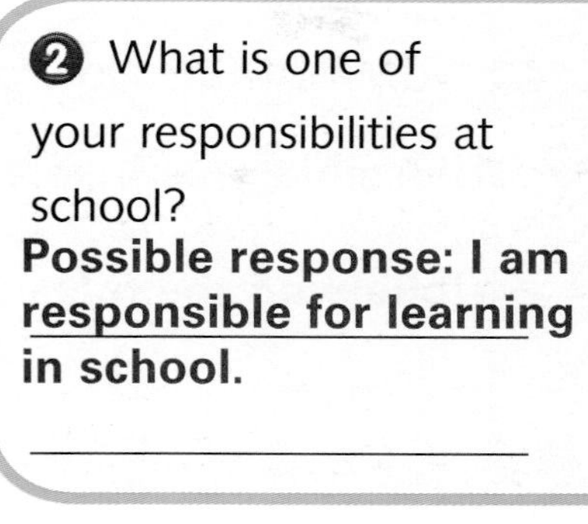

❷ What is one of your responsibilities at school?

Possible response: I am responsible for learning in school.

I am responsible for . . .

learning in school.

caring for my community.

cleaning up my room.

43

TextWork

❷ Comprehension

Review/Reflect Remind students that a responsibility is something that they should do. Have them think about what they should do at school. Guide them to look at the pictures at the bottom of the page. Ask: What does the boy say that he is responsible for at school? When students write their responses, they may vary. Responses should reflect a responsibility the student has at school.

SOCIAL STUDIES STRANDS

Government and Active Citizenship Poll students to find out what kinds of responsibilities they have at home. List their responses on the board. Have them use the list to write two sentences about students' responsibilities at home.

BUILD SKILLS

Chart and Graph Skills Construct a table on the bulletin board with the headings *Rights* and *Responsibilities*. Provide each student with two sheets of paper. Have each student draw one picture on each sheet—one showing a responsibility and the other showing a right. To ensure some variety, assign rows of students different settings for their rights and responsibilities, such as school, home, and a friend's home.

Lesson Review

Summary Have students work individually to summarize the key content before they complete the Lesson Review.

- Citizens of the United States have rights and responsibilities.
- People in the United States also have freedoms.
- Good citizens are responsible in many different ways.

1. **SUMMARIZE** How can you be a good citizen?

   Possible response: I can be a good citizen by volunteering, following the rules, and helping others.

2. What is one **right** that you have?

   Possible response: One right that I have is freedom of speech. Other responses are freedom of the press or freedom of assembly.

3. How can you show respect for others?

   Possible response: I can show respect by treating others well.

Writing

Make a list of some of your responsibilities.

44

WRITING RUBRIC

Score 4
- clearly demonstrates an understanding of responsibilities
- lists at least four responsibilities
- has very few or no errors

Score 3
- demonstrates an understanding of responsibilities
- lists two to three responsibilities
- has a few errors

Score 2
- demonstrates some confusion between rights and responsibilities
- lists at least two items
- has some errors

Score 1
- demonstrates much confusion between rights and responsibilities
- lists only one or two items
- has many errors

Build Background

Make It Relevant Explain to students that adults choose government leaders, such as the President, through voting. Point out that children sometimes vote, too. They may vote for a classroom leader or for a person to choose a game on the playground.

Preview the Lesson

Guide students in previewing the lesson. Point out the following features on Student Edition pages 45–48:

- **Page 45** Direct students to preview the photo and caption. Ask: Why do you think the people would be willing to wait in such a long line in order to vote?
- **Page 46** Have students read the heading on this page. Ask them whether they have ever heard of a ballot. Explain that a ballot shows people's choices so that they can vote.
- **Page 47** Have students preview the images on the page. Point out the ballot in the student's hand. Ask: Does your class have a class leader? What does he or she do?

Preteach Vocabulary

- Explain that a **vote** is a choice a person makes that gets counted. Tell students that there are different ways of voting. In a classroom, students might cast votes by raising their hands, allowing a teacher to count the number of votes. When adults vote for government leaders, they may use a paper ballot or a variety of mechanical or electronic methods.
- A **government** is a group of people that makes laws. Tell students that there are different kinds of governments in different communities. A school might have a student government, in which students can make decisions about certain parts of student life. A city or town also has a government to make laws for that community.
- Remind students that a **ballot** shows choices. Have them think about a quiz or a test in which they must choose an answer to a multiple-choice question by marking or circling the correct number or letter. Tell them that a ballot would offer a similar kind of choice.

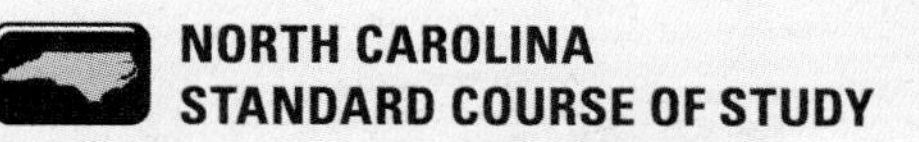

Objective 2.03 Participate in democratic decision-making.

Key Content Summary

- **People vote for leaders who make laws.**
- **People use ballots in order to vote.**
- **Classes can vote on leaders.**

Vocabulary

- **vote,** p. 45
- **government,** p. 45
- **ballot,** p. 46

Use North Carolina Interactive Presentations, Unit 2, Lesson 5, to access prior knowledge and build background.

Reach All Learners

ESL/Language Support

Scaffolding Content Have students use words and pictures to complete a K-W-L chart. Provide students with information about voting to fill in the first column. Then have students use words and pictures to fill in the second and third columns of the chart.

What I Know	What I Want to Know	What I Learned
When you vote, you make a choice that gets counted.		

Extra Support

Repeat the Words Create a Word Wall to provide additional practice in reading and identifying lesson vocabulary words. Have students repeat the words after you. Then invite volunteers to point to words you name. Have students add words to the wall as they read the lesson.

Extension Activity

Read a Ballot Show students a sample ballot with three choices. Then show them a tally sheet from a mock election, showing the results. Invite students to read the tally sheet to tell which choice won.

Integrate the Curriculum

Mathematics

Counting Votes Have volunteers suggest a game that the class could play. List the suggestions on the board. Then have each child write on a sample ballot or blank sheet of paper the game from the list that he or she would most like to play. Count students' votes and tally the results on the board. Have students determine which game received the most votes.

Make a Choice by Voting

When you **vote**, you make a choice that gets counted. Americans vote for many leaders in our government. A **government** is a group of people who make the laws. **What do you think you will read about voting?**

Possible response: I will read about how to vote for government leaders.

People wait in line for their turn to vote.

NORTH CAROLINA STANDARD COURSE OF STUDY
2.03 Participate in democratic decision-making.

45

Start with the Objective

Objective 2.03 Participate in democratic decision-making.

Set a Purpose for Reading

Read and discuss the lesson objective with students. Then have students read the lesson introduction on their own. Have students answer the question to set a purpose for reading. Model thinking for students by using the Think Aloud below.

Think Aloud

I know that Americans vote for their leaders. I also know that these leaders make laws. I will read to learn more about how leaders are elected to government.

BACKGROUND

Voting Rights The first Americans given the right to vote were white men who owned property. Women won the right to vote in 1920. In 1965, the government passed the Voting Rights Act. This law said that any citizen old enough to vote must be given an equal chance to do so. The act was passed after Dr. Martin Luther King, Jr., held demonstrations in the South demanding fair treatment for all citizens.

BACKGROUND

Polling Places Explain that the locations at which people vote are called polls. Tell them that polls can be housed in many different places, including churches, schools, and other public buildings. Point out that in this photograph, people are waiting outside a community building to vote.

SSSMART™ SUPPORT

TextWork

1 Vocabulary

Understand Vocabulary Direct students to review the first paragraph, in which the word *ballot* is defined and highlighted. Tell students to read each sentence in both paragraphs and circle the details they give about a ballot. When they have done this for each sentence, have them read the circled text and find the details that explain what a ballot is used for.

1 What do you use a ballot for?
Possible responses: voting, marking your choice.

How to Vote

You can use a ballot to vote. A **ballot** shows all the choices. A ballot can be on paper. It can also be on a voting machine.

You mark your choice on a ballot. The choice that gets the most votes wins.

Biography
Citizenship

Elizabeth Dole

Elizabeth Dole is a United States senator. She is from Salisbury, North Carolina. She has worked with six United States Presidents. She was also the President of the American Red Cross. The Red Cross helps people when bad things such as floods happen.

46

TEACHING YOUR SOCIAL STUDIES

SOCIAL STUDIES STRANDS

Technological Influences Some people want to vote with computers. They think it will make it easier to cast ballots and count votes. Others worry that computers can break down. They also fear that the votes might be changed.

BACKGROUND

Elizabeth Dole Elizabeth Dole is a native of Salisbury, North Carolina. She graduated from Duke University in 1958 and earned a degree from Harvard Law School in 1965. She served under President Nixon as the Deputy Assistant for Consumer Affairs. She also served as the Secretary of Transportation in the Reagan administration and as the Secretary of Labor in the Bush administration. She was first elected to the Senate in 2002.

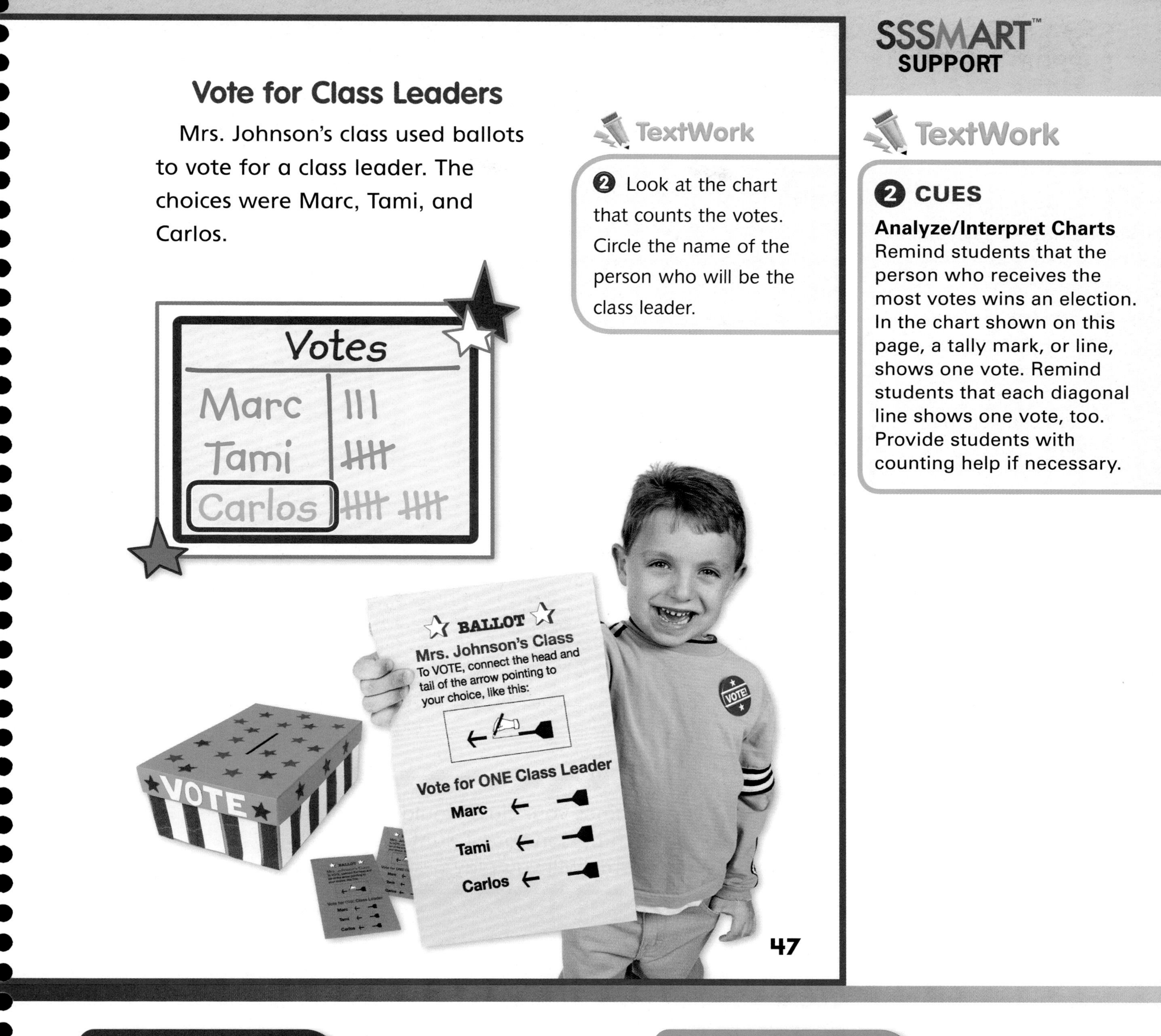

Vote for Class Leaders

Mrs. Johnson's class used ballots to vote for a class leader. The choices were Marc, Tami, and Carlos.

TextWork

❷ Look at the chart that counts the votes. Circle the name of the person who will be the class leader.

47

SSSMART™ SUPPORT

TextWork

❷ **CUES**

Analyze/Interpret Charts Remind students that the person who receives the most votes wins an election. In the chart shown on this page, a tally mark, or line, shows one vote. Remind students that each diagonal line shows one vote, too. Provide students with counting help if necessary.

SOCIAL STUDIES STRANDS

Government and Active Citizenship Give your class the opportunity to vote on a new class rule. Prepare a shoe box like the one shown on this page to collect votes. Give students ballots that show three choices. Guide students through the democratic decision-making process of voting anonymously and tallying the votes. You can tally the votes on the board, using marks like those in the chart on this page.

BUILD SKILLS

Decision Making Have students participate in the process of setting up a democratic vote. Tell students to choose an issue that they can vote on with their friends or family. Then have students create a ballot. Remind students to include at least three choices on the ballot. Ballots should also have instructions. Point out the ballot on this page as an example. Encourage students to hold a vote with their friends or family, using the materials they have created.

Lesson Review

Summary Have students work individually to summarize the key content before they complete the Lesson Review.

- People vote for leaders who make laws.
- People use ballots in order to vote.
- Classes can vote on leaders.

1. **SUMMARIZE** How can you make a choice that gets counted?

   Possible response: You can make a choice by voting.

2. What does a **government** do?

   Possible response: A government makes laws.

3. What are two kinds of ballots?

   Possible response: Two kinds of ballots are a paper ballot and a ballot on a voting machine.

Activity

List games your class would like to play. Have each person vote. Count the votes. Which game will you play?

48

ACTIVITY RUBRIC

Score 4
- lists three to four games that the class would like to play
- collects votes from all class members
- makes no errors when counting the votes

Score 3
- lists two to three games that the class would like to play
- collects votes from most class members
- makes few errors when counting the votes

Score 2
- lists one to two games that the class would like to play
- collects votes from some class members
- makes some errors when counting the votes

Score 1
- fails to list games or lists only one or two
- collects votes from few class members
- makes many errors when counting the votes

Review and Test Prep

The Big Idea

It is important to be a good citizen in your community. Good citizens help others. They also vote for their community leaders.

Summarize the Unit

Main Idea and Details Fill in the chart. Show what you have learned about voting.

Main Idea

Good citizens vote for leaders in their community.

Details

They use a ballot to vote.	They make a choice that gets counted.	The person with the most votes wins.

49

Unit Review

PAGES 49–52

The Big Idea

Ask students to review the unit's Big Idea. Remind students why it is important to follow the rules and laws of their community. Discuss ways that they can contribute to their community as good citizens.

Summarize the Unit

Main Idea and Details Invite students to review the Reading Social Studies at the beginning of the unit. Ask students to think about why good citizens vote for leaders in their community. Then ask them to brainstorm details that would support this main idea.

READING FOCUS SKILLS

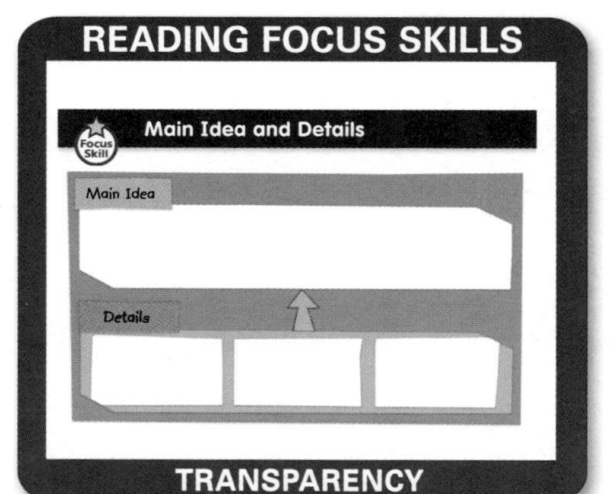

TRANSPARENCY

Graphic Organizer Write-On/ Wipe-Off Cards available

ASSESSMENT

Use the **UNIT 2 TEST** on pages 5–8 of the Assessment Program.

Use Vocabulary

Fill in the blanks with the correct words.

Word Bank
citizen p. 29
law p. 31
leader p. 33
vote p. 45
government p. 45

When I grow up, I will ❶ **vote** in elections. By voting, I will help choose the people who run our community. This group of people, called a ❷ **government**, helps everyone get along. I am a good ❸ **citizen** in my community. I follow every ❹ **law**, or rule. One day, I want to be a ❺ **leader** in my community.

50

VOCABULARY POWER

Word Web Write the word *vote* on the board. Remind students that *vote* means a choice that gets counted. Have students add words and phrases to the web to clarify their understanding of the word. For example, students could write *I vote for our class game. I will vote for government leaders when I am older.* Have students create a word web for each vocabulary word in the Unit Review.

Think About It

Circle the letter of the correct answer.

6. Which is the leader of a school?
   - **(A)** the principal
   - **B** the government
   - **C** a teacher
   - **D** the mayor

7. Which does a leader help a community do?
   - **A** read books
   - **B** plant trees
   - **(C)** make laws
   - **D** make food

8. What is respect?
   - **A** to speak about ideas
   - **(B)** to treat someone or something well
   - **C** to write about ideas
   - **D** to belong to groups

9. Which shows all of the choices you can vote for?
   - **A** a teacher
   - **B** a government
   - **(C)** a ballot
   - **D** a freedom

READ MORE

Encourage independent reading with these books or books of your choice.

Basic

Vote! by Eileen Christelow. Clarion Books, 2004. This lively introduction to voting covers every step in the process, from the start of the campaign all the way to the voting booth.

Proficient

Following Rules by Robin Nelson. Lerner Publications, 2003. This book shows the importance of following rules at home, at school, and in the community.

Advanced

Serving Your Community by Christin Ditchfield. Children's Press, 2004. Students learn ways to reach out and help others.

Unit Review

PAGES 49–52

Show What You Know

Writing

Write a List

Ask students to write a list of school rules. Suggest numbering or lettering to organize their thoughts.

Activity

Plan a Campaign Rally

Discuss in detail the different roles students will play during the campaign rally, including the two candidates, slogan writers, and poster makers.

North Carolina Adventures

Remind students that this game will review the concepts in the unit.

Spotlight on Goals and Objectives

Use North Carolina Interactive Presentations, Unit 2, to review concepts from the unit.

Answer each question in a complete sentence.

10. Who are some leaders in your community?

    Possible response: Some leaders in my community are teachers, police officers, and the mayor.

11. What are some freedoms that Americans have?

    Possible response: Some freedoms that Americans have are freedom of speech, freedom of assembly, and freedom of the press.

12. What happens when people break laws?

    Possible response: People have to face consequences for breaking laws because laws are made to keep members of a community safe.

Show What You Know

Writing Write a List
Imagine that a new child has joined your class. Write a list of class rules to help the new child.

Activity Plan a Campaign Rally
Choose two people to run for Class Safety Monitor. Make posters and signs. Tell about safety rules at the rally.

GO online To play a game that reviews the unit, join Eco in the North Carolina Adventures online or on CD.

52

WRITING RUBRIC

Score 4
- clearly identifies several school rules
- provides strong details that convey the importance of rules
- prints legibly and creates well-developed sentences

Score 3
- somewhat identifies a few school rules
- provides some details that convey the importance of rules
- prints somewhat legibly and creates developed sentences

Score 2
- identifies at least one school rule
- provides a few details that convey the importance of rules
- prints illegibly and creates minimally developed sentences

Score 1
- does not identify any school rules
- provides few or no details that convey the importance of rules
- prints illegibly and creates undeveloped sentences

ACTIVITY RUBRIC

Score 4
- is well-organized
- is completed in an orderly and timely manner
- shows clear understanding of a rally's purpose

Score 3
- is organized
- is completed in a somewhat orderly and timely manner
- shows some understanding of a rally's purpose

Score 2
- is somewhat organized
- is completed with some difficulty
- shows little understanding of a rally's purpose

Score 1
- is disorganized
- is not completed as planned
- shows no understanding of a rally's purpose

Unit 3
Changing People and Places

NORTH CAROLINA STANDARD COURSE OF STUDY

COMPETENCY GOAL 3

The learner will recognize and understand the concept of change in various settings.

OBJECTIVES

3.01 Describe personal and family changes, past and present.

3.02 Describe past and present changes within the local community.

3.03 Compare and contrast past and present changes within the local community and communities around the world.

3.04 Recognize that members of the community are affected by changes in the community that occur over time.

LESSON	TOTAL: 25 DAYS	NORTH CAROLINA STANDARD COURSE OF STUDY
Introduce the Unit **Unit Preview,** pp. 53–54 **The Big Idea,** p. 54 **Reading Social Studies,** pp. 55–56 Focus Skill Sequence	2 DAYS	COMPETENCY GOAL 3 **The learner will recognize and understand the concept of change in various settings.** **Spotlight on Goals and Objectives** Unit 3
1 **People Long Ago and Today** pp. 57–62 **past** p. 57 **present** p. 57 **change** p. 58 **communication** p. 61	5 DAYS	**Objective 3.01** Describe personal and family changes, past and present. **Spotlight on Goals and Objectives** Unit 3, Lesson 1
2 **My Community's History** pp. 63–66 **history** p. 63	4 DAYS	**Objective 3.02** Describe past and present changes within the local community. **Spotlight on Goals and Objectives** Unit 3, Lesson 2
3 **Technology in Communities** pp. 67–72 **technology** p. 67 **tool** p. 67 **transportation** p. 70	5 DAYS	**Objective 3.02** Describe past and present changes within the local community. **Objective 3.04** Recognize that members of the community are affected by changes in the community that occur over time. **Spotlight on Goals and Objectives** Unit 3, Lesson 3

TEACHING YOUR SOCIAL STUDIES	SSSMART SUPPORT
	Comprehension, Sequence, pp. 55–56
Background, Early Schools, p. 57 Azalea Festival, p. 60 History of Telephones, p. 61 **Social Studies Strands,** Individual Development and Identity, pp. 57, 60 Historical Perspectives, p. 58 Technological Influences, pp. 59, 61 Economics and Development, p. 59 **Build Skills,** Chart and Graph Skills, p. 58	**Skim and Scan,** p. 58 **Comprehension,** Review/Reflect, p. 59 Main Idea and Details, p. 60 **Vocabulary,** p. 61
Background, Duke University, p. 63 Stanford L. Warren Library, p. 64 Interviewing, p. 65 **Social Studies Strands,** Historical Perspectives, p. 63 Government and Active Citizenship, p. 64 Technological Influences, p. 65	**Skim and Scan,** p. 64 **Comprehension,** Review/Reflect, p. 65
Background, Statesville, North Carolina, p. 67 George S. Parker, p. 68 **Social Studies Strands,** Technological Influences, pp. 67, 69 Historical Perspectives, p. 68 Global Connections, p. 70 Economics and Development, p. 71 Government and Active Citizenship, p. 71 **Build Skills,** Chart and Graph Skills, p. 69 Decision Making, p. 70	**CUES,** pp. 68, 69 **Comprehension,** Sequence, p. 70 Draw Conclusions, p. 71

Print Resources

Student Edition, pp. 53–82
Teacher Edition, pp. 53A–82
Leveled Readers
Leveled Readers Teacher Guides
Document-Based Questions
Primary Atlas

Technology/Digital Resources

Spotlight on Goals and Objectives
North Carolina Interactive Presentations CD
North Carolina Interactive Presentations Online

Online Teacher Edition with ePlanner
Leveled Readers Online Database
North Carolina Adventures CD
North Carolina Adventures Online
Multimedia Biographies CD
Multimedia Biographies Online
Social Studies Music Collection CD

Hands-On Resources

Reading Focus Skills Transparencies
Social Studies Skills Transparencies
Graphic Organizer Write-On/Wipe-Off Cards
Interactive Atlas
Interactive Desk Maps
Interactive Map Transparencies
Picture Vocabulary Cards
Primary Source Kit
TimeLinks: Interactive Time Line
Social Studies in Action, pp. 38, 72–75, 76–79, 80–81, 82–83, 144, 151

Assessment Options

1 Unit 3 Test
Assessment Program, pp. 9–12

2 Writing
Write a Story, p. 82

3 Activity
Unit Project: Make a Scrapbook, p. 82

LESSON		NORTH CAROLINA STANDARD COURSE OF STUDY
4 **Changes in Communities** pp. 73–78 **country** p. 73	5 DAYS	**Objective 3.03** Compare and contrast past and present changes within the local community and communities around the world. **Spotlight on Goals and Objectives** Unit 3, Lesson 4
Unit 3 Review and Test Prep pp. 79–82	4 DAYS	**North Carolina Adventures** Unit 3

TEACHING YOUR SOCIAL STUDIES

Background,
- Asheville, North Carolina, p. 73
- Restoration of Historic Cities, p. 74
- Piazza Venezia, p. 75
- Harbin, China, p. 76
- Accra, Ghana, p. 77
- Cuzco, Peru, p. 77

Social Studies Strands,
- Geographic Relationships, p. 73
- Historical Perspectives, p. 75
- Cultures and Diversity, p. 76

Build Skills,
- Map and Globe Skills, p. 74

SSSMART™ SUPPORT

Comprehension,
- Sequence, p. 74
- Review/Reflect, p. 76
- Compare and Contrast, p. 77

CUES, p. 75

Summarize the Unit,
- Sequence, p. 79

Print Resources

- Student Edition, pp. 53–82
- Teacher Edition, pp. 53A–82
- Leveled Readers
- Leveled Readers Teacher Guides
- Document-Based Questions
- Primary Atlas

Technology/Digital Resources

Spotlight on Goals and Objectives

North Carolina Interactive Presentations CD
North Carolina Interactive Presentations Online

- Online Teacher Edition with ePlanner
- Leveled Readers Online Database
- North Carolina Adventures CD
- North Carolina Adventures Online
- Multimedia Biographies CD
- Multimedia Biographies Online
- Social Studies Music Collection CD

Hands-On Resources

- Reading Focus Skills Transparencies
- Social Studies Skills Transparencies
- Graphic Organizer Write-On/Wipe-Off Cards
- Interactive Atlas
- Interactive Desk Maps
- Interactive Map Transparencies
- Picture Vocabulary Cards
- Primary Source Kit
- TimeLinks: Interactive Time Line
- Social Studies in Action, pp. 38, 72–75, 76–79, 80–81, 82–83, 144, 151

Assessment Options

1 Unit 3 Test
Assessment Program, pp. 9–12

2 Writing
Write a Story, p. 82

3 Activity
Unit Project: Make a Scrapbook, p. 82

Leveled Readers

BELOW-LEVEL

Moving Ahead

Summary *Moving Ahead.* This Reader looks at how people's lives, communities, schools, and means of transportation have changed over time and how they have stayed the same.

Vocabulary Power Have students define the following words. Help them write one sentence for each word as it relates to our changing world.

change
past
communication
technology

Critical Thinking Lead students in a discussion about how their community might change in the future.

Write a Headline Have students write a newspaper headline describing an important event or change they learned about in the Reader.

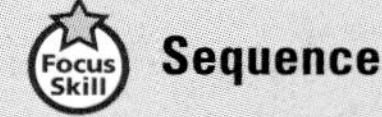

Sequence

ON-LEVEL

News Travels Fast

Summary *News Travels Fast*. This Reader identifies how inventions such as the printing press and the telephone have made communicating over long distances easier and faster.

Vocabulary Power Have students define the following words. Help them write one sentence for each word as it relates to our changing world.

change
past
share
communication

Critical Thinking Lead students in a discussion about how telephones have changed over time.

Write a Description Have students write about what they think life would be like without televisions.

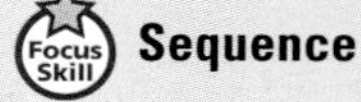

Sequence

ABOVE-LEVEL

Boomtowns and Ghost Towns

Summary *Boomtowns and Ghost Towns.* This Reader examines how, in the past, boomtowns grew very quickly and how, just as quickly, they could turn into ghost towns.

Vocabulary Power Have students define the following words. Help them write one sentence for each word as it relates to our changing world.

change
past
today

Critical Thinking Lead students in a discussion about how Rhyolite, Nevada, might be different if the gold had not run out.

Write a Report Have students research a ghost town in the United States. Have them write short reports about their ghost towns.

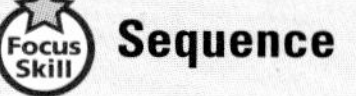

Sequence

Complete a Graphic Organizer

Have students complete the graphic organizer to show that they understand how to sequence events.

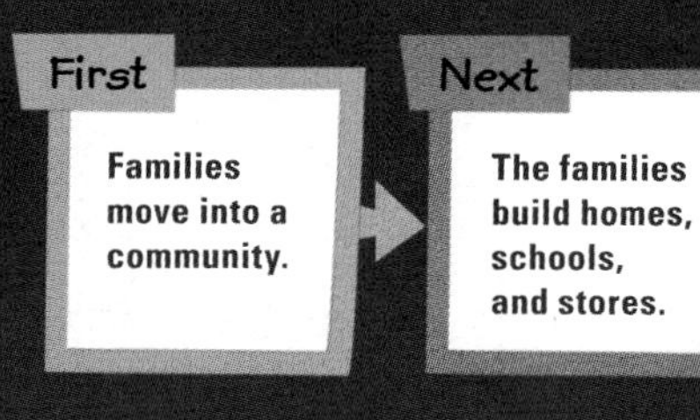

Leveled Readers Teacher Guides include complete lesson plans, copying masters, and project cards.

Harcourt Leveled Readers Available Online!
www.harcourtschool.com

A family looks at pictures from long ago in a scrapbook.

Unit 3 Preview

PAGES 53–54

Start with the Competency Goal

Competency Goal 3 The learner will recognize and understand the concept of change in various settings.

Make It Relevant

Read and discuss the unit competency goal. Help students think about ways in which people and things change.

Discuss the Photograph

Have students look at the photograph and discuss what is taking place. Explain that people experience change differently.

Q Why might the grandparents in the photograph view the scrapbook differently than their grandchildren?

A They may be able to remember certain past events portrayed in the scrapbook.

Instructional Design

START WITH THE GOAL AND OBJECTIVES

NORTH CAROLINA STANDARD COURSE OF STUDY

- competency goal
- objectives

PLAN ASSESSMENT

Assessment Options

- Option 1–Unit 3 Test
- Option 2–Writing: Write a Story, p. 82
- Option 3–Activity: Make a Scrapbook, p. 82

PLAN INSTRUCTION

Spotlight on Goals and Objectives
North Carolina Interactive Presentations, Unit 3

Unit 3 Teacher Edition
- resources
- activities
- strategies

Unit 3 Leveled Readers Teacher Guides

Unit 3 Preview

PAGES 53–54

The Big Idea

Have students read The Big Idea question and then preview how people and places change.

Access Prior Knowledge

Draw a two-column, two-row table listing the four seasons. Ask students to name some common characteristics for each season. For example, students may say that in the spring, new leaves grow on trees. Record their responses under each season. Discuss the changes that take place from season to season. Then have students read the paragraph and complete the activity.

How do people and places change?

To change is to become different. The ways people dress, work, and play can change over time. Some places change, too. People may build new roads and buildings. Some changes, such as changing clothes, happen every day. Some changes, such as growing up, happen over a long time.

Draw a picture of how you have changed over a long time.

Drawing should show that student understands the concept of change.

54

READ MORE

Encourage independent reading with these books or books of your choice.

Basic

Abe Lincoln's Hat by Martha Brenner. Random House Books for Young Readers, 1994. A simple telling of events in Abraham Lincoln's daily life.

Proficient

A Country Schoolhouse by Lynne Barasch. Farrar, Straus and Giroux, 2004. A grandfather describes the country schoolhouse that he attended in the 1940s.

Advanced

My Friend Grandpa by Harriet Ziefert. Blue Apple Books, 2004. A girl's grandfather teaches her that different generations can have fun together.

Reading Social Studies

Sequence

Focus Skill

Learn

- Sequence is the order in which things happen. What happens first? What happens next? What happens last?
- Look for sequence words such as first, next, then, later, last, and finally.

First
What happens first

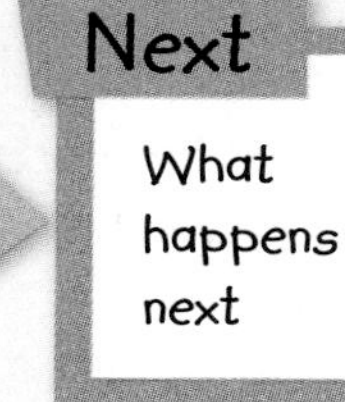

Next
What happens next

Last
What happens last

Practice

Read the paragraph below. Underline the sentence that tells what happens after Justin puts the letter into an envelope.

Justin wrote a letter to his grandmother. He needs to mail it to her. First, Justin puts his letter into an envelope. Next, he puts a stamp on the envelope. Last, Justin puts his letter into the mailbox.

Sequence

55

Learn

Have students read the Learn section and look at the graphic organizer. Explain that sequence is the order in which different events happen in time. By understanding sequence, students can better understand how events are related. Point out that sequence is usually shown within a text by the use of dates or time words such as *then* or *next*.

Practice

Read the paragraph with students. Point out the words *first, next,* and *last*. Ask students for the sequence of events. Help them write the sequence in a graphic organizer.

READING FOCUS SKILLS

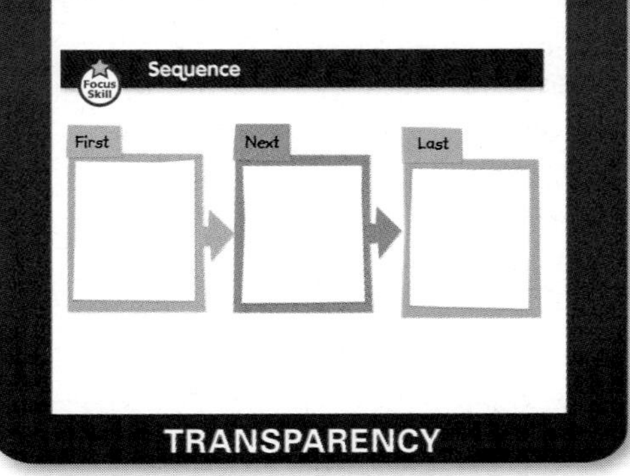

TRANSPARENCY

Graphic Organizer Write-On/ Wipe-Off Cards available

INTEGRATE THE CURRICULUM

ENGLISH LANGUAGE ARTS Tell a Story Have each student write or dictate three to five sentences about something that happened to him or her recently. Remind students to include sequence words to show the order of events. Students might talk about helping a parent make dinner, taking a trip to the store, or playing a game at school. Ask volunteers to read their stories to the class.

ELA 4.02 Use words that describe, name characters and settings (who, where), and tell action and events (what happened, what did ______ do) in simple texts.

Reading Social Studies PAGES 55–56

Apply

This selection explains the sequence of events in a school day long ago. Help students determine the order of events by looking at the time words. Point out the first event in the sequence. Then, ask students what event came next. How did they know? Direct students to fill in the graphic organizer based on the sequence indicated by the time words.

Unit 3 provides many opportunities for students to practice identifying sequence. As students read the unit, challenge them to think about the order in which things happen.

Apply

Read the paragraph.

Long ago in North Carolina, the school day was not like your school day. All the grades shared one classroom. First, they all read out loud. Next, each grade was called up for a lesson while the other children worked quietly. Last, the children helped the teacher do chores. They cleaned the classroom and got wood for the fire.

This chart shows the order in which things happened on a school day long ago. What can you add to the chart?

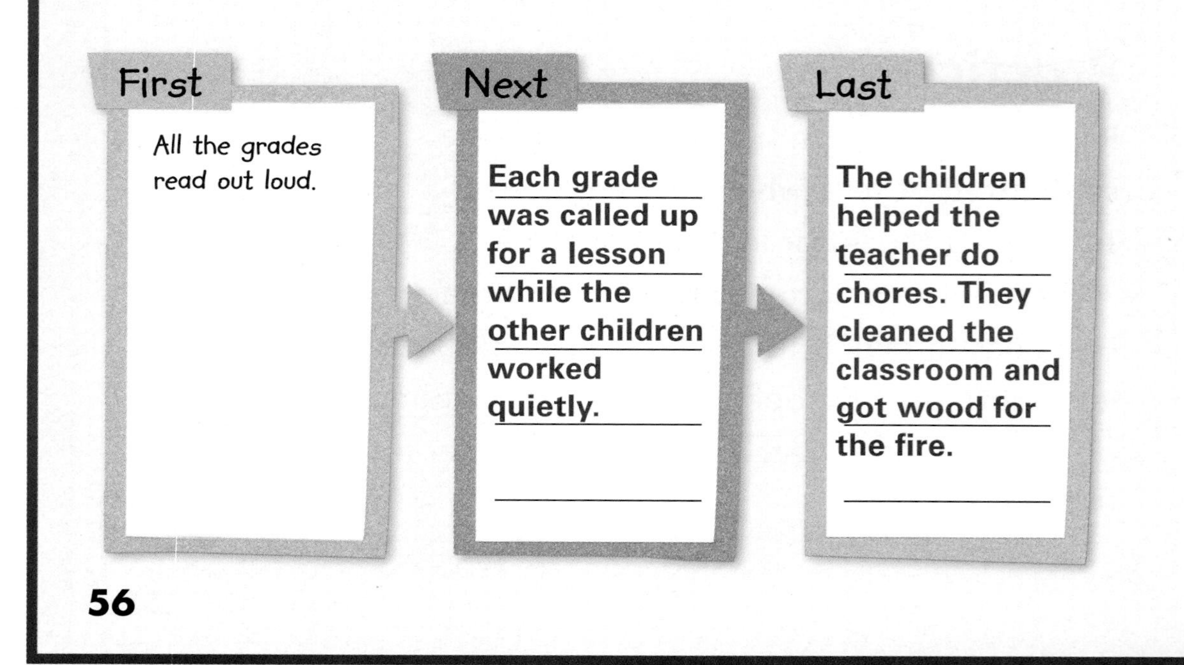

56

ESL/LANGUAGE SUPPORT

Vocabulary Development Ask students to think about words that relate to changes. Have students make a word web around the word *change*. As they read the unit, students should enter words into their webs to describe things that have changed over time.

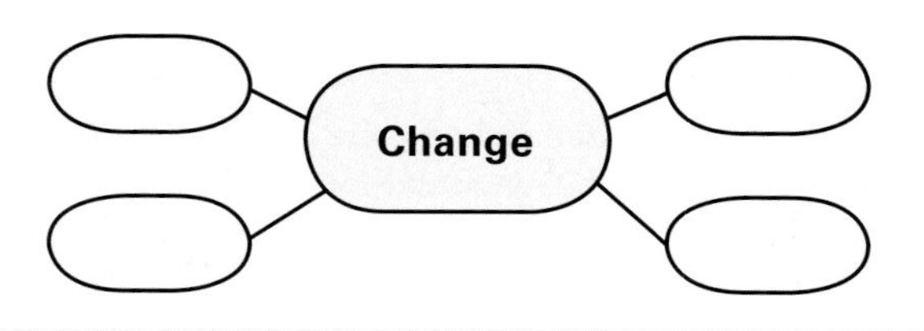

Prior Learning and Experiences As they read the unit, ask students to think about ways families change over time. Have volunteers share stories with the other students about their grandparents or other older adults they know who might do things differently now than they did in the past.

Build Background

Make It Relevant Ask students to describe the word *change* in their own words. Ask the following question to help students think about the role of change in their own lives: "How have you changed since you were a baby?" Students might mention changes in their physical appearance and their abilities.

Preview the Lesson

Guide students in previewing the lesson. Point out the following features on Student Edition pages 57–62:

- **Page 58** Ask students to think about change. Invite students to name something that is different now from what it was when they were younger.
- **Page 59** Invite students to preview the photograph. Draw students' attention to specific details, especially those that reinforce the idea of change. Encourage them to share their own observations.
- **Page 60** Have students preview the photographs. Ask how they know these photographs were taken in the past.
- **Page 61** Ask students to name some ways people communicate with one another today. List their responses on the board. Which communication methods are the same today as they were in the past? Which methods are different?

Preteach Vocabulary

- Write the words **past** and *before*. Explain that these two words are synonyms because they have the same meaning. Ask students to give an example of a game, toy, or food that they enjoyed in the past.
- Point out that the word *past* is an antonym, or opposite, of the word **present**. Ask students to name some synonyms for the word *present*.
- Invite students to explain the word **change** in their own words. Encourage students to share impressions they may have formed of schools of long ago based on movies or books. Then ask them to look around the classroom and point out some changes.

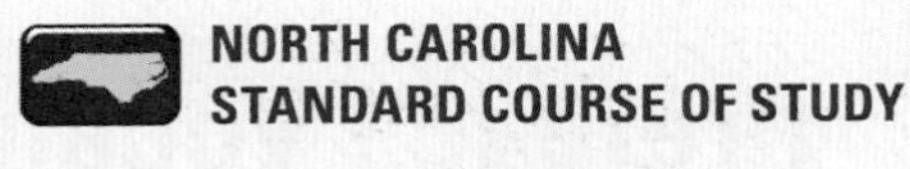

Objective 3.01 Describe personal and family changes, past and present

Key Content Summary

- **The past is the time before now. The present is the time now.**
- **Parents' roles have changed over time.**
- **The ways people dress and communicate have changed over time.**
- **Families change over time.**

Vocabulary

- **past,** p. 57
- **present,** p. 57
- **change,** p. 58
- **communication,** p. 61

Spotlight on Goals and Objectives

Use North Carolina Interactive Presentations, Unit 3, Lesson 1, to access prior knowledge and build background.

Preteach Vocabulary *continued*

- Explain that people use tools to help with **communication**. Ask students to list tools that help people communicate with one another.

Reach All Learners

ESL/Language Support

Active Learning Write the words *Past* and *Present* on separate index cards, and distribute a set of both cards to each student. Display photographs to represent objects from both the past and the present. Point to each photograph, and have students hold up the appropriate index card to tell if the object is from the past or the present.

Extra Support

Make a Poster Provide students with pictures of items or places from the past and present. Invite students to fold a piece of posterboard in half and label one side *Past* and one side *Present*. Have students select an item or place that has changed over time. Then ask students to draw a picture of the item or place as it appeared in the past and as it looks now. Display the posters in the classroom.

Extension Activity

Create a Collage Provide students with photographs, magazine pictures, and photocopies of people, places, and objects from the past and present, such as games, buildings, or cars. Label pieces of posterboard with those object names (games, buildings, cars). Have students paste pictures of the objects onto the posterboard, showing some pictures from the past and some from the present. Encourage students to write captions for their pages using vocabulary words. Display collages in the classroom.

Integrate the Curriculum

Healthful Living

Play Historic Games Help students find out more about games that children played in the past. Use the library or Internet resources to find out more about games such as Kick the Can and hopscotch. Have students choose one of these games and then learn it as a class.

People Long Ago and Today

Lesson 1

Grandma Mary tells Darla about when she was a child. Grandma Mary was a child in the **past**, the time before now. Darla is a child in the **present**, the time now. **What do you think you will learn about the past and the present?**

Possible response: I will learn how people lived in the past and how they live in the present.

A school in Wayne County, North Carolina, from the past

NORTH CAROLINA STANDARD COURSE OF STUDY

3.01 Describe personal and family changes, past and present.

Lesson 1

PAGES 57–62

Start with the Objective

Objective 3.01 Describe personal and family changes, past and present.

Set a Purpose for Reading

Read aloud the text with students. Point out the highlighted words *past* and *present*. Invite volunteers to give examples and definitions of the words in their own words. Then read aloud the question and ask volunteers to share their answers. Use the Think Aloud to model thinking about the past and present.

Think Aloud

I know that some people in my family were alive before I was. I have seen old photographs of them as children. I've seen our family change as new babies are born and people move. I will read to find out how families change.

BACKGROUND

Early Schools Schools were different in the past. Children ages 5 to 18 were taught in the same room. Students often stood at the podium and recited their math facts and spelling words. Students brought in wood for the wood-burning stove, which kept the one-room schoolhouse warm.

SOCIAL STUDIES STRANDS

Individual Development and Identity To reinforce the concepts of past, present, and change, have students create an illustrated time line showing different stages in their life. For example, students can draw pictures of themselves crawling, learning to ride a bicycle, and learning in school today. Have students display the illustrations sequentially on the board's ledge. Have students describe their pictures using the words *past*, *present*, and *change*.

TextWork

❶ Skim and Scan

Remind students that scanning the text is a fast way to find information. First, students should locate words in the TextWork item to determine the information they need to find (clothes, Grandma Mary, little girl). Then have students scan the text to locate the answer.

❷ Skim and Scan

Now tell students that they need to scan the text to find different information. Repeat the procedure above to help students locate the type of clothes that Darla likes to wear.

❶ Underline the clothes Grandma Mary wore when she was a little girl.

❷ Circle the clothes that Darla likes to wear.

Clothes in the Past

Darla watches old home movies with Grandma Mary. The movies show how people dressed in the past. "I always wore dresses when I was a little girl," Grandma Mary says.

Darla has dresses, but she likes to wear jeans and T-shirts. The clothes people wear change over time. To **change** means to become different.

TEACHING YOUR SOCIAL STUDIES

BUILD SKILLS

Chart and Graph Skills Draw a Venn diagram on the board. Label the left circle *Past* and the right circle *Present*. After reading the text on the page, have students assist as you complete the diagram for the topic of clothing. Continue adding to the diagram as you read the remainder of the lesson. Encourage students to discuss the completed diagram using terms such as *past, present, same,* and *different*.

SOCIAL STUDIES STRANDS

Historical Perspectives Explain that Grandma Mary and Darla are watching old home movies. Some people enjoy watching movies with their family for fun. Encourage students to share family activities they think are fun. Then ask students if they think that families long ago enjoyed the same activities for fun. Ask students to share their thinking and describe how they think leisure activities might have changed.

SSSMART™ SUPPORT

Families Past and Present

Grandma Mary tells Darla about her family. "Like many other women in the past, my mother worked at home. She took care of my brothers and me."

Today, both men and women work at home. Men and women also have jobs outside the home.

TextWork

3 Underline the sentence that tells where Grandma Mary's mother worked.

59

TextWork

3 Comprehension

Review/Reflect Read the TextWork item aloud with students. Ask, "Are we looking for information about the past or present?" (past) Have students volunteer the answer and then locate and underline it in the text. Make sure students underline the complete sentence. Point out that the period signals the end of the sentence in the text.

SOCIAL STUDIES STRANDS

Technological Influences Have students study the images on the spread. Make sure that students understand that the image projected on the screen on page 59 comes from the film projector on page 58. Ask students how movie recording and showing have changed over time. Discuss VCRs, DVD players, and movie theaters.

SOCIAL STUDIES STRANDS

Economics and Development Invite students to describe how the roles of women have changed over time. Make sure that they understand that in the past, most mothers stayed home taking care of the children. Today, many mothers work both at home and outside the home.

SSSMART™ SUPPORT

TextWork

4 Comprehension

Main Idea and Details
Tell students that the main idea of the page is that families change. Ask them to read the first paragraph to locate three different details that support the main idea. The details should be examples of how families change.

4 Underline some of the ways families change.

Family Life

Families change in the present just as they did in the past. Children grow into adults. People get married. Families move.

Grandma Mary tells Darla about the fun she had as a little girl. "Every year, we went to see the Azalea Festival. The festival is in Wilmington, North Carolina," she says. "People still go to it today."

60

TEACHING YOUR SOCIAL STUDIES

SOCIAL STUDIES STRANDS

Individual Development and Identity Reread the second paragraph about Grandma Mary and the annual Azalea Festival. Invite volunteers to describe an annual event that they attend with family or friends.

BACKGROUND

Azalea Festival Wilmington's Azalea Festival has been held annually for over 60 years. More than 300,000 people attend the April festival each year to enjoy Wilmington's culture, including arts and crafts, parades, music, and food.

Communication

Every day, people talk and write to share ideas and feelings. This sharing is called **communication**.

Long ago, Grandma Mary wrote letters to her friends. She also talked to them on the telephone. Today, Darla and Grandma Mary still communicate in these same ways. They also send letters and pictures by e-mail.

❺ Name one way you can communicate with people who live far away.

Possible response: Write letters, send e-mails, or talk on the phone.

61

TextWork

❺ Vocabulary

Understand Vocabulary Make sure students understand that the vocabulary word *communicate* means "to share ideas and feelings." Ask students how they would communicate with someone sitting next to them. Then have students complete the TextWork activity.

SOCIAL STUDIES STRANDS

Technological Influences Have students work in small groups to create communication murals. Provide each group with a piece of chart paper. Write the word *Communication* at the top. Invite students to cut out photographs, both historical and modern, of people communicating in different ways and paste them to the page.

BACKGROUND

History of Telephones Direct students' attention to the photograph of the girl on the telephone. Explain that Alexander Graham Bell started the first telephone company in the 1870s. Since then, telephones have changed. Have students study the image and compare the phone to a modern-day phone. Discuss differences in dialing, too. Point out that despite the improvements, telephone transmission still works in about the same way.

Lesson Review

Summary Have students work with a partner to summarize the most important ideas in the lesson. Tell them to use headings, highlighted words, and images to help them summarize. Then have students work independently to complete the Lesson Review.

- The past is the time before now. The present is the time now.
- Parents' roles have changed over time.
- The ways people dress and communicate have changed over time.
- Families change over time.

Lesson 1 Review

1. **SUMMARIZE** How is the way you live different from the way people lived long ago?

   Possible response: People long ago wore different clothes than I do, women worked at home, and people wrote letters to communicate.

2. Write a sentence that tells about **communication** between two people.

   Possible response: I use the telephone for communication with my grandmother.

3. What is one thing Grandma Mary did for fun as a little girl?

   Possible response: Grandma Mary went to see the Azalea Festival in Wilmington, North Carolina.

Writing

Write sentences about what you think it would have been like to live in the past.

62

WRITING RUBRIC

Score 4
- clearly understands the distinction between past and present
- provides at least three details about living in the past
- writes at least three sentences with no or very few errors

Score 3
- understands the distinction between past and present
- provides at least two details about living in the past
- writes at least two sentences with few errors

Score 2
- does not fully understand the distinction between past and present
- provides at least one detail about living in the past
- writing is not in sentence form

Score 1
- fails to differentiate between past and present
- examples provided are not relevant or are not related to the past
- writing is not in sentence form

Build Background

Make It Relevant Display a map of North Carolina. Then guide students to find Durham. Explain that Durham has changed over time. Ask students to name some changes that may take place in a community over time.

Preview the Lesson

Guide students in previewing the lesson. Point out the following features on Student Edition pages 63–66:

- **Page 63** Invite students to preview the photograph. Ask: What does Lily appear to be doing? Why can writing details about your community be helpful?
- **Page 64** Point out that Lily visits her library to learn about her community. Ask students to write a list of questions they have about their communities. Discuss with them the various ways a library may help them answer those questions. For example, historic photographs in reference books may show students a photograph of the first school in the community.
- **Page 65** Preview the title of this section. Ask: How is Lily finding out how her community has changed? Students will respond that she is asking her grandparents. Then ask: Why are older people a good resource for information?

Preteach Vocabulary

- Explain that all people and places have **history**. Ask: What does *history* mean? Then encourage students to give examples of events that happened in their own histories, such as receiving their first bike, starting school, or the birth of a younger sibling.

NORTH CAROLINA STANDARD COURSE OF STUDY

Objective 3.02 Describe past and present changes within the local community.

Key Content Summary

- **Every community has a history.**
- **You can learn about a community's history by visiting the local library and history museum and by talking to older people.**

Vocabulary

- **history,** p. 63

Spotlight on Goals and Objectives

Use North Carolina Interactive Presentations, Unit 3, Lesson 2, to access prior knowledge and build background.

Reach All Learners

ESL/Language Support

Scaffolding Content Explain to students that a time line shows the order in which things have happened. A time line can help a person review history. It can show days, weeks, months, or years. Provide students with an age time line. Invite them to record their history using words or pictures to indicate important events in their lives.

Extra Support

Write Descriptions Provide students with historic photographs of a community. Encourage students to study the photographs of the community. Then have students write descriptions of the photographs. Ask volunteers to read their descriptions to the class. Encourage students to compare and contrast the community in the photographs with present-day communities.

Extension Activity

Retell a Story Encourage students to recall and briefly summarize stories they have heard older family members tell. Stress examples of change, such as in people's dress, manners, games, transportation, and work. Have students discuss how these stories teach people about things that happened in history.

Integrate the Curriculum

Arts

Act Out a Story Tell students that some theaters and libraries have programs in which people can enjoy the retellings of stories. Invite students to practice and perform simple reenactments of their own stories. For example, have one volunteer tell the story as others mime what people in the story do and repeat what they say.

Lesson 2
PAGES 63–66

My Community's History

Lesson 2

Lily's class is learning about her community. Every community has a history. **History** is the story of what happened in the past. Lily will learn how her community has changed. **What might you learn about your community?**

Possible response: I might learn how my community has changed.

Lily visits different places in her community, Durham, North Carolina.

NORTH CAROLINA STANDARD COURSE OF STUDY

3.02 Describe past and present changes within the local community.

63

Start with the Objective

Objective 3.02 Describe past and present changes within the local community.

Set a Purpose for Reading

Ask a volunteer to read aloud the text. Provide support as needed. Direct students' attention to the highlighted word *history* and read the definition. Have students suggest similarities and differences between the meaning of *history* and *past*. Then read aloud the question and have students share their ideas. Model thinking for the students by using the Think Aloud.

Think Aloud

I know that a new neighborhood was built in my community. I remember when woods were there. I will read to learn more about how communities change.

BACKGROUND

Duke University Lily lives in Durham, North Carolina. This city is the home of Duke University, shown in the photograph on the page. The university was named after Washington Duke. More than 11,000 students are enrolled at Duke. In addition to traditional studies, such as law, business, and nursing, the university offers classes in environmental issues and microelectronics. Universities change to meet students' changing needs.

SOCIAL STUDIES STRANDS

Historical Perspectives Throughout the lesson, talk about the history of your local community. Ask students to share what they know about the community in the past. Encourage them to talk to family members and bring in historical family photographs showing changes in the community.

SSSMART™ SUPPORT

TextWork

1 Skim and Scan

Read the TextWork item aloud, and ask students what information they will scan the text to find. Explain that the places Lily goes to learn about her community's history are the same places they can visit in their own community.

TextWork

1 Underline the places you can visit to learn about your community's history.

Learning About the Past

Lily visits some places in her community to learn about its history. She visits the library. She also visits the history museum. People at these places tell Lily about her community's history.

Lily goes to the library in Durham.

64

TEACHING YOUR SOCIAL STUDIES

BACKGROUND

Stanford L. Warren Library The Stanford L. Warren Library in Durham, shown in the photograph on this page, opened in 1940. The library is known for the Selena Warren Wheeler Collection. This collection highlights and celebrates historical and contemporary African American literature, culture, and history.

SOCIAL STUDIES STRANDS

Government and Active Citizenship Explain to students that many people want to preserve, or save, North Carolina's history. Many groups work to accomplish this. One such group is Preservation North Carolina. This statewide organization works to preserve buildings and other sites in the state. With students, use available resources to see if your community has a historical site or society. Ask students why preservation is important.

A Changing Community

Lily finds books and photographs at the library. She also talks to older people in the community. They talk to her about her community's past. She also learns about her community's present.

Lily will use what she has learned to write about her community. You can learn and write about your community, too.

TextWork

❷ What is one thing you can find at a library?

books, photographs

Lily talks to her grandparents.

65

TextWork

❷ Comprehension

Review/Reflect Ask students to name things you can find in a library. Encourage them to extend their answers beyond books. Explain that thinking about what you already know can help you answer a question about new information in a text. Students' responses may include something found in the library that is not mentioned in the text. Accept all reasonable responses.

SOCIAL STUDIES STRANDS

Technological Influences With students, discuss how technology, or tools we use to make our lives easier, can help them learn about the history of the community. Discuss technology such as the Internet, e-mail, and historical films and photographs. Review the photographs in the lesson, and have students suggest ways Lily might use technology to learn about her community's history in each location. Note that the highlighted word *technology* is introduced in the next lesson.

BACKGROUND

Interviewing If students will be conducting an interview, you may wish to share the following tips:

1. Write clear questions before the interview. Questions should be open-ended, not "yes/no" questions.
2. Use a tape recorder or digital voice recorder to record the interview if the interviewee agrees. You can also take notes.
3. Review the notes or recording after the interview to make sure you understand what was said.

Lesson Review

Summary Have students review the images and text headings to summarize the lesson's main ideas. Then have them complete the Lesson Review.

- Every community has a history.
- You can learn about a community's history by visiting the local library and history museum and by talking to older people.

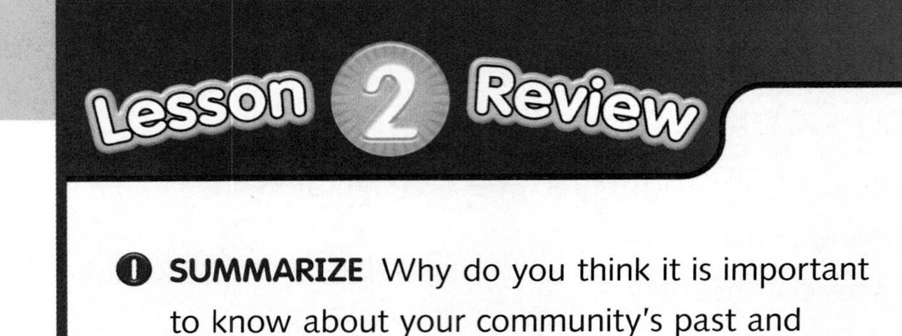

1. **SUMMARIZE** Why do you think it is important to know about your community's past and present?

   Possible response: It is important to know about my community's past and present because it helps me learn about the people in my community.

2. How might you learn about the **history** of your community?

   Possible response: I might learn about the history of my community by going to the library or a museum. I can also ask older people in my community.

3. What are some of the ways Lily finds out about her community's past?

   Possible response: Lily visits the library and the history museum and talks to older people in her community.

Draw a picture to show what your community might have looked like in the past.

66

ACTIVITY RUBRIC

Score 4
- fully understands the distinction between past and present
- illustration includes at least four realistic aspects of the community's past
- illustration is extremely well planned

Score 3
- understands the distinction between past and present
- illustration includes at least three realistic aspects of the community's past
- illustration is well planned

Score 2
- does not fully understand the distinction between past and present
- illustration includes at least two realistic aspects of the community's past, but key details are missing
- illustration is not well planned

Score 1
- fails to differentiate between past and present
- illustration is not relevant or does not include enough details to represent the past
- illustration is not well planned

Build Background

Make It Relevant Ask students to name examples of transportation, both old and new. Help students consider the different kinds of transportation people might need to get from one place to another. Create a class list naming these modes of transportation. Explain that transportation in the past is different from transportation in the present.

Preview the Lesson

Guide students in previewing the lesson. Point out the following features on Student Edition pages 67–72:

- **Page 67** Explain that technology makes our lives easier. Then ask students to look at the photograph and identify types of technology that they see.
- **Page 68** Ask students to preview the photographs, and explain that the photographs represent objects found in homes of the past. Ask students to list objects in their homes that make life easier.
- **Page 69** Ask students to preview the title of the section. Ask: What type of classroom does the photograph represent? Have students compare and contrast classrooms of the past with classrooms of today.
- **Page 70** Point out that technology has helped change transportation. Ask students: How did people in the past travel around their communities? How do people today travel around their communities?
- **Page 71** Ask students to list some common jobs. Discuss how technology may have improved each of the jobs listed.

Preteach Vocabulary

- Explain that **technology** is the tools people use to make life easier. Have students look around the classroom and point out examples of technology that make learning easier.
- Ask students to define **tool** in their own words. Point out that tools can help people with household chores, jobs, and school. Ask students to draw a picture of a tool that is helpful for learning.

NORTH CAROLINA STANDARD COURSE OF STUDY

Objective 3.02 Describe past and present changes within the local community.

Objective 3.04 Recognize that members of the community are affected by changes in the community that occur over time.

Key Content Summary

- **Changes in technology have made our lives easier at home, at school, and in the community.**
- **Technology has improved transportation.**
- **Technology has changed the ways people work and the jobs that they do.**

Vocabulary

- **technology,** p. 67
- **tool,** p. 67
- **transportation,** p. 70

Spotlight on Goals and Objectives

Use North Carolina Interactive Presentations, Unit 3, Lesson 3, to access prior knowledge and build background.

Preteach Vocabulary *continued*

- Ask students: How did you arrive at school this morning? Explain that whether they walked, took the bus, or rode in a car, they were using a form of **transportation**.

Reach All Learners

ESL/Language Support

Content and Language Objectives On the board, draw a graphic organizer with three columns and three rows. Head the columns *Word*, *Meaning*, and *Sentence*. Write each highlighted word in a separate row, and help students scan the text to find the meanings. Then orally model each word in a sentence. Ask students to come up with their own sentences for each highlighted word and enter them in the graphic organizer.

Extra Support

Brainstorm Ideas Encourage students to brainstorm ways transportation might change in the future. Work with students to list some current transportation problems. For example: some transportation is too crowded, some transportation is too slow, and some transportation uses too much fuel. Discuss how technology might help solve these problems.

Extension Activity

Create a Commercial Have students make a list of tools or modes of transportation that show improvements in technology. Then have students act out a radio or television commercial advertising the benefits of their tool or mode of transportation. Ask volunteers to act out their commercials in front of the class.

Integrate the Curriculum

Arts

Draw a Book Cover Have students draw a cover for a book that relates to one of the highlighted words from the lesson. Have students write a title, draw a picture, and add other details related to the word. Then have students trade their covers with partners to see if they can tell which highlighted word the book cover represents.

Technology in Communities

Technology is the tools we use to make our lives easier. A **tool** is something that people use to do work. Over time, changes in technology bring changes to communities. **What will you learn about how technology has changed?**

Possible response: I will learn how technology has changed communities by making people's lives easier.

Statesville, North Carolina

3.02 Describe past and present changes within the local community.
3.04 Recognize that members of the community are affected by changes in the community that occur over time.

67

Start with the Objectives

Objective 3.02 Describe past and present changes within the local community.

Objective 3.04 Recognize that members of the community are affected by changes in the community that occur over time.

Set a Purpose for Reading

Read aloud the introduction. Point out the highlighted words *technology* and *tool*. Have students provide examples of each. Then read the question aloud and have volunteers share their thoughts. Model thinking for students by using the Think Aloud.

Think Aloud

I know we got new computers at school. Our teachers do different things with the computers to teach us. I will read to learn how technology changes communities.

BACKGROUND

Statesville, North Carolina This photograph shows Statesville, a historic community in western North Carolina. Statesville preserves its history while incorporating modern changes. The community has modern businesses housed in historic buildings. Many people live in historic neighborhoods, too.

SOCIAL STUDIES STRANDS

Technological Influences Throughout the lesson, point out how technology has changed communities. For example, point out the cars in the photograph on the page. Ask students how families got from place to place before cars. Then ask them how cars changed the way families live.

SSSMART™ SUPPORT

TextWork

1 CUES

Analyze/Interpret Primary Sources Read the caption aloud and have students match the item name to the correct picture. Then have them think about how each item looks today. Tell students to circle the picture of the tool that they think looks like that tool today. When responding to the question, some students may circle the clothespins instead of the iron. This is acceptable.

1 Circle the picture of the tool that looks most like a tool people use today.

Changes in Home Tools

Homes are filled with tools. Some of these are toasters, washers, and dryers. People are always making new tools. Tools make work easier. Over time, new and better tools are made.

Clothespins, an iron, and a washer from long ago

Children in History

George S. Parker

George S. Parker was good at thinking up new games. In 1883, when he was 16 years old, he sold his first game. He and his brothers started a company. They made many of the board games that we play today.

TEACHING YOUR SOCIAL STUDIES

BACKGROUND

George S. Parker When Parker was a teenager, he invented a game he called Banking. He used his own money to print the game and sold it successfully. At the age of 16, he started his own game publishing company later called Parker Brothers. The company's biggest success came with the introduction of Monopoly in 1935. Parker did not invent Monopoly, but his company marketed and sold it. By the time of his death in 1953, Parker had invented or marketed more than 100 games.

SOCIAL STUDIES STRANDS

Historical Perspectives If possible, have students each invite an older person, such as a grandparent or a neighbor, to the classroom for an interview. Prior to the interview, have students write or dictate several questions about how technology changed families' lives. Ask the interviewee to bring in photographs or items from the past to deepen students' understanding of life in the past.

SUPPORT

Schools Long Ago and Today

Schools have changed over time. Long ago, schools had only one room and one teacher. Children of all ages learned together.

Today, schools have many rooms and many teachers. Some ways of learning are the same as in schools long ago. Some ways are different.

TextWork

2 Circle something in the picture of the classroom of long ago that is also in your classroom.

One-room school, 1917

School Tools

Long Ago	Today
A B C	

69

TextWork

2 CUES

Analyze/Interpret Photographs Ask students to look around the classroom. Then have them look at the photograph on the page and name items that appear both in the photograph and in their classroom. Point out that the items, such as desks, may look different but their purpose is the same. Student answers may vary. They can circle the chalkboard, desks, students, teacher, and books.

SOCIAL STUDIES STRANDS

Technological Influences After reading the page and completing the TextWork item, ask students to make predictions about how schools will change in the future. Record students' ideas on the board or on chart paper. Ask them how they know that technology will continue to change.

BUILD SKILLS

Chart and Graph Skills Have small groups of students conduct a survey about the number of computers in different school locations. For example, students can record the number of computers in each first-grade classroom. For a more challenging activity, students can record the number of computers in each elementary grade. Assist students as they transfer the information to a simple graph.

TextWork

3 Comprehension

Focus Skill **Sequence** Have students look at the images of different kinds of transportation in order from those used long ago to those used today. Explain that the images show the sequence of the changes to transportation technology. Then have students circle the types of transportation used long ago.

3 Circle the kinds of transportation people used long ago.

Transportation Long Ago and Today

Transportation is ways of moving people and things from place to place. In the past, transportation was very slow. Many people never went far from where they were born.

Technology has changed this. Boats, trains, cars, and planes are safer and faster. Today, people can travel far away—even into space!

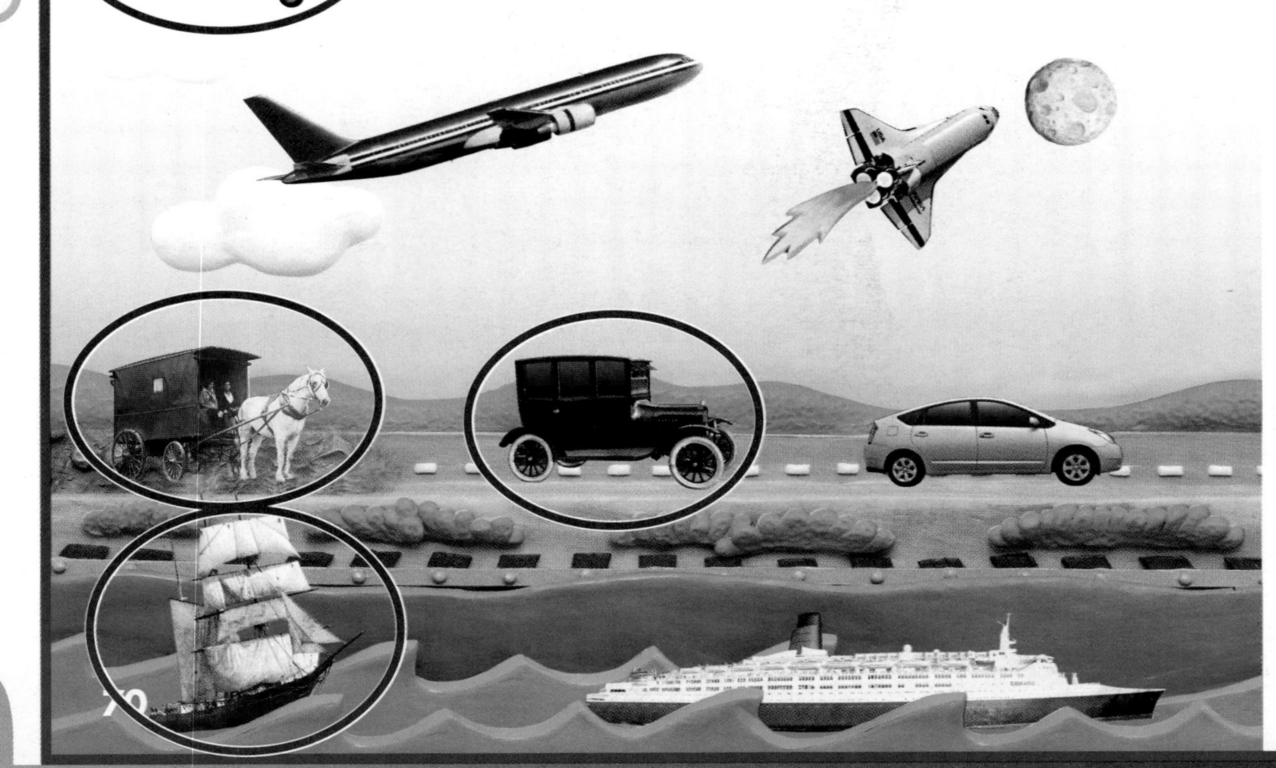

TEACHING YOUR SOCIAL STUDIES

SOCIAL STUDIES STRANDS

Global Connections Discuss with students how changes in transportation have linked communities around the world. Have students study the label of their school supplies, backpack, or clothing. Help them read the "Made in" label. Locate the different places on a world map and discuss how the items traveled from that country to North Carolina.

BUILD SKILLS

Decision Making After reading the text on the page, draw and label pictures of various types of transportation: a car, a plane, and a ship. Point out your hometown or a nearby city on a world map. Point out another location on the map, and ask students to decide which mode of transportation would be the fastest to reach that location. Continue the game by using different ending locations.

Jobs Long Ago and Today

New technology has changed the ways people work. Some jobs are no longer needed. Workers no longer take milk and ice to people's homes. Grocery stores now have refrigerators and freezers.

New technology has also made new jobs. Workers now use robots to make some things. A robot is a machine that can do a job.

The way people tell the news has changed.

Long Ago

Today

TextWork

❹ What is one kind of job that is no longer needed because of new technology?

workers who take

milk and ice to homes

TextWork

❹ Comprehension

Draw Conclusions Reread aloud the first paragraph to students. Then have them answer the question. If students have difficulty, ask them to draw a conclusion about the job of a milk or ice delivery person.

SOCIAL STUDIES STRANDS

Economics and Development Reread the second paragraph aloud and discuss the use of robots in repetitive factory jobs.

Q How might the use of robots help a company make more products and more money?

A Robots can do the work faster than people. They can help workers make more products in less time.

SOCIAL STUDIES STRANDS

Government and Active Citizenship Explain to students that good citizens stay informed. They pay attention to the news and know what is happening in their community. Ask students to name the different ways citizens today can stay informed of the news (newspaper, Internet, television, radio). Then have students identify the types of media that did not exist long ago.

Lesson Review

Summary Have students work with a partner to review the headings in the lesson. Have partners take turns telling the most important idea for each heading. Then have students work independently to complete the Lesson Review.

- Changes in technology have made our lives easier at home, at school, and in the community.
- Technology has improved transportation.
- Technology has changed the ways people work and the jobs that they do.

Lesson 3 Review

1. **SUMMARIZE** How has technology changed the way people live in communities?

   Possible response: Technology has made work easier and transportation faster. It has made new jobs and ended other jobs.

2. Give examples of different kinds of **transportation**.

   Possible response: Some different kinds of transportation are airplanes, trains, cars, boats, and space shuttles.

3. Why do we no longer need workers to deliver milk and ice to homes?

   Possible response: Refrigerators and freezers were made. Grocery stores now have refrigerators and freezers. So, people can buy milk and ice at grocery stores.

Writing

Write sentences about a tool we use today that makes our lives easier.

72

WRITING RUBRIC

Score 4
- shows a clear understanding of the definition of *technology*
- identifies a tool and provides relevant details about how it makes lives easier
- sentences have very few or no errors

Score 3
- shows an understanding of the definition of *technology*
- identifies a tool and provides details about how it makes lives easier
- sentences have few errors

Score 2
- shows a working understanding of the definition of *technology*
- identifies a tool but fails to provide relevant examples of how it makes lives easier
- sentences have several errors

Score 1
- does not show an adequate understanding of the term *technology*
- describes or names a tool, but does not provide relevant details about its usefulness
- sentences have numerous errors

Build Background

Make It Relevant Explain that there are many different communities around the world. Point out that these communities have their own traditions. Prepare a list of possible schools willing to participate in a pen pal program with the class. Have students vote on the school with which they would like to exchange letters. Have each student write a brief letter introducing himself or herself and their community.

Preview the Lesson

Guide students in previewing the lesson. Point out the following features on Student Edition pages 73–78:

- **Page 73** Ask students to preview the photograph. Ask: What does this photograph tell you about Marc's community?
- **Page 74** Ask students to preview the title of the section. Ask them to predict what they think will follow in the text. Discuss with students that all communities change over time and many experience similar changes.
- **Page 75** Display a map of the world, and have students locate Asheville, North Carolina, and Rome, Italy. Explain that although the two cities are far away, they may share many similarities. They also have many differences.
- **Page 76–77** Have students preview the photographs and read the captions. Ask students how Ayi's country, Ghana, is similar to the United States.

Preteach Vocabulary

- Explain that the United States is the **country** in which the students live. Display a map of the United States, and have students locate North Carolina on the map.

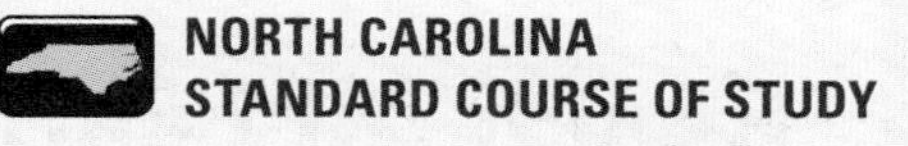

Objective 3.03 Compare and contrast past and present changes within the local community and communities around the world.

Key Content Summary

- **Communities around the world have changed over time.**
- **People in communities still do some things that they did long ago.**

Vocabulary

- **country,** p. 73

Use North Carolina Interactive Presentations, Unit 3, Lesson 4, to access prior knowledge and build background.

Reach All Learners

ESL/Language Support

Scaffolding Content Guide students to think of some features that are common within their community. Make a concept web in which to write these features. Have them complete the following sentence stem, "In my community..."

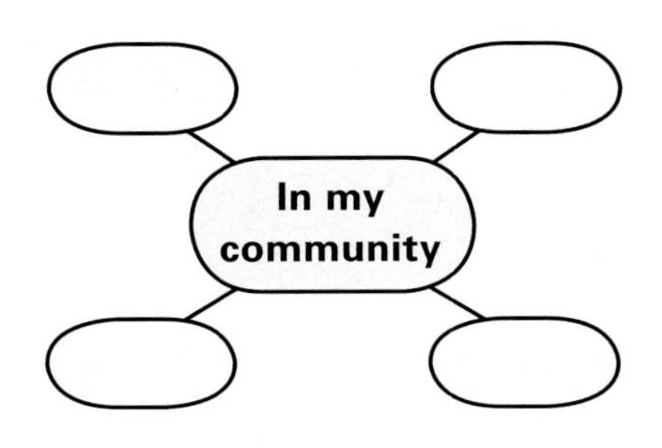

Extra Support

Create a Slogan Encourage students to brainstorm a list of distinctive features of their community. Then have students write a slogan that the community could use to show pride in its diversity, technology, and people.

Extension Activity

Create Questions Guide students in using school-approved resources to research the country the class will be pen pals with. Then have students write questions that they would like to ask the students in that country. Questions may include what a typical school day is like, what foods are popular, and what kinds of music people listen to.

Integrate the Curriculum

Science

Learn About Technology Show photographs of several different cities from around the world. Discuss with students the similarities and differences between these communities and their own. Have students pay special attention to buildings and modes of transportation.

Changes in Communities

Marc and Antonio are pen pals. They live in different countries. A **country** is a land with its own people and laws. The two boys share how their communities have changed. **What might you learn about how places change?**

Possible response: I might learn how Marc's and Antonio's communities have changed.

Marc lives in Asheville, North Carolina.

NORTH CAROLINA STANDARD COURSE OF STUDY
3.03 Compare and contrast past and present changes within the local community and communities around the world.

73

Start with the Objective

Objective 3.03 Compare and contrast past and present changes within the local community and communities around the world.

Set a Purpose for Reading

Read aloud the introduction with students. Review the highlighted word *country*. Have students identify the country in which they live. Then ask volunteers to share their answers to the question. Use the Think Aloud to model thinking about how places change.

Think Aloud

I have seen old photographs of my town. It has changed a lot. I will read to learn how other communities have changed. I wonder if they have changed in the same ways that my town has.

BACKGROUND

Asheville, North Carolina Asheville is a popular tourist attraction in western North Carolina. The arrival of the railroad in 1880 helped transform the small community into a bustling resort community. Asheville is home to George W. Vanderbilt's Biltmore Estate, the country's largest home.

SOCIAL STUDIES STRANDS

Geographic Relationships Explain to students that Asheville and other communities are always changing. People move into and out of communities. New homes and businesses are built.

Q How is your community changing?

A Possible response: People are moving in and out. New homes, stores, and parks are being built.

SSSMART™ SUPPORT

TextWork

1 Comprehension

Sequence To help students answer the question, have them scan the text for words, such as *long ago, soon,* and *today,* that indicate the sequence of life in past and present Asheville. Once students recognize the sequence words, have them scan the text for possible answers.

❶ What is one thing people in Asheville did long ago that they still do today?

People work in hotels.

Changes in Marc's Community

Long ago, families started to move to Asheville, North Carolina. They built homes, schools, and stores. The town grew.

Soon the railroad came to Asheville. People worked to help build it. They also began to build and work in hotels. Today, people in Asheville still work in hotels. They also make things such as chairs and tables.

Asheville, Long Ago

Asheville, Today

74

TEACHING YOUR SOCIAL STUDIES

BACKGROUND

Restoration of Historic Cities In addition to Asheville, many communities in North Carolina and across the United States are taking steps to preserve and restore their history. In North Carolina, the Restoration Branch of the State Historic Preservation Office helps people restore historic buildings. Groups in Rome, Italy, help preserve old buildings that symbolize the city's past.

BUILD SKILLS

Map and Globe Skills As you read the lesson, help children locate on a map the communities mentioned in the text. Use self-stick notes, pushpin flags, or removable stickers to mark the locations. Emphasize how Marc and Antonio use computers to communicate with each other.

SSSMART™ SUPPORT

Changes in Antonio's Community

Antonio liked learning about Asheville. Now he wants to tell Marc how Rome has changed.

Rome is a very old city in Italy. New buildings have been built. Old buildings have been made to look new on the inside. Other buildings have been made to look as they did in the past.

2 Circle something that is the same in both pictures of Rome.

Students may circle something other than the building that has stayed the same. Accept all reasonable responses.

Rome, Long Ago

Rome, Today

75

2 CUES

Analyze/Interpret Photographs Direct students to the two photographs on page 75. Explain that they both show the city of Rome. Make sure that students can identify which photograph of Rome is from long ago and which is from the present-day.

SOCIAL STUDIES STRANDS

Historical Perspectives Rome is a historic city. In Rome people can see characteristics of the past and the present.

Q How can you tell which photograph shows the past?

A Possible response: The photograph from the past has old cars and is in black and white.

BACKGROUND

Piazza Venezia These photographs show the Piazza Venezia in the heart of Rome. The buildings here represent Rome's rich history. One of the buildings was built in the 1400s. In the piazza, there is a huge, white marble monument. The monument honors Victor Emmanuel II, who was the first king of Italy after the country was unified in the mid-1800s. The long-ago photograph of Piazza Venezia was taken in the 1950s.

SSSMART™ SUPPORT

TextWork

③ Comprehension

Review/Reflect Remind students that Marc is using his web page to show the communities he has learned about. Point out the screen shots from the web page. Then have students answer the question.

③ What other communities has Marc learned about?

Harbin, China; Accra, Ghana; and Cuzco, Peru

Communities Around the World

Marc and Antonio want to learn about other communities around the world. Marc made a web page about the communities he has learned about. It tells how they have changed over time. Antonio plans to add more communities to the web page.

Li Ming lives in Harbin. Harbin is an old city in China. People built a railroad there. Harbin became very large!

TEACHING YOUR SOCIAL STUDIES

SOCIAL STUDIES STRANDS

Cultures and Diversity Have partners choose one community from the lesson. Guide them as they use the Internet to learn more about their community and how it has changed. Have students complete a simple report. Provide sentence frames, such as *Our community is __________. It is in the country of* __________. Students can present their reports to the class.

BACKGROUND

Harbin, China Harbin is the capital of a northeastern province in China. China is located on the continent of Asia. The city of Harbin grew when the Russians built the Chinese Eastern Railway through the region in the late 1800s. Today, railroads are still important in the city. In addition, railroads, ship channels, and an airport connect Harbin to places around the world.

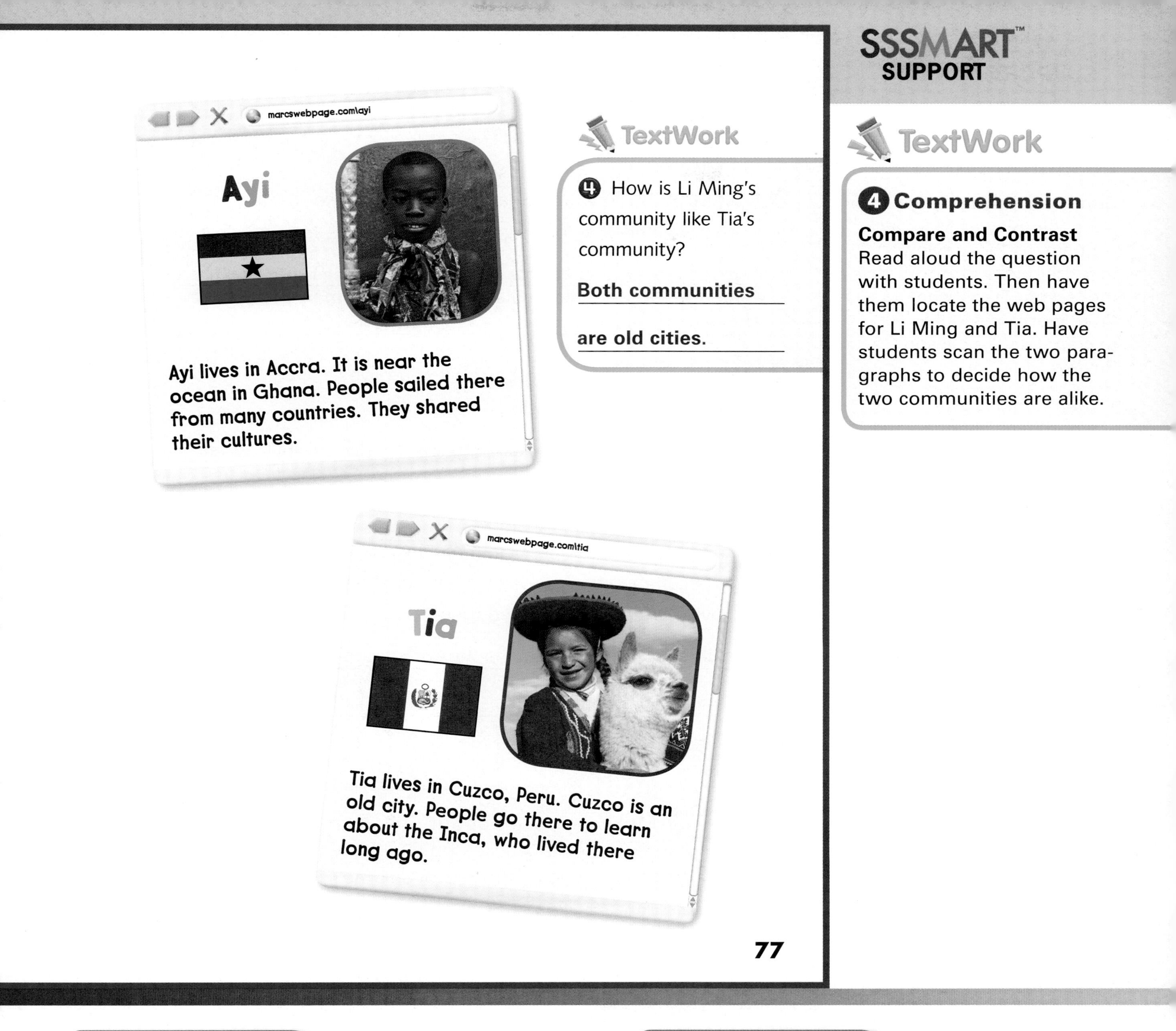

marcswebpage.com\ayi

Ayi

Ayi lives in Accra. It is near the ocean in Ghana. People sailed there from many countries. They shared their cultures.

marcswebpage.com\tia

Tia

Tia lives in Cuzco, Peru. Cuzco is an old city. People go there to learn about the Inca, who lived there long ago.

TextWork

4 How is Li Ming's community like Tia's community?

Both communities are old cities.

77

SSSMART™ SUPPORT

TextWork

4 Comprehension

Compare and Contrast Read aloud the question with students. Then have them locate the web pages for Li Ming and Tia. Have students scan the two paragraphs to decide how the two communities are alike.

BACKGROUND

Accra, Ghana Accra, a port city, is the capital of the country of Ghana in Africa. Like Harbin, Accra became an economic center of the area after the arrival of the railroad. Today, workers in the city manufacture food products, lumber, and clothing. Accra has various modes of transportation for its citizens, including cars and buses, railroads, ship channels, and airports.

BACKGROUND

Cuzco, Peru Cuzco is located in the country of Peru on the continent of South America. It is one of the oldest cities in the Western Hemisphere to be continuously inhabited. The Inca made it their home about 1,000 years ago. Many tourists come to Cuzco to study the ruins. Many hotels have been built to accommodate the travelers. Other than the tourism industry, Cuzco's chief economic activities are agriculture and mining.

Lesson Review

Summary Have student pairs role-play as Marc and Antonio as they review important ideas from the lesson. Then have them work individually to complete the Lesson Review.

- Communities around the world have changed over time.
- People in communities still do some things that they did long ago.

Lesson 4 Review

1. **SUMMARIZE** How are today's communities like the communities of long ago?

   Possible response: People live in communities that started long ago. Some buildings are the same. Some people have the same jobs.

2. Write a sentence about a **country** you have learned about in this lesson.

   Possible response: People go to the country of Italy to learn about the past.

3. Many years ago, people began moving to Marc's community, Asheville. What happened to Asheville after people moved there?

   Possible response: Asheville became bigger. People built a railroad and hotels.

Activity

Make a booklet about one of the communities in this lesson. Tell how that community has changed over time.

78

ACTIVITY RUBRIC

Score 4
- booklet includes relevant information about how one community has changed over time
- illustrations directly relate to community changes
- booklet has very few or no errors

Score 3
- booklet includes mostly relevant information about how one community has changed over time
- illustrations relate to community changes
- booklet has few errors

Score 2
- booklet includes some relevant information about how one community has changed over time
- some illustrations relate to community changes
- booklet has several errors

Score 1
- booklet contains little or no relevant information
- booklet contains few illustrations
- booklet has numerous errors

Unit 3

Review and Test Prep

The Big Idea

The ways people live change over time. Some places change, too. Some places stay the same.

Summarize the Unit

Sequence Fill in the chart. Show what you have learned about how transportation has changed.

First	Next	Last
Transportation was very slow long ago. Many people did not travel far from home.	Possible response: New technology helped change transportation. New kinds of transportation were made.	Possible response: Today, there are many kinds of transportation. People can go to places far away.

79

Unit Review

PAGES 79–82

The Big Idea

Ask students to review the unit's Big Idea. Invite students to share something they learned in this unit that supports the Big Idea. Write these ideas on the board. Students should give examples that accurately show how some things have changed over time, while other things have stayed the same.

Summarize the Unit

Sequence Invite students to review the Reading Social Studies at the beginning of the unit. Then ask students to think about what they have learned about changes in transportation in this unit. Charts should list in order items showing how transportation has changed for the better over time.

READING FOCUS SKILLS

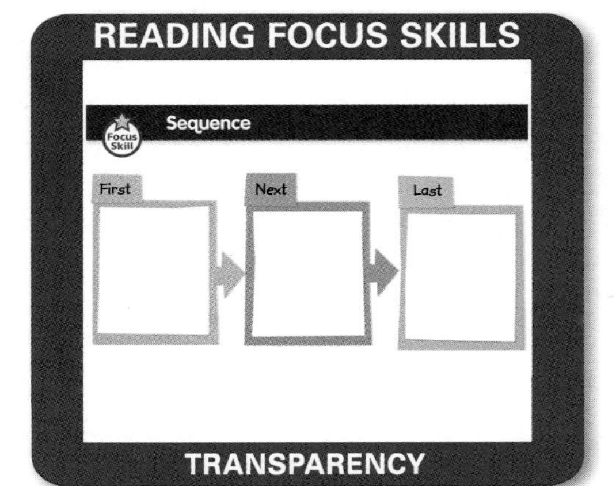

TRANSPARENCY

Graphic Organizer Write-On/ Wipe-Off Cards available

ASSESSMENT

Use the **UNIT 3 TEST** on pages 9–12 of the Assessment Program.

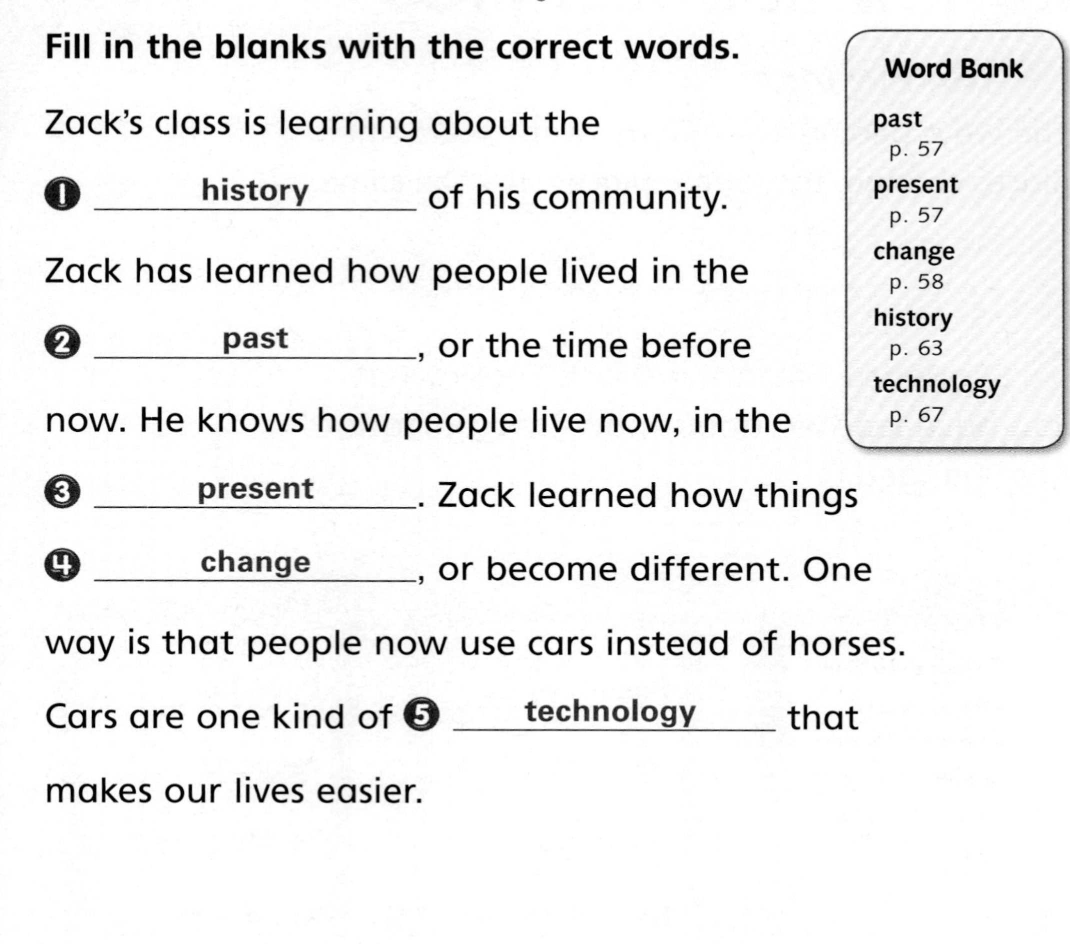

VOCABULARY POWER

Context Clues Explain to students that the words and images used throughout the unit will help them understand what the vocabulary words mean. For example, explain that the word *change* can have more than one meaning. Elicit from students another meaning for *change*, such as "coins." Then point out how the words and the images on the page where the vocabulary word is first defined show that *change* also means that things do not always stay the same—they become different.

Think About It

Circle the letter of the correct answer.

6 Which sentence tells about life long ago?
- (A) People lived in communities.
- B People went to space.
- C People used e-mail.
- D People used cell phones.

7 What is a country?
- A an ocean
- (B) a land with its own people and laws
- C a mountain
- D a valley

8 Which has made transportation safer and faster?
- A communication
- B e-mail
- C robots
- (D) technology

9 How did people communicate in the past?
- A They used cell phones.
- (B) They wrote letters.
- C They sent e-mails.
- D They drove cars.

81

READ MORE

Encourage independent reading with these books or books of your choice.

Basic

Abe Lincoln's Hat by Martha Brenner. Random House Books for Young Readers, 1994. A simple telling of events in Abraham Lincoln's daily life.

Proficient

A Country Schoolhouse by Lynne Barasch. Farrar, Straus and Giroux, 2004. A grandfather describes the country schoolhouse that he attended in the 1940s.

Advanced

My Friend Grandpa by Harriet Ziefert. Blue Apple Books, 2004. A girl's grandfather teaches her that different generations can have fun together.

Unit Review

PAGES 79–82

Show What You Know

Writing
Write a Story

Discuss with students what they were like when they were younger. Remind them of time-order words, such as *first, next, then, later, last*, and *finally*.

Activity
Make a Scrapbook

Students' scrapbooks should compare and contrast people, places, and things from their community's past and present.

North Carolina Adventures

Remind students that this game will review the concepts in the unit.

Spotlight on Goals and Objectives

Use North Carolina Interactive Presentations, Unit 3, to review concepts from the unit.

Answer each question in a complete sentence.

10. How has communication changed over time?

Possible response: Long ago, people wrote letters. Now, people can talk on cell phones or send e-mails.

11. What are some ways you can learn about how your community has changed?

Possible response: I can learn about how my community has changed by going to the library or history museum.

Show What You Know

Writing Write a Story
All things change. People change, too. Think about when you were younger. Write a story about a memory from that time.

Activity Make a Scrapbook
Make a scrapbook about your community's past and present. Draw or cut and paste pictures of life in the past and present on the pages. Then share your scrapbook.

GO online To play a game that reviews the unit, join Eco in the North Carolina Adventures online or on CD.

82

WRITING RUBRIC

Score 4
- reflects a strong understanding of how their life has changed over time
- includes a high level of detail and expression
- is well-written and complete

Score 3
- reflects an understanding of how their life has changed over time
- includes several details and good expression
- is mostly well-written and complete

Score 2
- reflects some understanding of how their life has changed over time
- includes some details and little expression
- written adequately but is minimally complete

Score 1
- reflects little understanding of how their life has changed over time
- includes little detail and no expression
- is poorly written and incomplete

ACTIVITY RUBRIC

Score 4
- has differences and similarities between past and present
- recognizes the many ways people and places change over time
- is well organized

Score 3
- has some differences and similarities between past and present
- recognizes some ways people and places change over time
- is somewhat organized

Score 2
- has few differences and similarities between past and present
- recognizes few ways people and places change over time
- is not very organized

Score 1
- has no differences and similarities between past and present
- does not recognize how people and places change over time
- is completely unorganized

Unit 4

Special Days

NORTH CAROLINA STANDARD COURSE OF STUDY

COMPETENCY GOAL 4

The learner will explain different celebrated holidays and special days in communities.

OBJECTIVES

4.01 Recognize and describe religious and secular symbols/celebrations associated with special days of diverse cultures.

4.02 Explore and cite reasons for observing special days that recognize celebrated individuals of diverse cultures.

4.03 Recognize and describe the historical events associated with national holidays.

4.04 Trace the historical foundations of traditions of various neighborhoods and communities.

Unit 4

LESSON	TOTAL: 25 DAYS	NORTH CAROLINA STANDARD COURSE OF STUDY
Introduce the Unit **Unit Preview,** pp. 83–84 **The Big Idea,** p. 84 **Reading Social Studies,** pp. 85–86 Focus Skill: Draw Conclusions	2 DAYS	COMPETENCY GOAL 4 **The learner will explain different celebrated holidays and special days in communities.** **Spotlight on Goals and Objectives** Unit 4
1 **Symbols** pp. 87–90 **symbol** p. 87 **flag** p. 87	4 DAYS	**Objective 4.01** Recognize and describe religious and secular symbols/celebrations associated with special days of diverse cultures. **Spotlight on Goals and Objectives** Unit 4, Lesson 1
2 **Celebrations** pp. 91–96 **celebration** p. 91 **holiday** p. 91 **religion** p. 92	5 DAYS	**Objective 4.01** Recognize and describe religious and secular symbols/celebrations associated with special days of diverse cultures. **Spotlight on Goals and Objectives** Unit 4, Lesson 2
3 **Holidays and Heroes** pp. 97–102 **national holiday** p. 97 **hero** p. 97	5 DAYS	**Objective 4.02** Explore and cite reasons for observing special days that recognize celebrated individuals of diverse cultures. **Objective 4.03** Recognize and describe the historical events associated with national holidays. **Spotlight on Goals and Objectives** Unit 4, Lesson 3

TEACHING YOUR SOCIAL STUDIES	SSSMART™ SUPPORT
	Comprehension, Draw Conclusions, pp. 85–86
Background, The Pledge of Allegiance, p. 87; Patriotic Symbols, p. 88; The State Flag, p. 89 **Social Studies Strands,** Economics and Development, p. 88; Geographic Relationships, p. 89 **Build Skills,** Chart and Graph Skills, p. 87	**Vocabulary,** p. 88 **CUES,** p. 89
Background, Folkmoot, p. 91; Christmas and Hanukkah, p. 92; Religious Holidays, p. 93; The Lantern Festival, p. 94; A Gift of Cherry Trees, p. 95 **Social Studies Strands,** Cultures and Diversity, pp. 92, 94 **Build Skills,** Chart and Graph Skills, p. 91; Map and Globe Skills, p. 95	**Vocabulary,** p. 92 **Skim and Scan,** pp. 93, 95 **CUES,** p. 94
Background, Parades, p. 97; George Washington, p. 98; Memorial Day and Veterans Day, p. 99; American Indians or Native Americans, p. 100; Patriot Day and Constitution Day, p. 101 **Social Studies Strands,** Government and Active Citizenship, p. 97; Cultures and Diversity, p. 98; Historical Perspectives, p. 100 **Build Skills,** Chart and Graph Skills, p. 99; Decision Making, p. 101	**CUES,** pp. 98, 101 **Skim and Scan,** p. 99 **Comprehension,** Draw Conclusions, p. 100

Print Resources

Student Edition, pp. 83–112
Teacher Edition, pp. 83A–112
Leveled Readers
Leveled Readers Teacher Guides
Document-Based Questions
Primary Atlas

Technology/Digital Resources

Spotlight on Goals and Objectives

North Carolina Interactive Presentations CD
North Carolina Interactive Presentations Online

Online Teacher Edition with ePlanner
Leveled Readers Online Database
North Carolina Adventures CD
North Carolina Adventures Online
Multimedia Biographies CD
Multimedia Biographies Online
Social Studies Music Collection CD

Hands-On Resources

Reading Focus Skills Transparencies
Social Studies Skills Transparencies
Graphic Organizer Write-On/Wipe-Off Cards
Interactive Atlas
Interactive Desk Maps
Interactive Map Transparencies
Picture Vocabulary Cards
Primary Source Kit
TimeLinks: Interactive Time Line
Social Studies in Action, pp. 48–49, 54–61, 64–65, 92–93, 98, 102–103, 105, 147

Assessment Options

1 Unit 4 Test
Assessment Program, pp. 13–16

2 Writing
Write a Poem, p. 112

3 Activity
Unit Project: Plan a Patriotic Party, p. 112

LESSON		NORTH CAROLINA STANDARD COURSE OF STUDY
4 **Remembering Our Past** pp. 103–108 **landmark** p. 103 **settler** p. 104	**5** DAYS	**Objective 4.04** Trace the historical foundations of traditions of various neighborhoods and communities. **Spotlight on Goals and Objectives** Unit 4, Lesson 4
Unit 4 Review and Test Prep pp. 109–112	**4** DAYS	**North Carolina Adventures** Unit 4

TEACHING YOUR SOCIAL STUDIES

Background,
- Bodie Island Lighthouse, p. 103
- Sacagawea, p. 104
- Town Creek Indian Mound, p. 105
- Latin American Festival, p. 106
- Scottish North Carolinians, p. 107

Social Studies Strands,
- Geographic Relationships, pp. 103, 105
- Cultures and Diversity, pp. 104, 106

SSSMART™ SUPPORT

Skim and Scan, p. 104

Vocabulary, p. 105

Comprehension,
- Draw Conclusions, p. 106
- Recall and Retell, p. 107

Summarize the Unit,
- Draw Conclusions, p. 109

Print Resources

- Student Edition, pp. 83–112
- Teacher Edition, pp. 83A–112
- Leveled Readers
- Leveled Readers Teacher Guides
- Document-Based Questions
- Primary Atlas

Technology/Digital Resources

Spotlight on Goals and Objectives

North Carolina Interactive Presentations CD
North Carolina Interactive Presentations Online

- Online Teacher Edition with ePlanner
- Leveled Readers Online Database
- North Carolina Adventures CD
- North Carolina Adventures Online
- Multimedia Biographies CD
- Multimedia Biographies Online
- Social Studies Music Collection CD

Hands-On Resources

- Reading Focus Skills Transparencies
- Social Studies Skills Transparencies
- Graphic Organizer Write-On/Wipe-Off Cards
- Interactive Atlas
- Interactive Desk Maps
- Interactive Map Transparencies
- Picture Vocabulary Cards
- Primary Source Kit
- TimeLinks: Interactive Time Line
- Social Studies in Action, pp. 48–49, 54–61, 64–65, 92–93, 98, 102–103, 105, 147

Assessment Options

1 Unit 4 Test
Assessment Program, pp. 13–16

2 Writing
Write a Poem, p. 112

3 Activity
Unit Project: Plan a Patriotic Party, p. 112

Leveled Readers

BELOW-LEVEL

Red, White, and Blue

Summary *Red, White, and Blue.* This Reader examines how we use songs, symbols, and holidays to honor the history and heroes of our country.

Vocabulary Power Have students define the following words. Help them write one sentence for each word as it relates to how we honor our country's history and heroes.

flag
hero
freedom
pledge
landmark

Critical Thinking Lead students in a discussion about why the colonists wanted to be free.

Write a Pledge Have students write a pledge about respecting their classmates and their school.

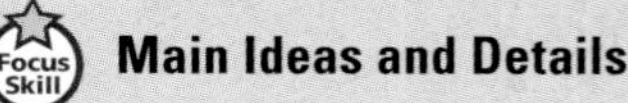

Focus Skill **Main Ideas and Details**

ON-LEVEL

The Star-Spangled Banner

Summary *The Star-Spangled Banner.* This Reader recounts the events that led up to Francis Scott Key's writing of the poem that became the national anthem of the United States.

Vocabulary Power Have students define the following words. Help them write one sentence for each word as it relates to how we honor our country's history and heroes.

flag
hero
country
poem

Critical Thinking Lead students in a discussion about why Francis Scott Key called the flag a star-spangled banner. Ask them what they would have called the flag.

Write a Diary Entry Have students write a diary entry describing how they feel when they see the American flag flying.

Focus Skill **Main Ideas and Details**

ABOVE-LEVEL

Hall of Heroes

Summary *Hall of Heroes.* This Reader describes the American heroes honored with statues in the National Statuary Hall at the Capitol building in Washington, D.C.

Vocabulary Power Have students define the following words. Help them write one sentence for each word as it relates to how we honor our country's history and heroes.

flag
hero
citizen
state
leader

Critical Thinking Lead students in a discussion about ways we honor heroes.

Write a Biography Ask students to research which citizens from their state are honored in the hall. Have them write a short biography about one of those citizens.

Focus Skill **Main Ideas and Details**

Complete a Graphic Organizer

Have students complete the graphic organizer to show they understand the main ideas and details about how we honor our country's history and heroes.

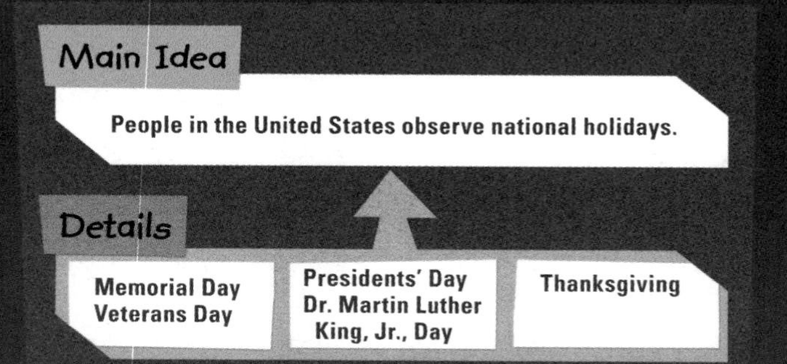

Leveled Readers Teacher Guides include complete lesson plans, copying masters, and project cards.

Harcourt Leveled Readers Available Online! www.harcourtschool.com

Plan a Patriotic Party

Getting Started

Introduce the Hands-On Activity on page 112 in the Unit Review as you begin Unit 4. Have students create a list of party ideas as they learn about heroes, holidays, symbols, and landmarks in our country. Explain that *patriotism* means "showing pride in our country." When the unit is complete, have students invite school administrators and family members to share in their party, which should reflect an understanding of the unit's Big Idea.

The Big Idea
How do we remember special days and people?

Project Management

- Organize students into pairs.
- Students should work with partners to research and find a way to celebrate one national holiday, symbol, landmark, or hero.
- Encourage partners to draw pictures, write poems, or create performances honoring their topic.

Materials: Social Studies textbook; posterboard; construction paper; markers, crayons, or colored pencils; pencil; paper; recordings of patriotic music

Organizer: Have students complete a K-W-L chart about their assigned hero, holiday, symbol, or landmark.

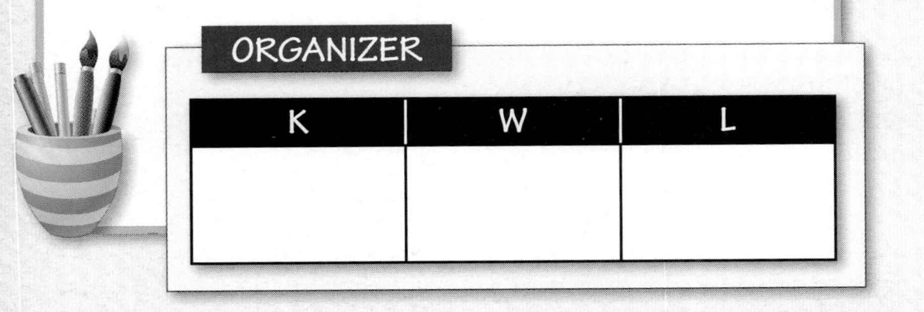

During the Unit

As students read Unit 4, they can begin work on their patriotic party. The party can include:

- Lesson Review activities
- Your own favorite activities
- Ideas students develop on their own

Complete the Project

Choose a time and place for the party. Then have small groups complete various assignments to prepare for the party, such as create and distribute invitations, make and hang decorations, and plan for patriotic refreshments. Allow pairs to deliver their presentations at the party.

What to Look For

For a scoring rubric, see page 112 of this Teacher Edition.

- Students understand the importance of patriotic symbols, landmarks, holidays, and heroes.
- Presentations are creative and well-prepared.
- Presentations, invitations, and other party elements relate to the party theme.

START

North Carolina Interactive Presentations

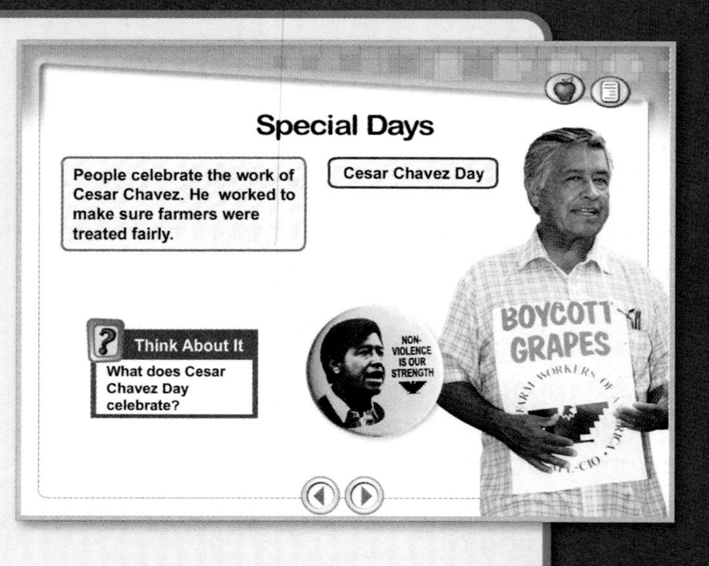

Purpose

The North Carolina Interactive Presentation Unit 4 can be used to preview Unit 4. This presentation provides a concise visual overview of Competency Goal 4 and its objectives. You can use it to preview the unit for the class, or throughout the unit to introduce and reinforce individual objectives.

Contents

The Unit 4 presentation includes an introduction to Competency Goal 4, including a vocabulary preview and a visual introduction to celebrating holidays and special days. In addition, the presentation covers all the unit's objectives lesson by lesson, giving students a broad overview of special days and the meanings behind them.

REVIEW

North Carolina Adventures

Purpose

The North Carolina Adventures games, offered both on CD and online, provide an entertaining first-person-player method of content review. When students have completed the unit, they can review its competency goal and all objectives through the Unit 4 game.

Contents

Tell students they will use their knowledge of special days to help Eco's family during a celebration at their house. Throughout, students will review what they have learned about holidays. Explain that the "Help" buttons in the game will refer them to pages in their textbooks if they need additional information.

Additional Resources

For Teachers

Free and Inexpensive Materials are listed on the Social Studies website at **www.harcourtschool.com/ss1**

- Addresses to write to for free and inexpensive products
- Links to unit-related materials
- Internet maps
- Internet references

The eTE with ePlanner provides the following components

- A calendar tool for scheduling Social Studies lessons and displaying all scheduled lessons and activities
- TE pages and additional resources for easy online reference

For Students

When students visit **www.harcourtschool.com/ss1** they will find internal resources such as

- Our Multimedia Biographies database
- Skills activities
- Additional research tools
- Information about all 50 states

A band plays at the Yam Festival in Tabor City, North Carolina.

Unit 4 Preview

PAGES 83–84

Start with the Competency Goal

Competency Goal 4 The learner will explain different celebrated holidays and special days in communities.

Make It Relevant

Read and discuss the unit competency goal. Ask the following question to help students understand in what ways holidays and special days in communities are celebrated.

Q In what ways do people celebrate holidays or special days?

A Students may mention gathering with friends and families, eating special foods, or watching a parade.

Discuss the Photograph

Explain to students that people may celebrate in many different ways. Have students look at the photograph and explain how people are celebrating at the Yam Festival.

Instructional Design

START WITH THE GOAL AND OBJECTIVES

NORTH CAROLINA STANDARD COURSE OF STUDY

- competency goal
- objectives

PLAN ASSESSMENT

Assessment Options

- Option 1–Unit 4 Test
- Option 2–Writing: Write a Poem, p. 112
- Option 3–Activity: Plan a Patriotic Party, p. 112

PLAN INSTRUCTION

Spotlight on Goals and Objectives
North Carolina Interactive Presentations, Unit 4

Unit 4 Teacher Edition

- resources
- activities
- strategies

Unit 4 Leveled Readers Teacher Guides

The Big Idea

Have students read The Big Idea question and then preview how holidays and special days are celebrated.

Access Prior Knowledge

Ask students to list the names of holidays that are observed by many people in the United States. Then have them give examples of how these holidays are celebrated. Point out that like Americans, people all over the world celebrate special days. Have students read the paragraph and complete the activity.

How do we remember special days and people?

A special day is a time to be happy about something that is important to you. Americans and people all over the world have many special days. On these days, we remember special times and people.

Draw a picture of a day that is special to you.

Drawing should show that student understands the concept of special days.

84

READ MORE

Encourage independent reading with these books or books of your choice.

Basic

You're a Grand Old Flag by George M. Cohan. Walker Books for Young Readers, 2007. Presents the complete text of this patriotic song with beautiful illustrations.

The Pledge of Allegiance: Symbols of Freedom by Lola Schaefer. Heinemann, 2002. A discussion of the Pledge of Allegiance and other symbols of America.

Advanced

Children Just Like Me: Celebrations! by Anabel and Barnabas Kindersley. DK CHILDREN, 1997. A multicultural look at holidays.

Reading Social Studies

Draw Conclusions

Focus Skill

Learn

■ A conclusion is something you figure out from facts in what you are reading.

■ Think about what you already know. Remember the new facts you learn.

■ Combine new facts with the facts you already know to draw a conclusion.

What You Learn		Conclusion
New facts you learn	→	What conclusion can you draw from reading the paragraph?
What You Know		
Information you already know	→	

Practice

Read the paragraph below. Underline the sentence that draws a conclusion.

Our flag is a symbol of the United States. We stand when we pledge allegiance to the flag. We honor the United States flag.

Fact

Reading Social Studies PAGES 85–86

Learn

Have students read the Learn section and look at the graphic organizer. Explain that drawing conclusions can help them determine the purpose of a text. It can also help students figure out something that is implied by the author, but not directly stated. Have students answer the following question to assess how well they draw conclusions.

Q Amy sees that it is raining. What might she need if she went outside?

A Amy might need an umbrella.

Practice

Read the paragraph with students. Point out the facts that might help them draw a conclusion. Ask students how that information relates to what they already know. What object is described?

READING FOCUS SKILLS

Draw Conclusions

What You Learn | Conclusion | What You Know

TRANSPARENCY

Graphic Organizer Write-On/ Wipe-Off Cards available

INTEGRATE THE CURRICULUM

ENGLISH LANGUAGE ARTS Drawing a Conclusion Organize students into pairs. Then have each student write a short description giving details of an object in the classroom, but not identifying the object. Have students exchange their descriptions with their partners. Each student should then try to draw a conclusion about what item is being described.

ELA 2.04 Use preparation strategies to anticipate vocabulary of a text and to connect prior knowledge and experiences to a new text.

Reading Social Studies PAGES 85–86

Apply

This selection gives several details that help lead students to the conclusion stated in the second sentence: *He is getting ready to go to a Fourth of July celebration with his family.* Ask students what details support the conclusion. How do those details relate to things they already know about the Fourth of July? Help students write the information in their graphic organizers.

Unit 4 provides many opportunities for students to practice drawing conclusions. As students read the unit, challenge them to draw conclusions from the information given in the text.

Apply

Read the paragraph.

Luke lives in Southport, North Carolina. He is getting ready to go to a Fourth of July celebration with his family. There will be a parade in the afternoon and fireworks at night. Luke makes sure to wear red, white, and blue. He practices singing patriotic songs. Luke takes an American flag with him.

What facts can you add to the chart? What conclusion can you draw?

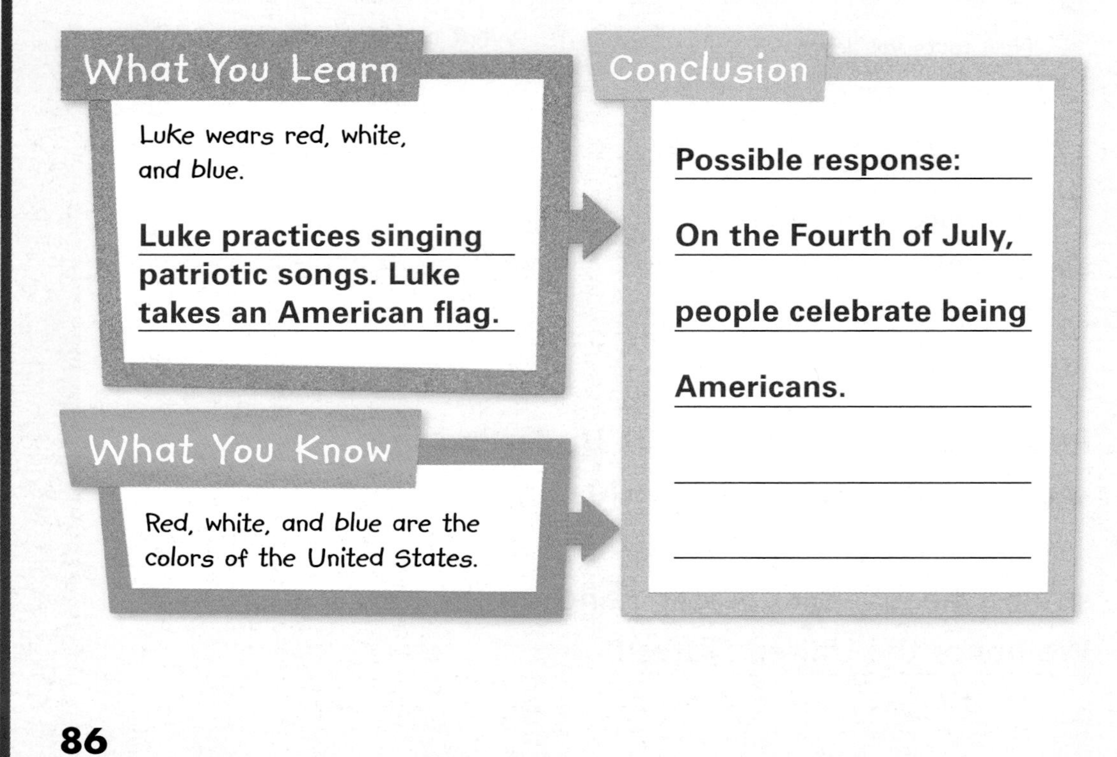

86

ESL/LANGUAGE SUPPORT

Vocabulary Development Have students draw a circle and place the phrase *American Traditions* in the center. Have them think of words such as *parade* or *holiday* that relate to cultural traditions in the United States. As they read the unit, students should add more words to their webs.

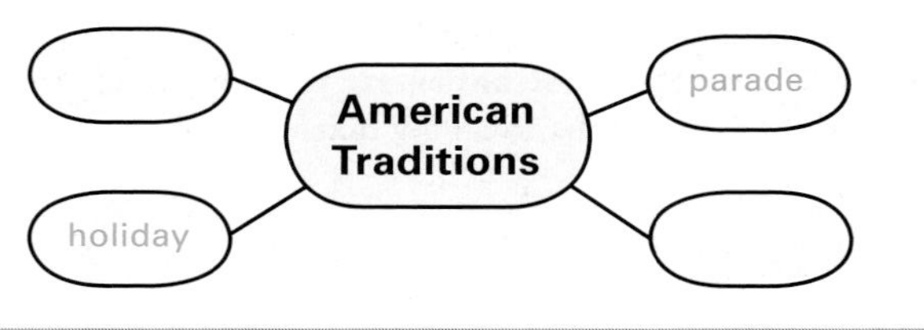

Prior Learning and Experiences As they read the unit, ask students about cultural traditions from another country with which they are familiar. The traditions may be ones that their families or friends practice. Have those traditions changed to blend with American traditions? Have volunteers tell the class about their holiday traditions.

Build Background

Make It Relevant Explain to students that our country's symbols represent the people who live here and the values that citizens hold. Ask students to name objects and places that make them think of the United States. Guide students to include landmarks such as the Statue of Liberty, Mount Rushmore, and the Washington Monument. Ask whether students have visited any of these places. Discuss their experiences and have them clarify how these symbols and locations remind them of our country.

Preview the Lesson

Guide students in previewing the lesson. Point out the following features on Student Edition pages 87–90:

- **Page 87** Invite students to preview the photograph. Ask students to explain what the students in the photograph are doing. How is the flag a symbol of the United States?
- **Page 88** Explain that certain symbols represent the United States. Ask students to look at the photograph of the dollar bill. Which President is on the dollar bill? How is his picture a symbol of the United States?
- **Page 89** Point out that North Carolina also has symbols. Some symbols are animals or plants that are found in the state. Ask students whether they have ever seen any of the symbols displayed on the page.

Preteach Vocabulary

- Ask students to define the word **symbol** in their own words. Point out that a symbol is something that represents another object or idea. Ask students to draw a symbol that makes them think of the United States.
- Ask students to locate the United States **flag** in the classroom. Have them describe what the flag looks like. Point out that the fifty stars represent the fifty states, and the thirteen stripes represent the thirteen original colonies.

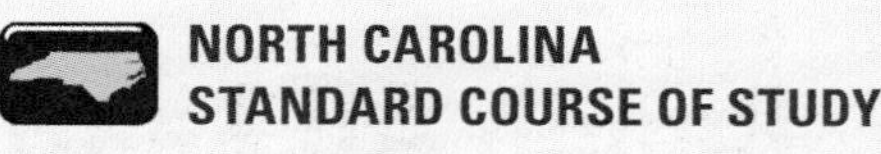

Objective 4.01 Recognize and describe religious and secular symbols/celebrations associated with special days of diverse cultures.

Key Content Summary

- **Symbols stand for ideas and other things that are important to people.**
- **The United States has symbols such as the American flag, the national flower, and the national bird.**
- **North Carolina has symbols like the state animal and the state flag.**

Vocabulary

- **symbol,** p. 87
- **flag,** p. 87

Spotlight on Goals and Objectives

Use North Carolina Interactive Presentations, Unit 4, Lesson 1, to access prior knowledge and build background.

Reach All Learners

ESL/Language Support

Scaffolding Content Use a word web to help students identify characteristics of the United States flag. Start with the words *United States Flag* in the center.

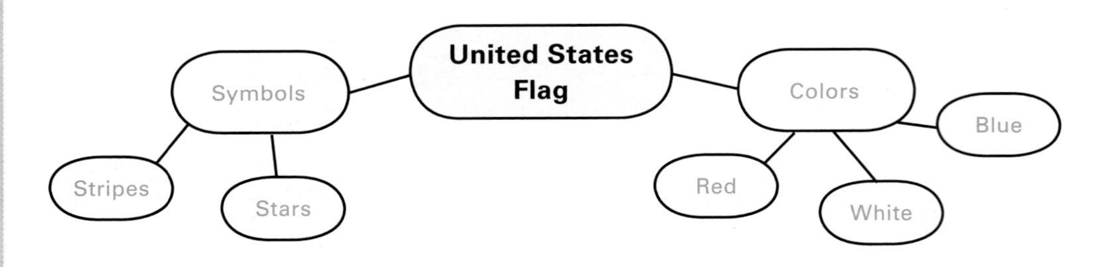

Extra Support

Research a Symbol Have pairs of students investigate one of the symbols named in the lesson. Have students use research materials or the school-approved websites to find or draw pictures of the symbol. Then have students write a description about the symbol's origin. Assist students in using the pictures to create a book of symbols.

Extension Activity

Act as a Tour Guide Explain that the Statue of Liberty is a symbol of our country. Have students use library and school-approved websites to research facts about the Statue of Liberty. As a class, list the facts on the board. Display a picture of the Statue of Liberty and have students act as tour guides presenting the class with different facts about the Statue of Liberty.

Integrate the Curriculum

Arts

Learn a Song Play a recording of the song "You're a Grand Old Flag" for students. Then display the words to the song. Ask students to explain how the song expresses American ideals. Teach students the words and then sing the song as a class. Then display the words of the Pledge of Allegiance next to the song. Review the Pledge of Allegiance, and ask volunteers to tell how this song and the Pledge of Allegiance are alike and how they are different.

Symbols

Lesson

A **symbol** is a picture that stands for an idea or a thing. The American flag is a symbol for the United States. A **flag** is a piece of cloth with symbols on it. **What will you learn about symbols?**

Possible response: I will learn about different kinds of symbols of the United States.

These children show respect for the flag by saying the Pledge of Allegiance.

NORTH CAROLINA STANDARD COURSE OF STUDY

4.01 Recognize and describe religious and secular symbols/celebrations associated with special days of diverse cultures.

87

Lesson 1

PAGES 87–90

Start with the Objective

Objective 4.01 Recognize and describe religious and secular symbols/celebrations associated with special days of diverse cultures.

Set a Purpose for Reading

Have the class read aloud the paragraph on this page. Ask students to identify school symbols. Discuss why symbols are important. Then have students answer the question to set a purpose for reading and use the Think Aloud below to model thinking.

Think Aloud

I know that symbols are things and ideas that have special meaning to people. I also know that both the United States and North Carolina have symbols. I think that I will read about what the symbols of our country and our state mean.

BACKGROUND

The Pledge of Allegiance The U.S. flag contains fifty stars and thirteen stripes. The stars represent the fifty states, and the stripes signify the thirteen original colonies. The students in this photograph are reciting the Pledge of Allegiance. The pledge was written for a children's magazine in 1892 by Francis Bellamy. The U.S. government officially recognized the pledge in 1942. Congress passed an act in 1954 that said a citizen reciting the pledge should stand with the right hand over the heart.

BUILD SKILLS

Chart and Graph Skills Have students identify symbols that they see at home and at school and list them in a chart like the one below. Ask students also to note what the symbols mean.

	Symbol	Meaning
At home		
At school		

SSSMART™
SUPPORT

TextWork

1 Vocabulary

Understand Vocabulary Tell students to reread the definition of the word *symbol* on the previous page. Have them write the definition in their own words. Then have students underline the symbols of the United States. Students may also underline the symbols mentioned in the captions, or they may underline the photographs as well.

TextWork

1 Underline the symbols of the United States.

American Symbols

The United States has many symbols. These symbols stand for ideas. These ideas are important to us.

Some symbols are plants. Some are animals. The rose and the bald eagle are American symbols.

The Liberty Bell stands for freedom.

The bald eagle is our national bird.

The pictures on our money are symbols, too.

88

TEACHING YOUR SOCIAL STUDIES

BACKGROUND

Patriotic Symbols The Liberty Bell was ordered in 1751 and cast in London. It was rung at the first public reading of the Declaration of Independence on July 8, 1776. The bald eagle is a symbol of strength and independence. The founders chose it as our national symbol because it is native to North America. John Adams planted the first roses on the White House grounds. In 1986, the rose was officially recognized as a national symbol. Show students a photograph of a rose.

SOCIAL STUDIES STRANDS

Economics and Development George Washington appears on the front of the $1 bill to honor his role in U.S. history. The color green is used because it makes it more difficult for people to copy, not because it has special meaning. Recently, more colors have been added to U.S. money because they are also difficult to copy. The symbols on money have stayed the same, however.

SSSMART™ SUPPORT

North Carolina Symbols

North Carolina has symbols, too. Some symbols are plants. Some are animals that live in North Carolina. The gray squirrel is the state animal. The box turtle is also a North Carolina symbol.

North Carolina has a flag. The colors and shapes on the flag are symbols, too.

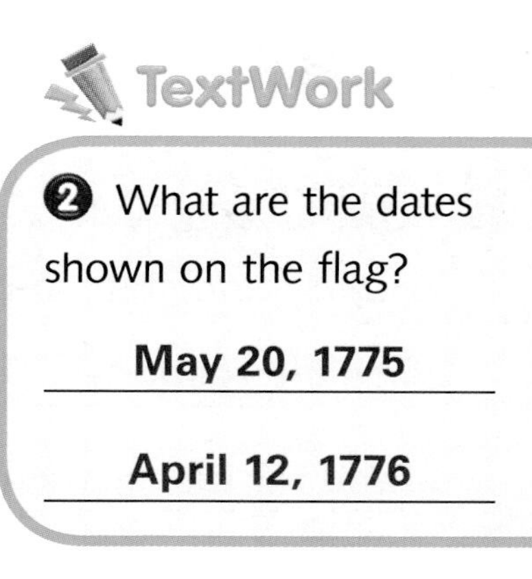

TextWork

❷ What are the dates shown on the flag?

May 20, 1775

April 12, 1776

Gray Squirrel

State Flag

Box Turtle

TextWork

❷ CUES

Analyze/Interpret Photographs Help students find the dates on the flag. Ask them to recall the parts of a date (month, day, year). Then tell students to find the two months, days, and years written on the North Carolina flag in the photograph. Tell students that the dates on the flag represent important times in North Carolina's history.

SOCIAL STUDIES STRANDS

Geographic Relationships Animals are chosen as state symbols both for their unique qualities and for their connection to the state. The gray squirrel is the state mammal. It lives in swamps and forests throughout the state. The box turtle is the state reptile. It can pull its head and legs into its shell and close the shell.

BACKGROUND

The State Flag North Carolina's flag uses letters, dates, and colors as symbols. The letters *N* and *C* stand for the state name. The date, May 20, 1775, is when Mecklenburg residents declared independence from England. April 12, 1776, is the date that the North Carolina delegates received permission to sign the Declaration of Independence. The colors were chosen to mirror those used on the national flag.

Lesson Review

Summary Have students work individually to summarize the key content before they complete the Lesson Review.

- Symbols stand for ideas and other things that are important to people.
- The United States has symbols like the American flag, the national flower, and the national bird.
- North Carolina has symbols that include the state animal and the state flag.

1. **SUMMARIZE** Why are the symbols for our country and state important?

   Possible response: Symbols are important because they stand for ideas, such as freedom, that are special to us.

2. Where have you seen our country's **flag**?

   Possible response: I have seen our country's flag in my classroom.

3. What do you think would be a good symbol for your community? Why?

   Answers will vary, but students should give an appropriate reason why they chose the symbol for their community.

Draw a flag for your class. Put symbols on it for things that are important to your class.

90

ACTIVITY RUBRIC

Score 4
- draws detailed, colorful class flag
- uses meaningful, original symbols

Score 3
- draws colorful class flag
- uses relevant symbols

Score 2
- class flag lacks detail
- uses irrelevant or meaningless symbols

Score 1
- does not draw class flag or draws flag without detail or care
- does not use symbols

Build Background

Make It Relevant Explain to students that because people are proud of their cultures and heritage, they share them with others through celebrations. Ask students to think about times they have celebrated something, such as birthdays, holidays, or family gatherings. Tell them that these celebrations show others what is important to their families. Guide students to see that in the same way, others can tell what is important to a group of people by studying the celebrations and traditions of their culture.

Preview the Lesson

Guide students in previewing the lesson. Point out the following features on Student Edition pages 91–96:

- **Page 91** Ask students to list some of their favorite holidays. Then ask students to describe the ways in which their families celebrate those holidays.
- **Pages 92–93** Invite students to preview the title of the section. Have them preview the photographs and describe what the people in the photographs are doing to celebrate.
- **Pages 94–95** Point out that people from different cultures bring their celebrations to the United States to share. Ask students to name some cultural celebrations in which they have participated.

Preteach Vocabulary

- Point out that the words *celebrate*, **celebration**, and *celebrating* are part of a word family. Ask volunteers to use each word in a sentence.
- Explain that sometimes a **holiday** is a celebration that connects to a certain religion, but there are many holidays that do not connect to any specific religion. Ask students to brainstorm a list of religious and nonreligious holidays.
- Ask students to define **religion**. Explain that different families practice different religions. Some families do not practice any religion. Ask: "What are some holidays on which people celebrate something in their religion?"

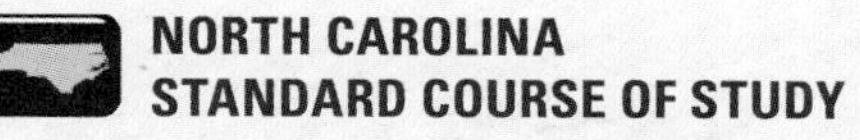

NORTH CAROLINA STANDARD COURSE OF STUDY

Objective 4.01 Recognize and describe religious and secular symbols/celebrations associated with special days of diverse cultures.

Key Content Summary

- **Celebrations are special days for friends and family.**
- **Some holidays are celebrated by everyone.**
- **Some people celebrate religious holidays. Some people celebrate holidays from their culture.**

Vocabulary

- **celebration,** p. 91
- **holiday,** p. 91
- **religion,** p. 92

Spotlight on Goals and Objectives

Use North Carolina Interactive Presentations, Unit 4, Lesson 2, to access prior knowledge and build background.

Reach All Learners

ESL/Language Support

Content and Language Objectives Have students use each photograph in the lesson to complete the sentence frame shown in the graphic organizer below.

The	[subject of the photograph]	is	[main idea of the photograph].
The	family	is	celebrating Hanukkah.

Extra Support

Draw a Conclusion Write a three sentence paragraph about celebrations on sentence strips. Leave out the conclusion of the paragraph. Mix up the sentences and allow the students to unscramble them. Pair students to write a conclusion to the paragraph. Invite partners to read their conclusions to the rest of the class.

Extension Activity

Write a Headline Show students examples of newspaper headlines that reference different holidays and celebrations. Brainstorm with the class a list of holidays and celebrations. Pair students and assign partners a holiday or celebration to research. Have pairs create a newspaper headline about their holiday or celebration. Encourage volunteers to read their headlines to the class. Record students' headlines on a posterboard and display it in the classroom.

Integrate the Curriculum

English Language Arts

Give an Oral Presentation Review the events surrounding a specific celebration or holiday, such as Thanksgiving or Independence Day. Have students write or dictate a sentence about why we celebrate this special day. Help them practice speaking their sentence. Encourage them to draw pictures to illustrate the holiday and to refer to their pictures as they deliver their oral presentations.

ELA 4.03 Use specific words to name and tell action in oral and written language (e.g., using words such as frog and toad when discussing a nonfiction text).

Lesson 2

PAGES 91–96

Lesson 2

Celebrations

A **celebration** is a time to be happy about something special. Some celebrations are just for family and friends. A **holiday** is a day of celebration for everyone. **What might you learn about celebrations?**

Possible response: I might learn how people take part in celebrations.

Dancers at the Folkmoot International Festival in Waynesville, North Carolina

NORTH CAROLINA STANDARD COURSE OF STUDY

4.01 Recognize and describe religious and secular symbols/celebrations associated with special days of diverse cultures.

91

Start with the Objective

Objective 4.01 Recognize and describe religious and secular symbols/celebrations associated with special days of diverse cultures.

Set a Purpose for Reading

Read and discuss the lesson objective and the lesson introduction with students. Draw students' attention to the highlighted words. Ask them to give an example of a celebration and a holiday. Then have students answer the question to set a purpose for reading. Model thinking for students by using the Think Aloud below.

Think Aloud

I know that a celebration is a special time for some people. I think that I will read about different examples of celebrations.

BACKGROUND

Folkmoot Folkmoot, which means "meeting of the people," began in 1984 after Waynesville resident Clinton Border attended a folk festival in the United Kingdom. He began traveling to festivals in other countries and meeting performers. Every summer for two weeks, different groups from different countries come to perform at the festival. Since 1984, hundreds of groups from many countries have entertained North Carolinians at the Folkmoot International Festival.

BUILD SKILLS

Chart and Graph Skills Have students fill in a Venn diagram like the one below to identify the similarities and differences between celebrations and holidays.

Celebrations	Both	Holidays
shared by family and friends	a time to be happy about something special	shared by everyone

SSSMART™
SUPPORT

TextWork

1 Vocabulary

Use Context Clues Help students identify the meaning of the word *religion*. Have them read the second sentence and circle the words that provide clues to the word's meaning. These words include *beliefs, God,* and *gods*.

1 Underline the meaning of religion.

2 Circle something special that people do on each holiday of a religion.

Holidays of Religion

On some holidays, people celebrate something in their religion. A **religion** is a set of beliefs about God or gods. Families eat special foods and do special things on these days.

Christmas

At Christmas, some Christian families put up Christmas trees. They celebrate the birthday of Jesus.

Hanukkah

At Hanukkah, Jewish families light candles on a menorah. Hanukkah is celebrated for eight nights.

92

TEACHING YOUR SOCIAL STUDIES

BACKGROUND

Christmas and Hanukkah On Christmas Day, some Christians go to church to celebrate the birth of Jesus. They also give presents to one another. During Hanukkah, Jewish families celebrate the time when an ancient temple was taken back from enemies by their ancestors. They say prayers and sing songs each night as another candle is lit on the menorah. Some Jewish people give gifts to each other during this holiday.

SOCIAL STUDIES STRANDS

Cultures and Diversity Remind students that a symbol is something that has meaning to people. Explain that religions often have symbols. Help students identify the symbols related to each religious celebration discussed on these pages.

Q Why do you think people use symbols in religious celebrations?

A Possible response: Because they want to bring meaning to their celebrations.

SSSMART™ SUPPORT

TextWork

2 Skim and Scan

Remind students that text features, such as captions, can help them find information. Have students scan the caption accompanying each photograph to help them identify something special that people do on each holiday.

BACKGROUND

Religious Holidays Remind students that holidays are usually a time for people to remember ideas that are meaningful to them. At Ramadan, Muslims remember that they received their holy book during that month. At Vesak, people remember the life of Buddha by giving food and gifts to Buddhist monks at the temple. At Holi, Hindus remember the new life that blooms in the spring by decorating themselves and others with spring colors.

SSSMART™
SUPPORT

TextWork

3 CUES

Analyze/Interpret Photographs To help students correctly identify the photograph that shows the Chinese New Year, have them read the caption for each photograph.

3 Circle the picture that shows Chinese New Year.

Celebrations of Culture

When people move to the United States, they still celebrate holidays from their culture. Celebrations help us learn about each other.

Irish Americans celebrate St. Patrick's Day with parades. They eat Irish foods.

The Chinese New Year lasts for 15 days. It ends with a Lantern Festival.

94

TEACHING YOUR SOCIAL STUDIES

BACKGROUND

The Lantern Festival The Lantern Festival is the last day of the Chinese New Year celebration. It is said that Buddhist monks used to light lanterns to honor Buddha each year and that the tradition spread throughout China. In addition to hanging lanterns, people place riddles inside of their lanterns. Anyone can try to guess the answer. If a person guesses the correct answer, the lantern owner will give him or her a small prize.

SOCIAL STUDIES STRANDS

Cultures and Diversity Tell students to examine the celebrations taking place in both of these photographs. Ask them to describe what they see.

Q What is similar about the celebrations shown in these two photographs? What is different?

A Similarities include: people are celebrating and enjoying parades. Differences include: the colors, the symbols, and the celebrations.

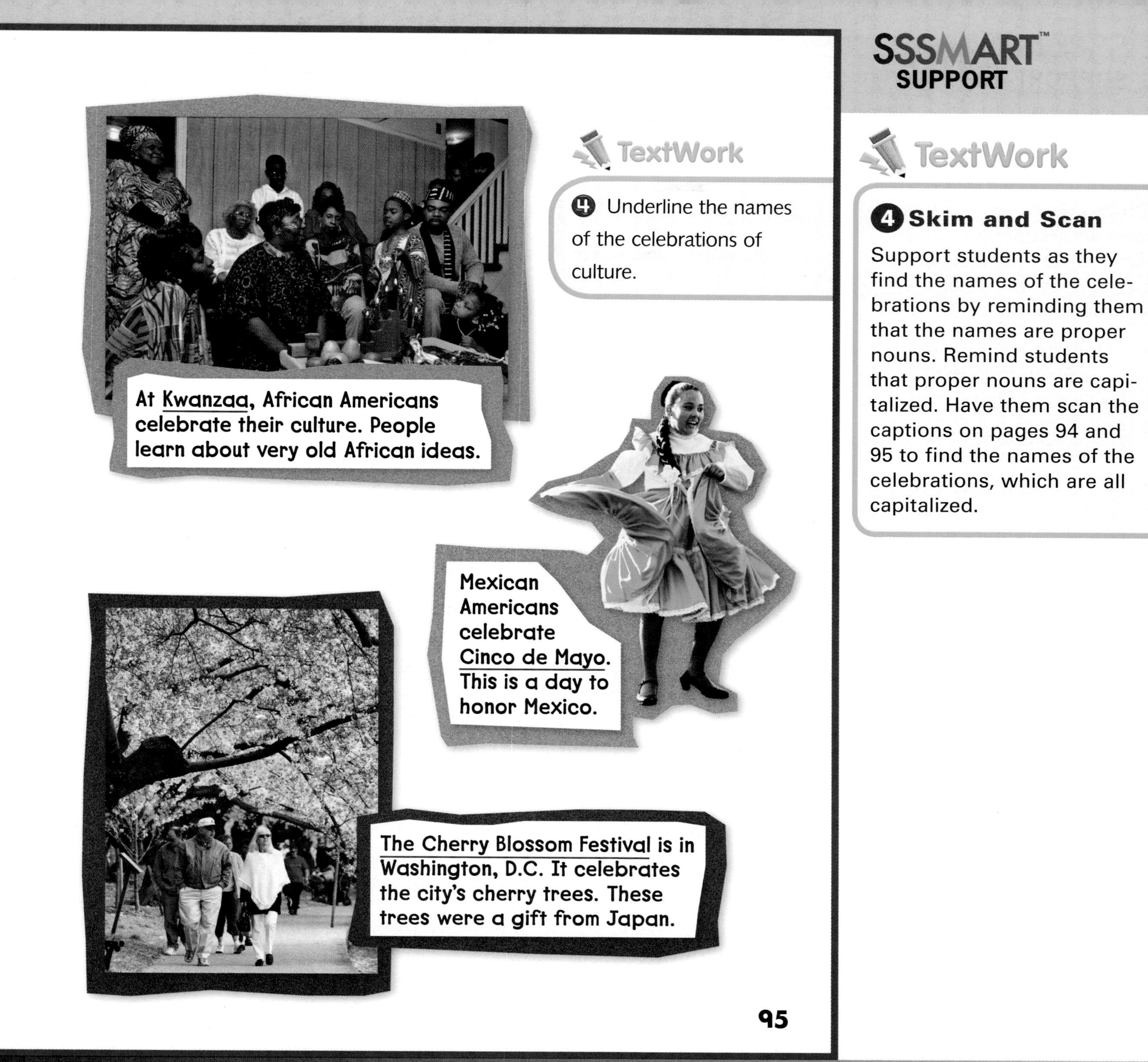

SSSMART™ SUPPORT

TextWork

4 Skim and Scan

Support students as they find the names of the celebrations by reminding them that the names are proper nouns. Remind students that proper nouns are capitalized. Have them scan the captions on pages 94 and 95 to find the names of the celebrations, which are all capitalized.

BACKGROUND

A Gift of Cherry Trees In the early 1900s, Japan and the United States began developing good relations. As a gesture of friendship, Japanese Mayor Yukio Ozaki gave 3,000 cherry trees to the United States. The first two trees were planted in 1912. In exchange for the cherry trees, the U.S. government gave dogwood trees to the Japanese. In 1981, after floods had damaged many cherry trees in Japan, the United States offered Japan clippings from the cherry trees that it had given us.

BUILD SKILLS

MAP SKILL **Map and Globe Skills** Prepare index cards with the names and dates of each holiday. Display a map of the world. Invite students to post the index cards near the country in which each celebration is from. St. Patrick's Day is March 17. The Chinese New Year starts at the beginning of the lunar year. Kwanzaa is celebrated from December 26 to January 1. Cinco de Mayo is celebrated on May 5. The Cherry Blossom Festival is held from late March through early April.

Lesson Review

Summary Have students work in groups to summarize the key content before they complete the Lesson Review.

- Celebrations are special days for friends and family.
- Some holidays are celebrated by everyone.
- Some people celebrate religious holidays. Some people celebrate holidays from their culture.

1. **SUMMARIZE** Why do people celebrate holidays?

   Possible response: People celebrate holidays to remember something special in their culture or religion.

2. What is one **holiday** your community celebrates?

   Answers will vary; students should name a holiday celebrated in their community.

3. Why do people in the United States celebrate holidays from different cultures?

   Possible response: Many people in the United States have moved here from other countries.

Writing

Write about a holiday that you learned about in this lesson.

96

WRITING RUBRIC

Score 4
- chooses holiday from the lesson
- includes accurate details and vivid description
- has no errors

Score 3
- chooses holiday from the lesson
- includes some details and clear description
- has few errors

Score 2
- chooses celebration instead of holiday
- includes few details and confusing description
- has some errors

Score 1
- chooses celebration instead of holiday
- lacks detail and description
- has many errors

Build Background

Make It Relevant Explain that some holidays are national holidays. Americans remember important people and events from our country's past on these special days. Ask students to share their experiences surrounding Independence Day. Elicit details of family and community events. Discuss how this national holiday celebrates our country's freedom.

Preview the Lesson

Guide students in previewing the lesson. Point out the following features on Student Edition pages 97–102:

- **Page 97** Explain to students that communities celebrate national holidays, like Independence Day, differently. Ask students how some communities may celebrate national holidays. Answers may include fireworks, parades, games, carnivals, or a day off from school or work.
- **Pages 98–99** Invite students to preview the title of the section. Ask, "How do we remember heroes?"
- **Pages 100–101** Point out that we learn about history when we celebrate important days in our country. Invite students to preview the picture, and ask, "Why do we celebrate Thanksgiving?"

Preteach Vocabulary

- Point out to students that a **national holiday** might be in honor of a person or people who have done something important for our country. Ask students whether they can name any national holidays that honor people.
- Tell students that the people who are honored by those national holidays are heroes. Explain that a **hero** is a person who does something brave or important. The United States has many heroes, both from the past as well as today. Ask students to name one of their heroes. Students may name a firefighter, a politician, a police officer, an athlete, a family member, or another person.

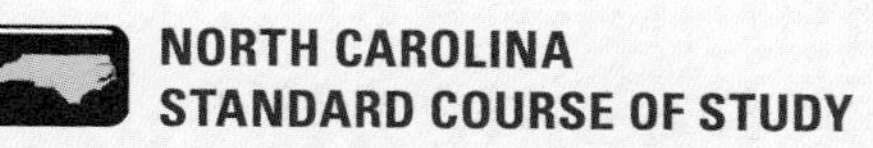

NORTH CAROLINA STANDARD COURSE OF STUDY

Objective 4.02 Explore and cite reasons for observing special days that recognize celebrated individuals of diverse cultures.

Objective 4.03 Recognize and describe the historical events associated with national holidays.

Key Content Summary

- **Holidays are days to celebrate important events and people in our history.**
- **We often remember heroes who have done important things to help others.**
- **We remember important days in our country's history.**

Vocabulary

- **national holiday,** p. 97
- **hero,** p. 97

Spotlight on Goals and Objectives

Use North Carolina Interactive Presentations, Unit 4, Lesson 3, to access prior knowledge and build background.

Reach All Learners

ESL/Language Support

Active Learning Help students make a word chart. Write the word *Hero* in the first column. Then have students write the meaning in the second column. Ask students to think about how a parent, soldier, firefighter, or police officer can be a hero. Then have students draw pictures of a hero performing an important duty in the third column or on a separate sheet of paper. Encourage students to write captions for their drawings and ask volunteers to share their drawings with the class.

Word	Definition	Picture
Hero	a person who does something brave or important	

Extra Support

Create a Puppet Provide students with materials to create a puppet. Have students create a puppet of an American hero. Students may choose heroes mentioned in the lesson or they may choose another hero such as a family member, a firefighter, or a teacher. Then have students write a description of their hero. For example, a student creating a puppet of George Washington may say, "I was the first President of the United States." Encourage students to practice their descriptions. Invite student groups to put on a puppet show for the class.

Extension Activity

Create a Calendar Guide students and help them create a list of national holidays along with the dates on which they are celebrated. Assign each student a holiday and have him or her create a calendar page for the holiday. Pages should include pictures and words that are associated with the holiday. Invite volunteers to share their calendar page with the class.

Integrate the Curriculum

Mathematics

Count Whole Numbers Display a calendar page of the current month for students to examine. Ask them to answer questions about the page. How many days are in a week? How many Wednesdays are in this month? Are there any national holidays in this month? Finally, ask students to name the last date on the calendar and tell on which day of the week that day falls.

Holidays and Heroes

Lesson 3

A **national holiday** is a day to remember an event that is important to our country. It may also remember a hero. A **hero** is a person who does something to help others. **What kinds of holidays might you read about?**

Possible response: I might read about different kinds of national holidays.

NORTH CAROLINA STANDARD COURSE OF STUDY

4.02 Explore and cite reasons for observing special days that recognize celebrated individuals of diverse cultures.

4.03 Recognize and describe the historical events associated with national holidays.

97

Lesson 3

PAGES 97–102

Start with the Objectives

Objective 4.02 Explore and cite reasons for observing special days that recognize celebrated individuals of diverse cultures.

Objective 4.03 Recognize and describe the historical events associated with national holidays.

Set a Purpose for Reading

Read and discuss the lesson objectives and the lesson introduction with students. Draw students' attention to the highlighted word *national holiday*. Have students keep in mind the highlighted word as they answer the question. Model thinking for students by using the Think Aloud below.

Think Aloud

I know that a holiday is a day everyone can celebrate. I think that I will read about holidays celebrated by everyone in the United States.

BACKGROUND

Parades This photograph shows a marching band in a parade. Parades are a common way that Americans celebrate national holidays. For example, parades are held on Thanksgiving Day, on Veterans Day, and on Independence Day—all national holidays. Ask students who have been to a parade to describe what took place.

SOCIAL STUDIES STRANDS

Government and Active Citizenship Lead a discussion about ways in which people celebrate national holidays. For example, people have parades and picnics, and may have the day off from work or school.

Q Why do people celebrate national holidays together?

A Possible response: to remember important people and events

SSSMART™ SUPPORT

TextWork

1 CUES

Analyze/Interpret Photographs Tell students that the captions contain information about the photographs. Have them read the captions to find out which person was once the President of the United States.

TextWork

1 Circle the picture of the person who was once President of the United States.

Remembering Heroes

Our country has many heroes. We have holidays to remember them.

Dr. Martin Luther King, Jr., Day honors Dr. King. He helped all Americans have the same rights.

Presidents' Day was once a holiday to remember our first President. His name was George Washington. Now it is a day to remember all of our Presidents.

Orville and Wilbur Wright flew the first airplane with a motor. On December 17, we remember the work they did.

98

TEACHING YOUR SOCIAL STUDIES

BACKGROUND

George Washington Before he became the first U.S. President, George Washington served our country in many ways. When the colonists decided to revolt against Britain, he led the colonial army. He also promoted drafting a new Constitution, after which his fellow leaders chose him to be the first President of the United States. George Washington and all of the other United States Presidents are honored on Presidents' Day. This day is celebrated on the third Monday of February.

SOCIAL STUDIES STRANDS

Cultures and Diversity In the 1950s and 1960s, Dr. Martin Luther King, Jr., worked to ensure equal rights for all people in our nation. He and other African American leaders used nonviolent protests to show Americans that some people were being treated unfairly in the United States. Congress made new laws to make voting, housing, and the workplace fairer for people of all races. Dr. King is honored on Dr. Martin Luther King, Jr., Day. This day is celebrated on the third Monday of January.

Cesar Chavez made sure farmers were treated fairly. We remember him on March 31.

Susan B. Anthony believed that all people should have the right to vote. The work she did helped make this happen. We remember her on February 15.

Memorial Day and Veterans Day are two national holidays. On these days, we remember those who have helped in our country's wars.

99

TextWork

2 Who worked so that all people could have the right to vote?

Susan B. Anthony

SSSMART™ SUPPORT

TextWork

2 Skim and Scan

Tell students that scanning means to look over a page quickly to find key terms. Ask students to scan the captions on this page for the key terms *right* and *vote*.

BUILD SKILLS

Chart and Graph Skills Make a calendar on the board showing the months of the year. Demonstrate to the class how to mark a holiday on the calendar, starting with Dr. Martin Luther King, Jr., Day on the third Monday of January. Then, call students to the board to mark the days on which Cesar Chavez and Susan B. Anthony are remembered. Students can use this calendar as a base when completing the lesson review activity.

BACKGROUND

Memorial Day and Veterans Day Explain to students the difference between Memorial Day and Veterans Day. Memorial Day is observed on the last Monday in May. It is a day to honor those who died while serving their country, particularly those who died in battle. Veterans Day is celebrated on November 11. It is a day to honor the living men and women who serve or have served in the military.

TextWork

3 Comprehension

Draw Conclusions Remind students that holidays are days to remember events from the past. Ask students to consider which of the foods that are listed were probably eaten in the past. Then have students study the photograph and identify which foods are being served.

3 Circle the food many Americans eat on Thanksgiving Day.

turkey (circled)
pizza

Honoring History

Some holidays help us remember important days in our country. To do this, we learn about history. For example, we learn about the Pilgrims. Long ago, the Pilgrims showed their thanks for a good harvest. They shared a dinner with the Wampanoag. The Wampanoag are American Indians. American Indians were the first people to live in North America.

We remember the dinner of the Wampanoag and the Pilgrims. We call this holiday Thanksgiving.

100

TEACHING YOUR SOCIAL STUDIES

BACKGROUND

American Indians or Native Americans Explain to students that American Indians also can be called Native Americans. These are considered to be equally respectful terms. However, it is preferable to use the tribal name whenever possible. For example, this page has information about the Wampanoag. It is more accurate and respectful to call them Wampanoag than Native Americans or American Indians.

SOCIAL STUDIES STRANDS

Historical Perspectives The Pilgrims were members of a religious group that left England seeking freedom to worship as they chose. The land and the climate in North America were very different from what the Pilgrims were used to, and they struggled to survive. American Indians taught them to fish and farm. Thanksgiving honors the successful harvest of the Pilgrims. Thanksgiving is celebrated on the fourth Thursday of every November.

July 4 is Independence Day. It is our country's birthday. On this day, we celebrate our country's freedom. Many communities have parades and fireworks.

TextWork

4 Circle the picture that shows Americans celebrating our country's birthday.

On Constitution Day, we remember the day when our country's first leaders signed the United States Constitution.

101

SSSMART™ SUPPORT

TextWork

4 CUES

Analyze/Interpret Photographs Ask students to recall how they usually celebrate the Fourth of July, which is our country's birthday. Tell them to find the photograph that shows people celebrating in that way.

BACKGROUND

Patriot Day and Constitution Day Patriot Day and Constitution Day are two of the newest federal holidays. In December 2001, President Bush declared September 11 Patriot Day. He wanted an official holiday to remember the people who died in the tragedy of September 11, 2001. Constitution Day began in 2005 and is observed on September 17. Schools that receive federal money are required to teach about the Constitution on or around that day each year.

BUILD SKILLS

Decision Making Have students choose a person or an event that they would like to have remembered by a national holiday. Ask them how officials should make such a decision. What qualities would the person or event need to have? What symbols would be used to represent the person or event? How would we celebrate? Help students move through the decision making process, then cast a vote to determine the most popular selection.

Lesson Review

Summary Have students work in pairs to summarize the key content before they complete the Lesson Review.

- Holidays are days to celebrate important events and people in our history.
- We often remember heroes who have done important things to help others.
- We remember important days in our country's history.

1. **SUMMARIZE** Why do we have national holidays?

   Possible response: We have national holidays to celebrate heroes and remember important days.

2. Name a person you think is a **hero**. Tell why you think he or she is a hero.

   Possible response: I think Dr. Martin Luther King, Jr., is a hero because he helped all Americans have the same rights.

3. Our country's birthday is July 4. What do we celebrate on this day?

   Possible response: We celebrate our country's freedom on July 4.

Activity

With your class, make a calendar showing our country's national holidays.

102

ACTIVITY RUBRIC

Score 4
- includes all national holidays
- uses accurate labels and symbols
- has no errors

Score 3
- includes most national holidays
- uses mostly accurate labels and symbols
- has few errors

Score 2
- does not include some national holidays
- uses inaccurate labels and symbols
- has some errors

Score 1
- does not include any national holidays
- does not use labels or symbols
- has many errors

Remembering Our Past

PAGES 103–108

Build Background

Make It Relevant Ask students what they know about the history of their neighborhood or community. Discuss important traditions of the students' neighborhood or community. Explain that a lot can be learned about a place by studying its traditions.

Preview the Lesson

Guide students in previewing the lesson. Point out the following features on Student Edition pages 103–108:

- **Page 103** Explain that it is important to remember the past. Ask students to list some ways in which the past can be remembered.
- **Pages 104–105** Point out that the American Indians were familiar with the land and showed settlers how to grow food. Ask students why the knowledge shared by the American Indians was helpful to the settlers.
- **Page 106** Invite students to preview the title of the section. Ask: "What might happen at the Latin American Festival?"
- **Page 107** Invite students to preview the photograph. Ask: "What culture do these musicians represent?" Explain that the bagpipe is a Scottish musical instrument.

Preteach Vocabulary

- Explain to students that a **landmark** is a place that people can visit. Landmarks are symbols and can help people remember the past. Ask students to list some landmarks in the United States.
- Point out that a **settler** is a person who makes a home in a new community. Ask students why settlers may need help from people who already live in the community.

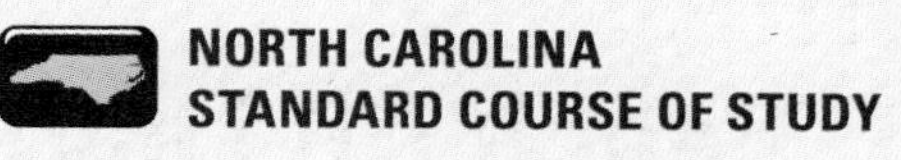

Objective 4.04 Trace the historical foundations of traditions of various neighborhoods and communities.

Key Content Summary

- **People remember the past by attending festivals and visiting landmarks.**
- **A landmark is a place that people visit. It is a symbol of an important event or idea.**
- **At festivals, people play games, watch performers sing and dance, and eat food that reminds them of their cultural traditions.**

Vocabulary

- **landmark**, p. 103
- **settler**, p. 104

Spotlight on Goals and Objectives

Use North Carolina Interactive Presentations, Unit 4, Lesson 4, to access prior knowledge and build background.

Reach All Learners

ESL/Language Support

Scaffolding Content Have students use words to complete a K-W-L chart. Provide students with information about the past to fill in the first column. Then have students use words to fill in the second and third columns of the chart.

What I Know	What I Want to Know	What I Learned
It is important to remember the past.		

Extra Support

Role-Play an Adventure Review the story of Sacagawea. Divide the class into groups of three. Guide students in researching Lewis and Clark's adventure. Then have students role-play their adventure to show how Sacagawea helped Lewis and Clark travel through the western part of North America.

Extension Activity

Write a Poem Encourage students to review the lesson. Then ask students to name important points from the lesson. For example, they may say that the settlers being helped by American Indians is an important point. Record their answers. Guide students in writing a brief poem about one of the important points listed. Invite them to draw pictures to go along with their poems. Have volunteers read their poems aloud to the class.

Integrate the Curriculum

Arts

Experiment with Paint Have students look at the image of Sacagawea on page 104. Ask students to tell what type of art this is most like. Have students describe the artwork as a painting. Then give students painting supplies. Have them experiment with painting to make a picture of something described in this lesson.

Lesson 4

PAGES 103–108

Lesson

Remembering Our Past

We know that it is important to remember the past. People have different ways of remembering the past. Some people visit landmarks. A **landmark** is a symbol that is a place people can visit. **What might you learn about the history of a community?**

Possible response: I might learn different ways people remember the past.

Bodie Island Lighthouse in North Carolina

NORTH CAROLINA STANDARD COURSE OF STUDY

4.04 Trace the historical foundations of traditions of various neighborhoods and communities.

103

Start with the Objective

Objective 4.04 Trace the historical foundations of traditions of various neighborhoods and communities.

Set a Purpose for Reading

Read and discuss the lesson objective with students. Then have them read the lesson introduction with a partner. Before students answer the question at the end of the introduction, model thinking by using the Think Aloud below.

Think Aloud

I know that some landmarks help remind us about important people and events that took place in the past. I think that I will read about landmarks found in North Carolina. I will also learn about other ways that people remember the past.

BACKGROUND

Bodie Island Lighthouse Point out the lighthouse in this photograph. Tell students that it is located on Bodie Island off the coast of North Carolina. This lighthouse is the third lighthouse built on the island. The first lighthouse began to tip over because it did not have a solid foundation. The second lighthouse was destroyed during the Civil War. The third lighthouse, the one in this photograph, was completed in 1872. Visitors may climb 214 steps to reach the top.

SOCIAL STUDIES STRANDS

Geographic Relationships Point out to students that *landmark* is a compound word made of the two words *land* and *mark*. They can use these two words to understand one meaning of *landmark*—a place where the land is marked by a symbol to remind us of an important person or event.

SSSMART™
SUPPORT

TextWork

1 Skim and Scan

Remind students that when they scan text, they read through it quickly, looking for important details. Point out the words *American Indians* and *showed* in the TextWork directions. Explain to students that they can scan the text to find these words. Doing so will help them find something that American Indians showed the new settlers how to do.

1 Name one thing American Indians showed new settlers how to do.

grow food

American Indians

American Indians helped new settlers. A **settler** is a person who makes a home in a new community. American Indians showed the settlers how to grow food. They grew corn and potatoes.

Biography

Trustworthiness

Sacagawea

Sacagawea was a Shoshone Indian. As a young woman, Sacagawea met Meriwether Lewis and William Clark. They wanted to go through the western part of North America. Sacagawea said that she would be their guide. She helped them in many ways.

104

TEACHING YOUR SOCIAL STUDIES

BACKGROUND

Sacagawea Sacagawea has long been celebrated as a heroine of American history. Her navigational abilities, along with her personal strength, have made her tale legendary. To honor her, a one-dollar gold coin bearing her image was created by the United States Mint. Though more statues, streams, lakes, landmarks, and poems have been named for this woman than any other woman in history, there is no record of her likeness.

SOCIAL STUDIES STRANDS

Cultures and Diversity The Shoshone are also known as the Snake Nation. They lived on both sides of the Rocky Mountains in the western part of the United States. Those who lived east of the mountains developed a culture based on the plains, where they lived. They hunted buffalo and lived in teepees. Sacagawea's family was part of this group of Eastern Plains Shoshone.

SSSMART™ SUPPORT

Today, many American Indians live in North Carolina. One of these groups is the Cherokee. There is a city in North Carolina called Cherokee.

There is a special landmark in Mount Gilead, North Carolina. It is called the Town Creek Indian Mound. Here, people can learn how American Indians lived long ago.

TextWork

2 Circle the name of one American Indian landmark that you can visit in North Carolina.

Cherokee Doll

TextWork

2 Vocabulary

Understand Vocabulary
Remind students that a landmark is a place that people can visit. Tell them to read the second paragraph to find such a place.

SOCIAL STUDIES STRANDS

Geographic Relationships Tell students that the Cherokee have a long history in North Carolina. According to legend, the Cherokee have lived in North Carolina since before European settlers arrived. Today, many Cherokee still live in North Carolina, blending tradition with modern ways of life.

BACKGROUND

Town Creek Indian Mound The Town Creek Indian Mound provides us with an example of early American Indian life. There, archaeologists have discovered that the Pee Dee built mounds in the center of their villages and used the mounds for religious purposes. They held meetings and ceremonies in the town center as well. Archaeologists have carefully dug up what is left of the old settlement so that people today can see what life was like for the Pee Dee who built it many years ago.

SSSMART™ SUPPORT

TextWork

3 Comprehension

Draw Conclusions Help students decide what the Latin American Festival shows about the culture. Have them read the last paragraph and circle the activities that take place at the festival. Tell them to use those details to draw a conclusion about what the Latin American Festival shows about the culture.

3 Look at the picture. What does it show about Latin American culture?

It shows dancing and clothes.

The Latin American Festival

The Latin American Festival is held each year in Charlotte, North Carolina. It celebrates Latin American culture and history.

The Latin American Festival has music and dancing. There is Latin American art. There is also food from Latin American culture.

Latin American Dancers

TEACHING YOUR SOCIAL STUDIES

BACKGROUND

Latin American Festival The first Latin American Festival was held in 1990. Point to the dancers in the photograph on this page. Tell students that each year, musicians and folk dancers from many different Latin American countries perform at the festival. The dancers wear traditional bright costumes. During the festival, people can see exhibits of Latin American art from the Mint Museum. There is also a special area with activities for children.

SOCIAL STUDIES STRANDS

Cultures and Diversity Point out to students that events like the Latin American Festival are a way for people to remember the parts of their culture that are important to them. Festivals are also a good way to learn about other cultures.

Highland Games

Highland Games celebrate Scottish culture and history. The Foothills Highland Games and Festival takes place every year in Hendersonville, North Carolina. At the Foothills Highland Games and Festival, people eat Scottish food and play Scottish games. They also wear special Scottish clothes and dance to Scottish music.

TextWork

4 What culture do people celebrate at the Foothills Highland Games and Festival?

Scottish

Scottish Bagpipe Players

TextWork

4 Comprehension

Recall and Retell Tell students to read the last two sentences of this paragraph. Ask them to recall the name of the culture celebrated at the Foothills Highland Games and Festival.

BACKGROUND

Scottish North Carolinians A long time ago, people from Scotland moved to the United States and brought their culture with them. Some of these people moved to North Carolina. Every year, the people of Hendersonville celebrate their Scottish traditions.

Lesson Review

Summary Have students work in pairs to summarize the key content before they complete the Lesson Review.

- People remember the past by attending festivals and visiting landmarks.
- A landmark is a place that people visit. It is a symbol of an important event or idea.
- At festivals, people play games, watch performers sing and dance, and eat food that reminds them of their cultural traditions.

Lesson 4 Review

1. **SUMMARIZE** Why do you think people celebrate their culture from long ago?

   Possible response: People celebrate their culture to remember the past and to have fun.

2. Tell about a **landmark** in your state.

   Possible response: The Town Creek Indian Mound is a landmark in North Carolina. People go there to learn about American Indians.

3. What are some of the ways people take part in the Latin American festival?

   Possible response: They play music. They dance, eat Latin American food, and look at Latin American art.

Writing

Write sentences about the ways different communities in North Carolina remember their past.

108

WRITING RUBRIC

Score 4
- sentences cover all of the topics covered in the lesson
- has no errors

Score 3
- sentences cover most of the topics covered in the lesson
- has few errors

Score 2
- sentences cover some of the topics covered in the lesson
- has some errors

Score 1
- sentences cover few of the topics covered in the lesson
- has many errors

Unit 4

Review and Test Prep

The Big Idea

On holidays, we remember special events and people.

Summarize the Unit

Draw Conclusions Fill in the chart. Show what you know about celebrations.

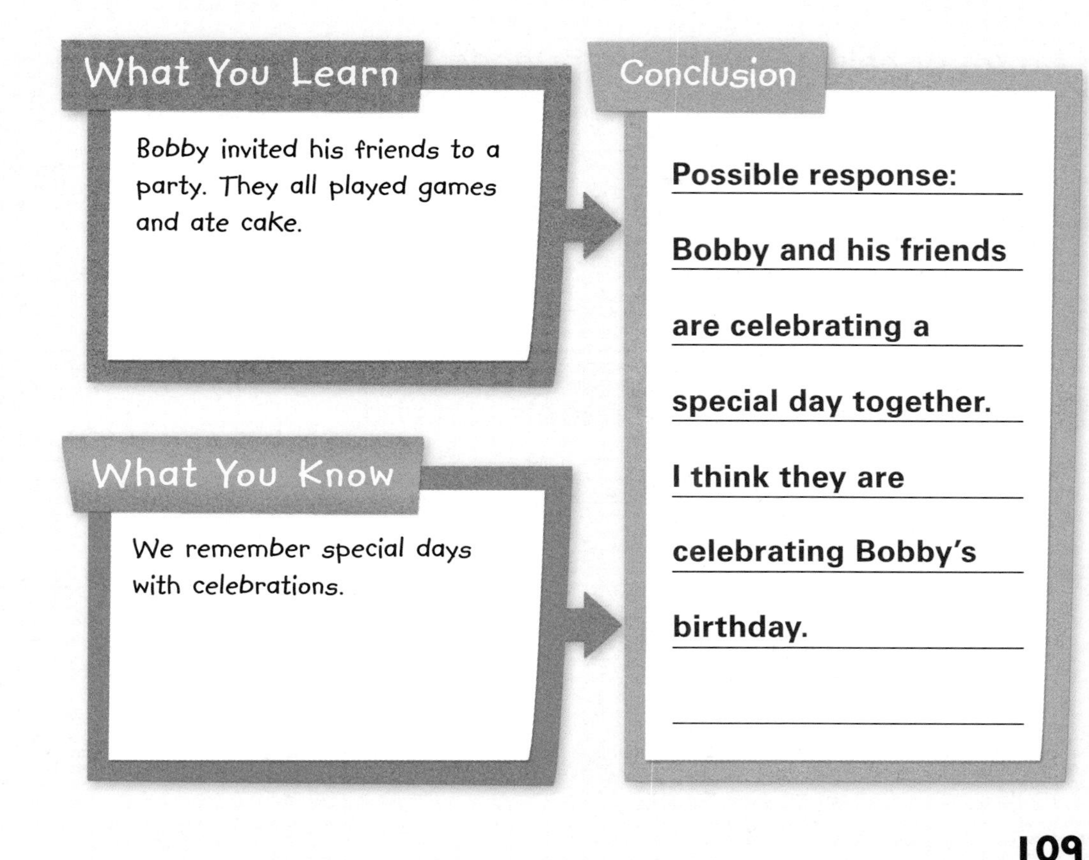

109

Unit Review

PAGES 109–112

The Big Idea

Ask students to review the unit's Big Idea. Invite students to share something they learned in this unit that supports the idea that holidays celebrate special events and people. Students should give examples that show what they have learned about symbols and heroes.

Summarize the Unit

Draw Conclusions Invite students to review the Reading Social Studies at the beginning of the unit. Ask students to think about what they already know about holidays and celebrations. Then ask them to think about what they have learned about holidays and celebrations from this unit. Help them use this knowledge to draw a conclusion on the graphic organizer.

READING FOCUS SKILLS

Draw Conclusions

What You Learn

What You Know

Conclusion

TRANSPARENCY

Graphic Organizer Write-On/ Wipe-Off Cards available

ASSESSMENT

Use the **UNIT 4 TEST** on pages 13–16 of the Assessment Program.

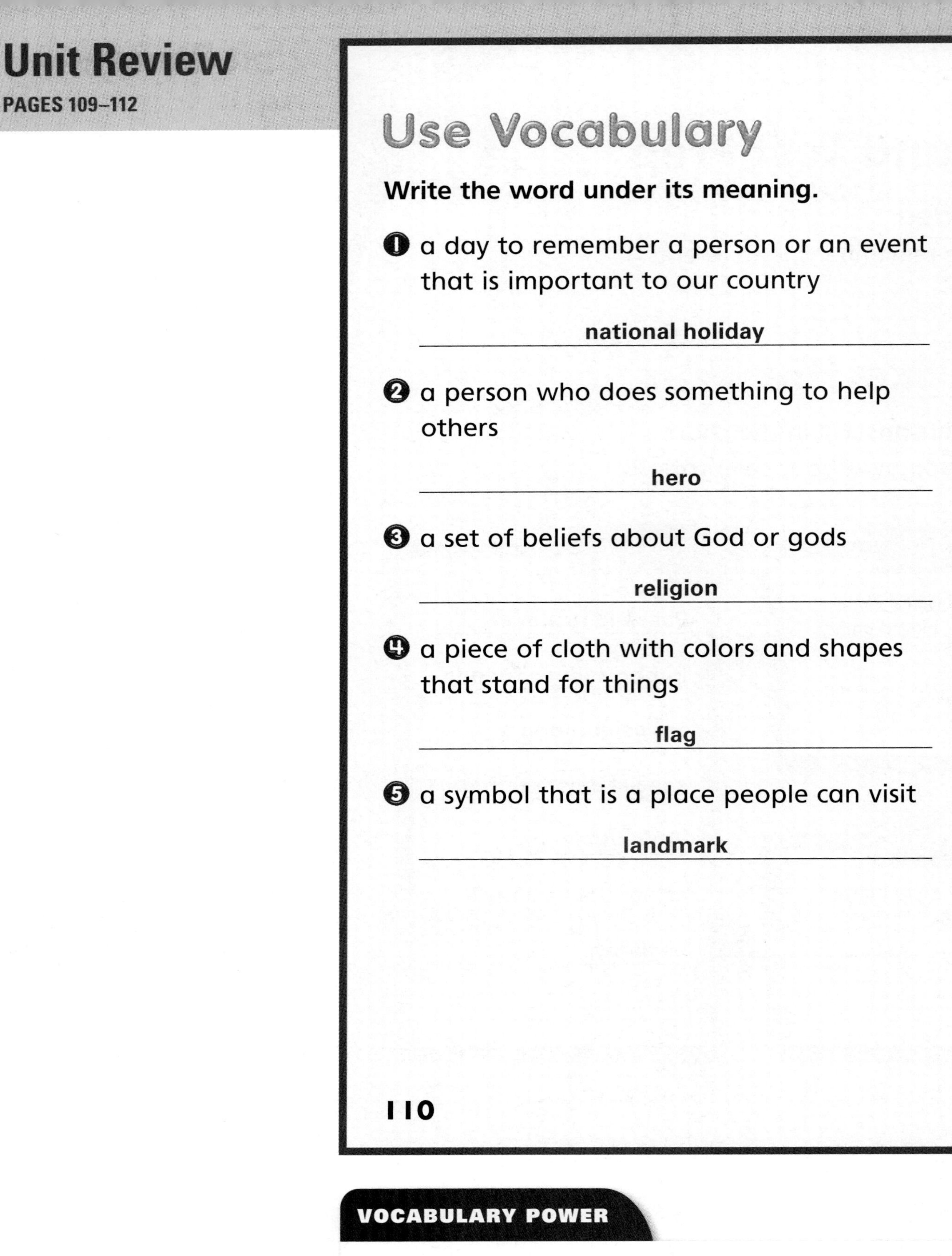

Use Vocabulary

Write the word under its meaning.

Word Bank
flag p. 87
religion p. 92
national holiday p. 97
hero p. 97
landmark p. 103

1. a day to remember a person or an event that is important to our country

   national holiday

2. a person who does something to help others

   hero

3. a set of beliefs about God or gods

   religion

4. a piece of cloth with colors and shapes that stand for things

   flag

5. a symbol that is a place people can visit

   landmark

110

VOCABULARY POWER

Word Parts Have students review the words *national holiday*, *landmark*, and *settler*. Show each word, one at a time. Ask students to find other words within the words. For example: *national* (*nation*), *landmark* (*land* and *mark*), and *settler* (*settle*). Point out that some unfamiliar words can be broken down into smaller, more recognizable words. Help students use the word parts as another way to find the meaning of each of these words.

Think About It

Circle the letter of the correct answer.

6. Which is a symbol of North Carolina?
   - **A** the rose
   - **B** the bald eagle
   - **C** the blue wolf
   - **(D)** the gray squirrel

7. Which holiday honors Mexico?
   - **(A)** Cinco de Mayo
   - **B** St. Patrick's Day
   - **C** the Cherry Blossom Festival
   - **D** Chinese New Year

8. Which is a national holiday?
   - **A** Vesak
   - **B** Kwanzaa
   - **(C)** Independence Day
   - **D** Holi

9. Which of these symbols is a landmark?
   - **A** flag
   - **(B)** Town Creek Indian Mound
   - **C** rose
   - **D** bald eagle

111

READ MORE

Encourage independent reading with these books or books of your choice.

Basic

You're a Grand Old Flag by George M. Cohan. Walker Books for Young Readers, 2007. Presents the complete text of this patriotic song with beautiful illustrations.

Proficient

The Pledge of Allegiance: Symbols of Freedom by Lola Schaefer. Heinemann, 2002. A discussion of the Pledge of Allegiance and other symbols of America.

Advanced

Children Just Like Me: Celebrations! by Anabel and Barnabas Kindersley. DK CHILDREN, 1997. A multicultural look at holidays.

Unit Review

PAGES 109–112

Show What You Know

Writing
Write a Poem

Ask students to think about our country's symbols and landmarks. Then review the structure of poems. Remind students of rhyme patterns and refer to examples.

Activity
Plan a Patriotic Party

Explain the meaning of patriotic. Then organize the class into pairs and explain each pair's responsibilities. During the party, make sure each child has a role to play in the presentation.

North Carolina Adventures

Remind students that this game will review the concepts in the unit.

Spotlight on Goals and Objectives

Use North Carolina Interactive Presentations, Unit 4, to review concepts from the unit.

Answer each question in a complete sentence.

10. What are some holidays that celebrate a religion?

Possible response: Some holidays that celebrate a religion are Christmas, Hanukkah, Ramadan, Vesak, and Holi.

11. Why do we celebrate national holidays?

Possible response: We celebrate national holidays to remember a time or a person who is important to our country.

12. What does a settler do?

Possible response: A settler is a person who makes a home in a new community.

Show What You Know

Writing **Write a Poem**
Think about a famous symbol or landmark. Why is it a good symbol or landmark? Write a poem about it.

Activity **Plan a Patriotic Party**
Plan to celebrate an American hero, holiday, symbol, or landmark. Make invitations and classroom decorations.

GO online To play a game that reviews the unit, join Eco in the North Carolina Adventures online or on CD.

112

WRITING RUBRIC

Score 4
- shows a clear understanding of symbols or landmarks
- describes many details clearly related to the symbol
- uses a creative poem structure that is easy to read

Score 3
- shows some understanding of symbols or landmarks
- describes some details related to the symbol
- uses a poem structure that is mostly easy to read

Score 2
- shows little understanding of symbols or landmarks
- describes details not always related to the symbol
- uses a poem structure that is incomplete and difficult to read

Score 1
- shows no understanding of symbols or landmarks
- does not describe details, or details are not related to the symbol
- does not use a poem structure

ACTIVITY RUBRIC

Score 4
- shows a clear understanding of patriotic symbols and holidays
- presents creative details that support a patriotic topic
- is well-prepared and very organized

Score 3
- shows some understanding of patriotic symbols and holidays
- presents some details that support a patriotic topic
- is prepared and organized

Score 2
- shows little understanding of patriotic symbols and holidays
- presents few details that support a patriotic topic
- is somewhat prepared and organized

Score 1
- shows no understanding of patriotic symbols and holidays
- presents no details to support a patriotic topic
- is ill-prepared and disorganized

Unit 5
Where People Live

NORTH CAROLINA STANDARD COURSE OF STUDY

COMPETENCY GOAL 5

The learner will express geographic concepts in real life situations.

OBJECTIVES

5.01 Locate and describe familiar places in the home, classroom, and school.

5.02 Investigate key features of maps.

5.03 Use geographic terminology and tools to create representations of the earth's physical and human features through simple maps, models, and pictures.

5.04 Analyze patterns of movement within the community.

5.05 Demonstrate responsibility for the care and management of the environment within the school and community.

5.06 Compare and contrast geographic features of places within various communities.

5.07 Explore physical features of continents and major bodies of water.

LESSON	TOTAL: 29 DAYS	NORTH CAROLINA STANDARD COURSE OF STUDY
Introduce the Unit **Unit Preview,** pp. 113–114 **The Big Idea,** p. 114 **Reading Social Studies,** pp. 115–116 Focus Skill Categorize and Classify	**2** DAYS	**COMPETENCY GOAL 5** **The learner will express geographic concepts in real life situations.** **Spotlight on Goals and Objectives** Unit 5
1 **At Home and at School** pp. 117–122 **location** p. 117	**5** DAYS	**Objective 5.01** Locate and describe familiar places in the home, classroom, and school. **Objective 5.03** Use geographic terminology and tools to create representations of the earth's physical and human features through simple maps, models, and pictures. **Spotlight on Goals and Objectives** Unit 5, Lesson 1
2 **Finding Where You Are** pp. 123–128 **neighborhood** p. 123 **state** p. 124 **border** p. 125 **continent** p. 126	**5** DAYS	**Objective 5.02** Investigate key features of maps. **Objective 5.03** Use geographic terminology and tools to create representations of the earth's physical and human features through simple maps, models, and pictures. **Spotlight on Goals and Objectives** Unit 5, Lesson 2
3 **Land and Water** pp. 129–134 **mountain** p. 130 **hill** p. 130 **valley** p. 131 **plain** p. 131 **ocean** p. 133	**5** DAYS	**Objective 5.06** Compare and contrast geographic features of places within various communities. **Objective 5.07** Explore physical features of continents and major bodies of water. **Spotlight on Goals and Objectives** Unit 5, Lesson 3

TEACHING YOUR SOCIAL STUDIES

Comprehension,
Categorize and Classify, pp. 115–116

Background,
North Carolina Zoo, p. 117
Maps and Safety, p. 120

Social Studies Strands,
Geographic Relationships, pp. 117, 118, 121
Individual Development and Identity, p. 119

Build Skills,
Map and Globe Skills, pp. 118, 119, 120

CUES, pp. 118, 119, 120

Vocabulary, p. 121

Comprehension,
Categorize and Classify, p. 121

Background,
Using Maps, p. 123
North Carolina Traffic Signs, p. 124
Continents, p. 126

Social Studies Strands,
Geographic Relationships, pp. 123, 125
Global Connections, pp. 126, 127

Build Skills,
Map and Globe Skills, pp. 124, 125, 127

CUES, pp. 124, 125, 126

Comprehension,
Monitor Understanding, p.127

Background,
Great Smoky Mountains, p. 129
Grandfather Mountain, p. 130
Maggie Valley, p. 131
Fontana Lake, p. 132
Oceans, p. 133

Social Studies Strands,
Geographic Relationships, p. 129
Global Connections, p. 130

Build Skills,
Map and Globe Skills, p. 131
Chart and Graph Skills, p. 132
Problem Solving, p. 133

Vocabulary, p.130

Skim and Scan, pp. 131, 133

CUES, p. 132

Print Resources

Student Edition, pp. 113–146
Teacher Edition, pp. 113A–146
Leveled Readers
Leveled Readers Teacher Guides
Document-Based Questions
Primary Atlas

Technology/Digital Resources

Spotlight on Goals and Objectives
North Carolina Interactive Presentations CD
North Carolina Interactive Presentations Online

Online Teacher Edition with ePlanner
Leveled Readers Online Database
North Carolina Adventures CD
North Carolina Adventures Online
Multimedia Biographies CD
Multimedia Biographies Online
Social Studies Music Collection CD

Hands-On Resources

Reading Focus Skills Transparencies
Social Studies Skills Transparencies
Graphic Organizer Write-On/Wipe-Off Cards
Interactive Atlas
Interactive Desk Maps
Interactive Map Transparencies
Picture Vocabulary Cards
Primary Source Kit
TimeLinks: Interactive Time Line
Social Studies in Action, pp. 28–36, 38–39, 143, 149, 152–156

Assessment Options

1. **Unit 5 Test**
   Assessment Program, pp. 17–20
2. **Writing**
   Write a Letter, p. 146
3. **Activity**
   Unit Project: Make a Mural, p. 146

LESSON		NORTH CAROLINA STANDARD COURSE OF STUDY
4 People and Places pp. 135–138 **city** p. 135 **suburb** p. 136 **farm** p. 137	**4 DAYS**	**Objective 5.04** Analyze patterns of movement within the community. **Spotlight on Goals and Objectives** Unit 5, Lesson 4
5 People Use Resources pp. 139–142 **resource** p. 139 **recycle** p. 141	**4 DAYS**	**Objective 5.05** Demonstrate responsibility for the care and management of the environment within the school and community. **Spotlight on Goals and Objectives** Unit 5, Lesson 5
Unit 5 Review and Test Prep pp. 143–146	**4 DAYS**	**North Carolina Adventures** Unit 5

TEACHING YOUR SOCIAL STUDIES

Background,
Raleigh, North Carolina, p. 135
Commuting, p. 136
Strawberry Farms, p. 137

Social Studies Strands,
Geographic Relationships, pp. 135, 137

Build Skills,
Chart and Graph Skills, p. 136

Background,
Gardens, p. 139
Conrad Reed, p. 140

Social Studies Strands,
Government and Active Citizenship, p. 139
Economics and Development, p. 140
Individual Development and Identity, p. 141

Build Skills,
Chart and Graph Skills, p. 141

SSSMART SUPPORT

Comprehension,
Focus Skill Categorize and Classify, p. 136

Skim and Scan, p. 137

CUES, p. 140

Skim and Scan, p. 141

Summarize the Unit,
Focus Skill Categorize and Classify, p. 143

Print Resources

Student Edition, pp. 113–146
Teacher Edition, pp. 113A–146
Leveled Readers
Leveled Readers Teacher Guides
Document-Based Questions
Primary Atlas

Technology/Digital Resources

Spotlight on Goals and Objectives
North Carolina Interactive Presentations CD
North Carolina Interactive Presentations Online

Online Teacher Edition with ePlanner
Leveled Readers Online Database
North Carolina Adventures CD
North Carolina Adventures Online
Multimedia Biographies CD
Multimedia Biographies Online
Social Studies Music Collection CD

Hands-On Resources

Reading Focus Skills Transparencies
Social Studies Skills Transparencies
Graphic Organizer Write-On/Wipe-Off Cards
Interactive Atlas
Interactive Desk Maps
Interactive Map Transparencies
Picture Vocabulary Cards
Primary Source Kit
TimeLinks: Interactive Time Line
Social Studies in Action, pp. 28–36, 38–39, 143, 149, 152–156

Assessment Options

1. **Unit 5 Test**
   Assessment Program, pp. 17–20
2. **Writing**
   Write a Letter, p. 146
3. **Activity**
   Unit Project: Make a Mural, p. 146

Leveled Readers

BELOW-LEVEL

My Town

Summary *My Town.* This Reader describes the different kinds of land, bodies of water, and communities where people live and the resources people use.

Vocabulary Power Have students define the following words. Help them write one sentence for each word as it relates to where people live.

location
resource
weather
state
shelter

Critical Thinking Lead students in a discussion about the location of their school. Encourage them to think about the nearby community, the land and water, the resources, and the weather.

Write a Story Have students write a story about a community that they have visited. Tell students to include a description of the buildings, land, and people.

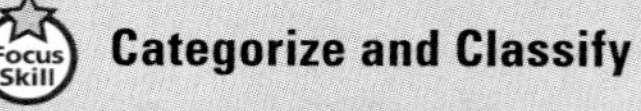
Categorize and Classify

ON-LEVEL

We Live Here

Summary *We Live Here.* This Reader describes the regions and lifeways of three unique peoples—the Inuit, the Tuareg, and the Yanomami.

Vocabulary Power Have students define the following words. Help them write one sentence for each word as it relates to where people live.

location
resource
village
rain forest

Critical Thinking Lead students in a discussion about how weather can affect how people live.

Write a Question Have students write a question that they would like to ask an Inuit, a Tuareg, or a Yanomami person. Encourage students to think of questions not answered in the Reader.

Categorize and Classify

ABOVE-LEVEL

Fighting Back the Sea

Summary *Fighting Back the Sea.* This Reader describes the challenges the Dutch face living on low, flat land next to the North Sea.

Vocabulary Power Have students define the following words. Help them write one sentence for each word as it relates to where people live.

location
resource
country
farm
dike

Critical Thinking Lead students in a discussion about why the Dutch needed to push back the sea.

Write a Description Ask students to write a short description of a dike. Tell them they can write about an early Dutch dike or a modern dike.

Categorize and Classify

Complete a Graphic Organizer

Have students complete the graphic organizer to show that they understand how to categorize and classify information about where people live.

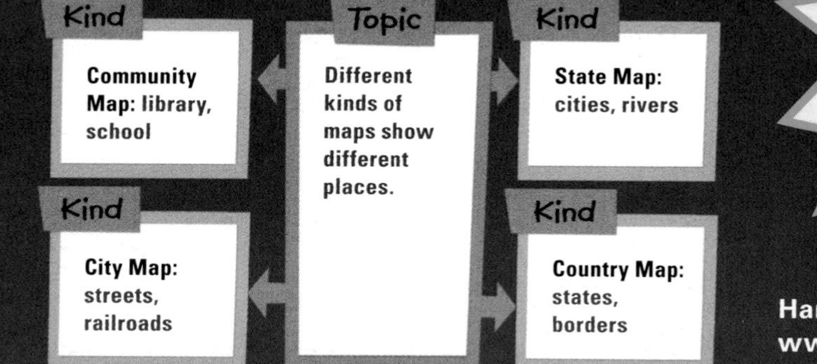

Leveled Readers Teacher Guides include complete lesson plans, copying masters, and project cards.

Harcourt Leveled Readers Available Online!
www.harcourtschool.com

Make a Mural

Getting Started

Introduce the Hands-On Activity on page 146 in the Unit Review as you begin Unit 5. Have students develop the project as they learn more about the ways in which location affects how people live. Explain that a mural is a large artwork in which pictures are used to show things related to a subject. The artwork should express the students' in-depth understanding of the unit's Big Idea.

The Big Idea
How do people use maps and globes to tell about places?

Project Management

- Have the class work together to brainstorm details for the mural.
- Encourage students to include physical characteristics of the places where they live and the things physical characteristics affect.

Materials: Social Studies textbook; wall panels made of posterboard; pencils; markers; paint; pictorial map or pictures of your area

Organizer: Have students use a chart to take notes as they brainstorm. Invite them to record important details.

ORGANIZER

What Our Mural Could Show	
Environment	**North Carolina**
Land and water	
Shelters and other buildings	
Transportation	
Foods	
Weather	
Recreation	

During the Unit

As students read Unit 5, they can begin work on their mural. Murals can include:

- Lesson Review activities
- Your own favorite activities
- Ideas students develop on their own

Complete the Project

Assist students in painting their mural by working with small groups to sketch a background for the mural. Have individuals or partners draw and color details on the mural. Encourage students to practice asking and answering questions about details on the mural.

What to Look For

For a scoring rubric, see page 146 of this Teacher Edition.

- Students can recall how location, weather, and physical features affect how they live.
- The mural is detailed and reflects physical characteristics of students' environment.

Technology/Digital Resources

START

North Carolina Interactive Presentations

Purpose

The North Carolina Interactive Presentation Unit 5 can be used to preview Unit 5. This presentation provides a concise, visual overview of Competency Goal 5 and its objectives. You can use it to preview the unit for the class, or throughout the unit to introduce and reinforce individual objectives.

Contents

The Unit 5 presentation includes an introduction to Competency Goal 5, including a vocabulary preview and a visual introduction to using geographic concepts. In addition, the presentation covers all the unit's objectives lesson by lesson, giving the students a broad overview of North Carolina's geography.

REVIEW

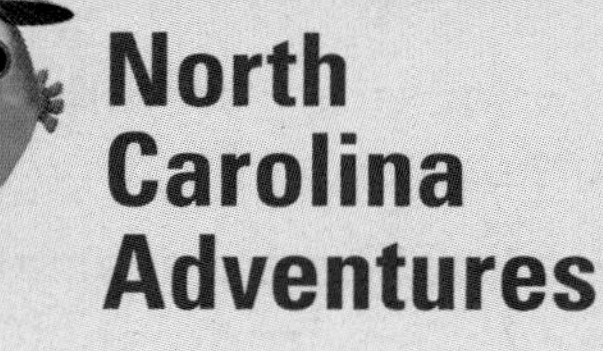

North Carolina Adventures

Purpose

The North Carolina Adventures games, offered both on CD and online, provide an entertaining first-person-player method of content review. When students have completed the unit, they can review its competency goal and all objectives through the Unit 5 game.

Contents

Tell students they will use their knowledge of geography to compete in events at field day. Throughout, students will review what they have learned about maps, cultures, and the environment. Explain that the "Help" buttons in the game will refer them to pages in their textbooks if they need additional information.

Additional Resources

For Teachers

Free and Inexpensive Materials are listed on the Social Studies website at **www.harcourtschool.com/ss1**

- Addresses to write to for free and inexpensive products
- Links to unit-related materials
- Internet maps
- Internet references

The eTE with ePlanner provides the following components

- A calendar tool for scheduling Social Studies lessons and displaying all scheduled lessons and activities
- TE pages and additional resources for easy online reference

For Students

When students visit **www.harcourtschool.com/ss1** they will find internal resources such as

- Our Multimedia Biographies database
- Skills activities
- Additional research tools
- Information about all 50 states

Where People Live

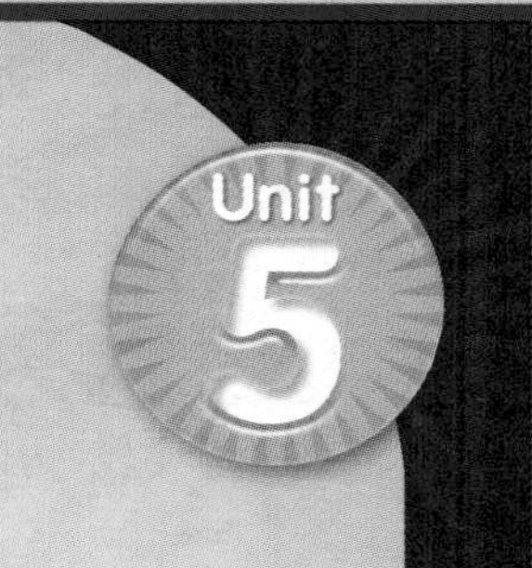

A family walks on the beach in Bald Head Island, North Carolina.

Spotlight on Goals and Objectives

North Carolina Interactive Presentations

NORTH CAROLINA STANDARD COURSE OF STUDY

COMPETENCY GOAL 5 The learner will express geographic concepts in real life situations.

113

Unit 5 Preview

PAGES 113–114

Start with the Competency Goal

Competency Goal 5 The learner will express geographic concepts in real life situations.

Make It Relevant

Read and discuss the unit competency goal. Ask the following question to help students understand the different places where people can live.

Q What are some things that people may live near?

A Students may mention that people may live near water, mountains, or farms.

Discuss the Photograph

Explain to students that some people live near bodies of water and beaches. Have students look at the photograph and point out that families can enjoy many different activities when visiting the beach. Discuss how this family is enjoying the beach.

Instructional Design

START WITH THE GOAL AND OBJECTIVES

NORTH CAROLINA STANDARD COURSE OF STUDY

- competency goal
- objectives

PLAN ASSESSMENT

Assessment Options

- Option 1–Unit 5 Test
- Option 2–Writing: Write a Letter, p. 146
- Option 3–Activity: Make a Mural, p. 146

PLAN INSTRUCTION

Spotlight on Goals and Objectives
North Carolina Interactive Presentations, Unit 5

Unit 5 Teacher Edition

- resources
- activities
- strategies

Unit 5 Leveled Readers Teacher Guides

Unit 5 Preview

PAGES 113–114

The Big Idea

Have students read The Big Idea question and then preview how people use maps and globes to tell about places.

Access Prior Knowledge

Display a map of the world. Ask students to name things on the map that are familiar to them. Point out the differences between countries, continents, and bodies of water. Have students read the paragraph and complete the activity.

The Big Idea

How do people use maps and globes to tell about places?

People live in many different places. Some people live near water. Other people live on hills. We can tell about where we live by using maps and globes. We can also use these tools to find out about new places.

Draw a picture of the place where you live.

Drawing should show that student understands the concept of places.

114

READ MORE

Encourage independent reading with these books or books of your choice.

Basic

Hello Ocean by Pam Muñoz Ryan. Charlesbridge Publishing, 2001. A young girl relates her experiences at the beach.

Proficient

Hottest, Coldest, Highest, Deepest by Steve Jenkins. Houghton Mifflin, 2004. Describes some of the remarkable places on Earth.

Advanced

Shelterwood by Susan Hand Shetterly. Tilbury House Publishers, 2003. While staying with her grandfather, Sophie learns about nature and the different kinds of trees.

Reading Social Studies

Focus Skill: Categorize and Classify

Learn

- When you categorize and classify, you sort things into groups.
- Decide what each group will be called.
- Place each thing in a group.

Practice

Read the paragraph below. Underline the category of places you go to shop. Then circle the places that can be classified as places to shop.

There are many different places in your community. There are places you go to learn, like schools and libraries. There are places you go to shop, like malls and grocery stores.

Categorize

Classify

Reading Social Studies PAGES 115–116

Learn

Have students read the Learn section and look at the graphic organizer. Explain to students that they can *classify* different things into *categories*. For example, a crayon could be classified as an art supply. Construction paper, paint, and markers could also be classified in the category of art supplies.

Practice

Read the paragraph with students. Ask students which two categories are mentioned in the text. What places can be classified to fit into each category? Help students fill in the graphic organizer with the information.

READING FOCUS SKILLS

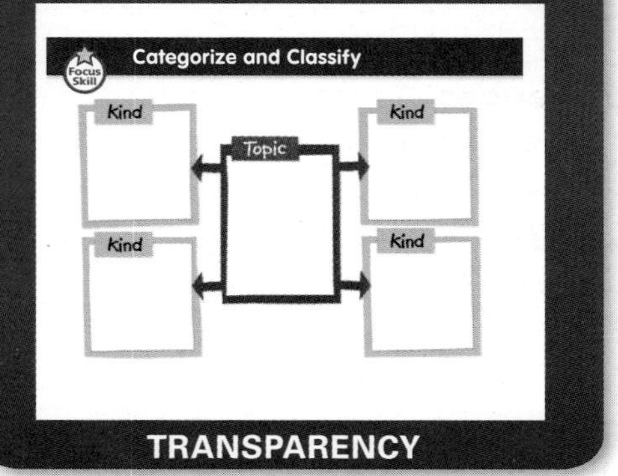

TRANSPARENCY

Graphic Organizer Write-On/ Wipe-Off Cards available

INTEGRATE THE CURRICULUM

ENGLISH LANGUAGE ARTS Make a Chart Ask students to think about the different kinds of landmark categories in their community. Students might suggest that there are buildings, parks, and houses. Have students make a chart identifying the different categories of landmarks and listing one or two examples within each category.

ELA 4.04 Extend skills in using oral and written language: completing graphic organizers.

Apply

This selection tells about some of the places in North Carolina that people might visit, including big cities and national parks. Ask students what four categories are mentioned in the text. Then, have them identify examples that can be classified into the categories. Help students write the information in their graphic organizers.

Unit 5 provides many opportunities for students to practice categorizing and classifying. As students read the unit, challenge them to think about how things from the lessons fit together into groups.

Apply

Read the paragraphs.

North Carolina has many places to visit. People go to cities like Raleigh and Charlotte. Families visit fun places like the North Carolina Zoo and the Jungle Rapids Family Fun Park.

Other people visit national parks such as the Blue Ridge Parkway or the Great Smoky Mountains. Some visit historic places like the Alamance Battleground or Fort Anderson.

The chart below shows places to visit. What can you add to the chart?

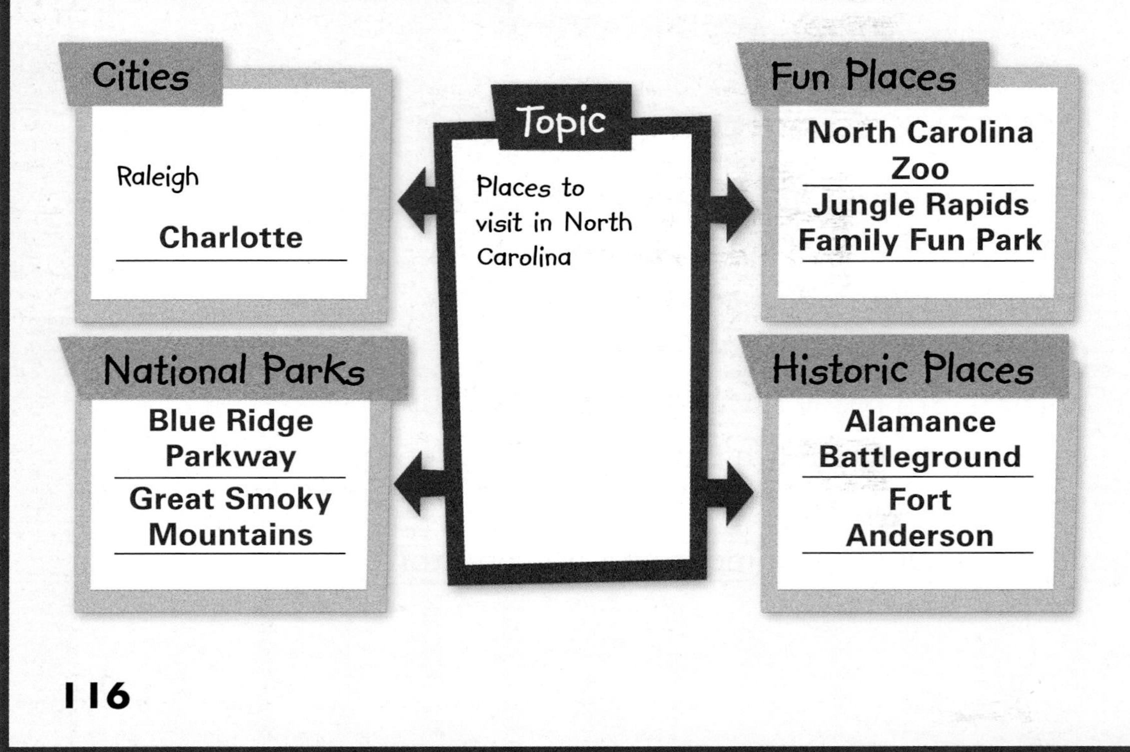

116

ESL/LANGUAGE SUPPORT

Vocabulary Development Ask students to identify some natural features, such as mountains or lakes, in their region. Make a display of the features on a wall or other large area in the classroom. As students read the unit, have them add words describing natural features to the word wall.

Prior Learning and Experiences As they read the unit, ask students to think about ways that people have adapted to different kinds of landscapes over time. How has life changed because of changes to the land? Have students write a sentence about one thing that is now different because of a change to the landscape.

At Home and at School

Lesson 1

PAGES 117–122

Build Background

Make It Relevant Display model airplanes, cars, and boats on a table next to photographs of these forms of transportation. Encourage students to discuss similarities and differences between the photographs and the models. Have students think about how photographs, maps, and models of places are the same and how they are different.

Preview the Lesson

Guide students in previewing the lesson. Point out the following features on Student Edition pages 117–122:

- **Page 117** Invite students to preview the photograph. Ask: "What is the girl in the photograph doing?" "Why would a map be helpful at a zoo?"
- **Page 118** Invite students to preview the photograph of Tim holding a map of his home. Ask why having a map of a home may be useful.
- **Pages 119–120** Explain that both classroom and school maps are helpful. Ask, "Why might a classroom map be helpful for a new student?" Then ask, "Why is it important for a school to have a map?" Point out that in case of emergencies, like a fire, it is important for teachers and students to know where to go.
- **Page 121** Invite students to preview the title of the section. Ask, "What is a model?" Encourage students to discuss models that they may have created.

Preteach Vocabulary

- Ask students to define the word **location** in their own words. Have students compose a list of locations where they have been that day or week. Encourage volunteers to describe those locations. Then ask students whether they have ever been to a location where they did not know their way around. Explain that maps help in those situations.

NORTH CAROLINA STANDARD COURSE OF STUDY

Objective 5.01 Locate and describe familiar places in the home, classroom, and school.

Objective 5.03 Use geographic terminology and tools to create representations of the earth's physical and human features through simple maps, models, and pictures.

Key Content Summary

- **Maps show locations in homes, classrooms, schools, and communities.**
- **Maps use symbols to show locations.**
- **Pictures and maps are flat, but you can look at a model from all sides.**

Vocabulary

- **location**, p. 117

Spotlight on Goals and Objectives

Use North Carolina Interactive Presentations, Unit 5, Lesson 1, to access prior knowledge and build background.

Reach All Learners

ESL/Language Support

Active Learning Create a map of the classroom. At the bottom of the map, write the names of the places in the classroom, such as coat closet, teacher's desk, and art center. Go over the map with students to determine which word goes with which place on the map. Then ask students to fill in the missing labels.

Extra Support

Complete a Word Web Provide students with short texts, such as brochures or pamphlets, that tell about specific locations. Direct students to underline the names of places. Guide them to create a word web about the location similar to the example shown.

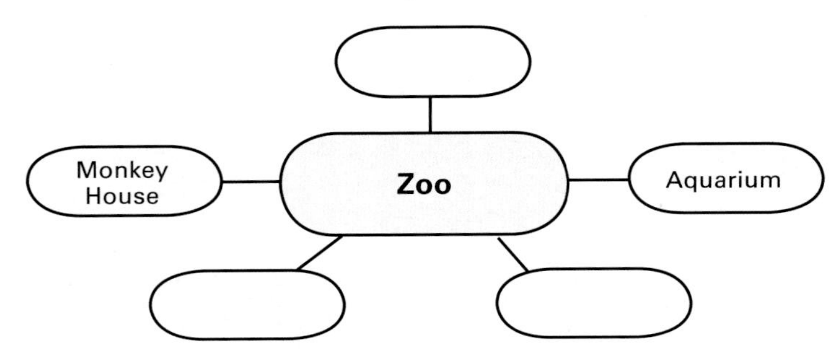

Extension Activity

Create a Map Provide students with materials to create a map. Have students make a map of their home and choose symbols for it. Encourage them to include features both inside and outside of the home, such as their bedroom, the kitchen, and the backyard. Have students clearly label their maps. Invite volunteers to share their maps with the class.

Integrate the Curriculum

English Language Arts

Classify Words Write the names of places in the community, at school, and at home on index cards. For example: store, first-grade classroom, and bedroom. Then write the following headings on chart paper: *Community*, *School*, and *Home*. Have students work in pairs to categorize the words appropriately and discuss their classifications.

ELA 4.04 Extend skills in using oral and written language: completing graphic organizers.

Lesson 1

PAGES 117–122

Lesson

At Home and at School

Maps show **location**, or where places are. Maps can show small places, such as parks. Maps can also show large places, such as communities. **What do you think you will learn about maps?**

Possible response: I might learn how to use maps to find locations in my home and my school.

Many people visit the North Carolina Zoo, in Asheboro.

NORTH CAROLINA STANDARD COURSE OF STUDY

5.01 Locate and describe familiar places in the home, classroom, and school.

5.03 Use geographic terminology and tools to create representations of the earth's physical and human features through simple maps, models, and pictures.

117

Start with the Objectives

Objective 5.01 Locate and describe familiar places in the home, classroom, and school.

Objective 5.03 Use geographic terminology and tools to create representations of the earth's physical and human features through simple maps, models, and pictures.

Set a Purpose for Reading

Read aloud the introduction with students. Introduce the highlighted word *location*. Have students identify the location of various places in the room. Then ask volunteers to share their answers to the question. Use the Think Aloud to model thinking about maps.

Think Aloud

We used a map when we drove to another town. I will read to learn more about how to use maps.

BACKGROUND

North Carolina Zoo The photograph shows the North Carolina Zoo in Asheboro. The zoo's website has downloadable maps of the zoo. The map shows the different exhibits in the two main sections of the zoo. Animals at the North Carolina Zoo are not kept in cages. They live on large tracts of land that are similar to their natural habitat.

SOCIAL STUDIES STRANDS

Geographic Relationships Display in the classroom a large map of the community. Help each student use a small circular sticker to mark different locations in the community, such as a store, a school, a library, or a post office.

SSSMART™ SUPPORT

TextWork

❶ CUES

Analyze/Interpret Maps With students, brainstorm a list of rooms in a home. Then read the map with students, identifying each room. Have students circle Tim's bedroom. Ask how they knew which room to circle.

❶ Circle Tim's room on the map he made.

At Home

You can use maps to show where things are in your home. Tim knows where to find things in his home. He drew a map of the inside of his home. The map shows the location of each room.

TEACHING YOUR SOCIAL STUDIES

BUILD SKILLS

MAP SKILL **Map and Globe Skills** Ask students to think of their bedroom at home or a bedroom they would like to have. Have them make a map of the room similar to Tim's map on page 118. You may consider having students complete the assignment as homework to encourage them to add more details that they may not recall at school.

SOCIAL STUDIES STRANDS

Geographic Relationships Review with students positional words such as *above, below, in front of, behind, right, left, over,* and *under*. Provide each student with a set of different-color cubes or other manipulatives. Give oral directions using positional words and have students carry them out. For example, you might say, "Put the blue cube beside the green cube."

In the Classroom

Tim knows the location of all the things in his classroom. Tim and his classmates are drawing a map of these places.

TextWork

❷ Look at the classroom map. Draw a box around the location of the reading area.

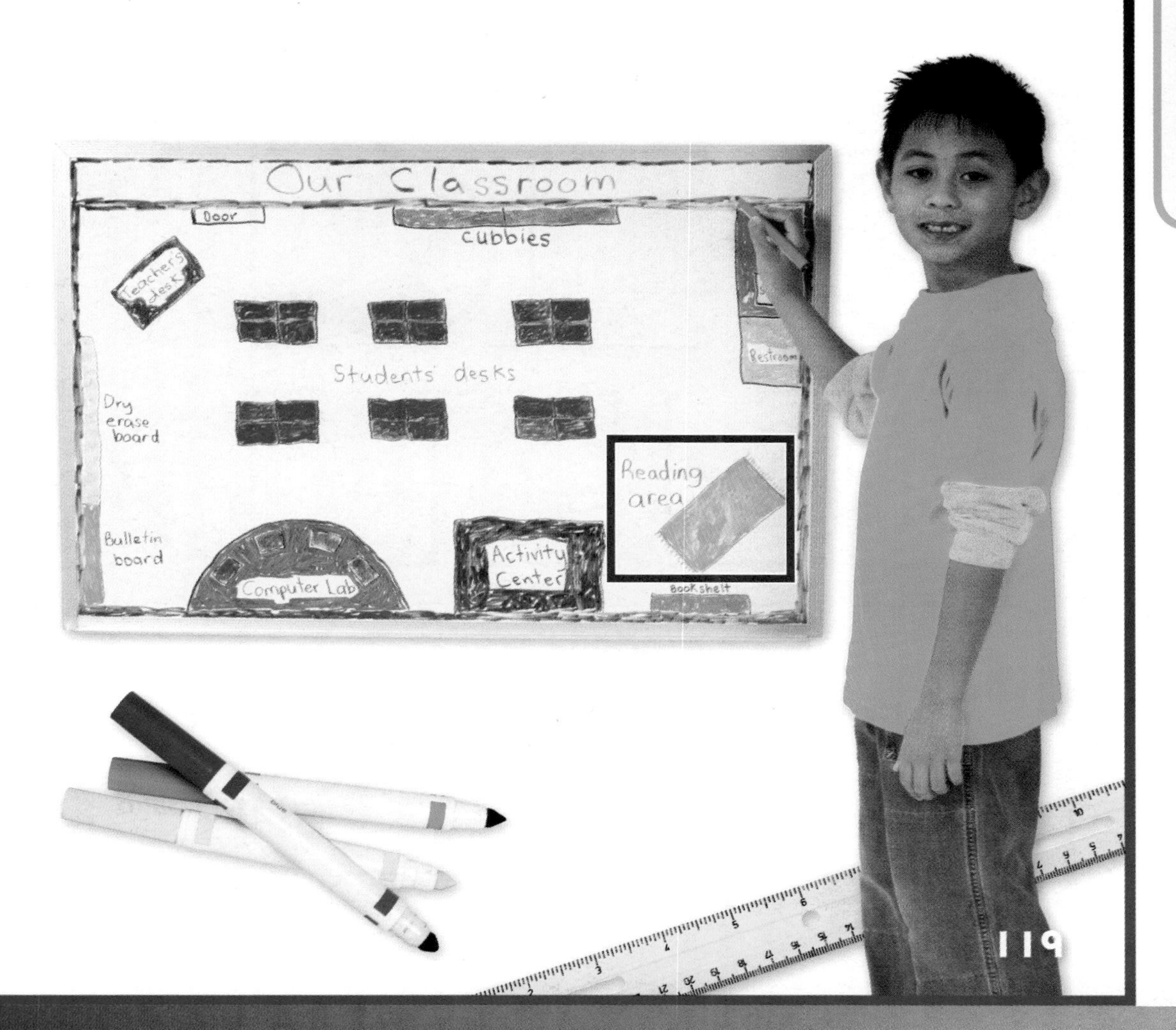

SSSMART™ SUPPORT

TextWork

❷ **CUES**

Analyze/Interpret Maps Read the map with students. Identify the location of the things on the classroom map. Then have students draw a box around the reading area. Have them describe the location. For example, students might say the reading area is to the right of the activity center.

SOCIAL STUDIES STRANDS

Individual Development and Identity Talk with students about times when you have used a map. Then encourage them to share descriptions of maps they have seen and describe the usefulness of those maps. Encourage dialogue about descriptions of how maps help us find our way.

BUILD SKILLS

MAP SKILL **Map And Globe Skills** Ask students to describe how the classroom looks when they walk in the door. Then ask them how it would look on a map. Explain that a map shows the classroom as though they were looking down into the room. Have them imagine that they could remove the roof of the classroom and peer in from above. This view would resemble a flat map of the classroom.

SSSMART™ SUPPORT

TextWork

3 CUES

Analyze/Interpret Maps After reading the text on the page, direct students' attention to the school map. Begin by reviewing the symbols in the Map Key. Then have students locate the symbol for the cafeteria on the school map. Ask them which rooms are next to the cafeteria. Have students circle those rooms. Encourage students to describe the location of those rooms to a partner.

3 Circle the rooms that are next to the cafeteria on the school map.

At School

Tim knows all the important places in his school. He even has a map of his school. The map of Tim's school has symbols. Symbols are pictures that stand for real things. The map key tells what the symbols mean.

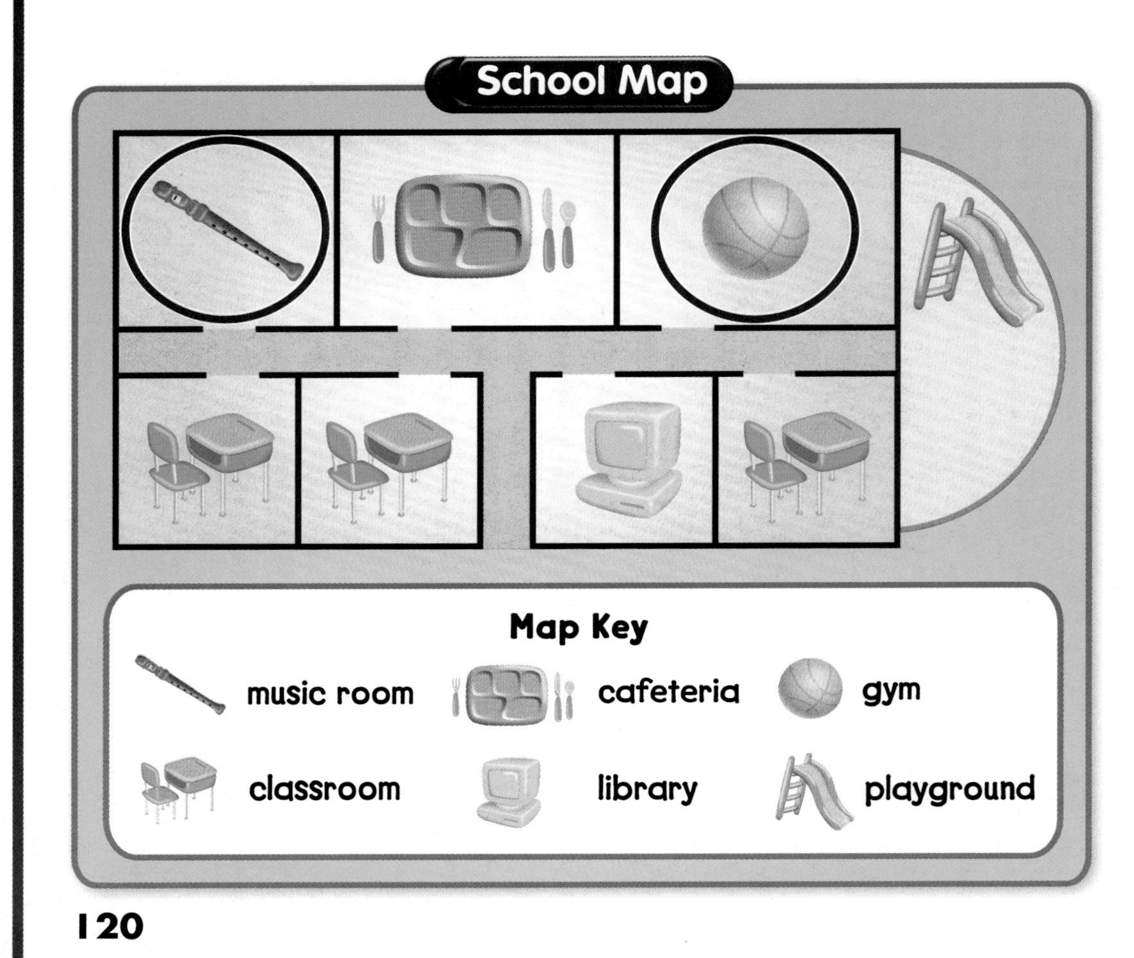

120

TEACHING YOUR SOCIAL STUDIES

BUILD SKILLS

MAP SKILL **Map and Globe Skills** Ask students questions about the map on the page. Questions should require students to use the Map Key. For example, you may ask, "Which symbol stands for the gym? What is across from the music room?"

BACKGROUND

Maps and Safety Maps are often used to show escape routes necessary to keep people safe in case of an emergency, such as a fire. Maps are often posted in hotels, schools, and other buildings to show the way to safety. Similar maps can be used for home safety plans.

Making a Model

Tim used the map of his classroom to make a model of his classroom. Pictures and maps are flat. You can look at a model from all sides. When you look down on it, it is like a map.

4 What flat items can be used to show a classroom?

pictures and maps

____

5 Underline the way a map is different from a model.

121

SSSMART™ SUPPORT

TextWork

4 Comprehension

Categorize and Classify Review the difference between a map and a model. Then have students identify which two flat items can be used to show a classroom.

5 Vocabulary

Use Context Clues
Have students provide definitions for *map* and *model,* using their own words. Then have them scan the text to find and underline the sentences that explain how a map is different from a model.

SOCIAL STUDIES STRANDS

Geographic Relationships Take students outside to study the layout of the playground. Encourage students to take notes or make sketches. Have partners or small groups of students work together to plan and make maps of the playground. Students should decide on at least three appropriate symbols to use in the map key. Invite groups to share their maps. Then have each group use its map to make a model of the playground. Invite volunteers to present their models. Display the finished models.

Lesson Review

Summary Have student pairs use the headings to review what they learned about maps. Then have them work individually to complete the Lesson Review.

- Maps show locations in homes, classrooms, schools, and communities.
- Maps use symbols to show locations.
- Pictures and maps are flat, but you can look at a model from all sides.

Lesson 1 Review

1. **SUMMARIZE** What can maps and models show about places?

   Possible response: Maps and models can show the location of places.

2. Tell about the **location** of a place in your school.

   Answers will vary, but students should accurately name the location of something in their school. Possible response: The location of the library is next to my classroom.

3. When might you need to use a map?

   Answers will vary, but students should accurately identify times they might need to use a map. Possible response: I might need to use a map when I visit a new place.

Activity

Make a map of your classroom. It should help new classmates find their way around. Show all the important places.

122

ACTIVITY RUBRIC

Score 4
- map includes a key and all relevant information
- map is accurate and has no errors

Score 3
- map includes a key and most of the relevant information
- map is mostly accurate and has few errors

Score 2
- map includes a key and includes some relevant information
- map has several errors

Score 1
- map does not include a key and includes little or no relevant information
- map has numerous errors

Build Background

Make It Relevant Display a map of the community or state. Ask students if they know what it is. Remind students that a map is a tool that people use to find where places are. Invite students to share what they know about maps. Encourage volunteers to point out places that they can identify on the community or state map.

Preview the Lesson

Guide students in previewing the lesson. Point out the following features on Student Edition pages 123–128:

- **Page 123** Invite students to preview the photograph and caption. Ask why a map of their neighborhoods may be useful.
- **Pages 124–125** Display a map of the United States. Explain that North Carolina is a state in the United States. Ask students to locate North Carolina on the map. Then ask students to identify the states that neighbor North Carolina.
- **Page 126** Display a globe. Inform students that the United States is located on the continent of North America. Have students locate North America on the globe.

Preteach Vocabulary

- Ask students where they live. Students may say they live in a house or an apartment. Explain that their homes may also be located in a **neighborhood**. Ask students to list some characteristics of a neighborhood.
- Explain that a **state** is part of a country. Ask students: "How many states are in the United States?" Encourage volunteers to discuss their experiences with visiting states outside of North Carolina.
- Point out that a **border** is not something that a person can see or touch. Explain that a border is a map tool that shows where one place ends and another begins.
- Ask students to define **continent** in their own words. Explain that there are seven continents on Earth. Use a globe to point out the seven continents. Say their names, and have students repeat their names after you.

NORTH CAROLINA STANDARD COURSE OF STUDY

Objective 5.02 Investigate key features of maps.

Objective 5.03 Use geographic terminology and tools to create representations of the earth's physical and human features through simple maps, models, and pictures.

Key Content Summary

- **A neighborhood is a part of a city or town.**
- **A state is a part of a country.**
- **A continent is a very large piece of land.**

Vocabulary

- **neighborhood,** p. 123
- **state,** p. 124
- **border,** p. 125
- **continent,** p. 126

Spotlight on Goals and Objectives

Use North Carolina Interactive Presentations, Unit 5, Lesson 2, to access prior knowledge and build background.

Reach All Learners

ESL/Language Support

Content and Language Objectives Write *map, border,* and *location* on the board. Ask "Why do these words go together?" Lead students to understand that a map shows locations and a border shows where one location (such as a state or country) ends and another begins. Demonstrate using a classroom map. Then point to other borders and locations and ask students to identify whether you are pointing to a border or a location.

Extra Support

Use a Globe Give each student a map that does not include labels. Provide students with a list of the seven continents. Have them use the classroom globe to locate each one. Then have them write in the correct locations on their maps.

Extension Activity

Find the Answers Use index cards to write questions for which students would use a globe or a map to find the answers. For example, ask: "What ocean is located above North America?" Have students write the question on the front of the index card. Allow pairs to use a globe or a map to find the answers. Then have pairs record their answers on the back of their index cards.

Integrate the Curriculum

Arts

Learn with Music Lead students in a rhythmic chant in which they echo the names of the continents and oceans as they locate them on a globe or map. For example, clap with the syllables as you chant, "Where, oh where, is the continent North America?" ("There, oh there, is the continent North America.")

Lesson 2 Finding Where You Are

A map can help us find our way around our neighborhood and community. A **neighborhood** is a part of a city or a town. A map can show our homes and other places. **How do you think this lesson will help you tell where you live?**

Possible response: This lesson will help me use maps to tell where I live.

You can use a map to show where you live.

NORTH CAROLINA STANDARD COURSE OF STUDY

5.02 Investigate key features of maps.

5.03 Use geographic terminology and tools to create representations of the earth's physical and human features through simple maps, models, and pictures.

123

Start with the Objectives

Objective 5.02 Investigate key features of maps.

Objective 5.03 Use geographic terminology and tools to create representations of the earth's physical and human features through simple maps, models, and pictures.

Set a Purpose for Reading

Read aloud the introduction with students. Have students share their knowledge of the highlighted word *neighborhood*. Then ask volunteers to share their answers to the question. Use the Think Aloud to model thinking about maps.

Think Aloud

I know that a map shows location. I've seen a map of my community and my state. I will read to learn more about using maps to show where I live.

BACKGROUND

Using Maps When people reach a four-way stop like the one shown in this photograph, they must choose which direction they want to go. Maps can help people choose the correct direction to get to their desired locations. The map on this page shows a community. Communities are different, yet they have many of the same features. These features, such as a school, park, post office, library, hospital, stores, and homes appear on many community maps.

SOCIAL STUDIES STRANDS

Geographic Relationships Encourage students to bring in maps. They may bring in a road map, an atlas, or a map they picked up while visiting a museum or other community location. When you have a collection of at least five maps, display them and have students compare the maps' key features.

TextWork

1 CUES

Analyze/Interpret Maps Have students point to the map on the page. Explain that the map shows their state, North Carolina. Demonstrate how each dot on the map corresponds to the name of the community it represents. Point out the difference between the star for Raleigh and the dots for other cities. Explain that Raleigh is the capital city of North Carolina. Tell students to find the word *Greenville* in the TextWork item and then find the dot that represents the community of Greenville on the map.

1 Look at the map. Find Greenville and circle it.

Your State

Maps can show many kinds of places. One map may show streets in a community. Another may show communities in a state. A **state** is a part of a country. North Carolina is a state. High Point is a community in North Carolina.

124

TEACHING YOUR SOCIAL STUDIES

BACKGROUND

North Carolina Traffic Signs The state uses different kinds of signs to help keep drivers safe and provide them with information. The signs on this page are examples of guide signs. These rectangular signs may be green, brown, or blue. They provide drivers with information about directions, such as those on an exit sign, and about distances to different locations.

BUILD SKILLS

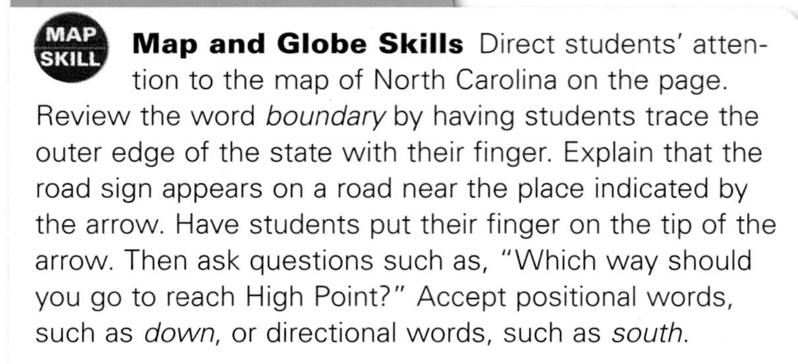

MAP SKILL **Map and Globe Skills** Direct students' attention to the map of North Carolina on the page. Review the word *boundary* by having students trace the outer edge of the state with their finger. Explain that the road sign appears on a road near the place indicated by the arrow. Have students put their finger on the tip of the arrow. Then ask questions such as, "Which way should you go to reach High Point?" Accept positional words, such as *down*, or directional words, such as *south*.

Your Country

Some maps show states and countries. A country is a land that has its own people and laws. The United States of America is our country. It has 50 states. North Carolina is one of these states.

Lines on a map show borders. A **border** is where a state or a country ends.

❷ Look at the map. Draw a circle around North Carolina.

TextWork

❷ CUES

Analyze/Interpret Maps Have students look back to the map of North Carolina on page 124. Explain that the map of the state is like a piece of a jigsaw puzzle. It fits into the map of the country on page 125. If students have difficulty locating the state, use positional words to describe its location.

SOCIAL STUDIES STRANDS

Geographic Relationships Have students trace the outline of the United States to become familiar with its shape. Discuss its most recognizable features including the Florida peninsula and the southern tip of Texas. Direct students' attention to the map on page 126 and have them quickly locate the United States by looking for the shape of the country.

BUILD SKILLS

MAP SKILL **Map and Globe Skills** Point out that Alaska and Hawaii are two states in the United States, yet they do not touch the rest of the land. Explain that their placement on the map on page 125 is not their true location. Point out the two states' locations on a world map. Have students look again at the map on page 125. Ask questions about the map, such as "Which states border North Carolina?"

TextWork

3 CUES

Analyze/Interpret Maps Refer students back to the map of the United States on page 125. Explain that that map is, again, like a piece of a larger jigsaw puzzle. It fits into the map of the world on page 126. If students have difficulty locating the country, use positional words to describe its location. Some students may circle Alaska as part of the United States. Hawaii may be too small for students to recognize.

3 Look at the map. Find the United States. Draw a circle around it.

Your Continent

Some maps show countries and continents. A **continent** is a very large area of land. There are seven continents on Earth. They are North America, South America, Europe, Africa, Asia, Australia, and Antarctica. The United States is on the continent of North America.

The World

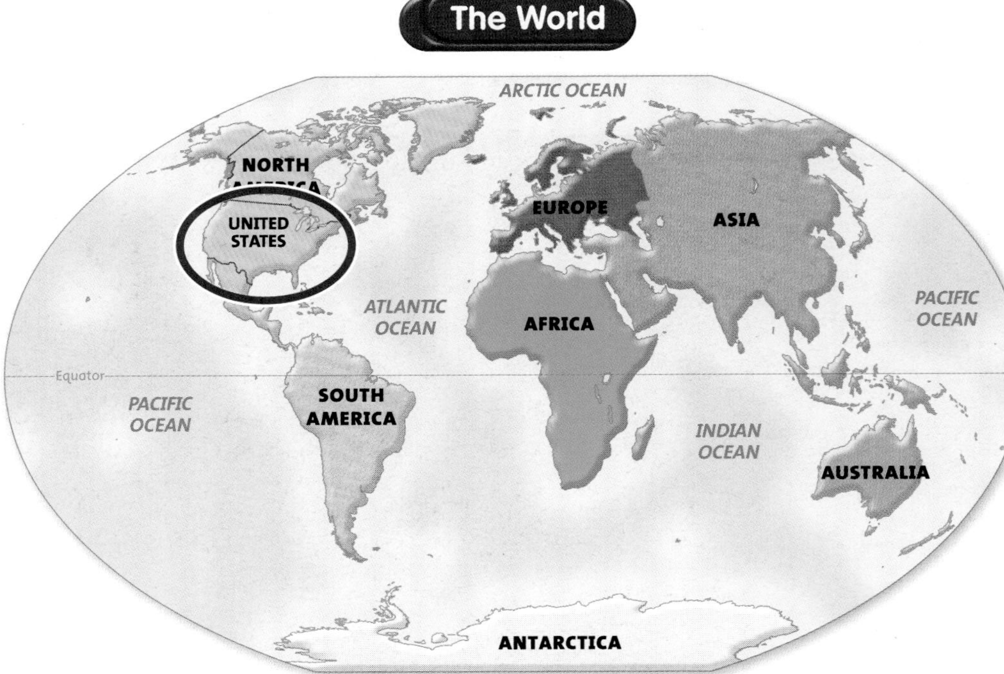

126

TEACHING YOUR SOCIAL STUDIES

BACKGROUND

CONTINENTS

Continents	Size	Population in 2005
Asia	17,139,445 sq. mi.	3,938,020,000
Africa	11,677,239 sq. mi.	922,011,000
North America	9,361,791 sq. mi.	332,245,000
South America	6,880,706 sq. mi.	373,679,000
Antarctica	about 5,500,000 sq. mi.	no residents
Europe	3,997,929 sq. mi.	731,087,000
Australia	2,967,909 sq. mi.	20,310,000

SOCIAL STUDIES STRANDS

Global Connections Remind students that transportation links communities around the world. Tell students that Asia sells some products to the United States. Have them trace different travel routes, both by air and by sea, from Asia to the United States. Repeat the scenario using different countries and continents.

Colors on a Map

Most maps use colors to show land and water. Different colors show land. Blue shows water. Rivers are blue lines on a map. Sometimes a river is a border of a state or a country.

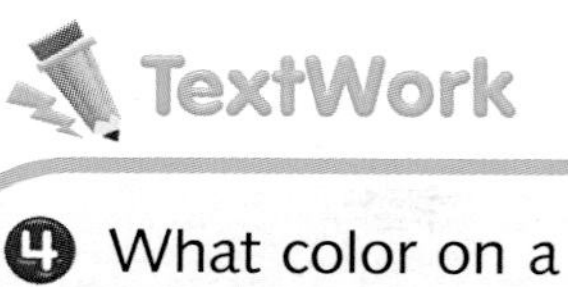

❹ What color on a map shows water?

blue

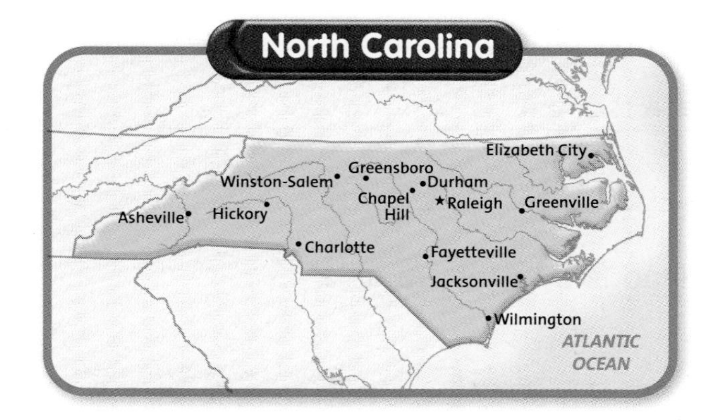

A globe is a model of Earth. A globe also uses colors to show land and water.

127

SSSMART™ SUPPORT

TextWork

❹ Comprehension

Monitor Understanding Read aloud the question. Ask students to write the answer. Tell students that if they have difficulty answering the question, they should reread the text to find the answer. Explain that good readers use this strategy when they have trouble understanding what they have read.

SOCIAL STUDIES STRANDS

Global Connections Invite students to share the names of places they have visited or read about, as well as places important to their family (for example, their ancestors' home country). Then help students find one of those locations on a world map or globe. Discuss the distinctions and relationships between communities, states, countries, and continents.

BUILD SKILLS

Map and Globe Skills Discuss with students the use of color on maps and globes. If possible, copy a map of the United States onto a transparency. Invite students to use transparency markers to color each state. Guide students to notice that if the same colors are used for adjoining states, their borders become less pronounced. Challenge students to determine the fewest number of colors that can be used so that no two adjoining states have the same color.

Lesson Review

Summary Have student pairs take turns explaining the relationships between a community, a state, a country, and a continent. Encourage them to use the images on the pages to help them. Then have students work individually to complete the Lesson Review.

- A neighborhood is a part of a city or town.
- A state is a part of a country.
- A continent is a very large piece of land.

Lesson 2 Review

1. **SUMMARIZE** How can a map help you tell where you live?

   Possible response: I can use maps to find the location of my neighborhood, state, country, and continent.

2. How are a **state** and a country different?

   Possible response: A state is a part of a country.

3. How can you tell where land and water are on a map?

   Possible response: I can tell the difference between land and water on a map. Different colors are used to show land. Blue is used to show water.

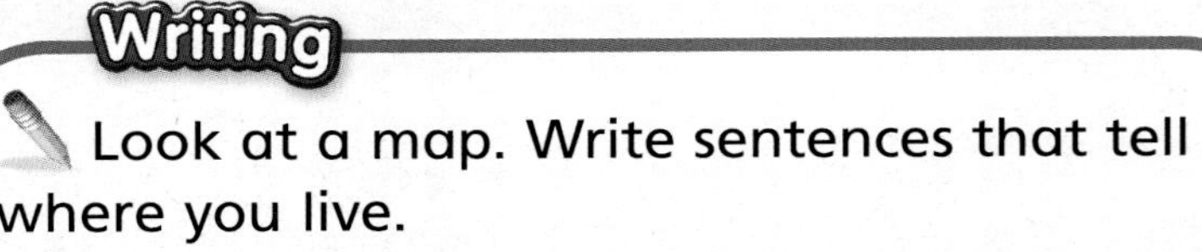

Writing

Look at a map. Write sentences that tell where you live.

128

WRITING RUBRIC

Score 4
- clearly understands the distinction between a community, state, country, and continent
- provides at least three details to describe location of home or community

Score 3
- understands the distinction between a community, state, country, and continent
- provides at least two details to describe location of home or community

Score 2
- does not fully understand the distinction between a community, state, country, and continent
- provides at least one detail to describe location of home or community

Score 1
- fails to understand the distinction between a community, state, country, and continent
- examples provided are not relevant or do not describe location of home or community

Build Background

Make It Relevant Discuss with students the term *environment*. Ask students what the environment in which they live is like. Encourage students to use vivid details. Ask students if the area in which they live is flat or hilly. Point out that North Carolina has many different types of environments including areas with mountains, lakes, rivers, and valleys.

Preview the Lesson

Guide students in previewing the lesson. Point out the following features on Student Edition pages 129–134:

- **Page 130** Invite students to preview the title of this section. Ask, "What is the difference between a mountain and a hill?" Explain that a mountain is the highest kind of land. Encourage students to discuss any trips they may have taken to the mountains.
- **Page 131** Point out to students that a plain is land that is mostly flat. Ask students why people might live on a plain. Answers may include that it is easy to grow food and easier to travel from place to place.
- **Pages 132–133** Ask students whether they have ever visited a lake, a river, or the ocean. What types of activities did they participate in when visiting? Ask what these bodies of water can be used for.

Preteach Vocabulary

- Ask students to define **mountain** in their own words. Display a map and point out the Great Smoky Mountains.
- Explain that a **hill** is a piece of land that rises above the land around it. Point out that many homes are built up on hills, and that sometimes communities are near hills. Ask students whether there are any hills in their community.
- Explain that a **valley** is the low land located between mountains. Have students draw a picture of a valley. Ask them to label the mountains and the valley.
- Ask students to differentiate between the words *plane* and **plain**. Point out that a plain is land that is mostly flat. Show students photographs of mountains and plains. Ask them to point to the picture of the plain.

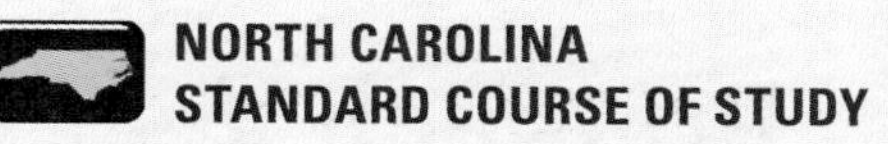

Objective 5.06 Compare and contrast geographic features of places within various communities.

Objective 5.07 Explore physical features of continents and major bodies of water.

Key Content Summary

- **Different parts of the United States have different kinds of land.**
- **Land may be mountains, hills, valleys, or plains.**
- **Communities may be near a lake, a river, or an ocean.**

Vocabulary

- **mountain,** p. 130
- **hill,** p. 130
- **valley,** p. 131
- **plain,** p. 131
- **ocean,** p. 133

Use North Carolina Interactive Presentations, Unit 5, Lesson 3, to access prior knowledge and build background.

Preteach Vocabulary *continued*

- Ask students whether they know which **ocean** borders North Carolina. Have students make a list of activities that take place near an ocean.

Reach All Learners

ESL/Language Support

Scaffolding Content Display a piece of posterboard divided into a two-column table with eight rows. The left column should be labeled *Photograph*, and the right column should be labeled *Word*. Paste seven photographs of the land and water types described in the unit into the first column. Point to a photograph and have students identify what it is. Record their answers in the column labeled *Word*.

Extra Support

Write a Sentence Remind students that North Carolina has many different types of land and bodies of water. Have students write descriptive sentences about one of the photographs in the lesson. Encourage volunteers to share their sentences with the class.

Extension Activity

Create a Riddle Explain that a riddle is a creative question or clue that takes thought to answer. Invite students to make up riddles about the land and bodies of water described in this lesson. Students should record each riddle and its answer on an index card. Then pair students to answer each other's riddles. Encourage pairs to present their riddles to the rest of the class.

Integrate the Curriculum

English Language Arts

Role-Play a Phone Call Invite pairs to role-play making calls to each other from different locations in North Carolina, such as from the beach to a nearby lake or a mountaintop to a riverbank. Challenge students to describe their environments in their conversations.

ELA 4.03 Using specific words to name and tell action in oral and written language (e.g., using words such as frog and toad when discussing a nonfiction text).

Lesson 3

PAGES 129–134

Land and Water

Lesson

Different parts of the United States have different kinds of land. Some communities are on land that is high. Some are on land that is low. Many communities are near water. **What do you think you will learn about land and water?**

Possible response: I think I will learn about different kinds of land and water.

The Great Smoky Mountains

NORTH CAROLINA STANDARD COURSE OF STUDY

5.06 Compare and contrast geographic features of places within various communities.

5.07 Explore physical features of continents and major bodies of water.

129

Start with the Objectives

Objective 5.06 Compare and contrast geographic features of places within various communities.

Objective 5.07 Explore physical features of continents and major bodies of water.

Set a Purpose for Reading

Have a volunteer read aloud the lesson title. Then read aloud the introduction. Talk about the land in your community. Then have students answer the question. Model the Think Aloud about land and water.

Think Aloud

There is a lake near my home. Most of the land in my community is flat. I wonder what land is like in other places. I will read to learn more about land and water.

BACKGROUND

Great Smoky Mountains The Great Smoky Mountains are part of the Appalachian Mountains. The "Smokies" have some of the tallest peaks in the Appalachian chain. The Great Smoky Mountains extend from Asheville, North Carolina, to Knoxville, Tennessee. The mountains were formed when continents collided millions of years ago.

SOCIAL STUDIES STRANDS

Geographic Relationships While learning about landforms and bodies of water, students can make a salt dough landform map. Have students use posterboard for the base and a mixture of 2 cups flour, 1 cup salt, and enough water to make the dough workable. They can use the mixture to create a landform map of North Carolina or of an imaginary state. When the landforms dry, have students paint their landforms an appropriate color.

TextWork

1 Vocabulary

Understand Vocabulary Explain to students that to complete this item, they must understand the word *mountain*. Ask a student to explain the meaning of the word. Then have students scan the text to find the answer.

1 Underline the mountains that are in North Carolina.

Mountains and Hills

Some communities are near mountains. A **mountain** is the highest kind of land. The Blue Ridge Mountains are in North Carolina. So are the Great Smoky Mountains.

Other communities are near hills. A **hill** is land that rises above the land around it. There are many hills in North Carolina.

mountain

hills

130

TEACHING YOUR SOCIAL STUDIES

BACKGROUND

Grandfather Mountain Tell students the mountain shown on this page is Grandfather Mountain. At an elevation of 5,964 feet, Grandfather Mountain is the tallest mountain in the Blue Ridge Mountains. However, it is not the tallest mountain in the Smokies. The mountain is famous for its mile-high swinging bridge. This suspension bridge is 5,305 feet above sea level. The bridge connects two tall peaks.

SOCIAL STUDIES STRANDS

Global Connections Provide students with a world map or globe and have them locate other mountain ranges in the United States and around the world. You may want to have students work with older students to use available resources to learn facts about mountain ranges around the world.

Valleys and Plains

Some people live in valleys. A **valley** is low land that is between mountains. Maggie Valley is in North Carolina. It is between some of the Great Smoky Mountains.

Other people live on plains. A **plain** is land that is mostly flat. The land in plains is good for growing food. North Carolina has many plains.

TextWork

❷ What kind of land is good for growing food?

the plains

SSSMART™ SUPPORT

TextWork

❷ Skim and Scan

Ask a volunteer to read the question aloud. Have students scan the second paragraph of the text to find the answer.

BACKGROUND

Maggie Valley Tell students that the valley shown on this page is Maggie Valley in North Carolina. This community in North Carolina lies in the Great Smoky Mountains. The community got its name in the early 1900s when Jack Setzer, a mail carrier, submitted the names of his three daughters to the postmaster for the name of a new post office in the area. The postmaster chose one of the names, Maggie.

BUILD SKILLS

Map and Globe Skills Show students various maps, including maps of North Carolina and the United States. Have them study the map keys to locate the symbols for various landforms and bodies of water. Then have students locate the various landforms on the maps.

SSSMART™ SUPPORT

TextWork

3 CUES

Analyze/Interpret Photographs
Ask a volunteer to read aloud the direction line. Then have another volunteer explain where to find the answer. Ask students to explain why they circled a certain photograph.

Lakes and Rivers

3 Draw a circle around the picture of a lake.

Many people live near water. Some live near lakes. Lakes can be big. Lakes can be small.

Other people live near rivers. People can use rivers to go places by boat.

lake

river

132

BACKGROUND

Fontana Lake The lake pictured on the page is Fontana Lake. The human-made lake is located in the Great Smoky Mountains. It is about 30 miles long and has deep, cold water, making it ideal for fishing. The lake and its dam were created to provide a source of hydroelectric power.

BUILD SKILLS

Chart and Graph Skills Provide students with magazines. Instruct them to cut out four or five photographs of different landforms or bodies of water. Have small groups of students work together to make a chart showing either types of landforms or bodies of water. Then have student groups explain their charts.

Oceans

The water in rivers moves across the land to the ocean. An **ocean** is a large body of water. The land near an ocean is mostly flat. The Atlantic Ocean and the Pacific Ocean are borders of the United States. Many people live near these oceans. North Carolina is next to the Atlantic Ocean.

TextWork

4 Name one ocean that is next to the United States.

Atlantic Ocean or

Pacific Ocean

ocean

SSSMART™ SUPPORT

TextWork

4 Skim and Scan

Read aloud the direction line with students. Remind students that they can identify key words in a question and scan the text looking for the words. Ask volunteers to identify words in the direction line that they can use to scan the text *(ocean, next to, United States).* Encourage students to identify the location of the possible answers and how they used the words to find the answer.

BACKGROUND

Oceans Earth has four oceans. They are the Arctic, Atlantic, Indian, and Pacific. Together, they cover over 70 percent of Earth's surface. The Pacific Ocean is the largest of the four oceans. The Pacific has both the tallest mountain (Mauna Kea of the Hawaiian Islands at more than 33,000 feet above the sea floor) and the deepest trench (Mariana Trench at more than 36,000 feet deep). Some people have delimited—defined the limits of—a fifth world ocean, the Southern Ocean.

BUILD SKILLS

Problem Solving Discuss the problem of water pollution in North Carolina with students. Have them work in small groups to devise a plan to raise awareness of the problem and promote conservation. Have groups share their problem-solving process and their plan to help clean up Earth's water.

Lesson Review

Summary Have students work with a partner. One student recalls information learned about land. The other partner recalls facts about water. Then, partners switch roles, refer to the lesson, and identify additional facts about land and water presented in the text. Have students work alone to complete the Lesson Review.

- Different parts of the United States have different kinds of land.
- Land may be mountains, hills, valleys, or plains.
- Communities may be near a lake, a river, or an ocean.

Lesson 3 Review

1. **SUMMARIZE** What kinds of land and water does North Carolina have?

   Possible response: North Carolina has mountains, hills, valleys, and plains. North Carolina has lakes and rivers. North Carolina is next to the Atlantic Ocean.

2. How are a **mountain** and a **valley** different?

   Possible response: A mountain is the highest kind of land. A valley is low land that is between mountains.

3. What are three kinds of land?

   Possible response: Three kinds of land are mountains, hills, and plains.

Activity

Make a chart showing the kinds of land and water in North Carolina.

134

ACTIVITY RUBRIC

Score 4
- chart is accurate and identifies at least four types of land and three bodies of water in North Carolina
- chart is extremely well organized and has very few or no spelling errors

Score 3
- chart is accurate and identifies at least three types of land and two bodies of water in North Carolina
- chart is well organized and has few spelling errors

Score 2
- chart is somewhat accurate and identifies at least two types of land and one body of water in North Carolina
- chart is organized and has several spelling errors

Score 1
- chart contains inaccurate information and identifies only one type of land and one body of water in North Carolina
- chart is poorly organized and has numerous spelling errors

Build Background

Make It Relevant Explain that people live in many different locations. People live in big cities, in suburban neighborhoods, or in rural areas. Ask students to describe the neighborhood in which they live. Then together come up with similarities and differences between living in cities, in suburbs, or in rural areas.

Preview the Lesson

Guide students in previewing the lesson. Point out the following features on Student Edition pages 135–138:

- **Page 135** Point out that communities can be different sizes. Some communities are very large while others are very small. Ask students to draw a picture of a community. They should label important places. Ask volunteers to share their drawings with the class.
- **Page 136** Ask students to preview the photograph. Ask, "In what type of community would you find this house?"
- **Page 137** Explain to students that some communities are far away from cities and are located in rural areas. Ask students to list some things a person may find in rural areas.

Preteach Vocabulary

- Show students a photograph of a **city**. Ask them what the photograph shows. Ask volunteers to share their experiences of visiting a city. Encourage them to use their senses to discuss details. What did they hear? What did they see?
- Explain that a **suburb** is a smaller community located near a big city. Ask students to list some characteristics of suburbs.
- Ask students to define **farm** in their own words. Explain to students that there are many different types of farms. Some farms grow fruits and vegetables; some have cattle, sheep, and pigs; and some grow grain such as wheat.

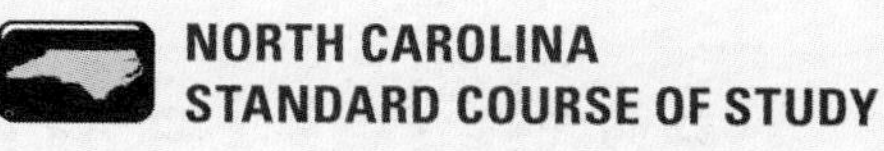

Objective 5.04 Analyze patterns of movement within the community.

Key Content Summary

- **Communities can be different sizes.**
- **A city is a large community.**
- **A suburb is a smaller community near a large city.**
- **Communities in the country are far from cities and suburbs.**

Vocabulary

- **city,** p. 135
- **suburb,** p. 136
- **farm,** p. 137

Spotlight on Goals and Objectives

Use North Carolina Interactive Presentations, Unit 5, Lesson 4, to access prior knowledge and build background.

Reach All Learners

ESL/Language Support

Active Learning Display photographs of a city, a suburb, and a farm. Ask students to draw a picture of an item found in each of these places. Encourage volunteers to share their pictures with the class.

Extra Support

Paint a Picture Provide students with materials to paint a picture of their community. Tell them to include specific characteristics. For example, if they live near an ice cream parlor, they may want to include it. Allow students to share their pictures with the class. Have them explain how their painting represents their community. Display the paintings in the classroom.

Extension Activity

Make Flash Cards Help students create a list of places found in the city, in the suburbs, and on a farm. Have students create flash cards by drawing pictures of the places on index cards. Have them write the location in which the place is found on the back of the index card. Then allow the class to play a game using the index cards to see whether they can determine if the place is found in the city, in the suburbs, or on a farm.

Integrate the Curriculum

Mathematics

Read Whole Numbers Find the populations of a nearby city, suburb, and rural community. Write each of the numbers on the board. Have students identify the individual digits. Then read the whole number aloud. Have students repeat the number after you. Tell them that this number represents an estimate of the number of people who live in this community.

People and Places

Communities can be different sizes. A town may be small. A **city** is a very large community. Cities have many people, many stores, and many streets. **What do you think you will learn about communities?**

Possible response: I will learn how communities can be different sizes.

Ron and his father live in the city of Raleigh, North Carolina.

NORTH CAROLINA STANDARD COURSE OF STUDY

5.04 Analyze patterns of movement within the community.

135

Start with the Objective

Objective 5.04 Analyze patterns of movement within the community.

Set a Purpose for Reading

Begin by having students preview the lesson photographs and captions. Ask a volunteer to read aloud the introduction. Ask students to explain the difference between a town and a city. Then ask student volunteers to share their answer to the question. Use the Think Aloud to model thinking about communities.

Think Aloud

I haven't always lived in this community. I moved here from a big city in another state. I know that the two communities are different, but they have many things in common. I will read to learn more about the sizes of communities.

BACKGROUND

Raleigh, North Carolina Tell students that the city shown in the photograph on this page is Raleigh, North Carolina. Point out that Raleigh is the second largest city in North Carolina. Raleigh is also the state's capital city. The city has a population of over 300,000 people. The city's transportation systems include highways, railroads, and airways. The city operates a public bus system for its citizens. Raleigh has seven colleges and universities and many historical sites and museums.

SOCIAL STUDIES STRANDS

Geographic Relationships Tell students that people move in and out of communities all the time. They also move within communities. As you read the lesson with students, ask them about modes of transportation that people use in cities, suburbs, towns, and rural communities.

SSSMART™ SUPPORT

TextWork

1 Comprehension

Categorize and Classify Remind students that when they categorize and classify, they sort similar information into groups. Explain that to answer the question, they need to understand the category: a smaller community that is near a large city.

TextWork

1 What do we call a smaller community that is near a large city?

a suburb

Living in the Suburbs

Kyle lives in Wake Forest. Wake Forest is a suburb of Raleigh, North Carolina. A **suburb** is a smaller community near a large city. It has fewer people, stores, and streets than a city does.

Kyle's family moved to Wake Forest from Raleigh. It is quieter in Wake Forest than in Raleigh. There is less traffic. The homes have bigger yards.

136

TEACHING YOUR SOCIAL STUDIES

BACKGROUND

Commuting Many people who live in a suburb work in a city. They commute from home to work and back again each day. According to the State Data Center, 26 percent of employed North Carolina residents work outside the county in which they live. Many of these people drive cars. Some of them ride buses.

BUILD SKILLS

Chart and Graph Skills Draw a two-column chart or a Venn diagram on the board with the headings *City* and *Suburb*. Have student volunteers suggest details for the chart to compare and contrast the two types of communities.

Q In which type of community would you find more tall buildings and apartment buildings?

A city

Living in the Countryside

Some communities are far from cities and suburbs. They are in the countryside. People in these communities often live on farms. A **farm** is a place for growing plants and raising animals.

Sara lives on a strawberry farm in North Carolina. The strawberries grown on her family's farm are sold in North Carolina's cities and suburbs. They are brought on trucks to larger communities.

TextWork

❷ Underline the kind of farm Sara lives on.

SSSMART™ SUPPORT

TextWork

❷ Skim And Scan

Have students skim the text. Then have them summarize what they have learned about where Sara lives. Then have students verify their summaries by scanning the text to locate the type of farm Sara lives on.

SOCIAL STUDIES STRANDS

Geographic Relationships Ask students to be silent for 60 seconds and listen to the sounds that they hear. This can be done outdoors or indoors. Record the sounds on paper. Then have students brainstorm a list of sounds they would expect to hear in a city. Then repeat the activity for sounds they would expect to hear on a farm. Discuss the differences.

BACKGROUND

Strawberry Farms North Carolina's strawberry production ranks fourth in the country. People can pick their own strawberries at farms across the state. Strawberries are also available at farmers' markets or in grocery stores. The strawberry season usually runs from April through June.

Lesson Review

Summary Have students review the images and text headings to summarize the lesson's main ideas. Then have them complete the Lesson Review.

- Communities can be different sizes.
- A city is a large community.
- A suburb is a smaller community near a large city.
- Communities in the country are far from cities and suburbs.

Lesson 4 Review

1. **SUMMARIZE** What kinds of communities did you read about in this lesson?

   Possible response: I read about cities, suburbs, and communities in the countryside.

2. What is the difference between a **city** and a **suburb**?

   Possible response: A city is a very large community. A suburb is a community near a large city.

3. Why might someone living in a city move to a suburb?

   Possible response: A person living in a city might move to a suburb to have a bigger yard.

Writing
Write about what it might be like to live on a farm.

138

WRITING RUBRIC

Score 4
- provides at least three details to describe living on a farm
- writes at least three sentences with no or very few errors

Score 3
- provides at least two details to describe living on a farm
- writes at least two sentences with few errors

Score 2
- provides details to describe living on a farm, but some details may be inaccurate or irrelevant
- sentences contain numerous errors

Score 1
- examples provided are not relevant or do not describe living on a farm
- writing does not follow correct sentence structure

Build Background

Make It Relevant Discuss with students the ways they can show that they care about a place. For example, people who care about their parks may volunteer to help pick up litter. Explain that it is our responsibility to take care of Earth. Ask students to create a list of ways in which they can help take care of the planet.

Preview the Lesson

Guide students in previewing the lesson. Point out the following features on Student Edition pages 139–142:

- **Page 139** Invite students to preview the photograph. Ask: "What are the people doing?" and "How are they using soil?"
- **Page 140** Ask students to preview the Children in History feature. Ask: "Who was Conrad Reed?" Discuss gold with students. Explain that gold is a resource.
- **Page 141** Display a recycle sign for students. Ask them if they know what the symbol stands for. Then discuss why they think it is important to recycle.

Preteach Vocabulary

- Explain to students that a **resource** is anything that people can use. Ask students to list possible resources. Students may say that trees, water, and metals are resources. Write the list on the board.
- Have students define **recycle** in their own words. Ask students to list things that can be recycled. Have students draw a picture of an item that can be recycled.

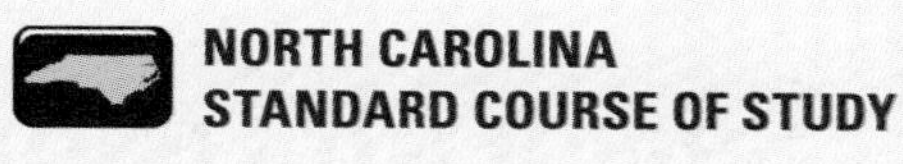

Objective 5.05 Demonstrate responsibility for the care and management of the environment within the school and community.

Key Content Summary

- People have the responsibility to take care of Earth's resources.
- People can reduce, reuse, and recycle to help save Earth's resources.

Vocabulary

- **resource,** p. 139
- **recycle,** p. 141

Use North Carolina Interactive Presentations, Unit 5, Lesson 5, to access prior knowledge and build background.

Reach All Learners

ESL/Language Support

Scaffolding Content Provide a blank word web with the words *Things That We Can Recycle* in the center circle. Have students use what they learn in the lesson to complete the word web.

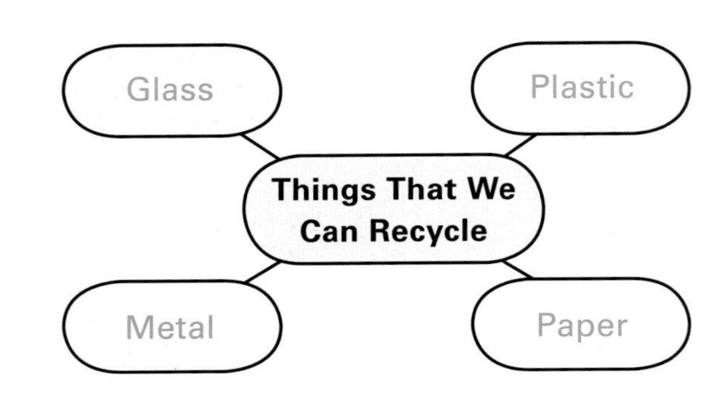

Extra Support

Identify the Resource Provide students with photographs of areas that contain specific resources, such as a forest. Have students identify the type of resource that comes from the area. Then have them write a sentence explaining something for which that resource is used. For example, trees can be used for wood to build houses.

Extension Activity

Reuse Milk Jugs Organize students in pairs. Give each pair a clean, one gallon milk jug. Have them think of a way in which their milk jug can be reused. For example, an empty milk jug can be used to hold bird seed. Encourage students to find ways in which the jug can be used in the classroom. Provide pairs with supplies, such as scissors and glue, to create a new container. Allow pairs to decorate and label their reusable milk jug.

Integrate the Curriculum

Arts

Make a Collage Organize students into small groups. Provide groups with magazines. Invite students to find pictures showing different kinds of resources. Then have them use those pictures to create a collage. Have each group write a caption to go with their collage. Display the finished collages in the classroom.

People Use Resources

Lesson

Soil, trees, and water are some of Earth's resources. A **resource** is anything that people can use. People often live near resources. **What do you think you will learn about how people use resources?**

Possible response: I think I will learn how people use and care for resources.

NORTH CAROLINA
STANDARD COURSE OF STUDY

5.05 Demonstrate responsibility for the care and management of the environment within the school and community.

139

Lesson 5

PAGES 139–142

Start with the Objective

Objective 5.05 Demonstrate responsibility for the care and management of the environment within the school and community.

Set a Purpose for Reading

Ask a volunteer to read aloud the text. Provide support as needed. Direct students' attention to the highlighted word *resource* and read the definition. Have students suggest resources that they use every day. Then read aloud the question and have students share their ideas. Use the Think Aloud to model thinking about caring for resources.

Think Aloud

We planted a garden at school. We also recycle. I know these are two ways to take care of Earth's resources. I will read to learn more about using and protecting Earth's resources.

BACKGROUND

Gardens Tell students that the woman and girl in the photograph are using Earth's resources to grow fruits and vegetables in a garden. People grow gardens in all kinds of locations including cities, the suburbs, and rural areas. Gardens can be flower gardens, water gardens, vegetable gardens, herb gardens, or cactus gardens. Growing or buying local fruits and vegetables helps Earth because resources are not needed to ship produce from other places.

SOCIAL STUDIES STRANDS

Government and Active Citizenship Discuss with students their responsibility to protect Earth. Have small groups of students plan and act out a short skit in which they decide to help Earth. For example, a group may dramatize one person dropping trash and another person passing by and picking it up, even though that person was not the one to litter. Invite students to share their skits with the class or with another class.

SUPPORT

TextWork

1 CUES

Analyze/Interpret Photographs Tell students that in order to circle the correct item, they must understand the word *resource*. Students can also use the word *planted* as a clue. Direct students' attention to the photograph at the top of page 140. Have students circle the resource that is being planted and identify it by name.

Taking Care of Earth

It is our responsibility to take care of Earth's resources. We can keep the land and water clean. We can plant trees to take the place of trees people have cut down.

Planting trees is one way to care for resources in your community.

Children in History

Conrad Reed

In 1799, 12-year-old Conrad Reed found a lump of gold in Cabarrus County, North Carolina. Gold is a resource. After his find, many people came to North Carolina to look for more gold. This was the first gold rush in the United States.

TEACHING YOUR SOCIAL STUDIES

BACKGROUND

Conrad Reed Young Conrad Reed saw something shining in the water in the creek on his family's farm. He picked up the heavy brick and took it to his father. Not knowing what it was, the family used the 17-pound gold brick as a doorstop for several years. A jeweler later identified the "brick" as gold and bought it from Reed's father.

SOCIAL STUDIES STRANDS

Economics and Development Draw a large tree on the board. On each branch, write a product made from a tree. Have students suggest products and add their ideas to the tree.

Q Why do people cut down trees?

A to make furniture, paper, and other products; to clear land to build homes and buildings

People can **recycle** old things to make new things. Plastic, paper, metal, and glass can be used again. People can reduce, or lower, the amount of resources they use. They can reuse things, or use them again.

We can do these things at school, too. We can reduce, reuse, and recycle to help save Earth's resources.

❶ Look at the pictures on page 140. Circle the resource that is being planted.

❷ Name one thing that you can recycle.
Possible responses: plastic, paper, metal, or glass

Use bins like these to recycle things in your community.

SSSMART™ SUPPORT

TextWork

❷ Skim and Scan

Remind students to identify words that can help them in the direction line *(can recycle)*. Tell students to scan to find the words. Have students identify the possible answers and their location in the first paragraph.

SOCIAL STUDIES STRANDS

Individual Development and Identity Provide students with common items that might typically be thrown away (shoe box, egg carton, soup can, etc.). Be sure the items are clean and have no sharp edges. Challenge students to use one or more items to create something new. For example, students might create a pencil holder or an art supply organizer.

BUILD SKILLS

Chart and Graph Skills Have students recycle items either at school or at home for one week. Help them to make a bar graph to show the number of each item recycled. Recycled items might include newspapers, magazines, plastic bottles, and aluminum cans. Remind students that when they are handling items to be recycled, they should take safety precautions. This includes wearing gloves when handling trash.

Lesson Review

Summary Have partners reread the question on page 139. Have them recall and retell the lesson's main ideas. Then have partners scan the headings and text to add to their summary. Have students work independently to complete the Lesson Review.

- People have the responsibility to take care of Earth's resources.
- People can reduce, reuse, and recycle to help save Earth's resources.

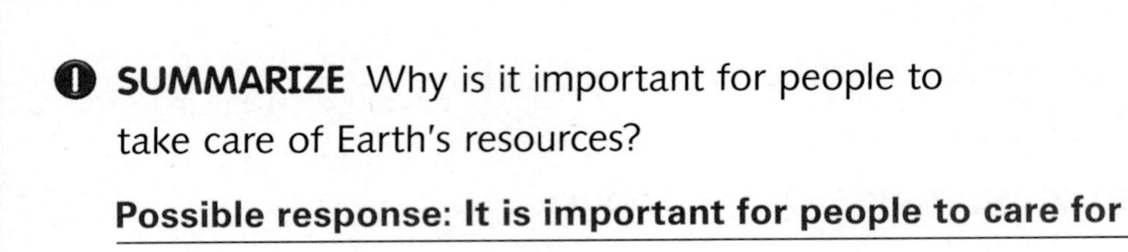

1. **SUMMARIZE** Why is it important for people to take care of Earth's resources?

   Possible response: It is important for people to care for Earth's resources in order to help save them.

2. What are some ways you can **recycle** in your home?

   Students should give an example of how they recycle something in their home. Possible response: I can save aluminum cans to recycle.

3. What are some ways you can help take care of the community?

   Possible response: I can help take care of my community by reducing, reusing, and recycling Earth's resources.

Activity

Make a poster to show people in your school what they can recycle.

142

ACTIVITY RUBRIC

Score 4
- poster is informative and identifies at least four examples of recyclable items
- poster is extremely well planned and presented

Score 3
- poster is informative and identifies at least three examples of recyclable items
- poster is well organized and neat

Score 2
- poster is somewhat informative and identifies at least two examples of recyclable items
- poster shows some evidence of planning

Score 1
- poster contains inaccurate or irrelevant information
- poster is not well thought out and/or is messy

Unit 5

Review and Test Prep

The Big Idea

People live in many different places. We can tell about where we live by using maps and globes.

Summarize the Unit

Categorize and Classify Fill in the chart. Show what you know about different places to live.

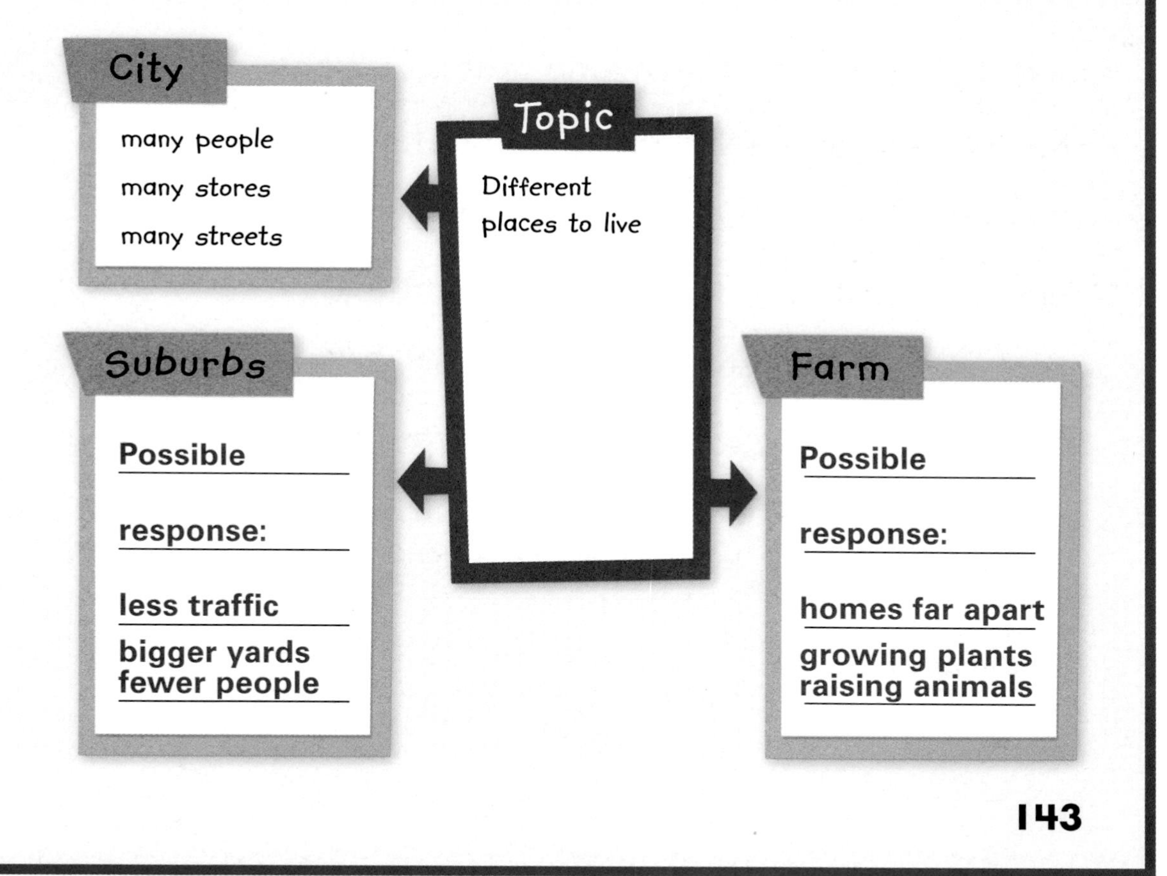

143

Unit Review

PAGES 143–146

The Big Idea

Ask students to review the Big Idea. Invite students to share something they learned in this unit that supports the idea that people live in many places.

Summarize the Unit

Categorize and Classify Invite students to review the Reading Social Studies at the beginning of the unit. Ask them to think of things that can be grouped together under one label. Then help students categorize and classify different places people live.

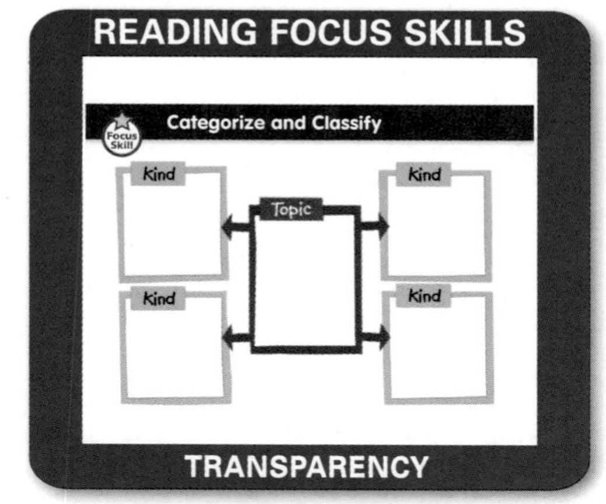

Graphic Organizer Write-On/ Wipe-Off Cards available

ASSESSMENT

Use the **UNIT 5 TEST** on pages 17–20 of the Assessment Program.

Use Vocabulary

Fill in the blanks with the correct words.

Word Bank
location p. 117
state p. 124
mountain p. 130
suburb p. 136
farm p. 137

Claire lives in a small community outside of Charlotte, North Carolina. This kind of community is called a ❶ suburb. Claire and her parents are going on a camping trip. They are visiting a park with a ❷ mountain, the highest kind of land. Claire has never seen land that is so high! She and her parents will use a map to find where they are, or their ❸ location. Then Claire will visit her grandparents. They grow plants and raise animals on their ❹ farm. It is far away from the city. By the end of her trip, Claire will have been all over the ❺ state of North Carolina.

144

VOCABULARY POWER

Categorize Vocabulary Copy the chart about land and water onto the board. Have students name three things that belong in each category, using the vocabulary that they learned in this unit. Be sure to discuss similarities and differences between the listed items.

Kinds of Land	Kinds of Water
mountain	lake
hill	river
valley	ocean

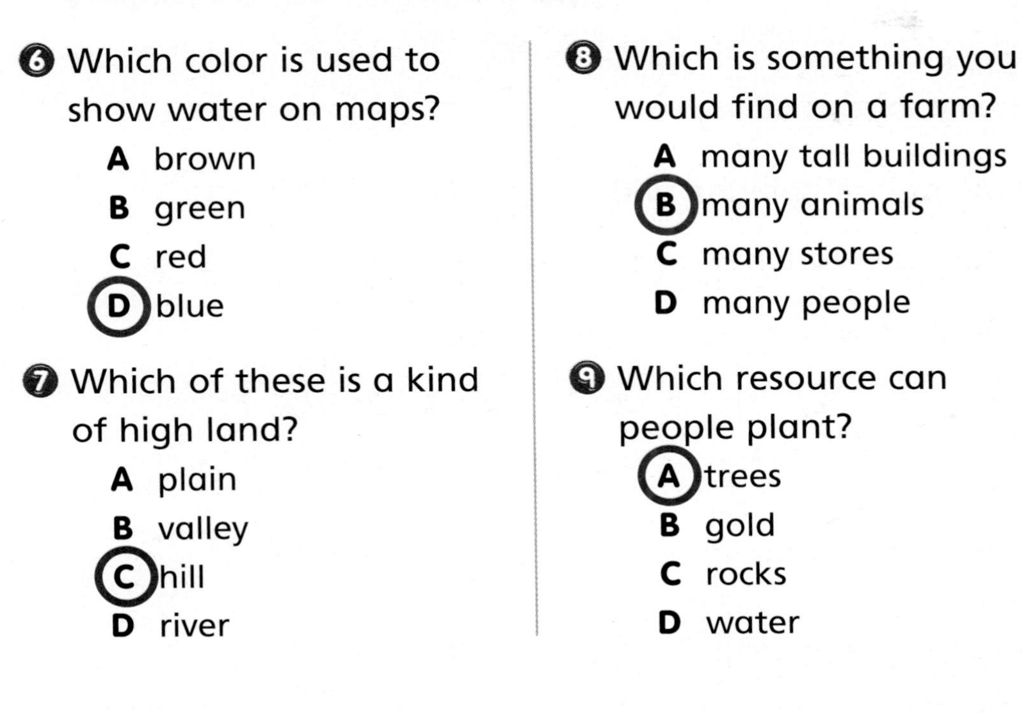

Think About It

Circle the letter of the correct answer.

6. Which color is used to show water on maps?
   - **A** brown
   - **B** green
   - **C** red
   - **D** blue (circled)

7. Which of these is a kind of high land?
   - **A** plain
   - **B** valley
   - **C** hill (circled)
   - **D** river

8. Which is something you would find on a farm?
   - **A** many tall buildings
   - **B** many animals (circled)
   - **C** many stores
   - **D** many people

9. Which resource can people plant?
   - **A** trees (circled)
   - **B** gold
   - **C** rocks
   - **D** water

145

READ MORE

Encourage independent reading with these books or books of your choice.

Basic

Hello Ocean by Pam Muñoz Ryan. Charlesbridge Publishing, 2001. A young girl relates her experiences at the beach.

Proficient

Hottest, Coldest, Highest, Deepest by Steve Jenkins. Houghton Mifflin, 2004. Describes some of the remarkable places on Earth.

Advanced

Shelterwood by Susan Hand Shetterly. Tilbury House Publishers, 2003. While staying with her grandfather, Sophie learns about nature and the different kinds of trees.

Unit Review

PAGES 143–146

Show What You Know

Writing

Write a Letter

Have students create a mental image of the place they live. Record responses on a word web. Ask children to use the words on the web to write a letter to a pen pal about the place they live.

Activity

Make a Mural

Suggest that small groups of students work on specific sections to allow everyone ample space to work. Guide students in art techniques as they add color.

North Carolina Adventures

Remind students that this game will review the concepts in the unit.

Spotlight on Goals and Objectives

Use North Carolina Interactive Presentations, Unit 5, to review concepts from the unit.

Answer each question in a complete sentence.

10. Why are maps important?

Possible response: Maps are important because they show location.

11. What kinds of land and water do people live near?

Possible response: People can live near hills, mountains, valleys, plains, rivers, lakes, and oceans.

Show What You Know

Writing **Write a Letter**
What words could you use to tell a pen pal about where you live? Write a short letter to your pen pal, telling about where you live.

Activity **Make a Mural**
With your class, create a mural to show where you live. Draw things in your community on the mural. Share your mural with another class.

GO online To play a game that reviews the unit, join Eco in the North Carolina Adventures online or on CD.

146

WRITING RUBRIC

Score 4
- clearly describes details about a place and its people
- uses many sensory words
- shows clear understanding of a friendly letter form

Score 3
- adequately describes details about a place and its people
- uses some sensory words
- shows some understanding of a friendly letter form

Score 2
- describes few details about a place and its people
- uses words related to only one sense
- shows little understanding of a friendly letter form

Score 1
- includes no details about a place and its people
- uses no sensory words
- does not use a friendly letter form

ACTIVITY RUBRIC

Score 4
- provides clear details about their community's land and people
- uses a variety of interesting colors and art techniques
- is well-organized

Score 3
- provides details about their community's land and people
- uses some interesting colors and art techniques
- is mostly organized

Score 2
- provides few details about their community's land and people
- uses few colors or only simple art techniques
- is somewhat organized

Score 1
- provides no details about their community's land and people
- uses no color or art techniques
- is disorganized

Unit 6
The Marketplace

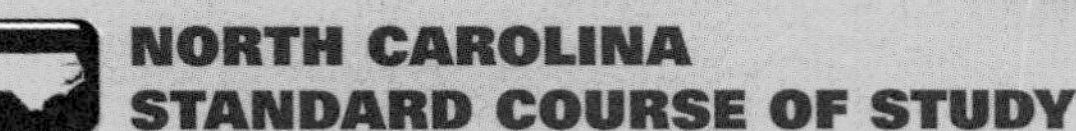

COMPETENCY GOAL 6

The learner will apply basic economic concepts to home, school, and the community.

OBJECTIVES

6.01 Examine wants and needs and identify choices people make to satisfy wants and needs with limited resources.

6.02 Describe how people of different cultures work to earn income in order to satisfy wants and needs.

6.03 Participate in activities that demonstrate the division of labor.

6.04 Explore community services that are provided by the government and other agencies.

6.05 Give examples of the relationship between the government and its people.

6.06 Identify the uses of money by individuals which include saving and spending.

6.07 Recognize that all families produce and consume goods and services.

LESSON	TOTAL: 29 DAYS	NORTH CAROLINA STANDARD COURSE OF STUDY
Introduce the Unit **Unit Preview,** pp. 147–148 **The Big Idea,** p. 148 **Reading Social Studies,** pp. 149–150 Focus Skill: Cause and Effect	**2** DAYS	**COMPETENCY GOAL 6** **The learner will apply basic economic concepts to home, school, and the community.** **Spotlight on Goals and Objectives** Unit 6
1 Goods and Services pp. 151–156 **goods** p. 151 **service** p. 151 **money** p. 153 **business** p. 153 **producer** p. 154 **consumer** p. 154	**5** DAYS	**Objective 6.07** Recognize that all families produce and consume goods and services. **Spotlight on Goals and Objectives** Unit 6, Lesson 1
2 Things We Use pp. 157–162 **need** p. 157 **want** p. 157 **scarce** p. 159 **job** p. 161	**5** DAYS	**Objective 6.01** Examine wants and needs and identify choices people make to satisfy wants and needs with limited resources. **Objective 6.02** Describe how people of different cultures work to earn income in order to satisfy wants and needs. **Spotlight on Goals and Objectives** Unit 6, Lesson 2
3 Spending and Saving pp. 163–166 **market** p. 163 **save** p. 163 **trade** p. 164	**4** DAYS	**Objective 6.06** Identify the uses of money by individuals which include saving and spending. **Spotlight on Goals and Objectives** Unit 6, Lesson 3

TEACHING YOUR SOCIAL STUDIES	 SUPPORT
	Comprehension, Cause and Effect, pp. 149–150
Background, Goods and Services, p. 151; Money, p. 153; Farmers' Markets, p. 154 **Social Studies Strands,** Economics and Development, pp. 151, 152, 154, 155; Individual Development and Identity, p. 152 **Build Skills,** Chart and Graph Skills, pp. 153, 155	**CUES,** p. 152 **Comprehension,** Make Inferences, p. 153; Cause and Effect, p. 155 **Vocabulary,** p. 154
Background, Wants and Needs, p. 157; Mongolian Yurt, p. 160; Guatemalan Cloth, p. 161 **Social Studies Strands,** Individual Development and Identity, pp. 158, 159; Cultures and Diversity, p. 160 **Build Skills,** Chart and Graph Skills, pp. 157, 161; Decision Making, p. 159	**Skim and Scan,** pp. 158, 160, 161 **CUES,** p. 159
Background, Carrboro Farmers' Market, p. 163; The History of Banks, p. 165 **Social Studies Strands,** Economics and Development, pp. 164, 165 **Build Skills,** Chart and Graph Skills, p. 163; Decision Making, p. 164	**Comprehension,** Make Inferences, p. 164; Cause and Effect, p. 165

Print Resources

Student Edition, pp. 147–180
Teacher Edition, pp. 147A–180
Leveled Readers
Leveled Readers Teacher Guides
Document-Based Questions
Primary Atlas

Technology/Digital Resources

Spotlight on Goals and Objectives
North Carolina Interactive Presentations CD
North Carolina Interactive Presentations Online

Online Teacher Edition with ePlanner
Leveled Readers Online Database
North Carolina Adventures CD
North Carolina Adventures Online
Multimedia Biographies CD
Multimedia Biographies Online
Social Studies Music Collection CD

Hands-On Resources

Reading Focus Skills Transparencies
Social Studies Skills Transparencies
Graphic Organizer Write-On/Wipe-Off Cards
Interactive Atlas
Interactive Desk Map
Interactive Map Transparencies
Picture Vocabulary Cards
Primary Source Kit
TimeLinks: Interactive Time Line
Social Studies in Action, pp. 22–23, 44–45, 66–67, 88–89, 105, 110–111, 114–121, 124–127, 132–133, 141

Assessment Options

1. **Unit 6 Test**
   Assessment Program, pp. 21–24
2. **Writing**
   Write a Story, p. 180
3. **Activity**
   Unit Project: Make a Classroom Market, p. 180

Unit 6 Planning Guide

LESSON		NORTH CAROLINA STANDARD COURSE OF STUDY
4 Working in a Factory pp. 167–172 **factory** p. 167	**5** DAYS	**Objective 6.03** Participate in activities that demonstrate the division of labor. **Spotlight on Goals and Objectives** Unit 6, Lesson 4
5 Government Helps Us pp. 173–176 **government service** p. 173	**4** DAYS	**Objective 6.04** Explore community services that are provided by the government and other agencies. **Objective 6.05** Give examples of the relationships between the government and its people. **Spotlight on Goals and Objectives** Unit 6, Lesson 5
Unit 6 Review and Test Prep pp. 177–180	**4** DAYS	**North Carolina Adventures** Unit 6

TEACHING YOUR SOCIAL STUDIES	SSSMART SUPPORT
Background, A Crayon Factory, p. 167 Division of Labor, p. 168 Crayons, p. 170 Protecting Children, p. 171 **Social Studies Strands,** Economics and Development, p. 167 **Build Skills,** Chart and Graph Skills, pp. 168, 171 Problem Solving, p. 169	**Skim and Scan,** p. 168 **Comprehension,** Cause and Effect, p. 169 Sequence, p. 171 **CUES,** p. 170
Background, Government Services, p. 173 **Social Studies Strands,** Government and Active Citizenship, pp. 173, 175 Individual Development and Identity, p. 174 **Build Skills,** Chart and Graph Skills, pp. 174, 175	**Comprehension,** Monitor Understanding, p. 174 **CUES,** p. 175
	Summarize the Unit, Focus Skill Cause and Effect, p. 177

Print Resources

Student Edition, pp. 147–180
Teacher Edition, pp. 147A–180
Leveled Readers
Leveled Readers Teacher Guides
Document-Based Questions
Primary Atlas

Technology/Digital Resources

Spotlight on Goals and Objectives
North Carolina Interactive Presentations CD
North Carolina Interactive Presentations Online

Online Teacher Edition with ePlanner
Leveled Readers Online Database
North Carolina Adventures CD
North Carolina Adventures Online
Multimedia Biographies CD
Multimedia Biographies Online
Social Studies Music Collection CD

Hands-On Resources

Reading Focus Skills Transparencies
Social Studies Skills Transparencies
Graphic Organizer Write-On/Wipe-Off Cards
Interactive Atlas
Interactive Desk Map
Interactive Map Transparencies
Picture Vocabulary Cards
Primary Source Kit
TimeLinks: Interactive Time Line
Social Studies in Action, pp. 22–23, 44–45, 66–67, 88–89, 105, 110–111, 114–121, 124–127, 132–133, 141

Assessment Options

1. **Unit 6 Test**
   Assessment Program, pp. 21–24
2. **Writing**
   Write a Story, p. 180
3. **Activity**
   Unit Project: Make a Classroom Market, p. 180

Leveled Readers

BELOW-LEVEL

Going Shopping

Summary *Going Shopping.* This Reader defines goods and services and examines the jobs that people do to provide goods and services to their communities.

Vocabulary Power Have students define the following words. Help them write one sentence for each word as it relates to the marketplace.

goods
jobs
services
market
factory

Critical Thinking Lead students in a discussion about why people save money.

Write a Business Plan Have students write a plan for a business they would like to own.

Recall and Retell

ON-LEVEL

All Kinds of Markets

Summary *All Kinds of Markets*. This Reader describes markets in North America, Europe, and Asia and the different goods sold in each place.

Vocabulary Power Have students define the following words. Help them write one sentence for each word as it relates to the marketplace.

goods
jobs
market

Critical Thinking Lead students in a discussion about how markets are different from stores.

Write a Description Have students write a description of a market. Have them describe the sounds, sights, and smells of the market.

Recall and Retell

ABOVE-LEVEL

All Twisted Up: Making Pretzels

Summary *All Twisted Up: Making Pretzels*. This Reader explains the history of pretzels and provides a recipe for making pretzels.

Vocabulary Power Have students define the following words. Help them write one sentence for each word as it relates to the marketplace.

goods
job
trade
today

Critical Thinking Lead students in a discussion about why some people decided to make pretzels with machines instead of by hand.

Write a Report Have students write reports about their favorite foods. Have them include the history of the foods in their reports.

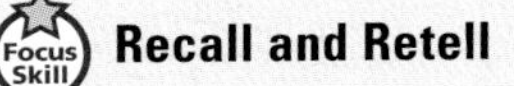
Recall and Retell

Complete a Graphic Organizer

Have students complete the graphic organizer to show that they understand how to recall and retell information about the marketplace.

Recall Detail
Communities have many kinds of stores that sell many kinds of goods.

Recall Detail
Buyers trade with sellers to get the goods and services they want.

Retell
Stores sell goods. Buyers and sellers trade for what they want.

Leveled Readers Teacher Guides include complete lesson plans, copying masters, and project cards.

Harcourt Leveled Readers Available Online!
www.harcourtschool.com

Make a Classroom Market

Getting Started

Introduce the Hands-On Activity on page 180 in the Unit Review. Have students develop project components as they learn about basic concepts of economics. Explain that a market is a place where people buy and sell goods and services. Discuss with students the goods and services that they would like to buy or sell. Have students act out different jobs necessary to make a good or a service in order to demonstrate the division of labor. The final project should express students' understanding of the unit's Big Idea.

The Big Idea
How do people make choices about how to spend money?

Project Management

- Organize students into pairs.
- Guide the research and, if possible, have other adult helpers available to assist students.

Materials: Social Studies textbook; tables or boxes for store counters; drawing paper; posterboard; colored markers; scissors; tape; glue

Organizer: For each booth that students plan, have students fill out an organizer like the one below. This process will help them complete their project.

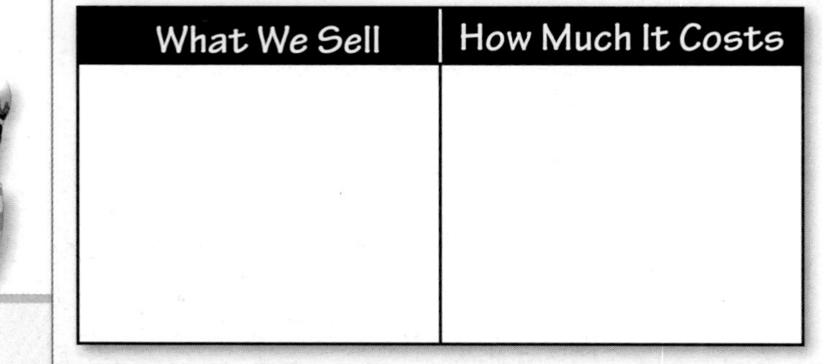

ORGANIZER

What We Sell	How Much It Costs

During the Unit

As students read Unit 6, they can begin work on their market booths. Booths can be based on:

- Lesson Review activities
- Your own favorite activities
- Ideas students develop on their own

Complete the Project

Invite other classes to come to the market to "shop." Encourage students to interact with their customers in a polite and appropriate manner. When the project is complete, provide students with an opportunity to share what they have learned from this unit.

What to Look For

For a scoring rubric, see page 180 of this Teacher Edition.

- Students demonstrate an understanding of basic economic concepts, including the division of labor.
- Students' booths reflect specific kinds of goods that people sell.
- Students can discuss basic economic concepts and then role-play transactions.

Technology/Digital Resources

START

North Carolina Interactive Presentations

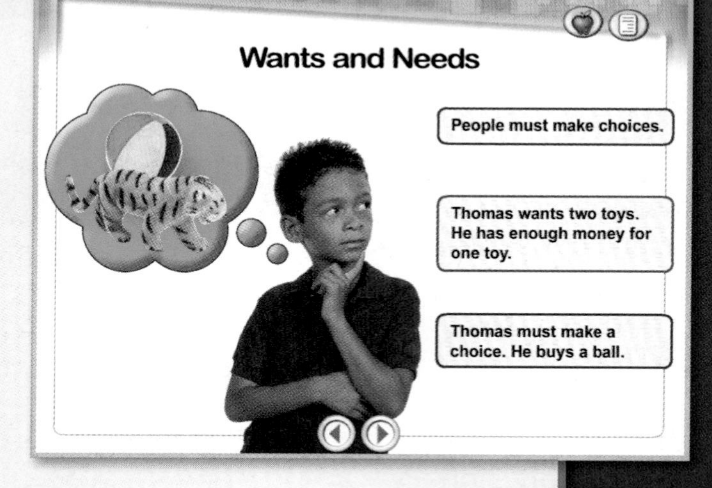

Purpose

The North Carolina Interactive Presentation Unit 6 can be used to preview Unit 6. This presentation provides a concise, visual overview of Competency Goal 6 and its objectives. You can use it to preview the unit for the class, or throughout the unit to introduce and reinforce individual objectives.

Contents

The Unit 6 presentation includes an introduction to Competency Goal 6, including a vocabulary preview and a visual introduction to basic economic concepts. In addition, the presentation covers all the unit's objectives lesson by lesson, giving a broad overview of wants, needs, and how people obtain them.

REVIEW

North Carolina Adventures

Purpose

The North Carolina Adventures games, offered both on CD and online, provide an entertaining first-person-player method of content review. When students have completed the unit, they can review its competency goal and all objectives through the Unit 6 game.

Contents

Tell students they will use their knowledge of wants and needs during a trip with Eco to Japan and Guatemala. Throughout, students will review what they have learned about wants, needs, and the ways people satisfy them. Explain that the "Help" buttons in the game will refer them to pages in their textbooks if they need additional information.

Additional Resources

For Teachers

Free and Inexpensive Materials are listed on the Social Studies website at **www.harcourtschool.com/ss1**

- Addresses to write to for free and inexpensive products
- Links to unit-related materials
- Internet maps
- Internet references

The eTE with ePlanner provides the following components

- A calendar tool for scheduling Social Studies lessons and displaying all scheduled lessons and activities
- TE pages and additional resources for easy online reference

For Students

When students visit **www.harcourtschool.com/ss1** they will find internal resources such as

- Our Multimedia Biographies database
- Skills activities
- Additional research tools
- Information about all 50 states

A mother and daughter buy things in a grocery store.

Unit 6 Preview

PAGES 147–148

Start with the Competency Goal

Competency Goal 6
The learner will apply basic economic concepts to home, school, and the community.

Make It Relevant

Read and discuss the unit competency goal. Help students answer the following question:

Q What are some things that people might buy?

A Students may suggest that people buy goods, such as food, and services, such as baby-sitting.

Discuss the Photograph

Explain to students that the mother and daughter in the photograph are buying goods at a grocery store.

Q How are the mother and daughter paying for their groceries?

A They are using money.

Instructional Design

START WITH THE GOAL AND OBJECTIVES

NORTH CAROLINA STANDARD COURSE OF STUDY
- competency goal
- objectives

PLAN ASSESSMENT

Assessment Options
- Option 1–Unit 6 Test
- Option 2–Writing: Write a Story, p. 180
- Option 3–Activity: Make a Classroom Market, p. 180

PLAN INSTRUCTION

Spotlight on Goals and Objectives
North Carolina Interactive Presentations, Unit 6
Unit 6 Teacher Edition
- resources
- activities
- strategies

Unit 6 Leveled Read…
Teac…

Unit 6 Preview

PAGES 147–148

The Big Idea

Have students read The Big Idea question and then preview ways in which basic economic concepts apply to home, school, and the community.

Access Prior Knowledge

Draw a word web.

- Label the center circle *Things We Buy*.
- Invite students to add words.
- Talk about which words are things that students can actually touch (goods). Circle those words in red.
- Point out that the other things on the web are things that people do for them (services). Circle those words in blue.

Then have students read the paragraph and complete the activity.

How do people make choices about how to spend money?

People in a community buy things from one another. They need money to buy things. People do work to get money for their families. Families must make choices about how to spend their money.

Draw a place where you go to buy things. Show some things that the place sells.

Drawing should show that student understands the concept of spending money.

READ MORE

Encourage independent reading with these books or books of your choice.

Basic

ABC of Jobs by Roger Priddy. Priddy Books, 2003. An easy alphabetical introduction to the different jobs people do.

Proficient

How It Happens at the Boat Factory by Dawn Frederick. Clara House Books, 2002. A boat factory is described and shown with photographs.

Advanced

Grandpa's Corner Store by DyAnne DiSalvo-Ryan. HarperCollins, 2000. Lucy brings together the neighborhood to save her grandfather's grocery store.

Reading Social Studies

Cause and Effect

Learn

- A cause is an event or action that makes something happen.
- What happens is the effect.

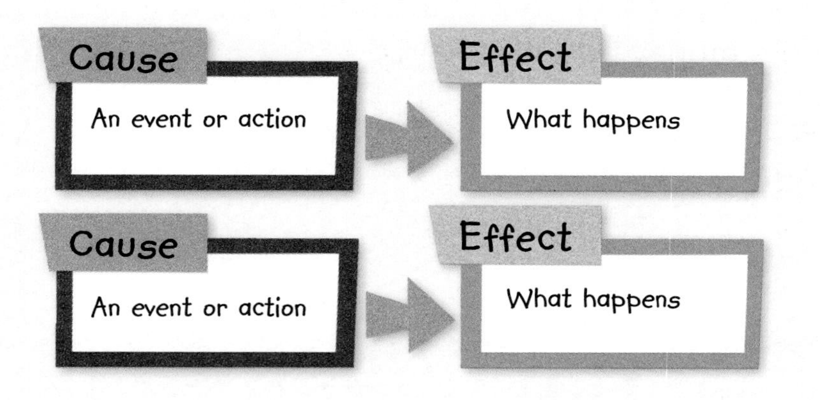

Practice

Read the paragraph below. Underline the effect of Carol's saving money.

Carol does chores every weekend. She earns money. Carol has saved a lot of money, so now she can buy a bicycle.

Cause

Effect

149

Reading Social Studies PAGES 149–150

Learn

Have students read the Learn section and look at the graphic organizer. Explain that a *cause* is what makes an *effect* happen. Students can often identify cause-and-effect relationships because of words and phrases such as *because, so*, and *as a result*.

Practice

Read the paragraph with students, pointing out the word *so*. Ask students to identify the causes in the paragraph. Then help them find the information that follows the word *so*. Explain that this is an effect. Make sure students underline the complete text of the effect of Carol's saving money.

READING FOCUS SKILLS

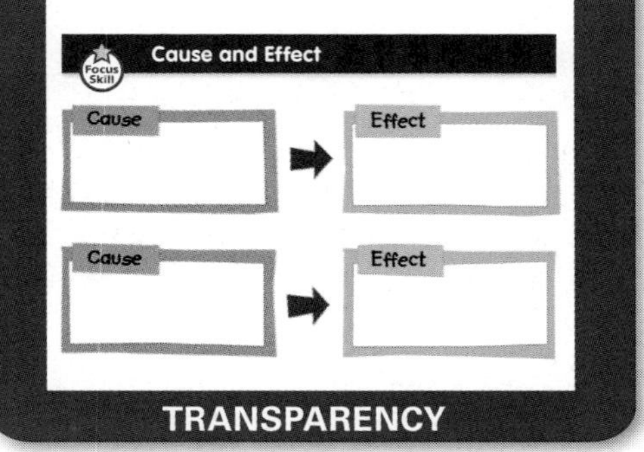

TRANSPARENCY

Graphic Organizer Write-On/ Wipe-Off Cards available

INTEGRATE THE CURRICULUM

ENGLISH LANGUAGE ARTS Write a Dialogue Have students work in pairs to write a short dialogue in which one student purchases an item from another student. Tell students to practice reading aloud the written parts until they can read them clearly and without mistakes. Then ask pairs to perform the dialogue for the class.

ELA 4.04 Extend skills in using oral and written language: clarifying purposes for engaging in communication.

Reading Social Studies PAGES 149–150

Apply

Read the selection with students. Explain how Simon doing chores is the cause of his earning money, as shown in the graphic organizer. Ask students what other events take place in the story. Are those events causes or effects? Help students select one cause and one effect to add to the graphic organizer.

Unit 6 provides many opportunities for students to practice identifying cause and effect. As students read the unit, challenge them to think about how different events described in the unit might cause other events.

Apply

Read the paragraph.

Simon wants to buy his mother a gift for her birthday. He earns money for doing chores around the house. He keeps his money in a jar so that it does not get lost. Simon goes to the Gibsonville Fall Festival in Gibsonville, North Carolina. At the festival, Simon buys a gift for his mother with the money he saved.

The chart below shows causes and effects. What can you add to the chart?

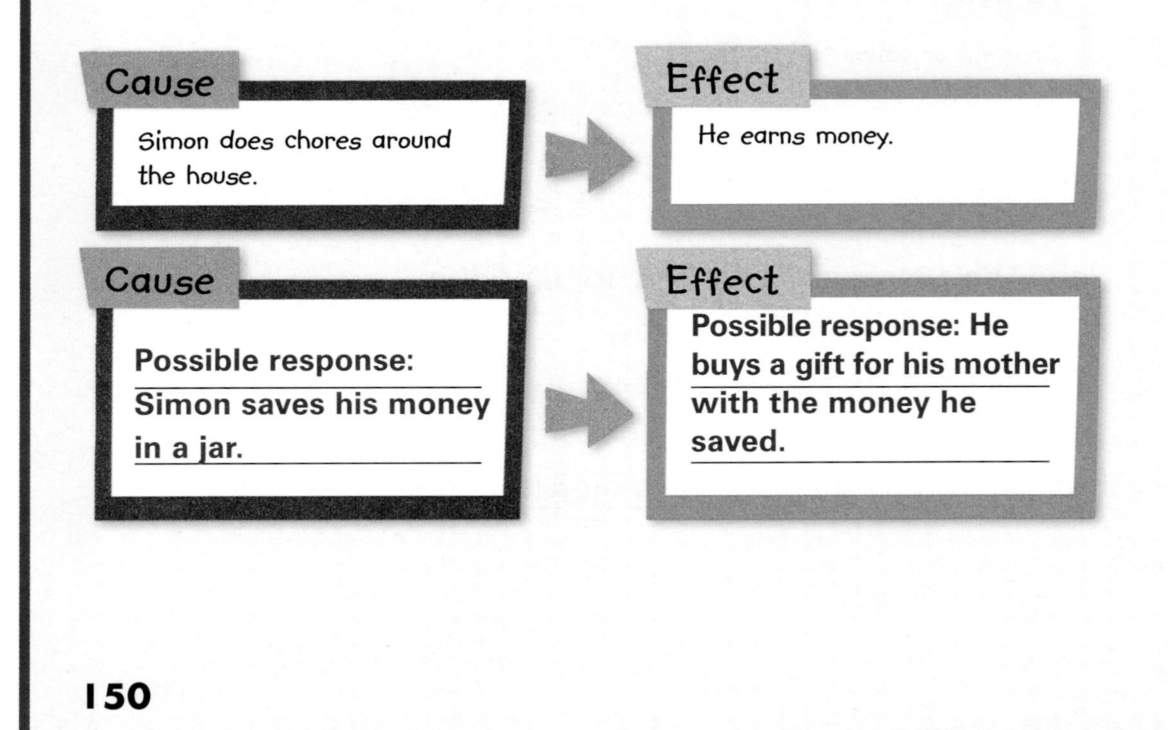

150

ESL/LANGUAGE SUPPORT

Vocabulary Development Help students create a word sort. Tell students to write on a sheet of paper the headings *Products, Jobs*, and *Money* or other category names you select from the unit. As they read the unit, have students list related words under the headings. Remind them to add to their lists as they read the lessons and learn more about economics.

Prior Learning and Experiences Ask students whether they have ever been to a school or community fundraising event, such as a bake sale or carnival. How might community groups make money from such events? What goods and services do the events provide? As they read the unit, ask volunteers to tell the class about experiences they have had at such events.

Build Background

Make It Relevant Ask students to think of a time when they made something, such as an art project or baked goods. Explain that when they make something, students are producers. Then explain to students that they and their families are also consumers because they buy goods made by other people. They also buy services provided by other people. Help students understand that all people are both producers and consumers.

Preview the Lesson

Guide students in previewing the lesson. Point out the following features on Student Edition pages 151–156:

- **Pages 152–153** Point out the goods and services that the people in the photographs are making or providing. Ask students to compare and contrast the goods and services.
- **Page 154** Ask students to explain what is happening in the picture. Point out that the man is using money to pay for the goods that he is purchasing.
- **Page 155** Have students look at the photograph of the mother dropping off her son at school. Ask volunteers to talk about the different jobs their parents may have.

Preteach Vocabulary

- Tell students that **goods** are things that are made. Explain that the books, pencils, paper, and other school supplies that students use are all goods.
- Ask students to think about the last time they got a haircut or visited the dentist. Tell them that these are examples of **services**.
- Explain that **money** includes coins and bills. Have students suggest reasons why people use money to pay for goods and services.
- Have students name places that they visit in order to buy goods or services. Tell students that these places are called **businesses**.

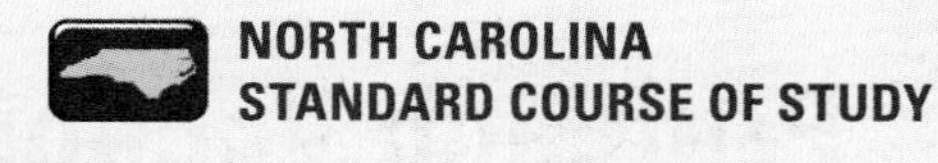

Objective 6.07 Recognize that all families produce and consume goods and services.

Key Content Summary

- **Goods are things made or grown by workers. Services are kinds of work that people do for others.**
- **A producer sells goods or services. A consumer buys goods or services.**
- **People earn money to pay for goods and services.**

Vocabulary

- **goods,** p. 151
- **service,** p. 151
- **money,** p. 153
- **business,** p. 153
- **producer,** p. 154
- **consumer,** p. 154

Use North Carolina Interactive Presentations, Unit 6, Lesson 1, to access prior knowledge and build background.

Preteach Vocabulary *continued*

- Remind students that goods and services are sold. Then tell students that **producers** are people who make the goods and services that people buy.
- Ask students to list some things they own, such as games or clothes. Explain that buying goods such as these makes them **consumers**.

Reach All Learners

ESL/Language Support

Scaffolding Content On the board, draw a T-graph with the word *Business* at the top level. Beneath it, make two columns headed *Producers* and *Consumers*. Help students brainstorm words that relate to producers and consumers to add to the graphic organizer. Discuss ways in which both producers and consumers support businesses.

Business	
Producers	**Consumers**

Extra Support

Learn About Jobs People Do Explain that in most families, at least one person works in order to buy goods and services. Remind students that people work in different jobs. Have the class suggest different jobs. Then ask each student to draw and label a picture of someone doing a job.

Extension Activity

Research Businesses Have students research different kinds of businesses. Then ask them to write a sentence or two explaining why one of the businesses they learned about is both a producer and a consumer.

Integrate the Curriculum

Mathematics

Making Change Give students small amounts of play money. Then lead them through an exercise in which they use the money to make change for various amounts. Help students understand that together, smaller bills make up larger amounts.

Goods and Services

Lesson 1

There are many kinds of workers. Some workers make goods. **Goods** are things that people make to sell. Some workers sell services. **Services** are the kinds of work people do for others. **What might you learn about working?**

Possible response: I might learn about how different people work. Some make goods. Some sell services.

Pet stores sell services and goods.

NORTH CAROLINA STANDARD COURSE OF STUDY

6.07 Recognize that all families produce and consume goods and services.

151

Start with the Objective

Objective 6.07 Recognize that all families produce and consume goods and services.

Set a Purpose for Reading

Read and discuss the lesson objective with students. Then have students read the lesson introduction on their own. Before they answer the question at the end of the introduction, model the thinking process by using the Think Aloud below.

Think Aloud

I know that some workers make goods. I also know that some workers sell services. I think that I will read about the people who make or grow different goods and who sell different services.

BACKGROUND

Goods and Services Tell students that this photograph shows people grooming dogs. Point out that there are examples of goods and services at a pet-grooming business. Groomers offer services for pets, such as washing, nail trimming, and hair cutting. Many groomers also sell goods, such as shampoo, nail trimmers, and collars.

SOCIAL STUDIES STRANDS

Economics and Development Tell students that some goods are made, such as clothes and cars. Other goods are grown, such as fruits and flowers.

Q What other goods are made? What other goods are grown?

A Students should demonstrate an understanding of the difference between goods that are made and goods that are grown.

TextWork

1 CUES

Analyze/Interpret Photographs Help students find the goods in these pictures. Point out that a good is something that people grow or make to sell. Have students find the things that were made to sell in each photograph.

TextWork

1 Circle the goods in the pictures.

Workers Make Goods

Some workers make goods. People can buy these goods in stores. Communities have many kinds of stores. These stores sell many kinds of goods.

Potter

Baker

Carpenter

152

TEACHING YOUR SOCIAL STUDIES

SOCIAL STUDIES STRANDS

Individual Development and Identity Point out that each of the people in these photographs makes a different type of good. Ask students to work in pairs to answer the following questions about what type of work they would like to do when they grow up: What do you like to do? What do you like to make? What would you like to learn to make? What kinds of jobs can a person who makes such things do?

SOCIAL STUDIES STRANDS

Economics and Development Point out to students that each person in these photographs has made something to sell. The potter used clay and water to make pots. The baker made bagels from ingredients such as flour, water, and butter. The carpenter used tools and wood to make a chair. Workers make all kinds of goods for people to use.

Q What kinds of goods can you find in your classroom?

A Students should identify desks, notebooks, pens, and so on.

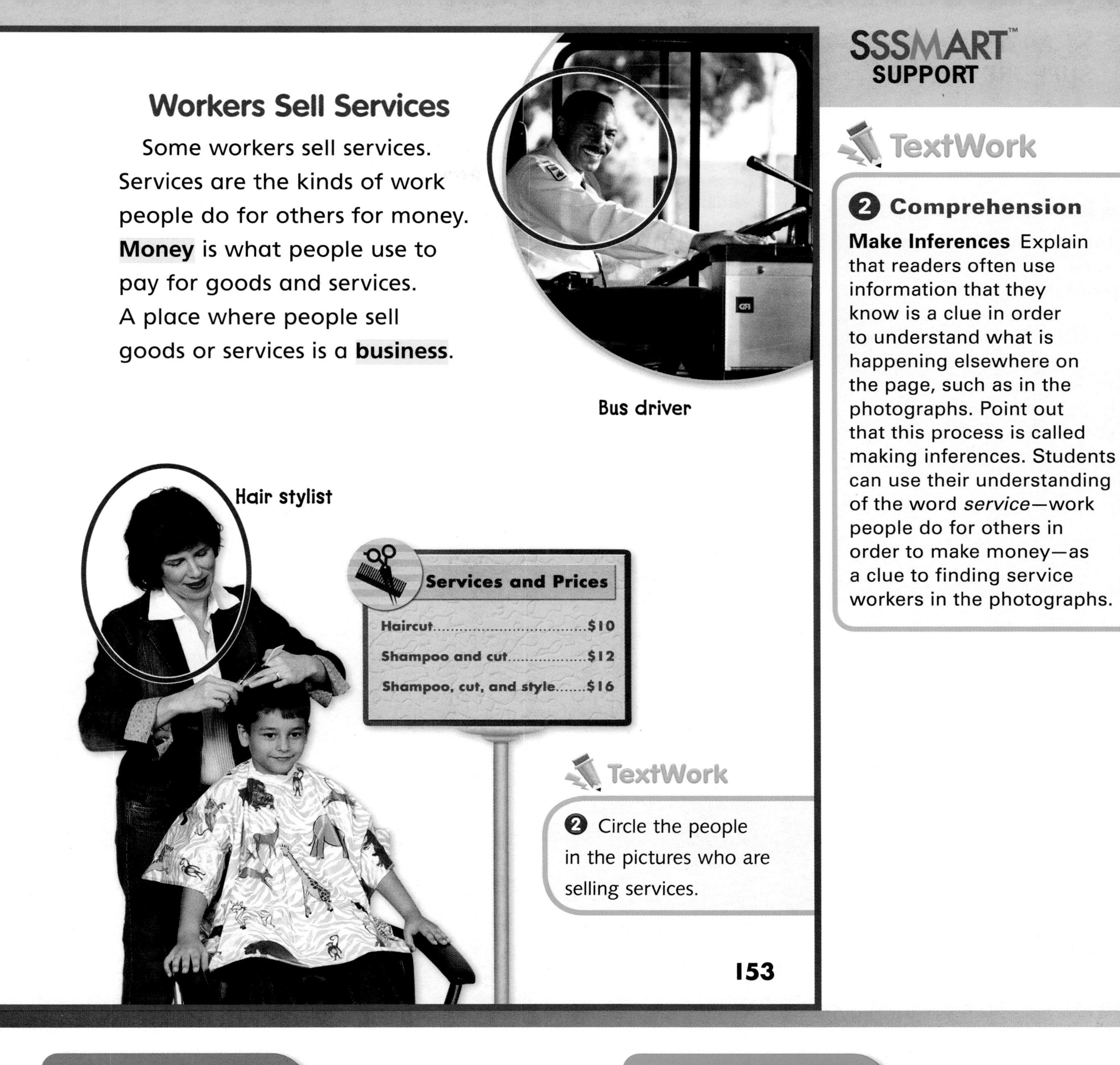

Workers Sell Services

Some workers sell services. Services are the kinds of work people do for others for money. **Money** is what people use to pay for goods and services. A place where people sell goods or services is a **business**.

Bus driver

Hair stylist

TextWork

2 Circle the people in the pictures who are selling services.

SSSMART™ SUPPORT

TextWork

2 Comprehension

Make Inferences Explain that readers often use information that they know is a clue in order to understand what is happening elsewhere on the page, such as in the photographs. Point out that this process is called making inferences. Students can use their understanding of the word *service*—work people do for others in order to make money—as a clue to finding service workers in the photographs.

BACKGROUND

Money The money we use today comes in the form of coins and paper bills. Money has been used for thousands of years to buy goods and services, but it was not always in the form of coins and bills. Some American Indians, for example, the Montauk, used beads made from shells as money. Some colonists used tobacco. In Fiji, whale teeth were used for money. Shells have been used in India. Cows, too, have been used as money in many places throughout history.

BUILD SKILLS

Chart and Graph Skills Have students work in pairs to draw diagrams that illustrate what goes on in a business. Tell them to include the information presented on this page in their diagrams. Encourage pairs to label the workers, the services, the money, and the business that they draw in their diagrams.

TextWork

3 Vocabulary

Understand Vocabulary Point out that the base word in the vocabulary word *producers* is *produce*. Explain that *produce* means "to make." Have students find the person in this photograph who has produced something.

3 Circle the producer in the picture.

Producers and Consumers

Some people work at making goods. Other people work at selling goods or services. All of these people are **producers**. People use money to buy goods and services. These people are **consumers**.

Consumers use money to buy fruits and vegetables.

154

TEACHING YOUR SOCIAL STUDIES

BACKGROUND

Farmers' Markets Tell students that this photograph shows a producer and two consumers at a farmers' market. In North Carolina, the government runs five farmers' markets. They are located in Asheville, Charlotte, Raleigh, Lumberton, and Piedmont Trail. These markets give local farmers a place to sell their goods. The markets give consumers a place to buy locally-grown fresh fruits and vegetables. Both families and businesses, such as restaurants, shop at farmers' markets.

SOCIAL STUDIES STRANDS

Economics and Development Remind students that some goods are made and that others are grown. Point out that one person in this photograph is selling fruit to the man and the girl. The fruits are goods that this producer has grown to sell to consumers. Ask students to identify the producer, the consumers, and the goods in this photograph.

Families Working

In your family, people work and buy goods and services. Families are made up of both producers and consumers. One or more of the people in your family may work. They use the money they earn to buy things for the family.

Your parents may drop you off at school on their way to work.

SSSMART™ SUPPORT

TextWork

4 Comprehension

Cause and Effect Tell students that this question is asking them to think about a cause-and-effect relationship. A cause is what makes something happen. In this question, working people are the cause. To answer the question, students must determine the effect. The effect will be what happens when people work. To help students think about this cause-and-effect relationship, have them write *People work because* in the first blank. Then have them complete that sentence.

SOCIAL STUDIES STRANDS

Economics and Development Tell students that the older members of the family are usually producers because they are able to go to work. Both older and younger family members may buy things, a fact that makes them consumers.

Q Who is a producer in your family? Explain what makes that person a producer.

A Students should demonstrate knowledge that a producer works, providing goods or services to others.

BUILD SKILLS

Chart and Graph Skills Help students further their understanding of the meaning of the words *producers* and *consumers* by filling in a Venn diagram like the one below.

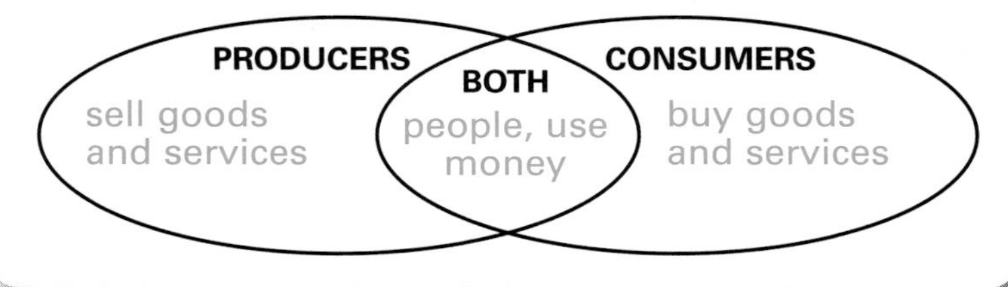

Lesson Review

Summary Have students work individually to summarize the key content before they complete the Lesson Review.

- Goods are things made or grown by workers. Services are kinds of work that people do for others.
- A producer sells goods or services. A consumer buys goods or services.
- People earn money to pay for goods and services.

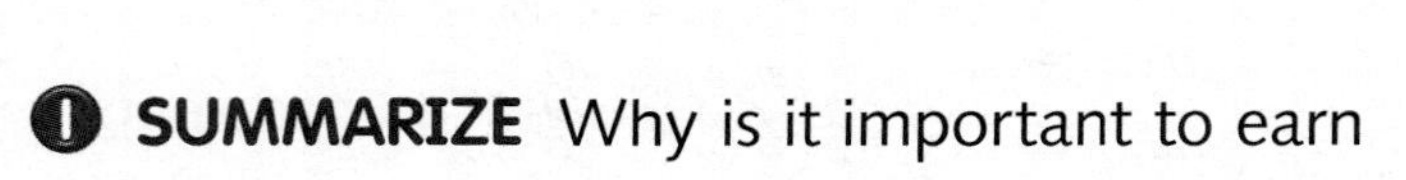

1. **SUMMARIZE** Why is it important to earn money?

   Possible response: It is important to earn money so that you can buy goods and services.

2. How are **goods** and **services** the same?

   Possible response: Workers can sell goods and services. People can buy goods and services.

   How are they different?

   Possible response: People make goods and people do services for others.

3. Why does a community need both producers and consumers?

   Possible response: Communities need producers to make and sell things. They need consumers to buy things.

Writing

Write sentences about a good or a service that you would like to buy.

156

WRITING RUBRIC

Score 4
- identifies a good or a service correctly
- includes detailed explanation of purchase
- has no errors

Score 3
- identifies a good or a service correctly
- includes general explanation of purchase
- has few errors

Score 2
- identifies a good or a service incorrectly
- includes unclear explanation of purchase
- has some errors

Score 1
- does not identify a good or a service
- lacks explanation of purchase
- has many errors

Build Background

Make It Relevant Have students think about their favorite food and their favorite game. Then ask them to decide which of those items they need to live and which item they want for fun. Explain that needs differ from wants.

Preview the Lesson

Guide students in previewing the lesson. Point out the following features on Student Edition pages 157–162:

- **Pages 157 and 158** Preview the photographs by having students describe what is happening in each. Then ask students whether food is something they need or something they want.
- **Page 159** Ask students which goods the boy might purchase. Then take an informal poll to find out who would purchase each item if he or she could buy only one of the things shown.
- **Page 160** Have students describe the content of the photographs. What do they show? Is a home a need or a want? Why?
- **Page 161** Point out the different activities in each photograph. Are these people providing goods or services?

Preteach Vocabulary

- Explain that **needs** are things people must have to live. Help students think of some items that are needs.
- Tell students that in addition to needs, people can also buy goods or services that are **wants**. Ask students to name some things many people have that are wants, such as televisions or cars.
- Help students understand that no one can have everything he or she wants, especially when there is not enough of a thing for everyone. Tell students that when there are very few items, they are called **scarce**.
- Tell students that a **job** is work that a person does for money. Have students name jobs that people they know have.

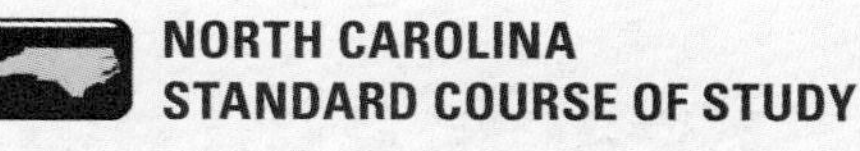

Objective 6.01 Examine wants and needs and identify choices people make to satisfy wants and needs with limited resources.

Objective 6.02 Describe how people of different cultures work to earn income in order to satisfy wants and needs.

Key Content Summary

- **Needs are things that people must have in order to live, such as food, clothing, and shelter.**
- **Wants are things that people would like to have but that they do not need in order to live. People must make decisions about what to buy.**
- **When something is scarce, there is very little of it.**

Vocabulary

- **need,** p. 157
- **want,** p. 157
- **scarce,** p. 159
- **job,** p. 161

Spotlight on Goals and Objectives

Use North Carolina Interactive Presentation, Unit 6, Lesson 2, to access prior knowledge and build background.

Reach All Learners

ESL/Language Support

Content and Language Objectives Draw a two-column graphic organizer on the board. Ask students to list some words in their native language that describe homes or jobs. Write those words in the left column. Then ask students for the corresponding English words. Write those words in the right column. Help students refer to dictionaries or other resources if needed.

Words in Native Language	Words in English

Extra Support

Find Advertisements Explain that businesses want to sell both items that are needs and items that are wants. Distribute magazines, and tell students to find three advertisements showing needs and three advertisements showing wants.

Extension Activity

Research Jobs Around the World Organize students into small groups. Help them use a map or an atlas to choose a country. Then have each group conduct research to find common jobs in that country.

Integrate the Curriculum

Healthful Living

Locate Nutrition Information Tell students that although everyone needs food, some foods are better at fulfilling that need than others. Help students locate information about nutrition on the Internet or in the library. Then have each student make a chart that shows healthful and unhealthful foods.

Things We Use

Lesson

All people have needs. **Needs** are things we must have to live. People also have wants. **Wants** are things people would like to have. People earn money to buy things they want and need.

What will you learn about wants and needs?

Possible response: I will learn about some kinds of wants and needs.

People shop for wants and needs.

NORTH CAROLINA STANDARD COURSE OF STUDY

6.01 Examine wants and needs and identify choices people make to satisfy wants and needs with limited resources.

6.02 Describe how people of different cultures work to earn income in order to satisfy wants and needs.

157

Lesson 2

PAGES 157–162

Start with the Objectives

Objective 6.01 Examine wants and needs and identify choices people make to satisfy wants and needs with limited resources.

Objective 6.02 Describe how people of different cultures work to earn income in order to satisfy wants and needs.

Set a Purpose for Reading

Read aloud the lesson introduction. Point out the highlighted words *needs* and *wants*. Tell students that they will be learning about the difference between these words. Have students answer the question to set a purpose for reading. Model thinking for students by using the Think Aloud below.

Think Aloud

I know that a need is something that I must have, such as water and a place to live. I know that wants are things that are extra. I think I will learn more about the differences between needs and wants.

BACKGROUND

Wants and Needs The people in this photograph are shopping for groceries. Some of the things for sale at the grocery store are things that we need, such as vegetables, fruits, and milk. Other goods are things that we want, such as candy or cake. We do not have to have things like that in order to survive. Ask students to identify more needs and wants they may find in a grocery store.

BUILD SKILLS

Chart and Graph Skills Have students make a chart like the one below. Tell them to fill it in with wants and needs.

Wants	Needs
bike, doll, soccer ball	food, clothing, a place to live

SSSMART™ SUPPORT

TextWork

1 Skim and Scan

Tell students to scan the text for the word *need*. When they find it, have them read the entire sentence that contains that word.

1 Underline the words for things people must have.

Things We Must Have

People need, or must have, food, clothing, and a place to live. Family members help one another meet their needs.

Family members share food with one another.

158

TEACHING YOUR SOCIAL STUDIES

SOCIAL STUDIES STRANDS

Individual Development and Identity There are many different kinds of families, but in all families people help one another take care of their needs.

Q How are the people in this photograph helping one another take care of their needs?

A Students should identify the ways that food, clothing, and shelter needs are being met in this photograph.

Things We Would Like

Families choose how to spend their money. They must first buy the things they need. Then they may use some of the money that is left for things they want. People can not buy everything they want. They must make choices.

Some things are scarce. When something is **scarce**, there is not much of it. It will cost more to buy.

TextWork

❷ Nicholas loves to play soccer. Circle the picture of what he might choose to buy.

159

SSSMART™ SUPPORT

TextWork

❷ CUES

Analyze/Interpret Photographs Point to each item in the photograph. Ask students to identify each item as you point to it. Ask students what might make Nicholas want to buy each item, based on what they were told about Nicholas in the TextWork question.

SOCIAL STUDIES STRANDS

Individual Development and Identity Ask students to take a survey of the class to learn what most of their classmates want to buy. Record their findings in a list on the board. Have students write two sentences about the list that explain what they learned about their classmates' wants and needs.

BUILD SKILLS

Decision Making Have students suppose that Nicholas has $10. The fishbowl costs $6, the soccer ball costs $11, and the checkerboard costs $4. Remind students that Nicholas loves soccer. Ask students to decide what he should do with his money. Should he buy the two items that he can afford right now? Should he wait until he can afford the soccer ball? Have students explain how they arrived at their decisions.

SSSMART™ SUPPORT

TextWork

3 Skim and Scan

Help students find the things in the paragraph that are needs. Tell them to scan the paragraph for the word *need*. Have them read the sentence that contains the word *need*. Tell students that the things that follow the word *need* are examples of needs.

3 Circle the words for things that are needs.

Homes Around the World

Families all over the world have the same needs. They need food, clothing, and a place to live. Many families meet their needs in the same ways your family does. Some meet their needs in different ways.

Mongolia

Tanzania

Sweden

160

TEACHING YOUR SOCIAL STUDIES

BACKGROUND

Mongolian Yurt Tell students that the home in the top left photograph is called a yurt. A *yurt* is a building made from wooden poles and covered with animal skins, blankets, or felt. Mongolian nomads live in yurts. Mongolian nomads are people who move their homes from place to place as they follow their herds of animals. Ask students why a home made of poles and skins would be good for nomads.

SOCIAL STUDIES STRANDS

Cultures and Diversity Ask students to think about the daily lives of the people in each of these photographs. Tell them to notice the types of clothes these people are wearing, the homes they live in, and the food that they are eating. Have students write a short paragraph about one of the photographs that describes how the people in it are meeting their basic needs.

Jobs Around the World

Many people work at jobs. A **job** is work that a person does to earn money.

There are many kinds of jobs around the world. Some are like the jobs in your community. Some are different.

TextWork

4 Underline the sentences that tell what kinds of jobs some people have.

Some people in Japan give music lessons.

Some people in Guatemala make cloth.

Some people in France work in restaurants.

TextWork

4 Skim and Scan

Tell students to scan the text for the word *job*. When they find it, have them read the sentence containing that word. Then have them scan the captions to find the jobs—the work that each person is doing to earn money. Tell students who are still looking for the answer that the words *give*, *make*, and *work* are all ways of describing different kinds of jobs.

BACKGROUND

Guatemalan Cloth Weaving cloth, as the Guatemalan woman is doing in this photograph, is an ancient Mayan tradition. The cloths are brightly colored and decorated with stripes, flowers, and different animals. Weavers use a backstrap loom. Its name comes from the strap that ties around the weaver's back. When weaving, the weaver leans back on the strap, which pulls the thread tight. The backstrap loom is light and easy to set up, so the weaver can take it with him or her from place to place.

BUILD SKILLS

Chart and Graph Skills Have students fill in a chart like the one below to describe the ways that each person in these photographs is earning money.

Job Name	Job Description
Piano teacher	gives music lessons to children
Weaver	makes cloth
Food server	takes orders and brings people food

Lesson Review

Summary Have students work individually to summarize the key content before they complete the Lesson Review.

- Needs are things that people must have in order to live, such as food, clothing, and shelter.
- Wants are things that people would like to have but that they do not need in order to live. People must make decisions about what to buy.
- When something is scarce, there is very little of it.

Lesson 2 Review

1. **SUMMARIZE** How do people get the things they use every day?

   Possible response: People work to get the things they use every day. People earn money at work. They use the money to buy things they need and want.

2. When is something **scarce**?

   Possible response: Something is scarce when there is not much of it.

3. What are some kinds of jobs that people can have?

   Possible response: People can give music lessons, work in restaurants, or make cloths.

Activity

Draw a picture of yourself doing a job that you might like to have one day.

162

ACTIVITY RUBRIC

Score 4
- draws detailed picture of future job
- picture is neat and colorful

Score 3
- draws detailed picture of future job
- picture is mostly neat and colorful

Score 2
- draws unclear picture of future job
- picture is somewhat neat and colorful

Score 1
- does not draw a job
- picture is not neat and colorful

Build Background

Make It Relevant Ask students to share their experiences of going to places to buy things. On the board, list the places that students name, such as malls, grocery stores, and convenience stores.

Preview the Lesson

Guide students in previewing the lesson. Point out the following features on Student Edition pages 163–166:

- **Page 163** Invite students to preview the photograph. Ask students to describe what type of market is shown and what the people are doing.
- **Page 164** Ask students to preview the title of this section. Ask students to define *spend* in their own words. Then ask students to list some things they have spent money on, such as gifts, games, or snacks.
- **Page 165** Explain that many people put the money they want to save in a bank. Ask students to describe a bank. Ask them to suggest why people put their money in banks.

Preteach Vocabulary

- Explain that a **market** is a place where people can buy or sell things. Have students draw a picture of a person buying or selling a good in a market. Encourage students to label their pictures.
- Ask students to discuss whether they have ever received money as a gift, for doing a chore, or for helping someone. Ask students what they do with the money they get. Explain that many people **save** some of the money they earn. Ask students where they could save some of their money. Answers may include a piggy bank, a special hiding place, or the bank.
- Point out that when people **trade** with one another, they are giving one thing to get another. Many people trade money to get a good or a service, but some people can trade other goods or services for something that they want. Have students list some goods and services that people might trade.

NORTH CAROLINA STANDARD COURSE OF STUDY

Objective 6.06 Identify the uses of money by individuals which include saving and spending.

Key Content Summary

- **People buy and sell goods at a market.**
- **People trade by giving one thing to get another.**
- **People save by keeping some of their money. Some people save their money in a bank.**

Vocabulary

- **market,** p. 163
- **save,** p. 163
- **trade,** p. 164

Spotlight on Goals and Objectives

Use North Carolina Interactive Presentations, Unit 6, Lesson 3, to access prior knowledge and build background.

Reach All Learners

ESL/Language Support

Active Learning Explain that many people make shopping lists to help them remember what they need or want to buy. Together, create a shopping list. Record students' answers when they name things that they need or want to buy. Then have students take turns pointing to items on the list and saying where they would go to buy each item.

Extra Support

Review the Lesson Review the lesson and the photographs within the lesson. Ask question such as these: "Where is Amy? Why is Amy at the market? What does Amy want to buy? What should Amy do with the money she has left?" Then encourage students to make picture cards that contain words and concepts from the lesson.

Extension Activity

Make a Flowchart Show students an example of a flowchart and explain how flowcharts are set up. Have students make a flowchart tracing the flow of money from buyers to sellers.

Integrate the Curriculum

English Language Arts

Compare Markets Discuss with students the many choices that people have when deciding where to shop for goods and services. Invite students to use a two-column chart to compare and contrast an outdoor market with another type of market, such as a chain supermarket or an online store. Suggest that students create categories such as Location, Goods, and People.

ELA 4.04 Extend skills in using oral and written language: producing written products.

Spending and Saving

Amy's community has a market. A **market** is a place where people buy and sell goods. Amy wants to spend some of her money. She also wants to save some. To **save** is to keep some money to use later. **What will you learn about spending and saving?**

Possible response: I will learn some ways people spend and save their money.

Farmers' Market in Carrboro, North Carolina

NORTH CAROLINA STANDARD COURSE OF STUDY

6.06 Identify the uses of money by individuals which include saving and spending.

163

Lesson 3

PAGES 163–166

Start with the Objective

Objective 6.06 Identify the uses of money by individuals which include saving and spending.

Set a Purpose for Reading

Read and discuss the lesson objective and the lesson introduction with students. Draw students' attention to the highlighted word *save*. Tell students to keep the highlighted word in mind as they answer the question to set a purpose for reading. Model the thinking process for students by using the Think Aloud below.

Think Aloud

I know that people use their money in two main ways: they spend it, and they save it. I think that I will read about how people make choices about spending and saving their money.

BACKGROUND

Carrboro Farmers' Market Tell students that this is a photograph of the Carrboro Farmers' Market in North Carolina. This market is open on Wednesdays and Saturdays from March through December. Farmers sell fruit, vegetables, flowers, and meats. Craftsworkers who make and sell jewelry, clothes, and decorative items are at the market, too. In 2006, a yearly Kids' Seedling Event was started. Farmers give tomato seedlings to children at the market. The following June, the children can show off their plants and win prizes.

BUILD SKILLS

Chart and Graph Skills Have students identify the consequences of spending and saving money by filling in a chart like the one below.

Cause	Effect
Spending	You have less money. You have more things.
Saving	You have more money. You have fewer things.

SSSMART™ SUPPORT

TextWork

1 Comprehension

Make Inferences Tell students that to make inferences, readers use clues from the text and from information that they already know to understand what they are reading. Have students recall the definitions of *producer* and *consumer* from Lesson 2 of this unit to help them answer the TextWork question.

TextWork

1 At the market, is Amy a producer or a consumer? Circle your answer.

producer (consumer)

Spending

Amy has money to spend at the market. She wants to buy a gift for her grandmother. Amy will think about things her grandmother likes. She will also think about how much money she has.

Buyers trade money for goods and services. When people **trade**, they give one thing to get another thing.

164

TEACHING YOUR SOCIAL STUDIES

BUILD SKILLS

Decision Making Point out that Amy is making a decision about how to spend her money for her grandmother's birthday. Have students work in pairs to identify the steps that Amy is taking in her decision-making process. They can do this by having one partner read the first paragraph, one sentence at a time, and having the other partner write out each step Amy is taking to make her decision.

SOCIAL STUDIES STRANDS

Economics and Development Tell students that before people used money, they often traded with one another. This is called bartering. Gradually, people decided to use money because they did not always have items of equal value to trade.

Q Have you ever bartered something? How did you decide whether the trade was fair?

A Answers will vary but should reflect an understanding of the meanings of the words *trade* and *barter*.

Saving

Amy does not spend all of her money at once. She saves some of it to use later.

Many people put the money they save in a bank. A bank is a business that keeps money safe.

TextWork

❷ Underline the sentence that tells why people keep money in a bank.

SSSMART SUPPORT

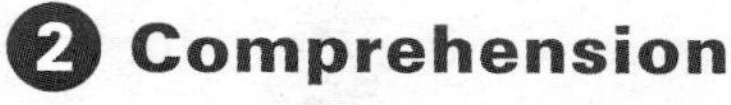

TextWork

❷ **Comprehension**

Focus Skill **Cause and Effect** Remind students that people often do one thing because they want another thing to happen. This process is called cause and effect. Have students underline what happens to the money that people put in a bank.

SOCIAL STUDIES STRANDS

Economics and Development Tell students that banks pay their customers money if their customers keep their money in savings accounts. The money that banks pay people for saving is called *interest*. If Amy put $1 in a savings account, the bank might pay her $.01 in interest. Ask students to determine how much interest money the bank would pay Amy if she put $5 in savings. $.05

Q Why is it better to save in a bank than at home?

A People can earn interest at a bank.

BACKGROUND

The History of Banks The only service that the earliest banks provided was changing money of one kind for another. This meant that a person with coins from one country could trade them for the type of coins used in another country that they were visiting. Banks later held accounts for businesspeople. This practice meant that store owners did not have to carry their money with them when they traveled to buy more goods because the banks kept both the money and careful records of how much money each person had.

Lesson Review

Summary Have students work individually to summarize the key content before they complete the Lesson Review.

- People buy and sell goods at a market.
- People trade by giving one thing to get another.
- People save by keeping some of their money. Some people save their money in a bank.

1. **SUMMARIZE** Why do people spend some of their money and save some of it?

   Possible response: People spend some of their money on things they want or need. People save some of their money for things they may want or need later.

2. What do people do at a **market**?

   Possible response: People buy and sell goods at a market.

3. Why do people put their money in a bank?

   Possible response: People put their money in a bank to save some for later. A bank helps keep their money safe.

Writing

Make a shopping list. Tell where you would go to buy the goods on your list.

166

WRITING RUBRIC

Score 4
- list is complete and very detailed
- stores match items on list
- work has few or no errors

Score 3
- list is complete
- stores match items on list
- work has few errors

Score 2
- list contains one or two items
- stores do not match items
- work has some errors

Score 1
- lists contains one or two items
- stores do not match items
- work has many errors

Build Background

Make It Relevant Encourage students to discuss the types of goods that are made in factories. Ask students to think about what it would be like to visit a factory. What would the factory look like and sound like? Explain that many goods that people use every day are made in factories.

Preview the Lesson

Guide students in previewing the lesson. Point out the following features on Student Edition pages 167–172:

- **Page 167** Invite students to preview the photograph. Ask students to predict the steps they will learn about in the crayon-making process.
- **Pages 168–169** Ask students to preview the photographs. Ask students what the man in the photographs is doing.
- **Page 170** Point out to students that factories have different machines to help with different jobs. Different people run these machines. Ask students to list reasons why machines in factories are helpful.
- **Page 171** Ask students to preview the Children in History section. Explain that long ago, children used to work in factories. Ask students to predict reasons they will learn why children do not work in factories today.

Preteach Vocabulary

- Explain to students that a **factory** is a place where different people use machines to make goods. Ask students to draw a picture of people working in a factory making a certain good. Have them label the product being made in the factory.

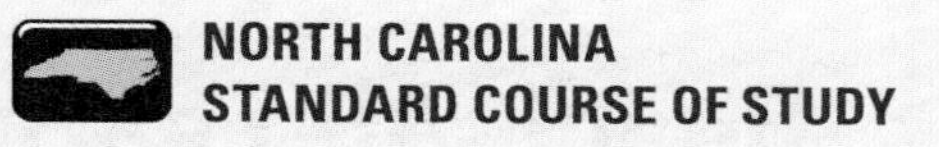

NORTH CAROLINA STANDARD COURSE OF STUDY

Objective 6.03 Participate in activities that demonstrate the division of labor.

Key Content Summary

- **A factory is a place where people use machines to make goods.**
- **Workers in a factory each do part of the job.**
- **If the job is very big, the factory needs many workers.**

Vocabulary

- **factory**, p. 167

Spotlight on Goals and Objectives

Use North Carolina Interactive Presentations, Unit 6, Lesson 4, to access prior knowledge and build background.

Reach All Learners

ESL/Language Support

Active Learning Invite students to share experiences they have had making things such as cookies, or building something such as a house of blocks. Ask: "What do you want to make?" Invite each student to role-play the steps in making an item for the class.

Extra Support

Learn Vocabulary List the words *factory*, *building*, and *workers* on the board. Tell students that these words go together. Ask: "Which words have meanings that are almost the same?" Then have students write a sentence describing why the word *workers* belongs in the group. A possible response might be "Workers have jobs in a factory."

Extension Activity

Write a Letter Give students the opportunity to find out more about a factory in North Carolina. Help them use school-approved resources to research a factory. Then work with students to write a class letter with questions to the public relations department of the factory.

Integrate the Curriculum

Mathematics

Conduct a Survey Have students conduct a survey to find out their classmates' favorite crayon colors. Provide a list of choices such as red, green, purple, brown, black, blue, or yellow. Allow pairs of students to survey other classes. When they have tallied the results, assist students in creating a large picture graph. Display the graph for the entire school to see.

Working in a Factory

Crayons are made in a factory. A **factory** is a building in which people use machines to make goods. Many people work at this crayon factory. In the factory, workers do different jobs. **What might you learn about factories?**

Possible response: I might learn about how crayons are made in a factory.

A crayon factory

NORTH CAROLINA STANDARD COURSE OF STUDY

6.03 Participate in activities that demonstrate the division of labor.

167

Lesson 4

PAGES 167–172

Start with the Objective

Objective 6.03 Participate in activities that demonstrate the division of labor.

Set a Purpose for Reading

As a group, read the lesson introduction aloud. Point out the highlighted word *factory.* Ask students to describe what happens in a factory. Then have students answer the question to set a purpose for reading. Model thinking for students by using the Think Aloud below.

Think Aloud

I know that goods like crayons are made in a factory. I also know that people use machines to make goods in factories. I think that I will read about the ways that people use machines to make crayons in a factory.

BACKGROUND

A Crayon Factory Tell students that this photograph shows a crayon factory. In a factory like this one, workers do different jobs. Some workers take orders from customers. Others workers run the factory. Still others work to make the crayons, pack them, and send them to stores. Explain how the different jobs in a factory are an example of the division of labor.

SOCIAL STUDIES STRANDS

Economics and Development Open a box of crayons and place them on a desk at the front of the class. Point out the different parts: the box, the crayons, and the labels on the crayons. Explain that different people are in charge of different steps of putting together a box of crayons.

SSSMART™ SUPPORT

TextWork

① Skim and Scan

Help students find out what gives crayons their color. Tell them to scan the first paragraph for the word *colors*. Model reading around that word to help students find the answer.

How Crayons Are Made

Step 1

Some factory workers mix hot, melted wax and colorings. The wax will give the crayons their shape. The colorings will give them their colors.

Other workers pour the hot, colored wax into molds. The molds shape the crayons.

TextWork

① What gives crayons their colors?

the colorings

168

TEACHING YOUR SOCIAL STUDIES

BACKGROUND

Division of Labor Tell students that people often split up a big job into smaller jobs. This is called the division of labor. Tell students that *labor* means "work." Division of labor is dividing up the work. Doing this uses each person's skills. It also helps people get a big job done faster. Perhaps students have had the experience of setting the table as their parents were making a meal. Point out that this is an example of the division of labor.

BUILD SKILLS

Chart and Graph Skills Help students keep track of the steps in the crayon-making process as they read. Draw this flowchart on the board. Have students copy it in their notebooks and fill it out as they read. Encourage them to use drawings and sentences.

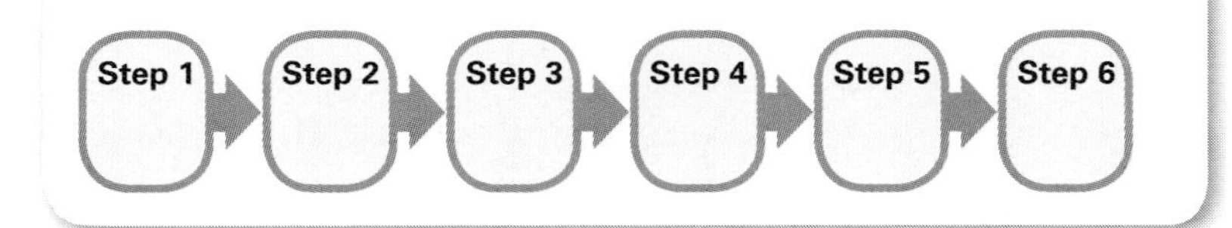

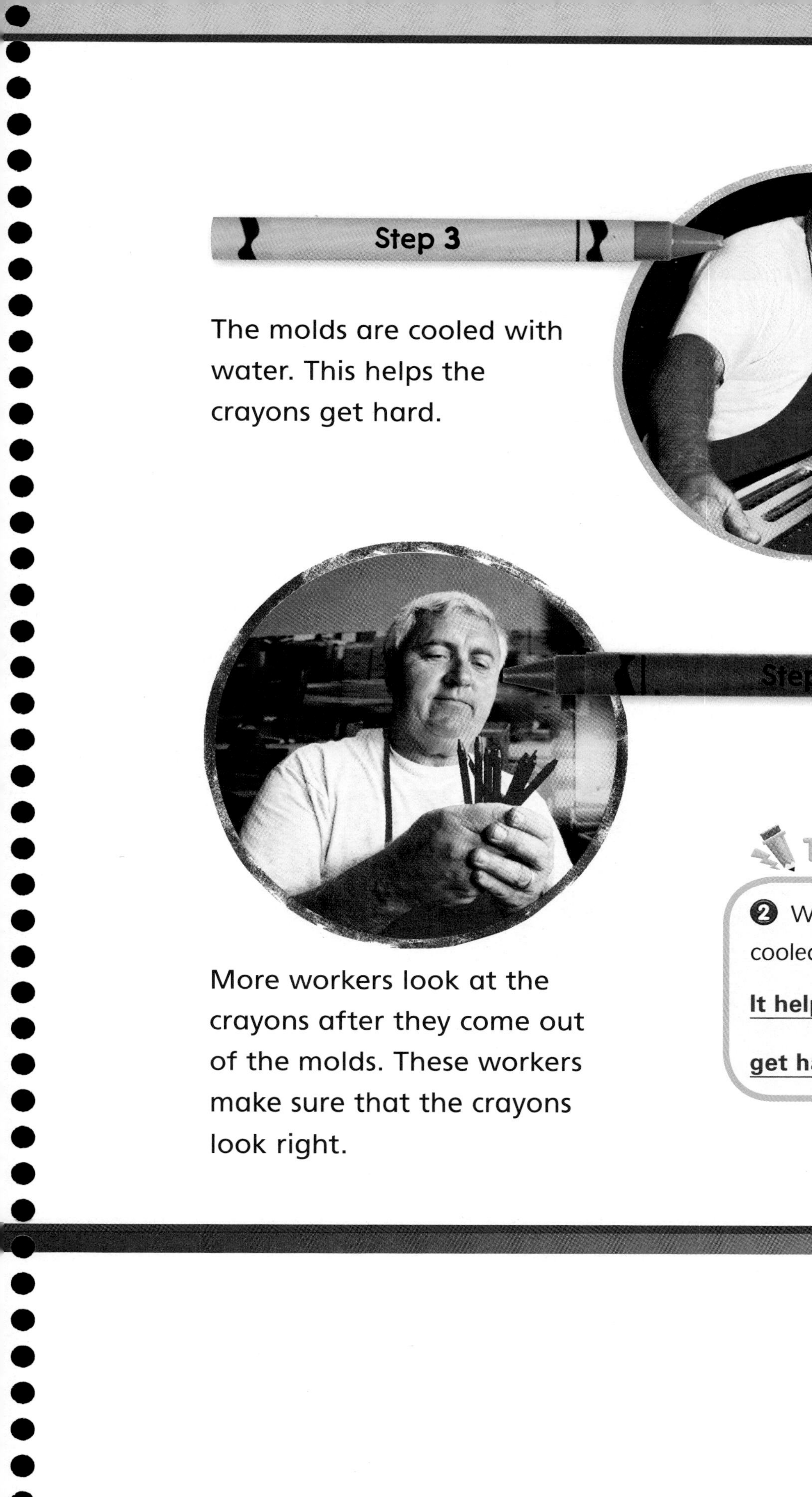

Step 3

The molds are cooled with water. This helps the crayons get hard.

Step 4

More workers look at the crayons after they come out of the molds. These workers make sure that the crayons look right.

TextWork

❷ Why are the molds cooled with water?

It helps the crayons get hard.

169

SSSMART™ SUPPORT

TextWork

❷ Comprehension

Cause and Effect
Tell students that this question is asking them to think about a cause-and-effect relationship. To answer the question, students must determine the effect. Have students look for what happens as a result of the molds being cooled with water. Tell them to write the effect in the TextWork box.

BUILD SKILLS

Problem Solving Have students participate in a task that involves the division of labor (for example, tidying the room). Work with students to identify the steps to complete the task. Then form groups and assign each group a step. When they have completed the steps, lead a discussion about using division of labor to complete a task. Prompt students to consider the difference between doing a task alone and dividing it up in terms of prep time, cooperation, and the finished product.

TextWork

3 CUES

Analyze/Interpret Photographs Help students identify the photograph of the machine that is making labels. Pair students and have them describe what is taking place in each photograph on this page. Then tell them to circle the photograph that shows a machine that is making labels.

Step 5

In another part of the factory, a worker uses a machine to make colored labels. Another machine pastes the labels on the crayons.

Step 6

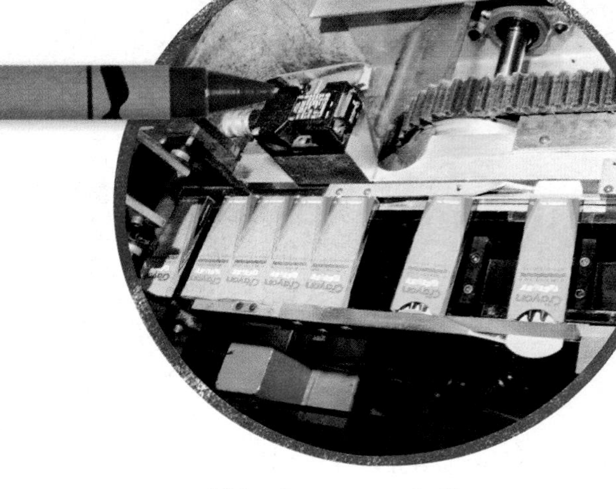

Workers put the crayons in boxes of different sizes. The boxes are then sent out to stores.

TextWork

3 Look at the pictures. Circle the picture that shows a machine making labels.

BACKGROUND

Crayons Tell students that a coloring crayon, shown in this lesson, is only one type of drawing tool. Chalk is another type of drawing tool. It is made of different ingredients and used in different ways. Pastels are made from both ingredients used for chalk and ingredients used for coloring crayons. Pastel crayons are waxy and chalky. Like coloring crayons, pastels come in many colors. Like chalk, pastels can be smudged. Many artists draw with pastels.

The crayons go to stores around the world. Your crayons went from the factory to a store near you. Then they came to your school.

TextWork

4 Where do crayons go after they leave the factory?

to a store

Children in History

Addie Laird

Addie Laird was a young girl who worked in a factory long ago. At that time, many children had jobs in factories. They worked hard all day at unsafe machines. Children got hurt. People who saw this picture of Addie wanted to pass new laws. Now a child's job is to learn in school.

TextWork

4 Comprehension

Sequence Remind students of sequence words such as *then* and *after*. Have students read the paragraph on this page to find out where crayons are sent after they leave the factory.

BACKGROUND

Protecting Children Almost 100 years ago, the U.S. government passed a law to protect child workers. One part of the law says that children under 14 cannot work during school hours, in dangerous jobs, or in factories.

Q Why do you think Congress passed this law?

A Possible response: so children could go to school; to keep children from getting hurt; to keep people from making children work

BUILD SKILLS

Chart and Graph Skills Help students understand where crayons are sent after they leave the factory. Pair students, and have partners draw a diagram that begins at the factory and ends at your school. Tell them to read the paragraph to find out what happens in between the factory and the school.

Lesson Review

Summary Have students work individually to summarize the key content before they complete the Lesson Review.

- A factory is a place where people use machines to make goods.
- Workers in a factory each do part of the job.
- If the job is very big, the factory needs many workers.

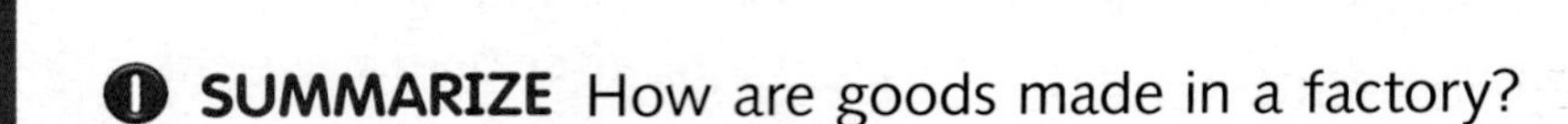

1. **SUMMARIZE** How are goods made in a factory?

   Possible response: Goods are made in a factory by workers who do different jobs.

2. How is a **factory** different from a market?

   Possible response: A factory is different from a market because people make things in a factory and sell things at a market.

3. Why do factories need many workers?

   Possible response: Factories need many workers because there are many kinds of jobs.

Activity

Draw a set of pictures that show how crayons are made. Show different workers doing each step.

172

ACTIVITY RUBRIC

Score 4
- each step in the process is completely clear and accurate
- different workers are shown in each step
- has no errors

Score 3
- each step in the process is clear and accurate
- different workers are shown in most steps
- has few errors

Score 2
- most steps in the process are shown
- different workers are shown in some steps
- has some errors

Score 1
- some steps of the process are shown
- few workers are shown in the steps
- has many errors

Build Background

Make It Relevant Explain to students that governments help communities. Point out that there are many different types of government services, such as schools, parks, and libraries. Ask students to list how people who work in a school, park, or library provide their services to other people. Record students' ideas.

Preview the Lesson

Guide students in previewing the lesson. Point out the following features on Student Edition pages 173–176:

- **Page 173** Point out that government workers help keep roads clear. Ask why this job is important for communities.
- **Page 174** Ask students to preview the photograph. Ask students whether they have seen people doing road work. Ask students to list reasons why the government might have people working on roads.
- **Page 175** Have students preview the two smaller photographs. Ask them to compare and contrast what is taking place in these photographs.

Preteach Vocabulary

- List various **government services**, such as schools, libraries, and parks. Have students explain why these services are provided by the government and how the services help the community.

NORTH CAROLINA STANDARD COURSE OF STUDY

Objective 6.04 Explore community services that are provided by the government and other agencies.

Objective 6.05 Give examples of the relationship between the government and its people.

Key Content Summary

- **Government services are things that the government does for the community.**
- **Government workers help keep the community safe and clean.**
- **There are different kinds of government workers, such as police officers, firefighters, teachers, librarians, and park rangers.**

Vocabulary

- **government service**, p. 173

Spotlight on Goals and Objectives

Use North Carolina Interactive Presentations, Unit 6, Lesson 5, to access prior knowledge and build background.

Reach All Learners

ESL/Language Support

Content and Language Objectives Provide students with photographs of a variety of government services. Use sentence strips to write a sentence about each of the photographs. Read the sentences aloud. Then have students repeat the sentence after you. When students are familiar with the words and sentences, ask volunteers to read aloud the sentences.

Extra Support

Fill in a Story Write a brief story about the services that the government provides, leaving out key words. For example, *People work as* ___police___ ___officers___ *to make sure that people follow the laws*. Read aloud the story to the class. Then ask volunteers to take turns reading aloud each sentence.

Extension Activity

Create a Bulletin Board Invite local government workers to visit the classroom. Encourage students to prepare meaningful questions to ask. Have students take notes during each visit. Then have students create a bulletin board to display information about the work that each person does.

Integrate the Curriculum

Arts

Make a Government Worker Scene Provide students with a blank scene of a community. Then give students magazines to find and cut out pictures of government workers at work, such as a librarian at a library. Have students glue their pictures to the community scene. Encourage students to include captions and labels for each worker or government setting.

Lesson 5

Government Helps Us

Government workers clear snow from roads.

Government services are the things that a government does to make a community a good place to live in. Government workers help keep communities safe and clean. **What do you think you will learn about government services?**

Possible response: I think I will learn how government services help communities.

NORTH CAROLINA STANDARD COURSE OF STUDY

6.04 Explore community services that are provided by the government and other agencies.

6.05 Give examples of the relationship between the government and its people.

Lesson 5

PAGES 173–176

Start with the Objectives

Objective 6.04 Explore community services that are provided by the government and other agencies.

Objective 6.05 Give examples of the relationship between the government and its people.

Set a Purpose for Reading

Read and discuss the lesson objectives with students. Then have them read the lesson introduction on their own. Before they answer the question at the end of the introduction, model thinking by using the Think Aloud below.

Think Aloud

I know that the government helps people by providing services. I also know that these services keep the community safe and clean. I think that I will read about the kinds of services that the government provides to the community.

BACKGROUND

Government Services Tell students that this photograph shows one of the services provided to the community by the government. Ask them to describe the service. Explain that the roads being cleared of snow by government workers were also built by government workers. Because roads are used by everyone in the community, people count on the government to make sure that they are kept clear and safe.

SOCIAL STUDIES STRANDS

Government and Active Citizenship Tell students that the government provides communities with many kinds of services, such as schools, buses, and trash collection.

Q What might happen if the government did not provide services to the community?

A Possible responses: Some things would not get done; only people who could afford services would get them.

SSSMART™ SUPPORT

TextWork

1 Comprehension

Monitor Understanding Tell students that readers often stop and think about what they are reading to make sure that they understand it. Model this skill for students. Read the first sentence aloud. Say, "The first sentence tells me that there are different kinds of government workers. I think the rest of the sentences will name some different kinds of government workers. I will read the next sentence to see whether I am correct." In their answers, students may list other government workers mentioned in the text or government workers not mentioned in the text.

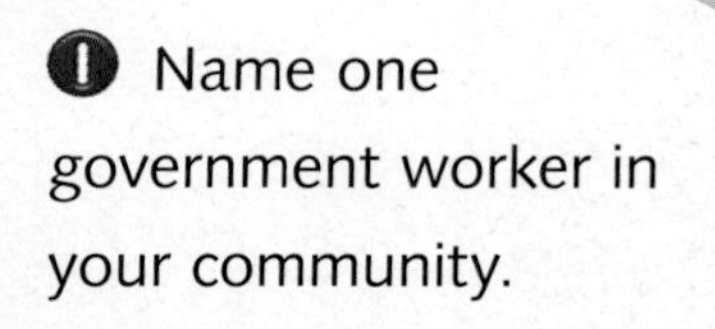

1 Name one government worker in your community.

Possible response: **police officer**

Government Workers

There are different kinds of government workers. Police officers make sure that people follow the laws. Firefighters help when there is a fire.

Schools are government services. Teachers help you learn. You go to school to learn how to be a good citizen in the community.

Some government workers build roads.

TEACHING YOUR SOCIAL STUDIES

BUILD SKILLS

Chart and Graph Skills Have students use a word web to identify workers who provide government services.

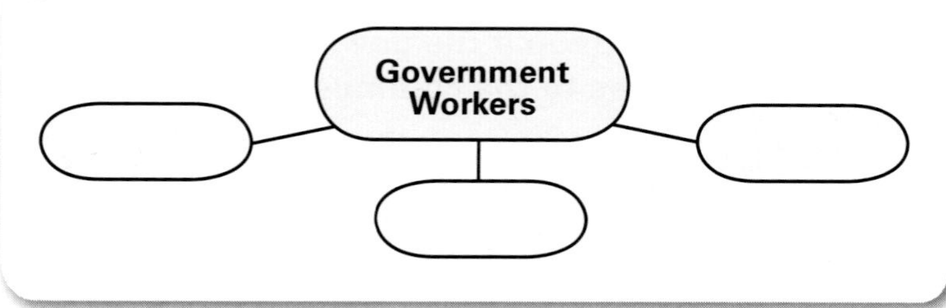

SOCIAL STUDIES STRANDS

Individual Development and Identity Have students talk with a partner about a job that they would like to do for the community as a government worker. Have partners tell each other why their chosen service is important. Tell them to explain how the job keeps the community safe or clean.

Park rangers make sure parks stay clean. They help visitors to the parks stay safe.

Libraries are government services, too. Librarians help you find books for school. They give you ideas for books to read for fun, too.

TextWork

❷ Circle the people who are government workers.

175

SSSMART™ SUPPORT

TextWork

❷ **CUES**

Analyze/Interpret Photographs Call on volunteers to describe what each person in the photographs is doing. Encourage students to include the children in their descriptions. Then have students circle the people who are working for the government.

SOCIAL STUDIES STRANDS

Government and Active Citizenship Tell students that libraries used to be private collections of books in the homes of people who could afford them or they were rooms in government and church buildings where important papers were stored. Today, public libraries are paid for by the government and contain books, magazines, newspapers, and computers for everyone in the community to use.

BUILD SKILLS

Chart and Graph Skills Use a chart to help students better understand the information.

Worker	Service
police officers	make sure people follow the laws
teachers	help students learn
park rangers	help park visitors stay safe
librarians	help people find books

Lesson Review

Summary Have students work individually to summarize the key content before they complete the Lesson Review.

- Government services are things that the government does for the community.
- Government workers help keep the community safe and clean.
- There are different kinds of government workers, such as police officers, firefighters, teachers, librarians, and park rangers.

1. **SUMMARIZE** How do government services help people?

   Possible response: Government services help keep roads clean and communities safe.

2. What is one **government service**?

   Possible response: Schools are a government service.

3. How do librarians help you?

   Possible response: Librarians help you find books and information you need from the library.

Writing

Write sentences about a government service that helps keep your community clean or safe.

176

WRITING RUBRIC

Score 4
- uses clear, descriptive sentences
- describes a service that keeps a community safe or clean
- has no errors

Score 3
- uses clear, descriptive sentences
- describes a service that keeps a community safe or clean
- has few errors

Score 2
- uses unclear or confusing sentences
- describes a service that does not keep a community safe or clean
- has some errors

Score 1
- uses unclear or confusing sentences
- does not identify a service
- has many errors

Review and Test Prep

Unit 6

The Big Idea

People trade goods and services with one another. They make choices about how to spend their money.

Summarize the Unit

Cause and Effect Fill in the chart. Show what you have learned about spending and saving money.

Cause		Effect
People work at jobs.	→	**Possible response: They earn money.**
Possible response: People save some of their money.	→	People use money they have saved to buy something they want.

177

Unit Review

PAGES 177–180

The Big Idea

Ask students to review the unit's Big Idea. Invite students to share something they learned in this unit that supports The Big Idea. Write students' answers on the board. Review the ideas of earning, spending, and saving money.

Summarize the Unit

Cause and Effect Invite students to review the Reading Social Studies at the beginning of this unit. Remind students that every action has a reaction. Ask them to give examples of causes and effects that they have read about in the unit.

READING FOCUS SKILLS

Cause and Effect

Cause		Effect
	→	
	→	

TRANSPARENCY

Graphic Organizer Write-On/ Wipe-Off Cards available

ASSESSMENT

Use the **UNIT 6 TEST** on pages 21–24 of the Assessment Program.

Use Vocabulary

Write the word under its meaning.

Word Bank
goods p. 151
services p. 151
market p. 163
trade p. 164
factory p. 167

1. a place where people buy and sell goods

   market

2. a building in which people use machines to make goods

   factory

3. things people make or grow to sell

   goods

4. work people do for others for money

   services

5. to give one thing to get another

   trade

178

VOCABULARY POWER

Synonyms Review the word *market* with students. Tell students that we call markets by many different names. Write *market* on the top of a piece of chart paper. Have students give other names of places where people buy and sell goods. Guide them by starting the list with examples such as *grocery store, mall, supermarket,* and *gift shop*. Reinforce the fact that these names are synonyms for the word *market*.

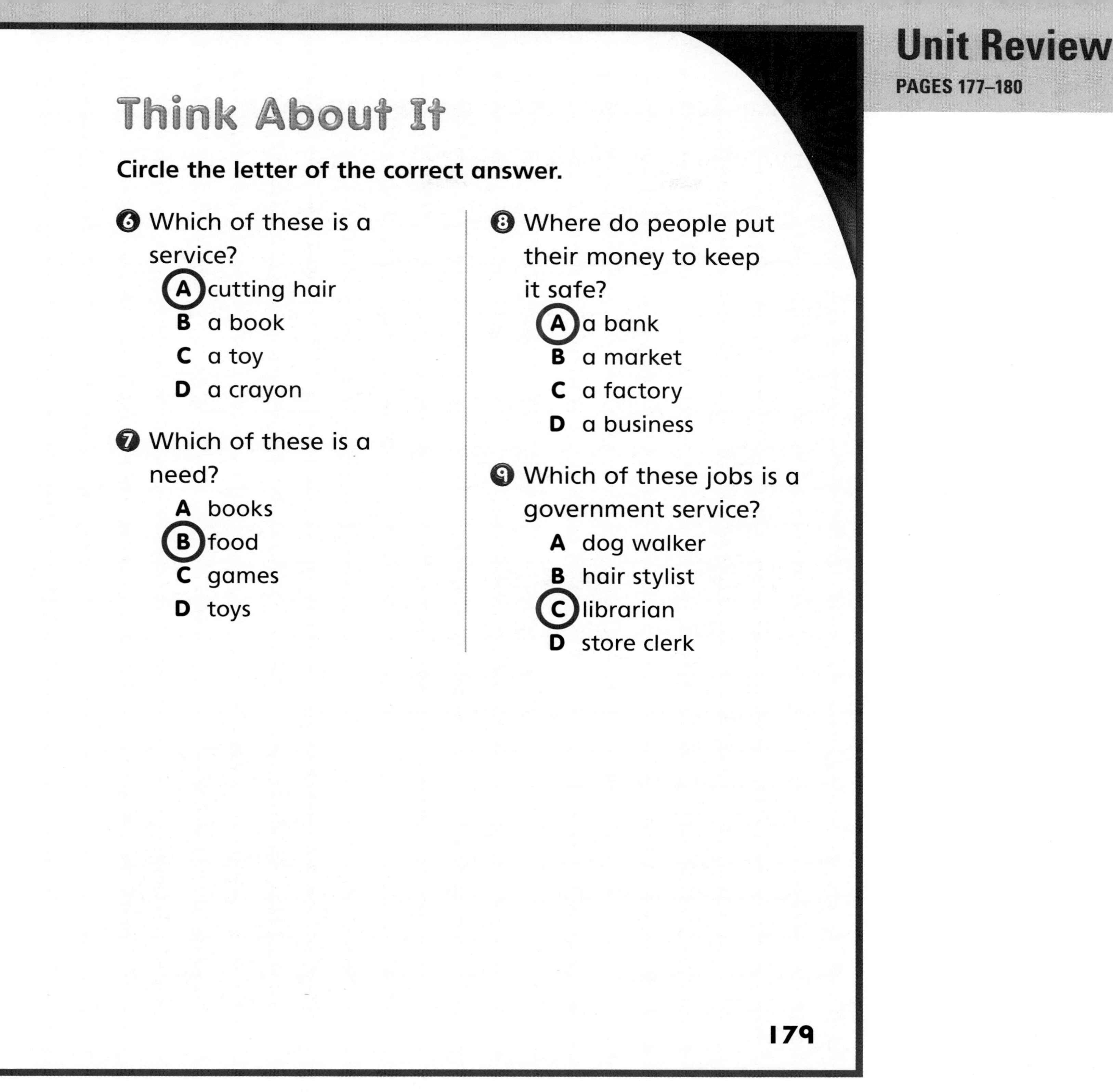

Think About It

Circle the letter of the correct answer.

6 Which of these is a service?

- **A** cutting hair
- **B** a book
- **C** a toy
- **D** a crayon

7 Which of these is a need?

- **A** books
- **B** food
- **C** games
- **D** toys

8 Where do people put their money to keep it safe?

- **A** a bank
- **B** a market
- **C** a factory
- **D** a business

9 Which of these jobs is a government service?

- **A** dog walker
- **B** hair stylist
- **C** librarian
- **D** store clerk

179

READ MORE

Encourage independent reading with these books or books of your choice.

Basic

ABC of Jobs by Roger Priddy. Priddy Books, 2003. An easy alphabetical introduction to the different jobs people do.

Proficient

How It Happens at the Boat Factory by Dawn Frederick. Clara House Books, 2002. A boat factory is described and shown with photographs.

Advanced

Grandpa's Corner Store by DyAnne DiSalvo-Ryan. HarperCollins, 2000. Lucy brings together the neighborhood to save her grandfather's grocery store.

Show What You Know

Writing
Write a Story

Ask students to list goods and services they would like to buy. The character in their story should make choices about what to buy.

Activity
Make a Classroom Market

Have pairs of students act as buyers while others sell their goods and services. To reinforce the concept of division of labor, explain that people have different jobs.

North Carolina Adventures

Remind students that this game will review the concepts in the unit.

Spotlight on Goals and Objectives

Use North Carolina Interactive Presentations, Unit 6, to review concepts from the unit.

Answer each question in a complete sentence.

10. Why do people work at jobs?

Possible response: People work at jobs so that they can earn money to buy goods and services.

11. Why is it important for people to save some of their money?

Possible response: It is important for people to save money so that they can have some for later.

Show What You Know

Writing Write a Story
Think about how you use your money. Make up a story about someone choosing how to use his or her money.

Activity Make a Classroom Market
Each person should act out a different job people have in a market. Choose what you will sell. Draw goods or services and money. Sell the goods or services so you can buy more.

HARCOURT

ECO

GO online To play a game that reviews the unit, join Eco in the North Carolina Adventures online or on CD.

180

WRITING RUBRIC

Score 4
- develops a character that makes good choices when buying
- includes numerous interesting story details
- is written in clear, well-structured sentences

Score 3
- develops a character that makes some choices when buying
- includes some interesting story details
- is mostly well written with complete sentences

Score 2
- develops a character that does not make a choice
- includes few story details
- is written with some complete sentences and some fragments

Score 1
- does not develop a story character
- includes no details
- is poorly written with incomplete sentences

ACTIVITY RUBRIC

Score 4
- clearly shows the concept of exchanging money
- clearly shows that people have different jobs at a market
- makes decisive and thoughtful choices when buying

Score 3
- shows the concept of exchanging money
- shows that people have different jobs at a market
- makes thoughtful choices when buying

Score 2
- shows some understanding of exchanging money
- somewhat shows that people have different jobs at a market
- make some thoughtful choices when buying

Score 1
- does not show the concept of exchanging money
- does not show that people have different jobs at a market
- does not consider any choices when buying

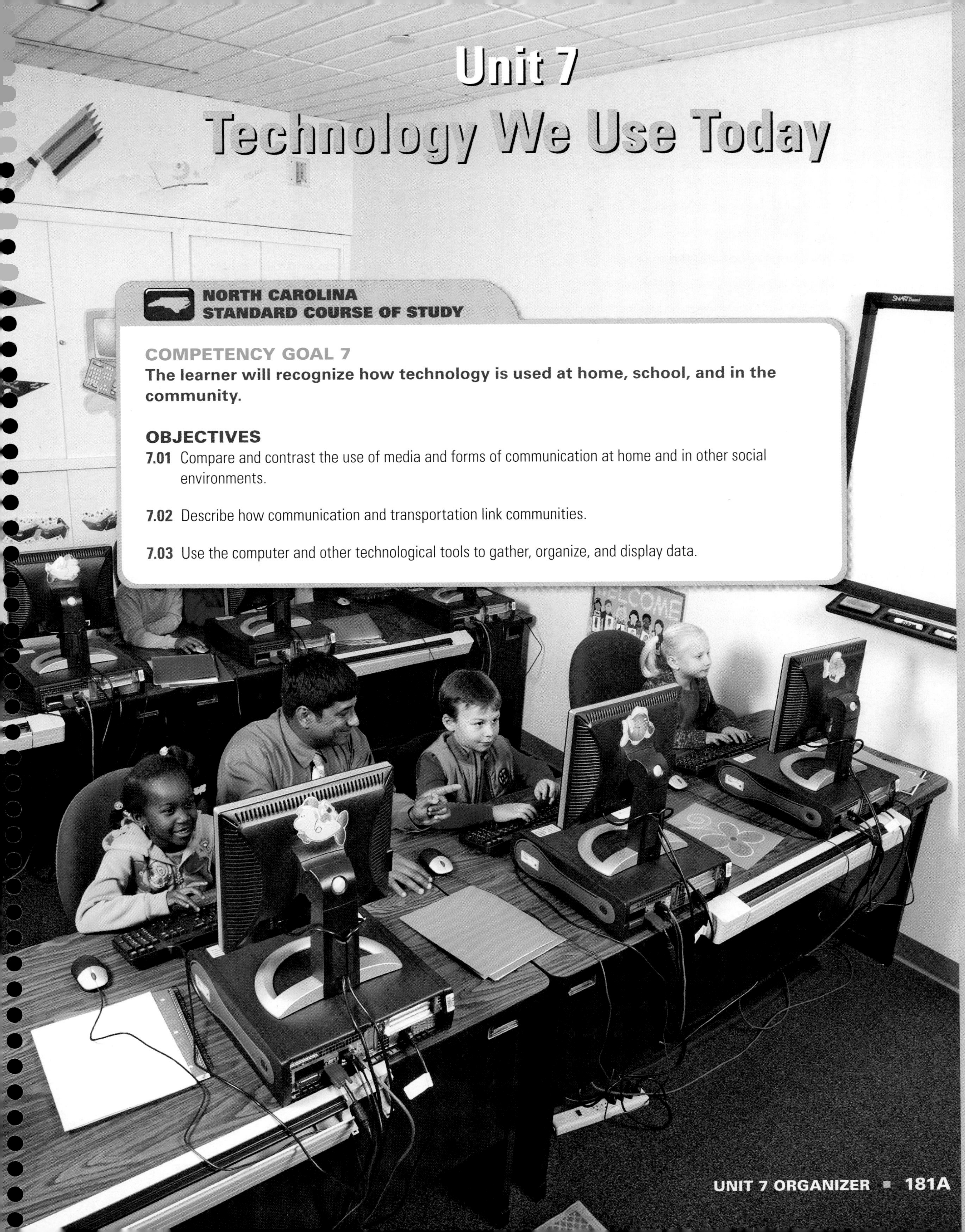

Unit 7
Technology We Use Today

NORTH CAROLINA
STANDARD COURSE OF STUDY

COMPETENCY GOAL 7
The learner will recognize how technology is used at home, school, and in the community.

OBJECTIVES

7.01 Compare and contrast the use of media and forms of communication at home and in other social environments.

7.02 Describe how communication and transportation link communities.

7.03 Use the computer and other technological tools to gather, organize, and display data.

LESSON	TOTAL: 18 DAYS	NORTH CAROLINA STANDARD COURSE OF STUDY
Introduce the Unit **Unit Preview,** pp. 181–182 **The Big Idea,** p. 182 **Reading Social Studies,** pp. 183–184 Focus Skill: Recall and Retell	2 DAYS	**COMPETENCY GOAL 7** **The learner will recognize how technology is used at home, school, and in the community.** **Spotlight on Goals and Objectives** Unit 7
1 **Communication** pp. 185–188 **Internet** p. 187	4 DAYS	**Objective 7.01** Compare and contrast the use of media and forms of communication at home and in other social environments. **Spotlight on Goals and Objectives** Unit 7, Lesson 1
2 **Connecting Communities** pp. 189–192 **future** p. 191	4 DAYS	**Objective 7.02** Describe how communication and transportation link communities. **Spotlight on Goals and Objectives** Unit 7, Lesson 2
3 **Using Technology** pp. 193–196 **fact** p. 193	4 DAYS	**Objective 7.03** Use the computer and other technological tools to gather, organize, and display data. **Spotlight on Goals and Objectives** Unit 7, Lesson 3
Unit 7 Review and Test Prep pp. 197–200	4 DAYS	**North Carolina Adventures** Unit 7

TEACHING YOUR SOCIAL STUDIES	SSSMART™ SUPPORT
	Comprehension, Recall and Retell, pp. 183–184
Background, Communication, p. 185 The Telephone, p. 186 Media, p. 187 **Social Studies Strands,** Technological Influences, p. 185 Historical Perspectives, p. 186 **Build Skills,** Chart and Graph Skills, p. 187	**CUES,** pp. 186, 187
Background, Computer-Based Communication, p. 189 The First Flight, p. 191 **Social Studies Strands,** Global Connections, p. 189 Cultures and Diversity, p. 191 **Build Skills,** Map and Globe Skills, p. 190	**Comprehension,** Recall and Retell, p. 190 **Skim and Scan,** p. 191
Background, Technology in the Classroom, p. 193 Learning Resources, p. 194 Television News Channels, p. 194 Internet Safety, p. 195 **Social Studies Strands,** Government and Active Citizenship, p. 193 Technological Influences, p. 195	**Vocabulary,** p. 194 **CUES,** p. 194 **Comprehension,** Recall and Retell, p. 195
	Summarize the Unit, Recall and Retell, p. 197

Print Resources

Student Edition, pp. 181–200
Teacher Edition, pp. 181A–200
Leveled Readers
Leveled Readers Teacher Guides
Document-Based Questions
Primary Atlas

Technology/Digital Resources

Spotlight on Goals and Objectives

North Carolina Interactive Presentations CD
North Carolina Interactive Presentations Online

Online Teacher Edition with ePlanner
Leveled Readers Online Database
North Carolina Adventures CD
North Carolina Adventures Online
Multimedia Biographies CD
Multimedia Biographies Online
Social Studies Music Collection CD

Hands-On Resources

Reading Focus Skills Transparencies
Social Studies Skills Transparencies
Graphic Organizer Write-On/Wipe-Off Cards
Interactive Atlas
Interactive Desk Map
Interactive Map Transparencies
Picture Vocabulary Cards
Primary Source Kit
TimeLinks: Interactive Time Line
Social Studies in Action, pp. 39, 76, 81, 108–109, 145

Assessment Options

1. **Unit 7 Test**
   Assessment Program, pp. 25–28
2. **Writing**
   Write a Paragraph, p. 200
3. **Activity**
   Unit Project: Make an Internet Safety Poster, p. 200

Leveled Readers

BELOW-LEVEL

Technology in Our World

Summary *Technology in Our World.* This Reader describes different types of technology and explains how technology helps make people's lives easier.

Vocabulary Power Have students define the following words. Help them write one sentence for each word as it relates to how technology helps people communicate.

technology
e-mail
computer
communication

Critical Thinking Lead students in a discussion about the different ways people communicate.

Write an Essay Have students write an essay describing how technology helps them communicate with others.

Focus Skill **Main Idea and Details**

ON-LEVEL

Communities Near and Far

Summary *Communities Near and Far.* This Reader explains how technology links communities near and far. It points out the different tools that help people share ideas.

Vocabulary Power Have students define the following words. Help them write one sentence for each word as it relates to how technology helps people communicate.

technology
communication
transportation

Critical Thinking Lead students in a discussion about how people today can share news faster.

Write a Report Have students write a report about a tool they use to communicate with their friends.

Focus Skill **Main Idea and Details**

ABOVE-LEVEL

Technology Today

Summary *Technology Today.* This Reader discusses how people use technology at home, at school, and at work.

Vocabulary Power Have students define the following words. Help them write one sentence for each word as it relates to how technology helps people communicate.

technology
communication

Critical Thinking Lead students in a discussion about how technology has changed the way we live.

Write a Description Have students write a description of a computer. Have them describe the mouse and keyboard.

Focus Skill **Main Idea and Details**

Complete a Graphic Organizer

Have students complete the graphic organizer to show that they understand the main idea and details about how technology has changed the way we live.

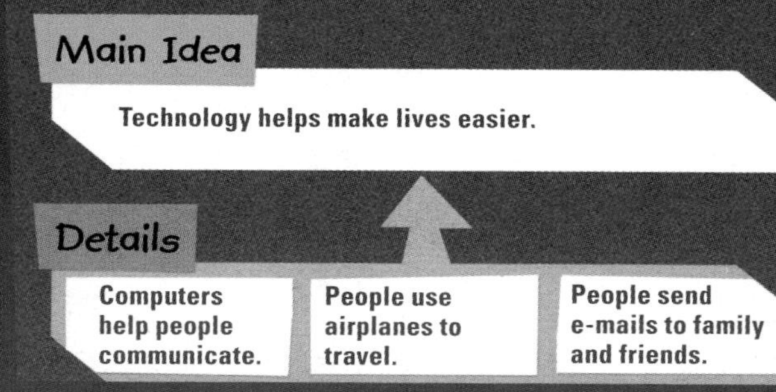

Leveled Readers Teacher Guides include complete lesson plans, copying masters, and project cards.

Harcourt Leveled Readers Available Online!
www.harcourtschool.com

Make an Internet Safety Poster

Getting Started

Introduce the Hands-On Activity on page 200 in the Unit Review as you begin Unit 7, and have students develop it as they consider the ways in which technology connects people in different parts of the world. Explain that the Internet is a public space and that as such, it requires the same kinds of safety precautions as those that apply to any other public place. The finished Internet safety posters should show students' understanding of how technology can be used safely.

The Big Idea
How does technology help connect communities?

Project Management

- Arrange for students to work independently.
- Guide the research and, if possible, have other adult helpers available to assist students.

Materials: Social Studies textbook; colored pens or markers; pencils; large sheets of poster-board

Organizer: For each safety guideline shown on the poster, have students fill out an organizer like the one below. This will help them complete their posters.

ORGANIZER

Safety Rule	How I Can Use It	Illustration

During the Unit

As students read Unit 7, they can begin work on their Internet safety posters. Posters can include:

- Lesson Review activites
- Your own favorite activities
- Ideas students develop on their own

Complete the Project

Invite students to share their posters with the class. Help students arrange their work in a large display area in the school so that the posters can provide Internet safety tips to others.

What to Look For

For a scoring rubric, see page 200 of this Teacher Edition.

- Students are able to create Internet safety posters that inform others of good safety tips.
- Students show an understanding of the ways in which technology connects people.
- Students work effectively and create eye-catching and interesting posters.

START

North Carolina Interactive Presentations

Purpose

The North Carolina Interactive Presentation Unit 7 can be used to preview Unit 7. This presentation provides a concise, visual overview of Competency Goal 7 and its objectives. You can use it to preview the unit for the class, or throughout the unit to introduce and reinforce individual objectives.

Contents

The Unit 7 presentation includes an introduction to Competency Goal 7, including a vocabulary preview and a visual introduction to using technology. In addition, the presentation covers the unit's objectives lesson by lesson, giving students a broad overview of technology and its impact on our daily lives.

REVIEW

North Carolina Adventures

Purpose

The North Carolina Adventures games, offered both on CD and online, provide an entertaining first-person-player method of content review. When students have completed the unit, they can review its competency goal and all objectives through the Unit 7 game.

Contents

Tell students they will use their knowledge of electronics to help a clerk at a computer store. Throughout, students will review what they have learned about technology and inventions. Explain that the "Help" buttons in the game will refer them to pages in their textbooks if they need additional information.

Additional Resources

For Teachers

Free and Inexpensive Materials are listed on the Social Studies website at **www.harcourtschool.com/ss1**

- Addresses to write to for free and inexpensive products
- Links to unit-related materials
- Internet maps
- Internet references

The eTE with ePlanner provides the following components

- A calendar tool for scheduling Social Studies lessons and displaying all scheduled lessons and activities
- TE pages and additional resources for easy online reference

For Students

When students visit **www.harcourtschool.com/ss1** they will find internal resources such as

- Our Multimedia Biographies database
- Skills activities
- Additional research tools
- Information about all 50 states

Unit 7

Technology We Use Today

Students work in a computer lab.

Spotlight on Goals and Objectives

North Carolina Interactive Presentations

NORTH CAROLINA STANDARD COURSE OF STUDY

COMPETENCY GOAL 7 The learner will recognize how technology is used at home, school, and in the community.

181

Unit 7 Preview

PAGES 181–182

Start with the Competency Goal

Competency Goal 7
The learner will recognize how technology is used at home, school, and in the community.

Make It Relevant

Read and discuss the unit competency goal. Point out the various forms of technology in your classroom.

Q Why do people use technology?

A Students may suggest that people use technology to make their lives easier.

Discuss the Photograph

Explain that the students in the photograph are using technology. Lead a class discussion on how students might use computers at school.

Instructional Design

START WITH THE GOAL AND OBJECTIVES

NORTH CAROLINA STANDARD COURSE OF STUDY

- competency goal
- objectives

PLAN ASSESSMENT

Assessment Options

- Option 1–Unit 7 Test
- Option 2–Writing: Write a Paragraph, p. 200
- Option 3–Activity: Make an Internet Safety Poster, p. 200

PLAN INSTRUCTION

Spotlight on Goals and Objectives
North Carolina Interactive Presentations, Unit 7

Unit 7 Teacher Edition

- resources
- activities
- strategies

Unit 7 Leveled Readers Teacher Guides

Unit 7 Preview

PAGES 181–182

The Big Idea

Have students read The Big Idea question. Then preview ways in which technology is used at home, at school, and in the community.

Access Prior Knowledge

Draw a concept web on the board. Write *Technology* in the center oval. Ask students to identify some types of technology that they use and their reasons for doing so. Help students form the information into complete sentences, such as *I use the telephone to call my grandparents*. Add the sentences to the concept web. Then have students read the paragraph and complete the activity.

The Big Idea

How does technology help connect communities?

Technology is all of the tools we use to make our lives easier. We use technology at home and in school. Communication and transportation connect us with communities all over the world.

Draw a picture of a kind of technology that you use.

Drawing should show that student understands the concept of technology.

182

READ MORE

Encourage independent reading with these books or books of your choice.

Basic

The Computer from A to Z by Bobby Kalman. Crabtree Publishing Company, 1998. Computer language, such as e-mail and the Internet, are explained.

Proficient

Robots by Darcy Lockman. Benchmark Books, 2000. This book discusses the new technology of robots and how we use robots in our everyday lives.

Advanced

Orson Blasts Off! by Raúl Colón. Atheneum/Anne Schwartz Books, 2004. Orson is forced away from his computer screen and takes a trip in a rocket ship.

Reading Social Studies

Recall and Retell

Learn

- To recall is to remember.
- To retell is to tell about something in your own words.

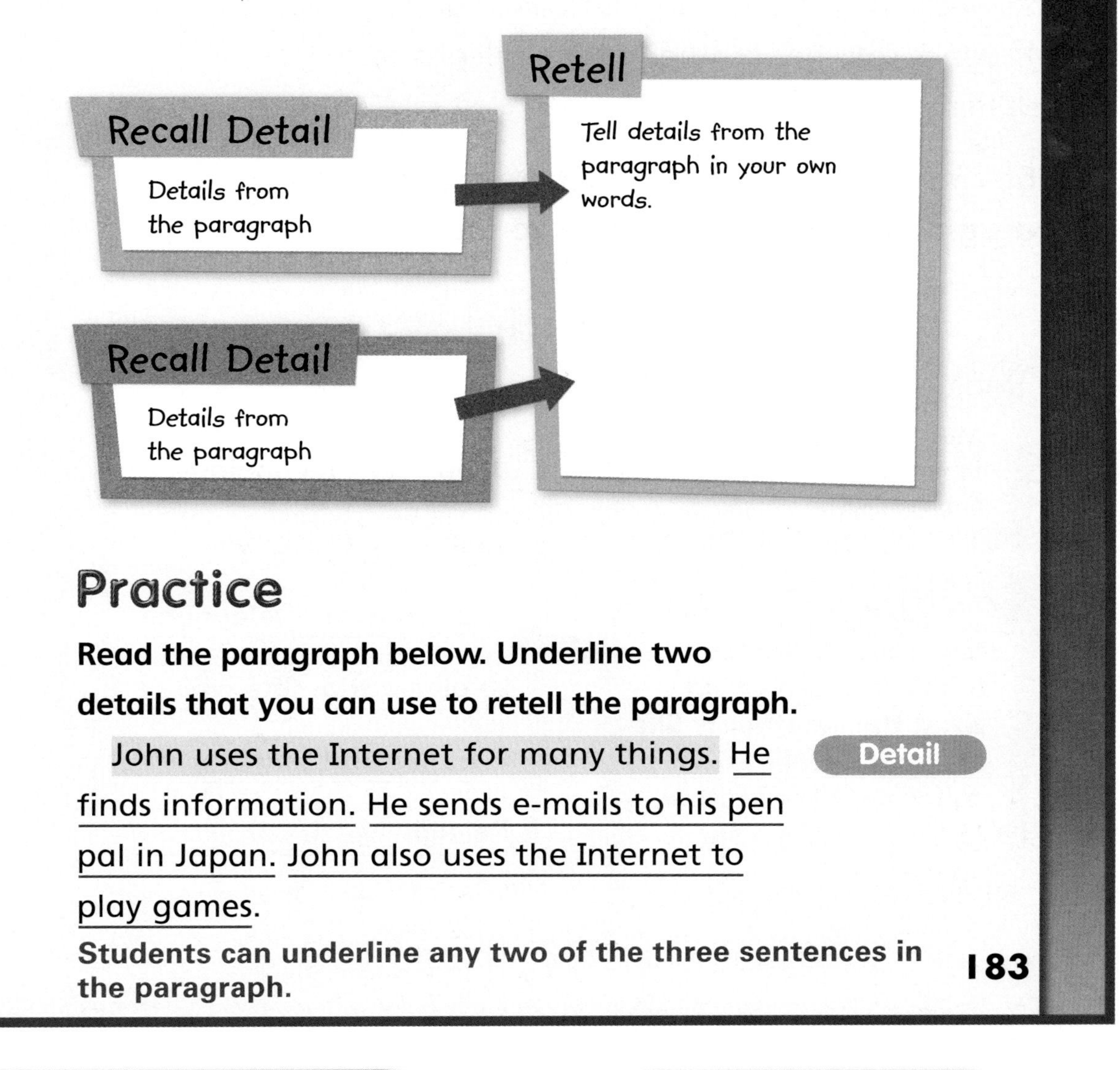

Practice

Read the paragraph below. Underline two details that you can use to retell the paragraph.

John uses the Internet for many things. He finds information. He sends e-mails to his pen pal in Japan. John also uses the Internet to play games.

Detail

Students can underline any two of the three sentences in the paragraph.

183

Reading Social Studies PAGES 183–184

Learn

Have students read the Learn section and look at the graphic organizer. Explain that recalling information helps students use the knowledge that they have learned. Then they can retell that information to someone else.

Q What time do you recall that school began this morning?

A Possible response: School began at 8 A.M.

Practice

Read the paragraph with students. Ask them what the paragraph is about. What details can they retell in their own words? Help students enter the information in the graphic organizer.

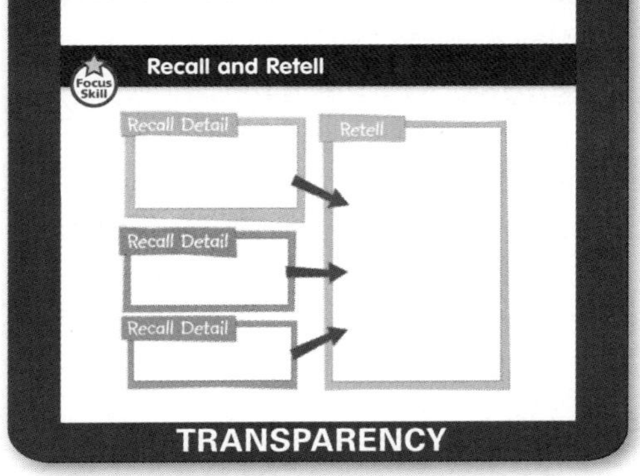

Graphic Organizer Write-On/ Wipe-Off Cards available

INTEGRATE THE CURRICULUM

ENGLISH LANGUAGE ARTS Remembering Stories Have students retell a familiar story, such as a fairy tale or nursery rhyme. Ask students to retell the story to the class without saying the name of the story. Encourage other students to identify the story from the details given by the storyteller.

ELA 2.06 Self-monitor comprehension by using one or two strategies (questions, retelling, summarizing).

Reading Social Studies PAGES 183–184

Apply

This selection provides details about a trip taken by Ms. Jones. Read the text with students, and then ask them what details they recall. Who is Ms. Jones visiting? In what city does that person live? Ask students to retell the story in their own words. Then help students write those retellings in the graphic organizer.

Unit 7 provides many opportunities for students to practice recalling and retelling. As students read the unit, challenge them to restate details from the text in their own words, either in writing or orally to a classmate.

Apply

Read the paragraph.

Ms. Jones is planning a trip to visit her brother in Raleigh, North Carolina. She uses the Internet to find information about airplane flights. She watches television to find out what the weather is like in North Carolina. Finally, Ms. Jones calls her brother on the telephone to tell him when she is coming.

The chart below recalls details from the paragraph. What can you add to the chart?

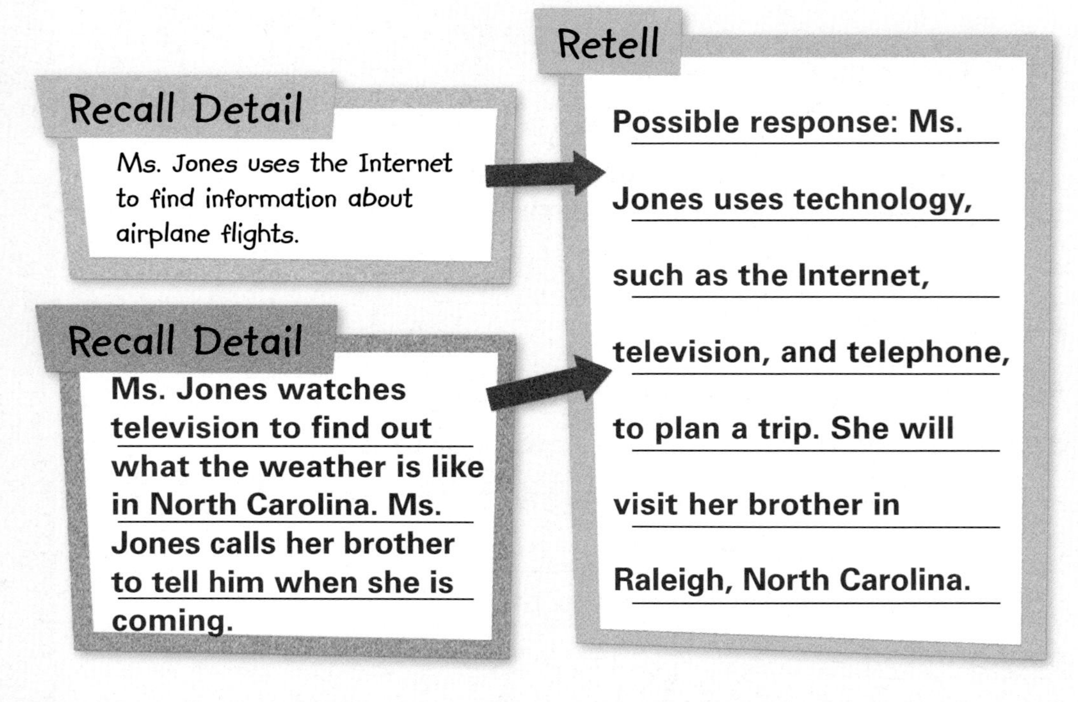

184

ESL/LANGUAGE SUPPORT

Vocabulary Development Ask students to think of words that describe technology or communication, such as *computer* or *telephone*. Help students write the words on cards and arrange them on a large wall or other display area in the classroom. As students read the unit, remind them to select new words to add to the word wall.

Prior Learning and Experiences Explain that technology includes items, such as microwaves and alarm clocks. As the students read the unit, tell them to think about the kinds of technology present in their homes. Ask them to write brief scripts that could be used to show a visitor from the past around their homes. Remind students to include the names of the technology items and their functions.

Build Background

Make It Relevant Ask students to name some ways in which they have communicated with people. Take an informal poll to find out how many students have written letters, talked on the telephone, sent e-mail, and used the Internet. Help students understand some of the differences among the communication processes that occur through those media.

Preview the Lesson

Guide students in previewing the lesson. Point out the following features on Student Edition pages 185–188:

- **Page 185** Ask the students how the girl in the photograph is communicating. What is she probably talking about? How can they tell from looking at the picture?
- **Page 186** Discuss the photographs of the telephones. Ask students to describe the different parts of the telephones shown. Then ask them why they think the telephones look different from one another.
- **Page 187** Explain that the machine in the photograph is an early type of computer. Point out the relative sizes of the woman and the computer. Ask students why computers were so much bigger years ago than they are today. Do they think that the smaller size of computers affects how people use them today?

Preteach Vocabulary

- Explain to students that the prefix *inter-* means "between or among." Then tell students that the **Internet** allows communication between or among computers in many different places all over the world.

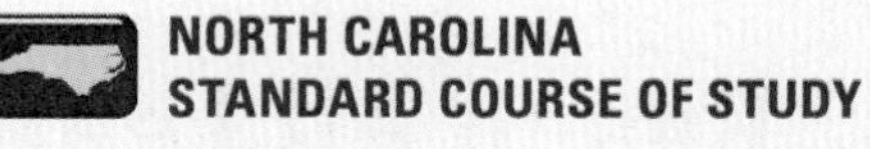

NORTH CAROLINA STANDARD COURSE OF STUDY

Objective 7.01 Compare and contrast the use of media and forms of communication at home and in other social environments.

Key Content Summary

- **People use telephones to communicate with others who are far away.**
- **Many people now use newer technology, such as computers and the Internet, for communication.**

Vocabulary

- **Internet,** p. 187

Spotlight on Goals and Objectives

Use North Carolina Interactive Presentations, Unit 7, Lesson 1, to access prior knowledge and build background.

Reach All Learners

ESL/Language Support

Scaffolding Content Draw a graphic organizer on the board with columns headed *Yesterday* and *Today.* Enter information about letters, telephones, computers, and the Internet in the appropriate columns. Ask students how the ways different media are used are the same and different.

Yesterday	Today

Extra Support

Learn About Communication Organize students in small groups, and give each group a variety of magazines or picture books. Ask students to find pictures of people communicating with others. Have each group select two or three pictures to share with the class. Students should explain the action in each picture.

Extension Activity

Role-Play Telephone Etiquette Tell students to ask teachers, parents, or other trusted adults what they think are the most important rules of telephone etiquette, or manners. Organize students in small groups, and tell them to discuss what they have been told about telephone etiquette. Have them decide on the three most important rules. Groups should then role-play these rules in front of the class.

Integrate the Curriculum

Science

Make Model Telephones Help students make simple "telephones," using string and empty cans or paper cups to do so. Have students work in pairs, taking turns talking and listening with the telephones. Explain that the telephones work because when the string is held tight between the cans or cups, the sound makes the string move back and forth a little. Tell students that modern telephones use electricity.

Lesson 1

PAGES 185–188

Communication

Lesson 1

Every day, people talk or write to share their ideas and feelings. This sharing is called communication. We use communication at home, at school, and at play. **What might you learn about communication?**

Possible response: I might learn about different ways people communicate.

NORTH CAROLINA STANDARD COURSE OF STUDY

7.01 Compare and contrast the use of media and forms of communication at home and in other social environments.

Start with the Objective

Objective 7.01 Compare and contrast the use of media and forms of communication at home and in other social environments.

Set a Purpose for Reading

Read the lesson introduction with students. Discuss the definition of the word *communication*. Ask students to list some of the ways they communicate. Ask volunteers to answer the question. Then use the Think Aloud to model thinking about communication.

Think Aloud

I know that people have always communicated with one another. I will read the lesson to learn more about the different ways people have communicated.

BACKGROUND

Communication Explain that sometimes a person communicates with only one person, and at other times with many people. The photograph on this page shows students participating in show and tell. The girl is communicating with many other students in her class. Those students, in turn, may ask her questions. Show and tell is a fun and important early communication process for students.

SOCIAL STUDIES STRANDS

Technological Influences Have students think of a time when they communicated with someone far away. Ask them how they communicated with that person. Explain that in recent years, communication with people in distant places has become much faster and easier because of technology such as the Internet. Point out that communication forms that were formerly somewhat limited, such as television, are now more interactive because of audience participation via the Internet.

SSSMART™
SUPPORT

TextWork

1 CUES

Analyze/Interpret Photographs Ask students to identify things that are the same and things that are different about the telephones in the photographs. Help students understand that items that look different can do the same thing. Most students will circle one of the cell phones, but accept the 1950s telephone as another possible response.

1 Circle the phone that you are most likely to use.

Telephones

Long ago, people could only write letters to communicate with people far away. Letters took a long time to get where they were going. When telephones were made, people could communicate by talking. Now people can use cell phones to send pictures, music, videos, and e-mail.

Early 1900s

Today

1950s

186

TEACHING YOUR SOCIAL STUDIES

BACKGROUND

The Telephone Tell students that in the mid-1800s, many people used new technology to find a way to send voices through wires. Alexander Graham Bell started the first telephone company in 1877. Explain that scientists later perfected the telephone into the device used today.

SOCIAL STUDIES STRANDS

Historical Perspectives Point out that when technologies are new, many people do not have them. Explain that for a long time after the first telephones were made, most people still communicated only in person or in writing. Have students think about the kinds of information that they share over the telephone. Then ask students to write short letters to friends that convey the same information.

Computers and the Internet

Today, people can send letters and pictures by e-mail. E-mail uses the Internet. The **Internet** links computers around the world.

Many people now have computers in their homes. Some use laptop computers when they are away from home. Students can use computers in schools.

❷ Circle the pictures of tools that you use every day.

In the past, computers were very large.

SSSMART™ SUPPORT

TextWork

❷ CUES

Analyze/Interpret Charts Ask students to explain how the pictures are organized within the graphic organizer. Engage the class in a discussion about how the items used in the past relate to the items used today. Have students consider why electronic communication today is faster than written communication was in the past. Note that even though the letter is listed as a type of communication used in the past, students who write letters may circle it.

BACKGROUND

Media Explain that the definition of *media* includes all types of communication that provide news and entertainment. Tell students that the media includes newspapers, radio, Internet, and television, all of which are often supported by advertising dollars.

BUILD SKILLS

Chart and Graph Skills Tell students that the chart on page 187 compares objects from the past and the present that people have used to communicate. It organizes items from the past in one column and items from the present in another.

Q What did people use to communicate before they had e-mail?

A People used the telephone and sent letters.

Lesson Review

Summary Have students work in pairs to summarize the key content from the lesson. Remind students to use headings and images to find the most important information. Then have each student complete the Lesson Review.

- People use telephones to communicate with those who are far away.
- Many people now use newer technology, such as computers and the Internet, for communication.

Lesson 1 Review

1. **SUMMARIZE** What are some ways to communicate?

   Possible response: I can communicate by talking on the telephone or sending an e-mail.

2. How do people use the **Internet**?

   Possible response: People can use the Internet to send e-mails and pictures.

3. What are some ways communication was different in the past?

   Possible response: In the past, people could not talk on the telephone or send e-mails on the Internet. They wrote letters.

Writing Write sentences about the ways you communicate with others.

188

WRITING RUBRIC

Score 4
- clearly understands how people communicate
- accurately describes ways of communicating
- shows a developed understanding of sentence structure

Score 3
- shows an understanding of ways people communicate
- generally describes ways of communicating
- shows a basic understanding of sentence structure

Score 2
- fails to fully understand communication
- describes an aspect of communicating, but does not identify specific ways
- shows a beginning understanding of sentence structure

Score 1
- does not understand the idea of communication
- fails to describe ways of communicating
- does not write in beginning sentence format

Build Background

Make It Relevant Help students think of the different methods of transportation that people in their communities use. Explain that cars, bicycles, airplanes, trains, and even walking are all forms of transportation. Ask students how they think being able to get to places faster can bring people from different communities together.

Preview the Lesson

Guide students in previewing the lesson. Point out the following features on Student Edition pages 189–192:

- **Page 189** Discuss with students the photograph of the family looking at the computer screen. Who do students think are the people on the screen? How might they be communicating with the people in the room?
- **Page 190** Direct students' attention to the illustration of the globe. What does the airplane represent? Ask students from what city the airplane is traveling and where it is going. How do they know?
- **Page 191** Point out the Biography feature subhead *Cooperation*. Ask students who they think might be cooperating in this biography. Help students think of times when cooperating with someone else has allowed them to complete a task.

Preteach Vocabulary

- Tell students that the **future** is any time that has not yet happened. Ask students what they will be doing in the near future. Will they play a game after school or do homework?

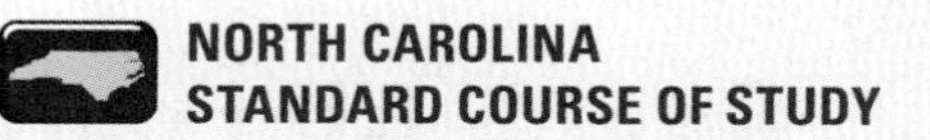

Objective 7.02 Describe how communication and transportation link communities.

Key Content Summary

- **People communicate and travel across long distances.**
- **Technology has brought about new forms of communication and transportation. It will continue to do so in the future.**

Vocabulary

- **future**, p. 191

Use North Carolina Interactive Presentations, Unit 7, Lesson 2, to access prior knowledge and build background.

Reach All Learners

ESL/Language Support

Active Learning Have students work in pairs to role-play what they know about traveling. For example, students could role-play asking someone else about ways to get to a certain city. Encourage students to be creative.

Extra Support

Play a Memory Game At the beginning of the lesson, have each student write the name of a type of transportation or communication on an index card and draw a picture of it on another index card. Collect all the cards and shuffle them. For each day that the lesson is taught, allow a different small group of students to use the cards to play a memory game. Students should arrange the cards face down and try to pair them correctly.

Extension Activity

Plan a Route Ask students to think of a person or place that they are interested in visiting. Then, using globes, maps, or atlases, students will plan a route that they could take to reach the person or place.

Integrate the Curriculum

Second Languages

Learn Names of Places Explain that the same country or city can have different names in different languages. Ask students to find a country on the map. Then help them use school-approved websites or library resources to learn the name of that country in the language spoken there. For example, Germany is known as *Deutschland* in German.

Science

Learn About Energy Help children create a three-column chart to group types of transportation by what makes them move: wind, electricity, gasoline.

Lesson 2

PAGES 189–192

Connecting Communities

Elena lives in Charlotte, North Carolina. Her grandparents live in Rio de Janeiro, Brazil. They use communication and transportation to connect their communities. **What might you learn about technology and communities?**

Possible response: I might learn about how technology connects communities.

Elena uses the computer to communicate.

NORTH CAROLINA STANDARD COURSE OF STUDY

7.02 Describe how communication and transportation link communities.

189

Start with the Objective

Objective 7.02 Describe how communication and transportation link communities.

Set a Purpose for Reading

Ask a volunteer to read aloud the lesson introduction. Point out that the introduction describes people who live far apart. Ask students which two cities are identified. Use the Think Aloud to model learning about technology and communites.

Think Aloud

I know that people can use technology to communicate with others. I also know that people can use transportation to visit people in other cities. Communication and transportation help bring people together. I will learn about the ways they do this.

BACKGROUND

Computer-Based Communication Tell students that some people use computers to communicate with others. People use computers to send e-mail and instant messages, as well as for video conferences. Point out that the family in the photograph is video-conferencing. The people are using a camera connected to the Internet to see those with whom they are speaking. Explain that it is important that students use technological communication only with a trusted adult present.

SOCIAL STUDIES STRANDS

Global Connections Show students a world map. Point out the locations of Charlotte, North Carolina, and Rio de Janeiro, Brazil. Ask students whether they know anyone who lives far away, and locate the places mentioned on the map. Explain that people all over the world use different methods of communication and transportation to communicate with family and friends.

TextWork

1 Comprehension

Recall and Retell Help students read the passage. Then ask them where to find the details about ways in which Elena communicates with her grandparents. Reread that section aloud. Ask what specific forms of communication are mentioned. Then help students write complete sentences that recall the information.

1 How does Elena communicate with her grandparents?

Possible response: She sends e-mails and talks on the telephone.

Connecting with People

Elena communicates with her grandparents. She sends e-mails and talks on the telephone. Elena's family also uses transportation. They go by airplane to visit one another.

190

BUILD SKILLS

Map and Globe Skills Direct students' attention to the illustration on page 190. Point out where the directions of north, south, east, and west would be on the globe. Explain that Charlotte is north of Rio de Janeiro. Ask students whether the Pacific Ocean lies east or west of the Atlantic Ocean.

Technology Connects Us

Technology has made communication easier. Television and the Internet connect us with people all over the world.

Technology has also made transportation easier. People go by car, bus, train, or airplane.

In the future, new technology will help connect us. The **future** is the time that has not yet come.

TextWork

❷ Underline the two things technology has made easier.

Biography

Cooperation

The Wright Brothers

Wilbur and Orville Wright were brothers who liked to make new things. They became the first people to fly an airplane. This happened on December 17, 1903, near Kitty Hawk, North Carolina. Today, people fly in airplanes all over the world.

SSSMART™ SUPPORT

TextWork

❷ Skim and Scan

Remind students that scanning text can help them locate information quickly. Have students scan the text. Then ask volunteers to point out the locations of details about two things technology has helped. Tell students to underline the two things in their books.

BACKGROUND

The First Flight The Wright brothers tried to fly many times before they were successful. They made their first sustained, powered flight on December 17, 1903. Orville Wright piloted the first flight, which covered 120 feet and lasted 12 seconds. Later that day, Wilbur Wright piloted the second powered flight, covering 175 feet in 12 seconds.

SOCIAL STUDIES STRANDS

Cultures and Diversity Explain that using transportation to go places can help students learn more about different cultures. Ask students to suggest the kinds of cultural aspects that they might encounter in other cities, states, or countries. Remind them that different cultures have different traditions.

Lesson Review

Summary Ask students to work independently to summarize the most important information from the lesson. Direct them to examine the images as well as text to write their summaries. Then have each student complete the Lesson Review.

- People communicate and travel across long distances.
- Technology has brought about new forms of communication and transportation. It will continue to do so in the future.

Lesson 2 Review

1. **SUMMARIZE** How does technology connect communities?

   Possible response: Technology connects communities by making new kinds of transportation and communication.

2. Use the word **future** in a sentence.

   Possible response: In the future, I will send an e-mail to my friend.

3. What kinds of transportation can help you go to places far away?

   Possible response: Airplanes, cars, trains, and buses can help me go to places far away.

Activity

Draw a picture that shows a kind of transportation you think people will use in the future.

192

ACTIVITY RUBRIC

Score 4
- clearly shows a kind of transportation
- shows a logical technological improvement
- is clean, neat, and well-illustrated

Score 3
- shows a kind of transportation
- shows a reasonable technological improvement
- is reasonably clean and clearly drawn

Score 2
- fails to depict clearly a kind of transportation
- does not show a reasonable technological improvement
- has some presentation errors that impede comprehension

Score 1
- does not show a kind of transportation
- shows no technological improvement
- has many presentation errors that impede comprehension

Build Background

Make It Relevant If your school has a computer lab or technology room, take your students on a tour of the resources. Point out the different kinds of technology available to them. Ask students to identify other kinds of technology with which they are familiar.

Preview the Lesson

Guide students in previewing the lesson. Point out the following features on Student Edition pages 193–196:

- **Page 193** Explain that the students in the photograph are using technology to learn. Ask students how computers can teach differently than books can.
- **Page 194** Point out the different parts of the illustration. What do the different kinds of media have in common? How are they different? Ask students to identify resources that they have used before and those that are new to them.
- **Page 195** Ask students to explain how the boy in the photograph obtained the picture he is holding. What is used to print pictures from a computer to paper?

Preteach Vocabulary

- Ask students to say something about themselves that is true, such as *My name is Emily* or *I am seven years old*. Point out that this information is a **fact**. Help students think of facts about their class, such as the number of boys or girls in class or the number of students whose names start with *L*.

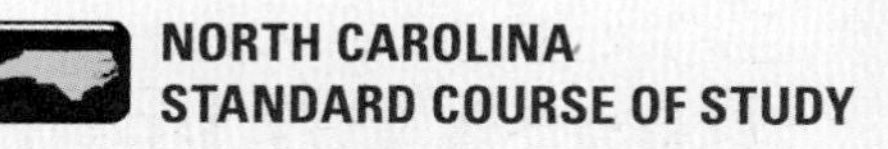

NORTH CAROLINA STANDARD COURSE OF STUDY

Objective 7.03 Use the computer and other technological tools to gather, organize, and display data.

Key Content Summary

- **Facts are available from technology resources.**
- **Use the Internet carefully and safely, with a trusted adult to help.**

Vocabulary

- **fact**, p. 193

Spotlight on Goals and Objectives

Use North Carolina Interactive Presentations, Unit 7, Lesson 3, to access prior knowledge and build background.

Reach All Learners

ESL/Language Support

Scaffolding Content Refer to the illustration on page 194 to create a graphic organizer that lists different types of media. Ask students to use the illustration and their own knowledge to identify facts about those types of media. Make another column to list the facts in the graphic organizer.

Media Types	Facts

Extra Support

Make a Technology Word Web On the board, draw a central oval containing the word *Technology*. Ask students to copy the oval and create a concept web around it that shows words related to technology. Have students share words from their webs to create a master class concept web.

Extension Activity

Choosing Key Words As a class, think of a topic that you would like to learn more about, such as your community or a cultural tradition. Ask students to think of some words relating to the chosen topic. Using the Internet, enter the words students have chosen in a search engine. Which words obtain the best results? Lead a class discussion on what makes some key words better than others. Make sure to use school-approved websites.

Integrate the Curriculum

Computer/Technology

Use the Computer Organize students into groups. Have each group pick a topic to research that interests them. Then have them use the computer to gather information on their selected topic. Have students use the computer and other technological tools to organize and display the data they found.

Using Technology

Lesson 3

Technology makes it easier for people to learn and to share. You can use computer technology to find facts about many things. A **fact** is something that is true. It is not made up.

What might you learn about using technology?

Possible response: I might learn about using technology to find facts.

North Carolina has many mountains.

Children use technology in school.

NORTH CAROLINA STANDARD COURSE OF STUDY

7.03 Use the computer and other technological tools to gather, organize, and display data.

193

Lesson 3

PAGES 193–196

Start with the Objective

Objective 7.03 Use the computer and other technological tools to gather, organize, and display data.

Set a Purpose for Reading

Read aloud the lesson introduction as students follow along. Point out the highlighted word *fact*. Explain the difference between a fact and an opinion. Use the Think Aloud to model thinking about using technology.

Think Aloud

I know that technology can be used for many things. I also know that there are many ways to use technology. In this lesson, I think I will learn about uses for technology. I will also learn about how to use technology.

BACKGROUND

Technology in the Classroom Draw students' attention to the photograph of the classroom, and explain that teachers may use different kinds of technology. Point out the laptop and the overhead projector in the photograph. Ask students what they think the class is doing. Point out that both teachers and students can use technology when learning in school.

SOCIAL STUDIES STRANDS

Government and Active Citizenship Explain that being informed about government is an important part of citizenship. Ask students how technology could help them stay informed about the government. Point out that the Internet has facts about elections and government. If possible, show students the website for your community.

SSSMART™ SUPPORT

TextWork

1 Vocabulary

Understand Vocabulary Review the definition of the word *fact*. Read aloud technological resources named in the paragraph. Any of the options on the graph are correct, but students should underline only one place to find facts.

2 CUES

Analyze/Interpret Charts Point out the different types of resources shown in the chart. Ask students to scan the text to find those resources identified as technology resources. Tell students to consider which of the resources would offer the most current information. Point out that a dictionary, an atlas, and other reference books contain information that does not change often.

TextWork

1 Underline one place to find facts.

2 Circle the resources that tell the latest news.

Technology Resources

Two technology resources you can use are the Internet and computer disks. Your school or community library may have CD-ROMs or DVDs. These have facts. You can also learn facts on television and radio.

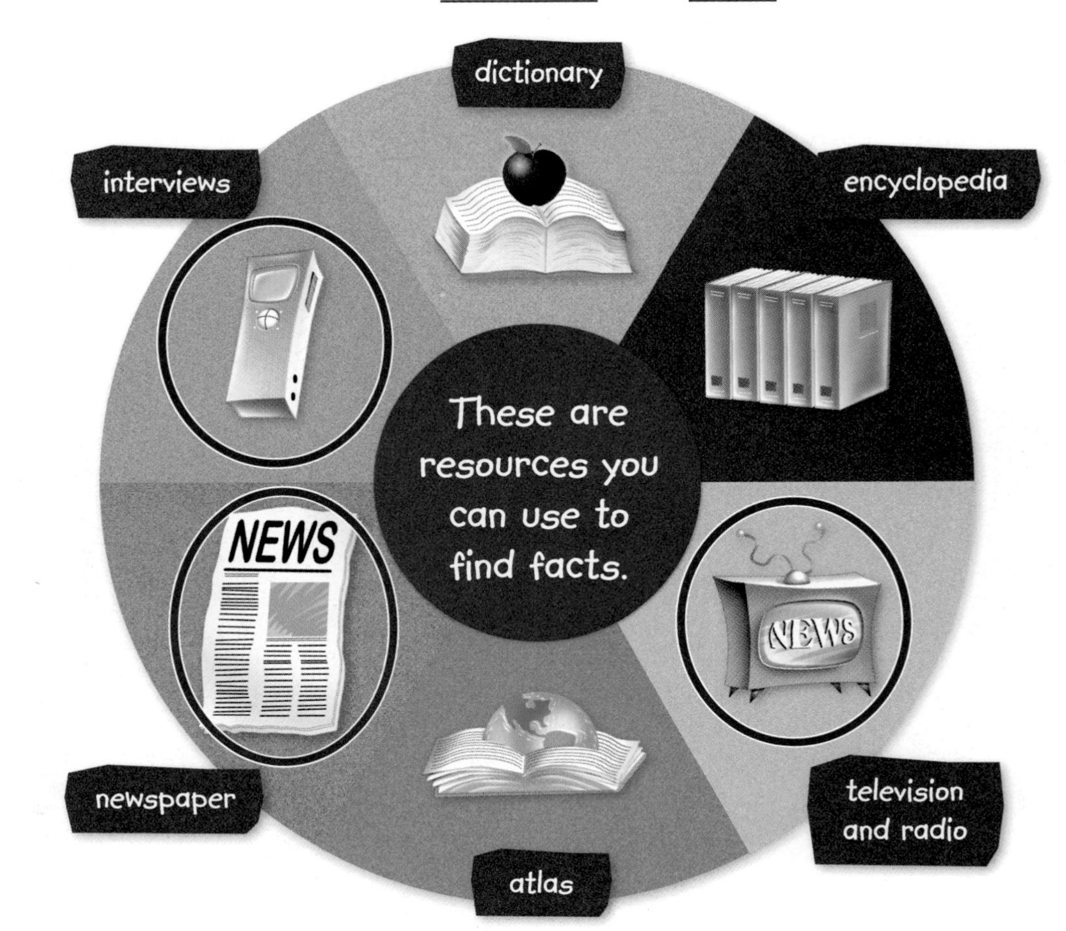

TEACHING YOUR SOCIAL STUDIES

BACKGROUND

Learning Resources The chart depicts six different learning resources. Three of these—the atlas, the dictionary, and the encyclopedia—provide basic information about places, words, and topics. As published books, these items typically contain information that is unlikely to change and do not provide current news. (Encyclopedias sometimes publish yearly updates.) The remaining three sources—newspaper, television, and interviews—are likely to be more contemporary and topical.

BACKGROUND

Television News Channels When it was launched in 1980, CNN became the first 24-hour, all-news television network. This format has made television a source of breaking news, with stories often being reported live. Following the success of CNN, other all-news networks such as MSNBC and Fox News have appeared, covering stories around the world from various viewpoints.

Using the Internet

Use Internet sites you know you can trust. Use the Internet only with an adult you trust.

- Use a mouse and a keyboard to look for facts.
- Type in key words.
- Read carefully and take notes.
- Print a paper copy.

TextWork

3 Who should always be with you when you are using the Internet?

an adult you trust

You can use computers to print out and show the information you find on the Internet.

TextWork

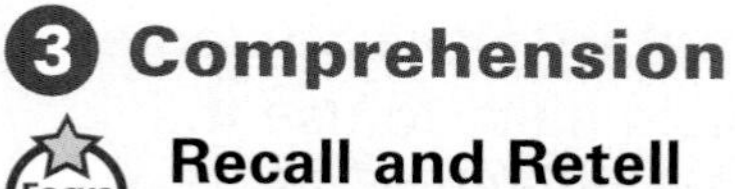

3 Comprehension

Recall and Retell (Focus Skill) Ask a volunteer to read aloud the passage. Then reread the section containing the information about who should accompany students when they use the Internet. Ask students to identify people who would be good choices to help them use the Internet.

SOCIAL STUDIES STRANDS

Technological Influences Show students a computer in your classroom, school library, or media center. Point out the computer's parts, such as the monitor, mouse, keyboard, CD-ROM drive, and tower or other hard drive location. Demonstrate proper ways to turn a computer on and off, use the keyboard and mouse, and navigate the operating system. After the demonstration, ask students to identify the different parts of the computer system.

BACKGROUND

Internet Safety When using the Internet, students should follow some basic safety rules:

- Do not give out personal information, such as name, address, or phone number.
- Do not talk to strangers online without a parent's or a guardian's permission.
- Tell a parent, teacher, or other trusted adult if someone on the Internet tells them something that makes them frightened or uncomfortable.

Lesson Review

Summary Have students work in pairs to use the lesson headings and images to summarize the lesson's main ideas. Then have students complete the Lesson Review independently.

- Facts are available from technology resources.
- Use the Internet carefully and safely, with a trusted adult to help.

1. **SUMMARIZE** What are some ways people can use technology to find facts?

   Possible response: People can use technology like the Internet or television to find facts.

2. Write one **fact** about technology resources that you learned from this lesson.

   Possible response: One fact I learned is that I can use the Internet and computer disks to find information.

3. Retell in your own words some tips for finding facts on the Internet.

   Possible response: When you look for facts on the Internet, you should use the mouse and keyboard to type in words, read carefully, and print a copy of what you found.

Use technology resources you read about in this lesson. Find facts about something. Write about what you find out.

196

WRITING RUBRIC

Score 4
- shows reliable and effective research obtained by using a technology resource
- accurately explains findings
- shows a developed understanding of sentence structure

Score 3
- shows adequate research obtained by using a technology resource
- generally explains findings
- shows a basic understanding of sentence structure

Score 2
- shows little research from a technology resource
- incompletely explains findings
- shows a beginning understanding of sentence structure

Score 1
- uses no research
- fails to explain findings
- does not write in beginning sentence format

Review and Test Prep

Unit 7

The Big Idea

The technology we use today connects people and communities around the world.

Summarize the Unit

Recall and Retell Fill in the chart. Show what you have learned about technology. Then retell the information in your own words.

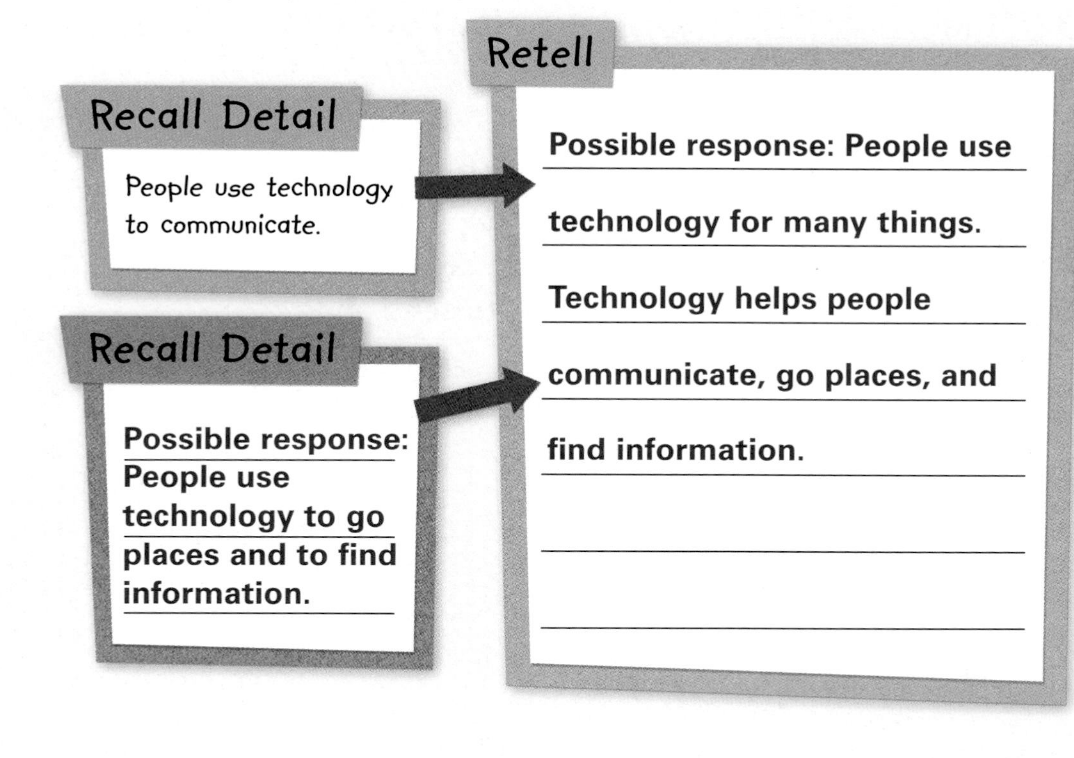

Unit Review

PAGES 197–200

The Big Idea

Ask students to review the unit's Big Idea. Invite students to share something from this unit that supports The Big Idea. Help students review the concept of how technology has helped connect communities around the world.

Summarize the Unit

Recall and Retell Invite students to review the Reading Social Studies at the beginning of the unit. Ask them to think about what they recall from this unit. Then have students retell what they remember in their own words.

READING FOCUS SKILLS

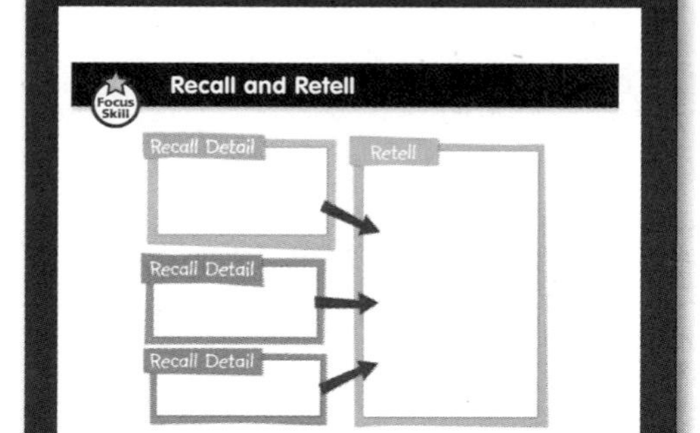

TRANSPARENCY

Graphic Organizer Write-On/ Wipe-Off Cards available

ASSESSMENT

Use the **UNIT 7 TEST** on pages 25–28 of the Assessment Program.

Use Vocabulary

Fill in the blanks with the correct words.

Word Bank
Internet p. 187
future p. 191
fact p. 193

1. We have many ways of finding a **fact**, or information that is true and not made up.

2. One way of finding information is by using the **Internet**, which links computers around the world.

3. In the **future**, we may have new ways of finding information.

4. Write a sentence that tells about how you use the **Internet**.

Possible response: I use the Internet to send and read e-mail.

198

VOCABULARY POWER

Nouns Remind students that nouns name people, places, and things. Write the word *fact* on the board. Explain to students that a fact is a noun because it is a thing. Review the rest of the vocabulary in this unit. Have students tell whether each vocabulary word in the unit is a person, place, or thing. As they categorize the words, reinforce the idea that these are all nouns. Ask students to give examples of other words that represent each type of noun.

Think About It

Circle the letter of the correct answer.

5 Which is a kind of technology we use for communication?

A car
B horse and wagon
C airplane
(D) cell phone

6 Which is a kind of transportation we use to go to places far away?

A walking
B horse and wagon
(C) airplane
D bicycle

7 Which is a kind of technology we can use to find information?

A train
B airplane
C car
(D) computer

8 Which is one of the steps for finding facts on the Internet?

(A) Type in key words.
B Call a friend.
C Read a book.
D Play a game.

199

READ MORE

Encourage independent reading with these books or books of your choice.

Basic

The Computer From A to Z by Bobby Kalman. Crabtree Publishing Company, 1998. Computer language, such as e-mail and the Internet, are explained.

Proficient

Robots by Darcy Lockman. Benchmark Books, 2000. This book discusses the new technology of robots and how we use robots in our everyday lives.

Advanced

Orson Blasts Off! by Raúl Colón. Atheneum/Anne Schwartz Books, 2004. Orson is forced away from his computer screen and takes a trip in a rocket ship.

Unit Review

PAGES 197–200

Show What You Know

Writing

Write a Paragraph

Ask students to list the kinds of technology we use today. Then brainstorm with them the kinds of technology we may use in the future.

Activity

Make an Internet Safety Poster

Review Internet safety guidelines with students. Students' posters should list Internet safety rules.

North Carolina Adventures

Remind students that this game will review the concepts in the unit.

Spotlight on Goals and Objectives

Use North Carolina Interactive Presentations, Unit 7, to review concepts from the unit.

Answer each question in a complete sentence.

9. How can technology help you find information?

Possible response: You can use technology like computers or CD-ROMs to find information.

10. How has the Internet changed the way people communicate?

Possible response: Internet technology has made it easier for people to communicate.

Show What You Know

Writing Write a Paragraph

What kinds of technology might we have in the future? Write about a new kind of technology for the future.

Activity Make an Internet Safety Poster

List safety rules for using the Internet. Make a poster showing the rules.

GO online To play a game that reviews the unit, join Eco in the North Carolina Adventures online or on CD.

200

WRITING RUBRIC

Score 4
- reflects a strong understanding of how technology connects people
- includes many creative and interesting details
- is well-written and complete

Score 3
- reflects an understanding of how technology connects people
- includes several interesting details
- is mostly well-written and complete

Score 2
- reflects some understanding of how technology connects people
- includes some details, but little creativity
- is minimally complete

Score 1
- reflects no understanding of how technology connects people
- includes few or no details
- is poorly written

ACTIVITY RUBRIC

Score 4
- shows a clear understanding of how to safely use the Internet
- uses a variety of rules that cover all aspects of Internet use
- is well-organized and legible

Score 3
- shows an understanding of how to safely use the Internet
- uses rules that cover most aspects of Internet use
- is somewhat organized and mostly legible

Score 2
- shows some understanding of how to safely use the Internet
- uses rules that cover some aspects of Internet use
- is not very organized and somewhat difficult to read

Score 1
- shows little or no understanding of how to safely use the Internet
- uses no rules, or rules used do not relate to Internet use
- is completely unorganized and illegible

For Your Reference

GLOSSARY

INDEX

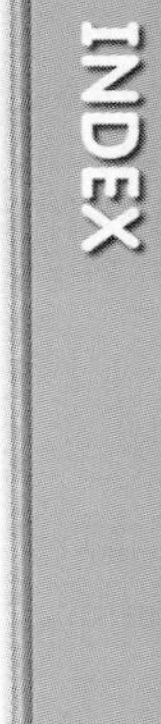

R1

Glossary

The Glossary has important words and their definitions. They are listed in alphabetical (ABC) order. The definition is the meaning of the word. The page number at the end tells you where the word is first defined.

B

ballot
A list that shows all the choices people can vote for. p. 46

border
The place where a state or country ends. pp. 18, 125

business
A place where people sell goods or services. p. 153

C

cardinal directions
The directions of north, south, east, and west. p. 19

celebration
A time to be happy about something special. p. 91

change
To become different. p. 58

citizen
A person who lives in and belongs to a community. p. 29

city
A very large community. pp. 15, 135

communication
The sharing of ideas and feelings. p. 61

community
A group of people who live and work together. It is also the place where they live. p. 11

compass rose
The symbol on a map that shows directions. p. 19

consequence
Something that happens because of what a person does or does not do. p. 39

consumer
A person who buys goods and services. p. 154

continent
One of the seven main land areas on Earth. pp. 14, 126

country
An area of land with its own people and laws. pp. 15, 73

culture
A group's ways of life. p. 14

custom
A way of doing something. p. 14

fact
Something that is true and not made up. p. 193

factory
A building in which people use machines to make goods. p. 167

fair
Acting in a way that is right for all. p. 37

family
A group of people who live together. p. 5

farm
A place for growing plants and raising animals. p. 137

flag
A piece of cloth with symbols on it. p. 87

freedom
A kind of right. p. 42

future
The time that has not yet come. p. 191

G

globe
A model of Earth. p. 14

goods
Things that people make or grow to sell. p. 151

government
A group of people who lead a community and make laws. p. 45

government service
A service that the government does for the community. p. 173

H

hero
A person who does something to help others. p. 97

hill
Land that rises above the land around it. p. 130

history
The story of what happened in the past. p. 63

holiday
A day of celebration for everyone. p. 91

I

immigrant
A person who comes from another place to live in a country. p. 18

inset map
A small map that is inside a larger map. p. 18

Internet
A system that links computers around the world. p. 187

J

job
Work that a person does to earn money. p. 161

L

landmark
A symbol that is a place people can visit. p. 103

law
A rule that people in a community must follow. p. 31

leader
A person who works to help a group. p. 33

location
The place where something is. p. 117

M

map
A flat drawing that shows where places are. p. 14

map key
The part of a map that shows what the symbols on the map mean. p. 19

map symbol
A small picture or shape on a map that stands for a real thing. p. 17

map title
The title of a map. pp. 17, 19

market
A place where people buy and sell goods. p. 163

mayor
The leader of a community. p. 35

money
What people use to pay for goods and services. p. 153

mountain
The highest kind of land. p. 130

N

national holiday
A day to remember a person or an event that is important to our country. p. 97

needs
Things we must have to live. p. 157

neighborhood
A part of a town or city. p. 123

ocean
A large body of water. pp. 14, 133

P

past
The time before now. p. 57

plain
Land that is mostly flat. p. 131

present
The time now. p. 57

principal
The leader of a school. p. 34

producer
A person who makes goods or sells goods and services. p. 154

R

recycle
To make something old into something new. p. 141

religion
A set of beliefs about God or gods. p. 92

resource
Anything that people can use. p. 139

respect
To treat someone or something well. p. 43

responsibility
Something that people should do. p. 41

right
Something people are free to do. p. 41

role
The part a person plays in a group or a community. p. 6

rule
Something that tells people how to act. p. 29

save
To keep something, such as money, to use later. p. 163

scarce
Not much of something. p. 159

services
Kinds of work people do for others for money. p. 151

settler
A person who makes a home in a new community. p. 104

share
To use something with others. p. 5

state
A part of a country. pp. 15, 124

suburb
A smaller community near a large city. p. 136

symbol
A picture that stands for an idea or a thing. p. 87

T

technology
All of the tools we use to make our lives easier. p. 67

tool
Something a person uses to do work. p. 67

trade
To give one thing to get another. p. 164

tradition
Something that is passed on from older family members to children. p. 15

transportation
Any way of moving people and things. p. 70

valley
Low land between mountains. p. 131

volunteer
A person who works without pay to help people. p. 43

vote
A choice that gets counted. p. 45

wants
Things we would like to have. p. 157

world
All the people and places on Earth. p. 17

Index

The index tells where information about people, places, and events in this book can be found. The entries are listed in alphabetical order. Each entry tells the page or pages where you can find the topic.

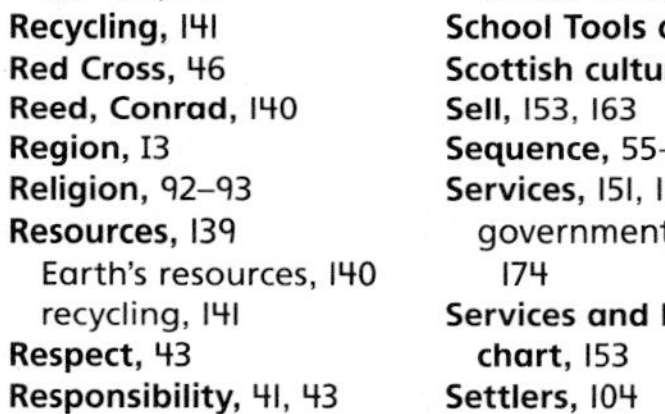

PHOTO CREDITS

Placement Key: (t) top, (b) bottom, (r) right, (l) left, (c) center, (bg) background, (fg) foreground, (i) inset.

Front Cover: (bg) Stock Images / Alamy; (bl) © Robert Dowling/CORBIS; (cr) Terry Heffernan Films; (cl) Media Bakery; (tbg) Photo Disc/Getty Images. Back Cover: (tl) Stockbyte/Getty Images; (bg) Stock Images / Alamy. Title page: (c) Stockbyte/ Getty Images; (bg) Stock Images / Alamy.

v (t) Museum of Flight/Corbis; v (b) Index Stock Imagery, Inc.; vi (bl) Image Works, Inc., The; vii (b) Lawrence Migdale; I3 (t) Big Cheese Photo/Picturequest; I3 (cr) ImageState; I3 (b) Getty Images; 5 (inset) (c) Patrick Molnar/Getty Images; 7 Laura Dwight / Photo Edit; I3 (bg) Visions of America, LLC / Alamy; 15 (br) Michael Ochs Archives/Corbis; 17 Patti McConville/Getty Images; 30 (bc) Getty Images; 39 (b) Getty Images; 41 (bg) © James Shaffer/PhotoEdit; 42 (b) David Young-Wolff/PhotoEdit; 42 (cr) Lisa Law/ The Image Works; 42 (tl) © Rob Bartee / Alamy; 45 (bg) Crandall / The Image Works; 46 (br) Georges DeKeerle/Getty Images; 53 (bg) Creatas Images (RF) Image; 57 (bg) Jim Hargan; 58 (cr) Corbis; 59 (inset) Retrofile.com; 60 (bl) Getty Images; 60 (br) Image from the Lower Cape Fear Historical Society Archives, Wilmington NC; 61 (bl) Retrofile.com; 63 (bg) Jon Arnold / DanitaDelimont.com; 64 (cl) Durham County Library; 67 (bg) JIM HARGAN; 68 (cr) Schenectady Museum; Hall of Electrical History Foundation/Corbis; 68 (c) Dave L. Ryan/Index Stock Imagery; 68 (cl) C Squared Studios/Photodisc Green(Royalty-free)/Getty Images; 69 (cl) Culver Pictures; 70 (tl) Museum of Flight/ Corbis; 70 (tc) Felix Clouzot/Getty Images; 70 (tr) Getty Images; 70 (bl) Bettman/Corbis; 70 (c) Hulton/Archive/Getty Images; 70 (cr) Robert Maust/Photo Agora; 70 (bl) Brown Brothers; 70 (br) John McGrail Photography; 71 (tr) Bettmann/CORBIS; 71 (bl) ©Jeff Greenberg/ The Image Works; 73 (bg) Gibson Stock Photography; 74 (bl) The Library of Congress; 74 (br) Chuck Burton/ASSOCIATED PRESS; 75 (cr) Bettmann/Corbis; 75 (bl) Patrick Batchelder Photography; 76 (br) Jon Arnold Images / Alamy; 77 (tl) Robert Estall photo agency / Alamy; 77 (br) Keren Su/China Span / Alamy; 83 (bg) The News Reporter; 88 (cl) Leif Skoogfors/Corbis; 88 (cr) Tom and Pat Leeson; 89 (tcr) Stockbyte/SuperStock; 89 (cl) Oxford Scientific/Bill Paton/Jupiterimages; 89 (br) Dick Spahr/Workbook Stock Image/ Jupiterimages; 91 (bg) Kelly Parris/Unicorn Stock Photos; 92 (cr) Thinkstock/Jupiter images; 92 (bl) Journal-Courier / Steve Warmowski / The Image Works; 93 (tl) ZUMA Press; 93 (cr) © Corbis. All Rights Reserved.; 93 (bl) Keren Su/China Span / Alamy; 94 A. Ramey/PhotoEdit; 95 (bl) Rob Crandall/The Image Work; 95 (tl) Dennis MacDonald / Alamy; 95 (tl) Lawrence Migdale/PIX / Alamy; 97 Index Stock Imagery; 98 (tr) Flip Schulke/Corbis; 98 Francis G. Mayer/Corbis; 98 Yogi/Corbis; 99 (b) Francisco Rangel/The Image Works; 99 (cr) Library of Congress; 101 (b) Michael Ventura; 101 (t) Tony Freeman/PhotoEdit; 103 (bg) Steve Murray/Picturesque.com; 104 ©William Ahrendt; 105 (cr) Marilyn Angel ynn/Nativestock.com; 106 Latin American Coalition; 106 (bl) PhotoObjects.net/Photographer: Zedcor Wholly Owned; 107 (bc) MIKE DIRKS/TIMES-NEWS; 113 (bg) Corbis; 117 North Carolina Zoo; 124 (bl) Image Works; 124 (cl) ECKERT IMAGES; 129 Donovan Reese/ Panoramic Images; 130 (bg) Vladpans/Panoramic Images; 130 (inset) Lester Lefkowitz/Corbis; 131 (br) James Schwabel/Panoramic Images; 131 (cl) PAT & CHUCK BLACKLEY; 132 (cl) Pat & Chuck Blackley; 132 (br) Open Door images/Jupiter Images; 132 (bg) Panoramic Images; 135 (br) Gibson Stock Photography; 136 (cr) Dana Hoff/Beateworks/Corbis; 137 (bg) Rex A. Stucky/Getty Images; 139 (bg) Corbis; 140 Marc Romanelli / Alamy; 141 Eastcott-Momatiuk / The Image Works; 152 (cl) Pixonnet.com / Alamy; 152 (tc) Paul Felix Photography / Alamy; 153 Jonathan Nourok/ PhotoEdit; 154 (b) Lawrence Migdale; 155 (tr) Matt Henry Gunther/Getty Images; 157 (bg) Brand X Pictures /Jack Hollingsworth/Jupiter Images; 158 (c) Benelux/zefa/Corbis; 160 (cl) Panorama Images / The Image Works; 160 (tr) © Travel Ink / Alamy; 160 (bc) Bo Zaunders/CORBIS; 161 (cl) Danita Delimont / Alamy; 161 (tr) Daj/Getty images; 161 (br) David R. Frazier Photolibrary, Inc. / Alamy; 163 (bg) Debbie Roos/Photographer; 164 (bc) Jeff Greenberg/PhotoEdit; 165 (bc) David Young-Wolff/PhotoEdit; 167 John Zoiner; 168 (tl) Gale Zucker Photography; 168 (br) Gale Zucker Photography; 168 (t) Gale Zucker Photography; 169 (t) Gale Zucker Photography; 169 (l) Gale Zucker Photography; 170 (t) Gale Zucker Photography; 170 (b) Gale Zucker Photography; 171 (b) Lewis Wickes Hine/ Corbis; 173 (bg) © Richard Hamilton Smith/ CORBIS; 174 (b) Gibson Stock Photo; 175 (cr) Jeffrey Greenberg /Photo Researchers, Inc.; 175 (bl) Digital Vision Ltd. / Superstock; 186 (bl) Judith Collins / Alamy; 186 (br) Kevin Dodge/Corbis; 187 SuperStock inc,/Superstock; 187 Dynamic Graphics / Jupiterimages; 191 (br) Corbis.

All other photos property of Harcourt School Publishers.

INDEX

Tabbed Section

Index

A

B

C

N

P

R

S

U

V

North Carolina

Bibliography

CONFIRMED AND CURRENT RESEARCH

READING EXPOSITORY TEXT

For students to be successful content-area readers, they need reading instruction that focuses on:

- a diverse range of reading material, emphasizing expository and informational texts as much as literature (Biancarosa and Snow, 2004; International Reading Association, 2006; National Reading Panel, 2000);
- comprehension, specifically the strategies and processes that proficient readers use (Biancarosa and Snow, 2004; Kamil, M.L., 2003; International Reading Association, 2006; National Reading Panel, 2000);
- vocabulary development (Kamil, M.L., 2003; International Reading Association, 2006; National Reading Panel, 2000);
- using and interpreting diagrams, graphs, and other nonlinguistic sources of information, such as maps and time lines, and using the parts of a textbook and other reference materials (International Reading Association, 2006).

Furthermore, assessment that is ongoing and varied, including both formative and summative tests, should serve as a basis for decision making about student literacy needs related to curriculum and instruction (Biancarosa and Snow, 2004; International Reading Association, 2006; National Governors Association, 2005).

References cited:

Biancarosa, G. & Snow, C.E. (2004). *Reading next—A vision for action and research in middle and high school literacy: a report to the Carnegie Corporation of New York.* Washington, DC: Alliance for Excellent Education.

International Reading Association. (2006). *Standards for middle and high school literacy coaches.* Newark, DE: author.

Kamil, M.L. (2003). *Adolescents and literacy: Reading for the 21st century.* Washington, DC: Alliance for Excellent Education.

National Governors Association. (2005). *Reading to achieve: A governor's guide to adolescent literacy.* Washington, DC: National Governors Association Center for Best Practices.

National Reading Panel. (2000). *Report of the National Reading Panel: Teaching Children to Read.* Washington, DC: National Institute of Child Health and Human Development, National Institutes of Health.

HISTORY AND HISTORICAL THINKING

Ashby, R., Lee, P., and Dickinson, A. (1997). How Children Explain the Why of History: The Chata Research Project on Teaching History. *Social Education, 61* (1), 17–21.

Barton, K. (1996). Narrative Simplifications in Elementary Students' Historical Thinking. *Advances in Research on Teaching, 6,* 51–83.

Barton, K. (1997a). History—It Can Be Elementary: An Overview of Elementary Students' Understanding of History. *Social Education, 61* (1), 13–16.

Berson, M.J. (2004). Digital Images: Capturing America's Past with the Technology of Today. *Social Education.* 68 (3).

Downey, M., and Levstik, L. (1991). Teaching and Learning History. In Shaver, J. P. (Ed.), *Handbook on Research in Social Studies Teaching and Learning.* New York: Macmillan.

Foster, S. (1999). Using Historical Empathy to Excite Students About the Study of History: Can You Empathize with Neville Chamberlain? *The Social Studies* (January/February), 18–24.

Garcia, J., and Michaelis, J. (2001). *Social Studies for Children: A Guide to Basic Instruction.* Needham Heights, MA: Allyn & Bacon.

Levstik, L. S., and Barton, K. C. (1997). *Doing History: Investigating with Children in Elementary and Middle Schools.* Mahwah, NJ: Lawrence Erlbaum Associates.

McDiarmid, G. W. (1994). Understanding History for Teaching: A Study of the Historical Understanding of Prospective Teachers. In Carretero, M., and Voss, J. F. (Eds.), *Cognitive and Instructional Processes in History and the Social Sciences*, 159–185. Hillsdale, NJ: Erlbaum.

National Council for the Social Studies (NCSS) (2004). *Powerful Teaching and Learning in the Social Studies* [online]. Available: http://www.ncss.org/standards/positions/powerful.html

Porter, P. H. (2005) Writing in the Content Areas: Warm-up, Build Muscle and Win the Championship. *Social Studies Review.* 44 (2).

Seixas, P. (1996). Conceptualizing the Growth of Historical Understanding. In Olson, D. R., and Torrance, N. (Eds.), *The Handbook of Education and Human Development: New Models of Learning, Teaching, and Schooling,* 765–783. Cambridge: Blackwell Publishers.

VanSledright, B. A. (2002). *In Search of America's Past: Learning to Read History in Elementary School.* New York: Teachers College Press.

Wilson, S., and Wineburg, S. S. (1988). Peering at History Through Different Lenses: The Role of Disciplinary Perspectives in Teaching History. *Teachers College Record, 89* (4), 525–539.

Wineburg, S. S. (1991a). On the Reading of Historical Texts: Notes on the Breach Between School and Academy. *American Educational Research Journal, 28* (3), 495–519.

Wineburg, S. S. (1991b). Historical Problem Solving: A Study of the Cognitive Process Used in the Evaluation of Documentary and Pictorial Evidence. *Journal of Educational Psychology, 83,* 73–87.

Yeager, E. A., and Davis, O. L., Jr. (1996). Classroom Teachers' Thinking About Historical Texts: An Exploratory Study. *Theory and Research in Social Education, 24,* 146–166.

Yeager, E. A., and Wilson, E. K. (1997). Teaching Historical Thinking in the Social Studies Methods Course: A Case Study. *The Social Studies,* May/June, 121–126.

Zarnowski, M. (2003). *History Makers: A Questioning Approach to Reading and Writing Biographies.* Portsmouth, NH: Heinemann.

Zinn, H. (1997). *A People's History of the United States.* New York: New Press.

MULTICULTURAL APPROACHES

Parker, W. C. (2005). *Social Studies in Elementary Education* (12th ed.). Upper Saddle River, NJ: Pearson.

Rényi, J., and Lubeck, D. R. (1994). A Response to the NCSS Guidelines on Multicultural Education. *Social Education 58* (1), 4–6.

PRIMARY SOURCES

Barton, K. C. (1997). I Just Kinda Know: Elementary Students' Ideas About Historical Evidence. *Theory and Research in Social Education, 25* (4), 407–430.

Trofanenko, B. (2002). Images of History in Middle-Grade Social Studies Trade Books. *New Advocate, 15* (2), 129–132.

Wineburg, S. S. (2001). *Historical Thinking and Other Unnatural Acts: Charting the Future of Teaching the Past.* Philadelphia, PA: Temple University Press.

SOCIAL PARTICIPATION

Sunal, C. S., and Haas, M. E. (2005). *Social Studies for the Elementary and Middle Grades: A Constructivist Approach* (2nd ed.). Boston, MA: Pearson.

Tornery-Purta, J., Schwille, J., and Amado, J. (1999). *Civic Education Across Countries: Twenty-Four National Case Studies from the IEA Civic Education Project.* Amsterdam, Netherlands: IEA.

SOCIAL STUDIES AND CROSS-CURRICULUM CONNECTIONS

Parker, W. C. (2005). *Social Studies in Elementary Education* (12th ed.). Upper Saddle River, NJ: Pearson.

USE OF GRAPHIC ORGANIZERS

Howard, J. (2001). Graphic Representations as Tools for Decision Making. *Social Education, 65* (4), 220–223.

North Carolina Standard Course of Study
First Grade Social Studies

Competency Goals and Objectives	Student and Teacher Edition Pages
Competency Goal 1 The learner will analyze how individuals, families, and groups are similar and different.	Unit 1, 1A–24
Objectives **1.01** Describe the roles of individuals in the family.	5A–8, 9A, 21, 23
1.02 Identify various groups to which individuals and families belong.	2, 9A–12, 22
1.03 Compare and contrast similarities and differences among individuals and families.	2–4, 5A, 7, 9A, 13A–16, 17B, 19
1.04 Explore the benefits of diversity in the United States.	9B, 13A–13B, 14, 17A–20, 24
Competency Goal 2 The learner will identify and exhibit qualities of good citizenship in the classroom, school, and other social environments.	Unit 2, 25A–52
Objectives **2.01** Develop and exhibit citizenship traits in the classroom, school, and other social environments.	26, 29A, 33A, 41A–44
2.02 Identify the roles of leaders in the home, school, and community such as parents, mayor, police officers, principal, and teacher.	33A–36
2.03 Participate in democratic decision-making.	45A–49, 52
2.04 Recognize the need for rules in different settings.	27, 29A–32, 37A–37B, 38, 52
2.05 Identify the need for fairness in rules by individuals and by people in authority.	29A, 33B, 37A–40
2.06 Predict consequences that may result from responsible and irresponsible actions.	29B, 37A–40
Competency Goal 3 The learner will recognize and understand the concept of change in various settings.	Unit 3, 53A–82
Objectives **3.01** Describe personal and family changes, past and present.	54, 57A–62, 63A–63B, 82
3.02 Describe past and present changes within the local community.	56–59, 63A–72, 73B, 79, 82
3.03 Compare and contrast past and present changes within the local community and communities around the world.	58–59, 63B, 67A, 73A–78
3.04 Recognize that members of the community are affected by changes in the community that occur over time.	59, 63, 67A–72
Competency Goal 4 The learner will explain different celebrated holidays and special days in communities.	Unit 4, 83A–112
Objectives **4.01** Recognize and describe religious and secular symbols/celebrations associated with special days of diverse cultures.	85–96, 112
4.02 Explore and cite reasons for observing special days that recognize celebrated individuals of diverse cultures.	97A–102
4.03 Recognize and describe the historical events associated with national holidays.	97A–102, 112
4.04 Trace the historical foundations of traditions of various neighborhoods and communities.	94, 97, 103A–108, 112

North Carolina Standard Course of Study First Grade Social Studies

Competency Goals and Objectives	Student and Teacher Edition Pages
Competency Goal 5 The learner will express geographic concepts in real life situations.	Unit 5, 113A–146
Objectives	
5.01 Locate and describe familiar places in the home, classroom, and school.	117A–122
5.02 Investigate key features of maps.	117, 119–120, 123A–128, 130–131, 146
5.03 Use geographic terminology and tools to create representations of the earth's physical and human features through simple maps, models, and pictures.	117A–122, 123A–128, 129
5.04 Analyze patterns of movement within the community.	124, 131, 135A–138
5.05 Demonstrate responsibility for the care and management of the environment within the school and community.	133, 139A–142
5.06 Compare and contrast geographic features of places within various communities.	116, 123, 129A–134, 135–137, 146
5.07 Explore physical features of continents and major bodies of water.	126, 129A–134, 146
Competency Goal 6 The learner will apply basic economic concepts to home, school, and the community.	Unit 6, 147A–180
Objectives	
6.01 Examine wants and needs and identify choices people make to satisfy wants and needs with limited resources.	157A–162
6.02 Describe how people of different cultures work to earn income in order to satisfy wants and needs.	149–150, 157A–162, 180
6.03 Participate in activities that demonstrate the division of labor.	153, 167A–172, 180
6.04 Explore community services that are provided by the government and other agencies.	173A–176, 179
6.05 Give examples of the relationship between the government and its people.	173A–176
6.06 Identify the uses of money by individuals which include saving and spending.	148, 150, 163A–166, 177, 180
6.07 Recognize that all families produce and consume goods and services.	151A–156, 158
Competency Goal 7 The learner will recognize how technology is used at home, school, and in the community.	Unit 7, 181A–200
Objectives	
7.01 Compare and contrast the use of media and forms of communication at home and in other social environments.	185A–188
7.02 Describe how communication and transportation link communities.	183, 189A–192, 200
7.03 Use the computer and other technological tools to gather, organize, and display data.	183–184, 193A–196, 198, 200

Correlations

North Carolina Standard Course of Study Social Studies Skills

Skills Competency Goals and Objectives	Student and Teacher Edition Pages
Skill Competency Goal 1 The learner will acquire strategies for reading social studies materials and for increasing social studies vocabulary.	
Objectives	
1.01 Read for literal meaning.	18, 41B, 43, 163B, 170
1.02 Summarize to select main ideas.	33B, 34, 38, 43, 60, 63B, 94, 163B
1.03 Draw inferences.	29, 33, 41, 45, 64, 67, 71, 89, 92, 97, 100, 106, 151, 164, 167, 171, 173, 175, 191
1.04 Detect cause and effect.	29, 37, 163
1.06 Recognize and use social studies terms in written and oral reports.	36, 91B, 96, 128, 146
1.07 Distinguish fact and fiction.	193
1.08 Use context clues and appropriate sources such as glossaries, texts, and dictionaries to gain meaning.	8, 18, 32, 40, 162
Skill Competency Goal 2 The learner will acquire strategies to access a variety of sources, and use appropriate research skills to gather, synthesize, and report information using diverse modalities to demonstrate the knowledge acquired.	
Objectives	
2.01 Use appropriate sources of information.	13B, 33B, 41B, 57B, 61, 63B, 64, 68, 73B, 75–76, 87B, 91B, 103B, 129B, 132, 139B, 157B, 167B, 173B, 185B, 189B, 193B
2.02 Explore print and non-print materials.	9, 13B, 41B, 57B, 61, 63B, 63–64, 68, 73B, 75–76, 91B, 103B, 129B, 132, 139B, 157B, 167B, 185B, 189B, 193B
2.03 Utilize different types of technology.	13B, 57B, 64, 73B, 76, 87B, 189B, 193B, 193, 195
2.04 Utilize community-related resources such as field trips, guest speakers, and interviews.	68, 173B
2.05 Transfer information from one medium to another such as written to visual and statistical to written.	57B, 103B
2.06 Create written, oral, musical, visual, and theatrical presentations of social studies information.	5B, 9B, 10, 15, 17B, 29B, 33B, 37B, 41B, 57B, 63B, 67B, 87B, 91B, 97B, 103B, 129B, 135B, 139B, 151B, 167B, 173B, 185B, 189B
Skill Competency Goal 3 The learner will acquire strategies to analyze, interpret, create, and use resources and materials.	
Objectives	
3.01 Use map and globe reading skills.	13, 17–18, 70, 95, 117B, 117–118, 120–121, 123B, 123–127, 130–131, 189B, 189–190
3.02 Interpret graphs and charts.	7, 11, 30, 39, 58, 69, 87, 97B, 99, 104, 132, 136, 141, 155, 157B, 157, 161, 163B, 163, 167B, 168, 174–175, 187, 193B
3.05 Interpret history through artifacts, arts, and media.	58, 61, 68, 71, 82, 103B

North Carolina Standard Course of Study Social Studies Skills

Skills Competency Goals and Objectives	Student and Teacher Edition Pages
Skill Competency Goal 4 The learner will acquire strategies needed for applying decision-making and problem-solving techniques both orally and in writing to historic, contemporary, and controversial world issues.	
Objectives	
4.01 Use hypothetical reasoning processes.	10
4.02 Examine, understand, and evaluate conflicting viewpoints.	38, 39
4.03 Recognize and analyze values upon which judgments are made.	15, 46–48, 52, 104, 191
4.04 Apply conflict resolutions.	29B, 39, 40, 159
4.05 Predict possible outcomes.	29, 39, 69, 159, 169
4.06 Draw conclusions.	10, 34, 45B, 71, 88, 91B, 100, 187
4.07 Offer solutions.	101, 133, 159
4.08 Develop hypotheses.	31, 66, 90, 108
Skill Competency Goal 5 The learner will acquire strategies needed for effective incorporation of computer technology in the learning process.	
Objectives	
5.01 Use word processing to create, format, and produce classroom assignments/projects.	1E, 1F, 24, 25E, 25F, 53F, 78, 82, 83E, 83F, 102, 113F, 134, 146, 147E, 147F, 181E, 181F, 193B, 196
5.04 Create nonlinear projects related to the social studies content area via multimedia presentations.	1E, 24, 25E, 78, 82, 83E, 102, 134, 146, 147E, 181E, 193B, 196